TOM PETTY

ROCK'N'ROLL GUARDIAN

Lyrics copyright information

TOM PETTY

ROCK 'N' ROLL
GUARDIAN

ANDREA M. ROTONDO

OMNIBUS PRESS

London / New York / Paris / Sydney / Copenhagen / Berlin / Madrid / Tokyo

Exclusive Distributors
Music Sales Limited,
14/15 Berners Street,
London, W1T 3LJ.

Music Sales Corporation
180 Madison Avenue, 24th Floor,
New York,
NY 10016,
USA.

Macmillan Distribution Services
56 Parkwest Drive
Derrimut, Vic 3030,
Australia.

Every effort has been made to trace the copyright holders of the photographs in this book but one or
two were unreachable. We would be grateful if the photographers concerned would contact us.

Printed in the EU

A catalogue record for this book is available from the British Library.

Visit Omnibus Press on the web at www.omnibuspress.com

Contents

Preface

My older sister was the smart one. My younger brother was the funny one. In 1976 at the age of seven, I was just the little girl in the middle. I hadn't yet discovered that special thing that would make me *me*. My parents – dad, a factory worker, and mom, a clerk for the Internal Revenue Service – had just announced that we'd be moving and I was devastated. We were living in the upstairs apartment of a two-family house with my grandfather and uncles living downstairs. My grandfather was my best friend and I couldn't imagine being separated from him. There was no way I'd find a friend like him in our new town. When the day of our dreaded departure came, my grandfather had a gift for me: a red transistor radio. He told me that today was just the first of many challenges I'd have to live up to and he was sure I'd find new friends. In the meantime, the music on the radio would keep me company.

From that day on, DJs were my constant companions. I was introduced to artists from diverse genres and backgrounds, such as Howlin' Wolf, Willie Dixon, Pink Floyd, the Eagles, Gloria Gaynor and The Bee Gees. Most nights I'd fall asleep with that radio tucked under my pillow.

To me, radio was an art form. I appreciated all types of music but traditional blues and rock spoke most clearly to me. In time, I came to

7

appreciate one voice above all others though. From the first moment I heard Tom Petty & The Heartbreakers' debut record – the now classic 'American Girl' and 'Breakdown' – I knew we were kindred spirits: the band and I were both on the verge of something. I'd twist that radio dial every day in the hopes of hearing a Tom Petty song and in later years I'd spend all the money I earned babysitting on the band's albums and singles.

One day in the early eighties – around the time that *Hard Promises* was released – I saw a classified ad in *Circus* magazine. A Petty fan was looking for pen pals that shared her obsession. I wrote her a letter and ended up with a dozen new friends that loved Tom Petty, The Heartbreakers and rock'n'roll in general. That may seem quaint but back in the day there was no Internet. No Facebook or Twitter. MTV had only just launched in 1980. The only connection I had to music was through the radio waves, magazines and my pen-pal network.

I clearly remember the day that *Southern Accents* – Tom Petty & The Heartbreakers' sixth studio album – was released in 1985. It had been three years since the band's previous effort, *Long After Dark*, and I could not wait to listen to the album. After school one day I raced to Newbury Comics in Boston to pick up a copy of the album. I had no way of knowing that one track, 'Dogs On The Run', would have such a profound effect on my entire outlook on life.

One lyric in particular – "There's ways of getting anything I want" – played over and over in my head. For some reason, this tiny thought stuck with me – became my mantra – and over the course of the next 29 years, I've found it to be absolutely true. I learned that if I strategised, made the right connections and worked hard, all that I desired – a life beyond my own "one-story town" – was possible.

On June 11, 1985, I found myself at the Worcester Centrum for a Tom Petty concert. I struck up a conversation with the mixing engineer at the front-of-house board. He told me a bit about his job – mixing the concert sound for the audience – and, from that night on, I decided that I would work toward becoming an engineer too. By 1991 I was living in New York City, following my dream to engineer records. By chance I met Shelly Yakus, the talented engineer who worked with producer Jimmy Iovine on Tom Petty's breakthrough album, *Damn*

The Torpedoes. He was kind enough to answer some of my questions and suggested ways in which I could learn more about the craft. He was so helpful that I decided to seek advice from other industry luminaries and one of them hooked me up with the publisher of *Pro Sound News* magazine. He and I clicked and I was hired as an editor. I had found my calling. I spent my days sitting in on recording sessions and writing about them – first for *Pro Sound News* and then for other magazines like *Billboard*, *Mix*, *EQ* and *Musician*.

As Tom Petty & The Heartbreakers continued to jump hurdles in their careers, I did in mine as well. I was also able to follow the band extensively over the years and have been lucky enough to see them perform in dozens of US cities as well as overseas – even attending their triumphant return to Paris in the summer of 2012 at Le Grand Rex theatre as well as an intimate outdoor gig in Italy at Piazza Napoleone in Tuscany's beautiful walled city of Lucca. Every single show always feels like going home.

When Omnibus Press UK came to me to ask if I'd write a bio of Tom Petty, one of the most respected rock'n'roll musicians and songwriters of our time, I hesitated. There are already some excellent books and films about the band, including the first authorised book – *Conversations With Tom Petty* – written by songwriting expert Paul Zollo. I acquired that book while I was an editor at Omnibus Press US in the early 2000s and it was a joy collaborating with Paul and Tom's team at East End Management. Zollo covered Tom's life history through a series of Q&A interviews and the book is a must-have for even casual fans.

Then, in 2007, director Peter Bogdanovich released the glorious four-hour *Runnin' Down A Dream* documentary. The film – and companion coffee-table book – is a masterful resource for all things Petty.

There's hope that Tom will write his own memoir at some point in the future – if he ever slows down long enough to take pen to paper (and I hope he does). But even if that doesn't happen, rock'n'roll historian and Ph.D. Warren Zanes is said to be working on another authorised tome, which will be well worth the wait.

What you hold in your hands now though is the first Tom Petty biography written by a (mostly) impartial third party. It's a record of

Tom Petty's childhood, his work with local bands in the late sixties and early seventies, his trek to Los Angeles with Mudcrutch in 1975 and his enduring body of work with The Heartbreakers and as a solo artist. It's my hope that this book is a useful addition to the lexicon.

★ ★ ★

These days I keep a photo of Tom Petty and Mike Campbell tacked above my computer. It was taken in 1999 at Irving Plaza in New York City. The band staged a three-night stand at this intimate venue in support of *Echo*, the band's first studio album since 1996. This was a watershed moment for Tom Petty. After a long, dark period getting through a divorce and all that goes with such a massive life change, Tom was back and happy. The photo speaks to this newfound joy – Tom and Mike playing their guitars and looking at each other with knowing smiles. I've kept this photo all these years to remind myself that happiness *always* returns – even after our stormiest voyages.

During the research for this book I was continually humbled by the power that music wields. In its purest form it can lift us up and help us navigate the most challenging circumstances. Both of my parents passed away during the creation of this book and my sorrow would have been overwhelming had it not been for music. I found that simple songs were the salve on my wound – one that felt like it just might never heal. Tom Petty's music in particular made my grief more bearable and, today, as I near completion of this project, I am once again thankful that I discovered his music when I was just a kid. It has meant the world to me, as it does to millions of fans around the globe. The Heartbreakers toured the United States over the summer of 2013 and at one show a fan held up a simple, hand-drawn sign that said, "I was raised on your music." This straightforward, heartfelt message holds true for so many people who embraced Tom Petty's music at an early age and have grown alongside The Heartbreakers over the years. This loyalty is a testament to Tom's music, his ability to connect with the audience and his desire to stay relevant as the sands of time continue to flow.

Introducing his own music to fans was never enough for Tom, though. He has spent his career offering a nod to all those who came before him by always inserting a few covers into his live set. These songs helped give the audience a peek into his own musical influences and acted as the departure point for fans to seek out more of that artist's music on their own. In 2005 Tom took this concept further by developing his own radio show for XM Radio (now SiriusXM Satellite Radio). *Buried Treasure*, now in its eighth season, showcases Tom as DJ and he shares gems from his personal – and extensive – record collection. While he heavily favors playing music from artists he discovered during his own childhood, he's also been known to play songs from a few contemporary artists like Jack White as well as Heartbreakers' deep cuts. *Buried Treasure* has introduced the fathers of rock'n'roll – Elvis Presley, Bo Diddley, Chuck Berry, Albert King and the Everly Brothers – to new music fans and Tom feels that it's his duty to curate this music for the next generation. This is the music that helped him build his career and create a unique brand of rock'n'roll that is beloved by fans all over the world. In February of 1980 – at the height of *Damn The Torpedoes'* popularity – music journalist Mitch Cohen described Tom's music this way in an issue of *Creem* magazine: "His messages were forthright and simple. His confidence brooked no argument, his hurts hurt, and that was that."

Perhaps what is most endearing about Tom Petty's brand of rock'n'roll is its authenticity. His music has liberated more than one generation. His lyrics put a voice to our darkest fears and deepest yearnings: love, betrayal, perseverance and – most importantly – our innate desire to carry on.

– Andrea M. Rotondo

Introduction

In 2016 Tom Petty will celebrate his 40-year tenure as the leader of one of America's preeminent rock'n'roll bands: The Heartbreakers. Like America's other long-running rock'n'roll outfit, Bruce Springsteen's E Street Band, The Heartbreakers are a band that has improved with age. They've been together for decades and it looks like they've got at least another 10 good years in them – if their recent streak of shows in 2013 at New York City's Beacon Theater and LA's Henry Fonda Theatre are any indication. Petty deftly kept this band together throughout the years and each Heartbreaker has been an integral ingredient to Petty's success in the music business.

Music industry insiders will no doubt point to tangible measures of that success – the number of records he's sold over the years (more than 60 million) or the gross of his band's sell-out concert tours or the popularity of his own radio show, *Buried Treasure*, on SiriusXM Satellite Radio. Those are impressive achievements, to be sure. But, ask fans to quantify Tom Petty's success and they'll likely describe it in more organic terms. "He cares about his fans." "His music encouraged me to pick up a guitar and learn how to play." "'I Won't Back Down' gave me the courage to quit my lousy job and go back to school." "Tom's records helped me pick up the pieces after a really messy breakup."

While platinum records are important, the true measure of someone's legacy lies in public opinion. In the case of Tom Petty, his fans have loved and respected him – and his music – since he first set foot on stage in Gainesville in the mid-sixties as a member of The Sundowners.

It's easy to look in the rear-view window now and say that Tom Petty's rise to stardom was a foregone conclusion, but that would be dismissing decades of backbreaking work that got him where he is today. Yes, Petty has an abundance of natural talent, songwriting acumen and business savvy but even armed with those skills, his success came only after many, *many* hard-fought battles.

I spent a year researching and writing this book and I was a fan of Tom Petty's music for more than three decades before that. I've come to believe that there are four elements to Mr. Petty's success: first and foremost is his undeniable passion for music; secondly, the early support and encouragement he received from his mother and grandmother; third, his innate never-give-in determination; and, finally, his sense of loyalty to those he cares about, to his fans and to the music itself.

After you read the first chapter devoted to Tom's childhood, you'll come away astonished by the depths of his passion for rock'n'roll. The genre consumed his every waking thought – and mostly likely his dreams as well – from the moment he had a chance encounter with Elvis Presley on the set of *Follow That Dream* in 1961. This single-minded devotion is admired by anyone who's ever struggled to figure where he or she belongs in life. Imagine instinctively knowing your path in life had only one trajectory. Tom knew from an early age that music was the key to his future. He couldn't imagine doing anything else and he vowed when he was just a teenager that he'd make music – even if his band never progressed beyond the garage. For Tom Petty, writing and playing music is as essential – and involuntary – as breathing.

Adria Petty, Tom's eldest daughter, talked about her father's blind devotion to music with *Interview* magazine reporter Angela Ledgerwood: "As a very young person, he was almost too obsessed with records and 45s. It's really adorable to hear him talk about how he would sneak into his neighbor's house and steal 45s and play them, and then sneak them back before anyone noticed. He was very determined to get his hands on music." This anecdote illustrates Petty's desperate need to absorb as much music as he could. It's almost as if he had no control of this desire to understand music. It was core to his being and could not be ignored.

This yearning to truly understand music of all genres has served him well throughout his lifetime and he's still playing records and discovering new music today.

Petty's late mother, "Kitty", plays an important role in his story, too. Although she passed away when her son was just 30 years old, her early support was vital. Likewise, his grandmother and aunts played pivotal roles in his early development. They encouraged him to be his own person and to pursue his dream of making a living as a working musician. Their blind devotion to his creativity somewhat assuaged the hurt that stemmed from a father that was volatile in the home and nearly impossible to please.

This support from the women in his life clearly taught him to value the female point of view and to respect the fairer sex. In fact, he often writes songs from the woman's perspective and he's crafted many in which the woman holds all the power. There is no sense of inequality in Tom Petty's music. Everyone comes to the table on an even footing.

As you learn more about Tom Petty and the trials he endured while building The Heartbreakers' legacy, you may find yourself thinking, "Did this guy intentionally go looking for trouble?" After all, throughout his career he hit more than his share of speed bumps. He threatened to withhold the band's sophomore record from his label Shelter/ABC unless they renegotiated his inequitable contract. When MCA bought out ABC, Tom bristled at the idea of being absorbed by this conglomerate that may or may not stand behind his music. He set out to record his third album, *Damn The Torpedoes,* without any financial backing from the label. He went bankrupt in the process and sued to get out of his contract and become a free agent. Just when you think things are going Petty's way in 1981, after the huge success of *Damn The Torpedoes*, he's embroiled in another disagreement with his record company. This time, it wanted to raise the retail price of the band's next album, *Hard Promises*, by one dollar to $9.98. The musician steadfastly refused the idea and started a write-in campaign with fans to dissuade the label from going through with the price hike. The people won that battle in the end.

Time and time again, Tom has fought crisis after crisis. Was he in the wrong place at the wrong time? Was "the man" picking on this advocate for underdogs everywhere? Or, are Tom Petty's convictions so steadfast that he just can't help himself in the face of perceived injustice and inequality? I believe the latter to be true.

Heartbreaker and lead guitarist Mike Campbell says his friend Tom Petty is not one to back down from a fight – ever. "Maybe the reason it's taken us so long to succeed is that Tom pisses people off. For as long as I've known him he's bugged people in authority," says Mike. "Once, we were playing really well at a festival in Florida. The band coming on next, who had an album out, got the promoter to pull the plug on us in mid-song. Tom ran backstage; he wanted to know who'd done it. It was a guy who looked like he played on the Florida Gators football team – six feet four, two hundred pounds. Tom, who's a wiry, skinny little guy, put his finger on the bruiser's chest. He poked him like a woodpecker. 'You goddamn son of a bitch!' he said. 'Don't you ever pull the plug on my band.' The guy could have crushed Tom, but he was so taken back that he just backed off. Tom's been like that for as long as I've known him."

Throughout these career hardships – as well as those closer to the heart, like the breakup of his 22-year-marriage to his high-school sweetheart Jane Benyo or the heart-trending death of his friend George Harrison – Tom Petty's proven his mettle and has somehow tapped in to a seemingly bottomless well of perseverance that's allowed him to fight his way back to equilibrium over and over again. It's a characteristic that fans have come to love and admire and only wish they could adopt more of that attitude in their own lives.

What stands out about Tom Petty the most though is his loyalty to his family, friends and band members. Since the early days of Mudcrutch and then The Heartbreakers, Petty has felt responsible not only for his own career and livelihood but that of his bandmates, managers and all others who work closely with him. If the rock'n'roll dream didn't pan out, it wasn't just his future on the line. His desire to protect those he loves no doubt helped him effectively maneuver inside the music industry from the very beginning.

Just look at the case of Ron Blair. The two were friends in Gainesville long before Ron signed on as the original bassist of The Heartbreakers in Los Angeles in 1975. When Blair decided to leave the business in the early eighties, there were no hard feelings. Petty would miss him on stage and in the studio but he understood why his friend needed to get off the music-business treadmill. Ron Blair returns to his post in The Heartbreakers years later though in cosmic fashion after the devastating death of his own replacement, Howie Epstein. In this book you'll hear Petty explain that The Heartbreakers would likely have hung it up altogether after Howie's untimely death had it not been for Ron's return. Ron had stayed close friends with Tom and Mike and the rest of the band throughout the years so when there was a void that he could fill, he stepped right in – almost as if no time had passed at all.

Petty demonstrated this same sort of long-term affection for his friends in 2007 when he resurrected the original Mudcrutch line-up for a studio album, mini-tour and live EP. The outing gave Mudcrutch guitarist Tom Leadon and drummer Randall Marsh a chance to see what might have been if Tom Petty's original band *had* made it big. They would have been rock stars alongside their mates Tom Petty, Mike Campbell and Benmont Tench.

Tom's commitment to friendship was also evident in everything he tried to do to help Howie Epstein break his addiction to drugs. There were stints at rehabs, kind support and tough love but nothing – absolutely nothing – worked. When Tom talks about Howie's struggle with drugs, his sadness is palpable. The sorrow of not being able to pull a friend out of despair appears to haunt him to this day.

On a lighter note, there's a fantastic segment in Peter Bogdanovich's *Runnin' Down A Dream* documentary about The Heartbreakers that shows Petty in the studio with friend and fellow musician Roger McGuinn. Roger's A&R guy is pushing him to record a song that lacks musical integrity. Tom takes on the A&R guy in defense of Roger, a musician that he feels should not compromise his standards by recording this subpar song. It's Petty at his best and most uncompromising. Some may interpret actions like this as brash or arrogant but it's simply part of Petty's quest for musicians to stay true to authentic music.

Many of these stores show that there is just about nothing that Tom Petty wouldn't do to protect his family and friends, his band and the very music that he holds so dear.

But, of course, all of Tom's finer points would have gotten him nowhere if the music that sprang from within him didn't connect on a very real level with his fans. Music journalist Jon Pareles summed it up best in a 1996 article for *The New York Times*: "Mr. Petty writes tunes that seem to have always existed. Behind the offhand delivery, the songs have the classic virtues of economy and directness." The soundtrack of many lives wouldn't be nearly as rich without Tom Petty's enduring body of work. Songs like 'American Girl', 'Listen To Her Heart', 'Refugee', 'The Waiting', 'I Won't Back Down' and 'Learning To Fly' resonate with individuals from all walks of life because what Tom sings about – love won or lost and overcoming hardship – is essential to everyone's journey in life.

Petty's songs are direct and personal and so easy to adopt as one's own anthem. The music has inspired millions of people the world over. Tom Petty may just see himself as a messenger of our times – not unlike Bob Dylan or Bruce Springsteen or John Mellencamp – but he's perhaps the messenger who's most respected by his fans and peers. Over the years he's not only brought his own music to the table but has reawakened our interest in our forebears like Bo Diddley, The Byrds and The Beatles who laid the very groundwork for rock'n'roll's development. It's Petty's fervent hope that his music – and that of his touchstones – lives on forever. It is in these simple acts of stewardship that Tom Petty has become the true guardian of rock'n'roll. He's proudly carried this weight on his shoulders for nearly 40 years and it's not a task he'll give up anytime soon.

CHAPTER 1

Searching For A Safe Place
(1950–1969)

"My life was very turbulent as a child and a little scary, and music made everything seem right."

$-$ T.P.

No child, anywhere, should ever feel afraid in his own home. Tom Petty's formative years were spent – like too many other kids across America – in a home with an abusive father and a caring mother who wasn't able to throw up enough of a barricade between her sons and volatile husband.

Tom's father, Earl, was the volcano that periodically erupted in the Petty home on NE 6th Terrace in Gainesville, Florida. Tom didn't talk much about his father until recent years when he admitted that his dad – who passed away in December of 1999 – was "incredibly verbally abusive" and "… would give me pretty good beatings most of my life". In fact, Tom has said that "the house could erupt into a fistfight" at any moment. "My dad was Jerry Lee Lewis with no talent," Tom explains. "He didn't play and sing, but he was that *wild*. That *crazy*. That *charming*. You know, how Jerry Lee has an incredible charm about him, but he still might shoot you."

These revelations weren't altogether surprising considering the anger, confusion and pain that is such an integral part of so many of Tom's earliest songs ('Fooled Again', 'Hurt', 'Century City', 'Don't Do Me Like That', etc.). Throughout a storied career in which he's often challenged authority, Tom has made a point of railing against injustice. "[It] just outraged me," he says. "I just couldn't contain myself." That need to stick up for the little guy comes from years of being the underdog himself, the child who was unable to deflect his father's verbal tirades, off-base criticism and physical assaults.

The adult Tom Petty has been fairly tight-lipped about his family for much of his life. He'd readily tell reporters how he fell in love with rock'n'roll, but he rarely discussed his father, mother or younger brother, Bruce. That changed around 2000. In interviews Tom has given in the past 10 years or so, he's been considerably more open about his father (with whom he never truly reconciled), his much loved mother who died too soon, his turbulent home life and how it all shaped him as an individual and as one of America's most respected songwriters.

Why the soul-searching now? For one thing: time. Now in his early sixties, Tom has a better understanding of time – or our tenuous grasp on how much time we all have left – and he's finally at a point in his life where he can reflect on and come to terms with all the things that he wished had turned out differently.

To better understand the man himself, we have to go back to fifties Gainesville.

★ ★ ★

The American South has always had a way of taking hold of people. It's an unspoken pull; equal parts nostalgia and a never-give-up-the-fight attitude that holds true in any adversity. The South takes care of its own and inspires daydreamers. But, for all its charms, it's also a place where the clock ticks just a bit more slowly than elsewhere in the United States, where opportunities may not be as plentiful and where some kids, like Tom Petty, grow into anxious teenagers wishing and praying that "there's a little more to life, somewhere else". The South and its traditions play an immensely important role in Tom's story, one that the songwriter revisits time and time again in his songs, even though he's resided in California for nearly 40 years now. The South helped shape the man Tom would become and it remains an ever-present force in his life and music.

Thomas Earl Petty – Tommy to his family and friends – was born on October 20, 1950, at Gainesville's Alachua General Hospital. He was the first child of Earl and Katherine "Kitty" Petty. The young couple – Kitty was just 23 when she gave birth to Tom – had married in 1947 and bought a modest home in the college town of Gainesville in north central Florida.

Earl and Kitty were Southerners through and through. Earl and his twin sister, Pearle, were born in Argyle, Georgia, on January 15, 1924, to William Kyler Petty and Sallie Henderson Lewis Petty. Earl also had two brothers, Wesley and Buck. Sallie was of Cherokee descent and their mixed race relationship raised the ire of many in their logging community. One night, sometime between 1924 and 1926, William got in a brawl with several men and, legend has it, killed a man. The next day the family gathered up everything they owned, packed it on their wagon and left Georgia for the greener pasture of Northern Florida. Once in the Sunshine State, the Pettys erased that ugly chapter from their lives, rarely mentioning it again. Tom himself didn't hear the story until the nineties when his father retold the tale while aboard the band's tour bus late one night after a gig.

Earl grew up in Florida and, like most men of his age, fought for his country during World War II; he was stationed in Egypt as an air force groundsman. After the war he returned to Gainesville and worked a truck route for the Eli Witt Company, a wholesale distributor of tobacco, candy and other household products. Earl named his business Petty's Wholesale Dry Goods Co. After marrying Kitty in 1947, he bought the house that year as well.

Tom recalls that his father "... did a lot of things. He drove a truck selling wholesale dry goods – anything from cigarettes to handkerchiefs on cardboard sheets." Earl's last job was selling insurance for the National Standard Life Insurance Company but at some point he also owned a retail store. "When I was growing up," says Tom, "my dad had a grocery store in the black part of town. They used to put me out to play with the black kids until the store closed.

"When I was eight my mom gave me this whole rap about how black people had their own movie theatres and bathrooms, and when I asked why, she said, 'They prefer it that way.' And I thought, 'I'm not buying that,'" Tom told *Q*'s Mike Blake in 2012. This was the beginning of Tom's perception of social justice (or injustice, as the case may have been in the South back in the day).

Kitty Avery Petty, three years younger than Earl, had grown up in Gainesville. After getting married, she devoted herself to homemaking before Tom was born in 1950. Bruce, Tom's younger brother, came along two years later. As the kids got older, Kitty went to work in the city's tax collector's office selling car registrations and license plates.

Kitty and Earl were both Sunday School teachers at Gainesville's North Central Baptist Church but it is the way of things down south that righteousness and a healthy respect for the Lord often go hand in hand with an equally healthy proclivity for sinfulness, in Earl's case gambling, drinking and running cars off the road. Though Kitty did everything she could to keep her two sons as happy and healthy as possible, her husband often upset the balance in the home. Outsiders probably had no idea that Tommy felt so disconnected from those closest to him.

"I remember thinking from a very early age that my parents might have been aliens and I landed in an alien family like one of those on *The Twilight Zone*," Tom once told *Harp*'s Jaan Uhelszki. "Even when I was really young, I knew that I was not like them at all. It was probably because TV had come into the picture when I was three or four. I loved the television so much. It would go off at night and sometimes I would wait for it to come on. I knew in there was a world that was not anything like the one I was in."

Despite Tom's firm belief that he didn't belong in Gainesville, it was an attractive place in which to live during the fifties and sixties and, in fact, still is today. The town blends quaint Southern charm with academia and the youthful exuberance that comes from the many students attending the University of Florida, the nation's seventh largest campus, as well as Santa Fe College. When Tom was growing up, there were two local music shops, Lipham Music and Lillian's Music Store, as well as aquatic events at the Glen Springs Pool, and other distractions. "I remember it fondly," says Tom. "It was just big enough that it had two movie theatres, which was great... There was a very Southern contingent there. There's kind of a farming element, and then there's the university so you have this mix of people. You could run across just about any kind of person there."

Tom spent his early years at Sidney Lanier Elementary School. When school wasn't in session, Tom was shooting sling shots, riding his bike up and down the street until dusk, visiting nearby Northeast Park and going to the movies, especially Westerns: "I was just obsessed with Westerns," he says.

After school the afternoons were spent playing with kids from the neighbourhood while his maternal grandmother, Troas F. Hale Avery, looked after Tom and Bruce. Kitty would return from work around six to make dinner and put the kids to bed. Earl Petty often didn't make an appearance until after the kids were asleep. Grandmother Avery was a calming force in an otherwise chaotic home and she grew especially close to her grandson, the only blond-haired, blue-eyed child in the family. Kitty's parents had divorced by this time, so Tom never met his grandfather, Earl Avery, but from an early age his grandmother encouraged Tom's aspirations and, as he notes now, "really tried to build up my confidence". Supportive throughout his childhood, she always told him, "You can do anything you set your mind to." Evidently, he believed her.

★ ★ ★

When Tom was 11, his very course in life changed. Every fan has heard the stories about his early encounter with Elvis Presley and how that one moment sparked an enduring passion for rock'n'roll, but there may have been an even earlier influence that perhaps set the stage for Tom's interest in music.

Tom admits, "When I was really young, I liked cowboys who played guitar. That's why I thought the guitar was cool. The guitar just always seemed like a kind of rebellious instrument to me. And then Elvis came along [and] he was kind of like a cowboy, too." This cowboy theme – coupled with his own Cherokee Indian heritage – has cropped up in Tom's work over and over again throughout the years. Consider some of the characters that appear in his songs. The 1999 album *Echo* mentions Billy The Kid in the song of the same name, Davy Crockett and Roy Rogers are namechecked in 'About To Give Out' and the character from 'Swingin'' is dressed in "boots and silver spurs". Let's also not forget the "Indian who shot out the lights" in "a barroom fight" from 'Crawling Back To You' on the *Wildflowers* album. The cowboy and Indian theme even presents itself onstage from time to time. Remember the totem pole that graced the stage each night of 1989's Strange Behavior tour or the rodeo-style artwork that touted the Way Out West tour of 2001?

So is it possible that country music pioneer Ernest Tubb and singer/cowboy actor Roy Rogers were Tom's first touchstones, years before his encounter with Elvis, seeing The Beatles on *The Ed Sullivan Show* and listening to early Rolling Stones albums? Perhaps.

There's no denying, though, that Tom's chance meeting with Elvis in the early sixties set a whole chain of events into motion – events that fueled Tom's insatiable craving for a life devoted to rock'n'roll.

It was a typical Saturday morning in 1961 and Tom was doing the usual: hanging around, sitting under a tree in his front yard, waiting for something exciting to happen – and it did. His Aunt Evelyn, Kitty's sister, pulled up in the driveway and asked if he'd like to take a drive to Ocala, 65 kilometers to the south, with her and his cousins Louise, Albert and Howard. Tom's uncle, Earl Jernigan, was a film processor – the only one in Northern Florida, in fact. When movies were shot in the area, his company – Jernigan's Motion Picture Service – was always on call. On this particular day, a movie called *Follow That Dream* was being made, and it starred Elvis Presley, not long released from the Army but still America's premier rock'n'roll performer. Elvis was also a good ole' Southern boy, Tupelo-born and Memphis-bred, and he felt at home in Ocala where, as ever, he was gracious to the fans that lined up by the chain-link fence that kept the locals off the set.

Tom, his cousins and his aunt arrived on the set before Elvis that day. Every time a young man walked by, Tom would ask his aunt if that was Elvis. She told him that he'd *know* when Elvis arrived. A few minutes later, a buzz broke out along the fence line as Elvis drove up. Tom remembers that The King absolutely glowed, his larger-than-life presence leaving an indelible mark on the 14 year old.

"Elvis appeared like a vision," Tom recalls. "Elvis didn't look like the people I'd known. He had a real glow around him, like a full-body halo. He looked like a god to me. After I saw Elvis that one time, I became obsessed. I can't tell you how much rock'n'roll consumed me. It wasn't a matter of choice. It was something that came over me like a disease.

"I went home a changed man," says Tom. "When I hit the street the next day, I was trying to find some Elvis Presley records. The music just hypnotised me, and I played these records to the point my parents began to worry that something was wrong with me."

From then on, Tom was on a quest to hear as many Elvis songs as possible, whenever possible. In fact, he traded his prize possession, a WHAM-O Slingshot, for a turntable and a box of 45s, many of which were Elvis singles. At the same time, Tom made full use of his family's transistor radio. "I always liked the radio, but at that point I became consumed with it. At night we could get WLS [890 AM in Chicago]. There, you got to hear all that great R&B stuff. I had to listen to everything. I became completely obsessed. There was a record shop, and there were a couple of five-and-dimes that had really good record departments. And I loved to browse there. I became so obsessed with it that my parents were worried – really worried that it was strange that I had no other interests than that."

The groundbreaking DJs that worked at WLS – one of the first stations to play contemporary music both night and day – may have inspired a young Tom Petty to expand his horizons and listen to a variety of musical acts. Prominent DJs Jim Dunbar, Ed Grennan, Mort Crowley, Gene Taylor, Bob Hale, Sam Holman (also the station's program director) and Dick Biondi were all spinning vinyl there in the early sixties. According to the station's own "Silver Dollar Survey" of

September 16, 1961, WLS was playing artists like Dick & Dee Dee, Troy Shondell, Bobby Vee, Lonnie Donegan, Jan & Dean, the Highwaymen, Fats Domino, the Lettermen, Ben E. King, Roy Orbison, Elvis Presley and Ray Charles – among others. Tom appreciated hearing all sorts of music and listening to the radio and buying records became one of his topmost priorities.

"The hook was in really deep," Tom admits of his passion for music at this time in his life. "I'm in about the fifth grade and I'm playing fifties records and it's all I want to talk about. Even the other kids thought it was weird."

That feeling of belonging that fans get when they first join the rock'n'roll fraternity helped fuel Tom's compulsion. He discovered that music consoled him when matters at home got out of control. "I never felt safe as a child," he admitted to *Harp*'s Jaan Uhelszki in 2006. "There is so much about my dad, looking back, that I like but I was so afraid of him. My father was such a loose cannon. I was never too at ease around him… I took refuge in the music – rock'n'roll was my safe place."

For the next few years Tom devoted all his time to music, listening to everything and anything he could. WLS DJ Dick Biondi is credited with being the first American DJ to play a Beatles song, 'Please Please Me', on the radio in February 1963 and it's entirely likely that Tom Petty was one of thousands of teenagers who heard the track on air. These years of listening to music on the radio coalesced into an important period in Tom's development, a time for discovering the type of man – and musician – he would become someday.

The world was changing fast in the early sixties and the politics of the era must have had an impact on Tom, albeit on the edge of his consciousness. The 1960 presidential race pitted charismatic Democrat John F. Kennedy, a Catholic from Boston, against then Vice President, Republican Richard Nixon. In the first televised presidential debate, Kennedy appeared to mop the floor with the older Nixon who was recovering from a leg injury and looked nervous and uncomfortable. Kennedy, on the other hand, went into the debate as if it were a movie soundstage, playing his part like a Shakespearean actor. It was the first time television played a major role in how the candidates conveyed their message to the voters. Soon, television would be the tastemaker of almost every aspect of American life.

While the changes of the day were uprooting American society, moving the country inexorably forward from the closed thinking of the fifties towards the free spiritedness that would characterise the next decade, Tom was sitting in his bedroom listening to every record he could get his hands on. "I spent the next two years, until The Beatles came, just literally listening to records every day. It never, *never* occurred to me to play or that I would sing, it was just, 'These are great!' I'd listen to 'em all day. When The Beatles came, that took over and Elvis moved to the back a little bit. Now I see, ah, you can do this. Here's a way out. Because even at 12, you gotta beat this place. Gotta get out of Gainesville.

"Elvis really did mean a lot to me as a child," Tom told *Pulse!* reporter Alan di Perna in a 1999 interview. "The whole idea that this person came from poverty, like me, and he got out and made something of himself. And that he did it by doing something pretty cool, rather than something that was devious, or being a crooked politician or any of the normal Southern ways out of things."

Changes had taken place in the world of rock'n'roll, too, where the first wave of US rockers had been largely silenced or neutered during the early, pre-Beatles sixties. Elvis had been drafted and when he emerged from the Army seemed a far less threatening proposition than when he went in; Chuck Berry had been jailed; Little Richard found God; Jerry Lee Lewis was in disgrace for marrying his 13-year-old cousin; and Buddy Holly, whom history now credits with having originated the concept of the 'rock band', had died in a plane crash. It seemed as if the music industry was clawing back control after the first wave of rock'n'roll rebels, and the charts were now the preserve of 'safer' music, though much of it, notably that which emanated from the Brill Building in New York, was certainly not lacking in quality. But it wasn't to last. On the horizon was a group from England called The Beatles and within a matter of days after their first US TV appearance America's young would see the light.

It is impossible to overemphasise the effect that The Beatles had on America's teenage population when they arrived in the country in February 1964. Millions watched their first appearance on *The Ed Sullivan Show*, and later that year Tom saw The Beatles' film *A Hard Day's Night*, which solidified his notion that music was his way out: "… that's obviously the way you go, you know; you've got farming over here, and on this side, The Beatles."

Tom almost got to see the band play live in concert. *Almost.* "I had a ticket to see The Beatles in Jacksonville [September 11, 1964], but two days before there was a hurricane and it was pissing with rain so my Mom said, 'There's no way you are driving to Jacksonville.' So I didn't get to see The Beatles." It wouldn't be until the following year that Tom went to his first live show. "The first concert I ever went to was headlined by The Beach Boys, but The Zombies and The Searchers were on the bill [July 24, 1965, at the Jacksonville Coliseum]," remembers Tom. "Quite a show. I really wanted to see the British bands, and The Zombies were mind-blowingly good while The Searchers had such beautiful voices, mesmerizing. And John McNally [founding member of The Searchers] played a Telecaster, the first time I'd seen one, and it had this bright, brittle sound. I remember thinking it sounds good."

★ ★ ★

As Tom became more and more infatuated with the music of the day, it wasn't long before he wanted a guitar of his own. Like a thousand teenage boys with stars in their eyes and hair that now flopped down almost to cover them, he convinced his mom to buy him a brand-new model from the Sears, Roebuck catalog. "It was one of these dollar-down, dollar-a-day jobs," he remembers. "She said, 'What songs are you going to play?' and I said we were going to write our own songs. She burst into laughter: 'You want to write songs, and you can't even play an instrument yet?' But I just thought, 'They can do it. Why can't I?'" Kitty Petty was puzzled by this notion but she loved her son and admired the persistence and tenacity he displayed while begging her to part with a few hard-earned dollars. This more than anything was what persuaded her to buy him the guitar.

To this day, Tom tells people that his mom "was a complete angel", eternally supportive of his dreams. "She was cool," said Tom. "She'd give me Rolling Stones albums." His brother Bruce also has incredibly fond memories of Kitty as he recounted in the *Runnin' Down A Dream* documentary: "My mother was always kind of the glue that held the family together."

By 1965 the extraordinary success of The Beatles had convinced Tom that it was time to start a band. For Tom, the Fab Four was the spark that put his future in focus. "It wasn't until The Beatles that there was a real bolt of lightning to the brain. You know, 'Oh, a self-contained band.' They had the singers and the band all in one thing. Then the kids around the neighbourhood would talk about, 'Let's form a group and be like The Beatles.' And it looked to me like a really good job – they were obviously young and in charge of their own lives. And it was a good way to have friends and meet girls, and I loved music so much that I hustled up a guitar and got in a group long before I could play. We hammered it out. And I've been in a group now since 1965."

Two kids from the neighbourhood – Richie Henson and Robert Crawford – actually taught Tom guitar basics, showing him the notes, chords and scales, and Tom took to the instrument quite easily. The first songs he learned and performed included 'Wooly Bully' by Domingo "Sam" Zamudio of Sam the Sham & The Pharaohs, Tommy Tucker's 'High Heel Sneakers' and 'Love Potion #9' by Jerry Leiber and Mike Stoller, a minor hit for The Clovers in 1959 but a number three hit by The Searchers in 1965. Once Tom had a guitar, he experimented and taught himself songs by ear, by trial and error. It came naturally to him, so much so that he even began writing his own tunes. The first song he wrote was called 'Baby, I'm Leaving'.

There was a second and equally strong force that persuaded Tom that music-making was a worthwhile endeavour. It was, naturally, a girl. Even at 14 or 15 Tom was already getting a handle on male bravado and posturing for the ladies. One night he went to a dance at Gainesville High and struck up a conversation about music with an appealing young classmate and told her that he was in a band. The fib backfired when, much to his surprise, she told him she was on the school dance committee and promptly booked his "band" to play a few songs at the next event. Too embarrassed to tell her that his band was a figment of his imagination, the next day Tom wasted no time in putting matters right. "I set about scouring the neighbourhood for anybody that owned instruments, that could play instruments and we just struck gold. I will never forget it. We went to my house, we all plugged into the same amplifier. We found something we all knew. *Wham!* The heavens split, like this sound was incredible! It was the biggest rush of my life. Wow, you know, we're doing it! You know, we're making this music."

Wearing matching blue shirts to the dance, despite their nerves Tom and his friends pulled it off. "We started to play and we were a huge success. Everybody dug it, and we played our three songs, and everybody yelled for more, so we played them again."

After the dance, a booker for frat-house parties in the area hired them for another gig under one condition: learn some more songs. Tom took the challenge to heart and never looked back.

Tom's first official band was called The Sundowners and consisted of Tom, Richie Henson and Robert Crawford, all on guitars, and Dennis Lee on drums. The group didn't have a bass player at first but Tom switched from guitar to bass soon after the band's formation. Tom's father stepped up and bought him a professional bass, a Gibson EB-2, and a Fender Tremolux amplifier around this time. It was an unexpected gesture of love and acceptance that meant a lot to Tom at the time and still does to this day.

The Sundowners went to work practising and learning more songs, among them 'House Of The Rising Sun', the traditional song that The Animals took to number one in 1964, and The Ventures' instrumental hit 'Walk Don't Run'. As their repertoire grew, so did the band's bookings at frat parties around town. They'd play songs by The Rolling Stones, The Animals and The Kinks, all of whose early albums featured cover versions of American R&B and blues songs, thus drawing Tom and his bandmates back into the American music that so inspired the first wave of British bands. Beatles songs weren't part of their stage act yet because the band members were unable to sing harmony. That skill would come in time.

Tom found it liberating to finally connect with people his own age that shared a love of music… especially the music that The Beatles

29

brought to America. "I'd been a collector of old music and when I hit the age of 13 The Beatles came and it was completely contemporary and all of a sudden my friends could share in this passion I had... which was really nice because until then my friends were not interested in rock'n'roll records," Tom says. "When garage bands started, everyone had a very similar set list; everyone played the current hits and when we went into the deeper tracks, it was usually The Rolling Stones, The Animals, learning blues and R&B through those acts. I didn't know Chuck Berry except I learned those songs through The Rolling Stones. It would be a while before I understood what he was about. It was a fantastic road map The Beatles and Stones laid down if you were a fanatic like I was; I'd see their names as songwriters, and I'd go find these guys, get the records and it was a whole other revelation."

Tom's search for these fathers of R&B, soul and rock'n'roll was a veritable master class in music theory. He studied the likes of Howlin' Wolf, Arthur "Big Boy" Crudup, Elmore James, Fats Domino, Otis Redding, John Lee Hooker and others. He had no way of knowing how important this knowledge base would be in the future.

★ ★ ★

When Tom was about 15 years old, his group competed in a "battle of the bands" competition. The prize was the chance to play the Moose Club dance every Friday night. The Sundowners easily trumped the competition and won the gig, which paid $100 per dance. Now things were getting serious. Dennis Lee's mom sewed actual uniforms for The Sundowners: pink collarless jackets with white ruffled shirts and black trousers. The guys also began wearing Beatle boots with Cuban heels. The band played gigs often and was making money. "The first time we got paid," recalls Tom, "my mom really thought I had stolen the money and was really concerned that I'd taken up a life of crime." Once he explained that he'd earned the money for playing music, she was surprised but proud. That said, she immediately told Tom not to set his sights on the local bars: "Don't think you're going to be down in the bars playing," she told him. But, mothers don't always get their way.

The Sundowners were becoming a well-respected band in town and the gigs – all types of gigs – kept coming.

Though only a freshman in high school, Tom was treating this adventure as a profession. Nevertheless it cost him some of the experiences that other high school kids were having. At one point, his love of music lost him a girlfriend, Jackie Taylor, because he had to play another school's prom on the same night of his own. He also eventually had to miss his own high school graduation ceremony due to a gig. To Tom, these sacrifices were worthwhile if it meant the band was moving forward in the Gainesville music scene.

The problem for Tom was that not all of The Sundowners were taking the band as seriously as he was. Even as a boy, Tom took everything about music to heart. He may have been one of the youngest guys in the band but he was taking most of the responsibility. "Gainesville was a wonderful place to be doing what we were doing," says Tom now. "There were a lot of venues to play because of the college. Frat parties, which weren't our favourite, clubs, functions. We were enterprising little kids."

At this point, Tom felt the need to explore other options. On a few occasions he sat in on bass for The Epics, another popular Gainesville mainstay, and they began lobbying for him to join them on a full-time basis. He resisted jumping The Sundowners' ship until he got into a fight with Dennis Lee, then promptly quit the band and joined The Epics on his sixteenth birthday – right after he went down to the Department of Motor Vehicles to get his driver's license.

The Epics – Rodney Rucker singing lead, Ricky Rucker and Tom Leadon on guitars and Dickie Underwood on drums – were even more successful than The Sundowners. Tom would join as their bass player. The members were older than Tom, who was in tenth grade at the time. Most of The Epics were in their senior year and others had graduated the year before.

Even in this band, though, Tom took all the initiative. He had business cards made up for The Epics that included his name and phone number and he booked gigs himself. The tagline on the cards noted, "For love or money." He'd play music just for the sheer joy but he wanted to

31

make a living too. In 2006, Rick Rucker – now a high-school teacher in Ocala, Florida – told *Gainesville Sun* staff reporter Alice Wallace that, "We [The Epics] realized Tom was the real musician of the band."

During his tenure as a member of The Epics, Tom took a part-time after-school job at Lipham Music. Don Felder, who would eventually join the Eagles, also worked at the store. These were important days for Tom and he was soon learning more about music than he could have ever imagined. His parents continued to worry about his single-minded obsession with music. His high school guidance counselor took him to task and asked why he wasn't interested in learning subjects at school. Tom coolly and honestly replied, "Rock is more fun." His dad was not amused by Tom's attitude. "My father thought I had the devil in me," he says. "I can understand him being a little concerned. I was kinda failing at school. I got this report card with all Fs, except for one D minus in crafts, and he broke all my records. What gets me is I showed up enough to get Fs instead of incompletes.

"I was a problem to society. My crafts teacher, the one who gave me the D minus, she wanted me to stop hanging out with musicians. 'Look at Elvis Presley,' she said. 'If he hadn't the talent and a good manager, he wouldn't have had a job to fall back on.' I always thought Elvis was kind of a poor example to prove her point."

In addition to his music, Tom did find gainful employment in other areas during his high school years and beyond. They were "straight" jobs, as Tom liked to call them, but he found he wasn't particularly good at any of them and certainly didn't enjoy the time he spent working in a barbecue restaurant, at a cemetery, on a construction site and as a grounds maintenance man at the local university. He didn't see any of those opportunities taking him very far.

When high school graduation day came in June 1968, Tom breathed a sigh of relief. Finally, he could focus all of his time and attention on his music career, one that would lead him to a new life, far away from Gainesville.

Following his dream to become a rock'n'roll musician meant founding a proper band with other like-minded musicians who also longed to leave Gainesville. "I discovered the limitations of the place early on," says Tom. "There's a lot of nice things about the town I grew up in, but I wasn't the kind of person who would have been content to settle and stay there. There's nothing wrong with that. Sometimes I wish I was that kind of person."

But Tom had found his calling and there was nothing he could do to stop it. "I feel like a lucky man," Tom concedes. "A lot of people really struggle to find out what they want to do in life, but I knew as soon as I saw Elvis Presley, when I was 11. From that point, music became my religion, my nourishment. It was also a safe haven for me. My life was very turbulent as a child and a little scary, and music made everything seem right."

CHAPTER 2

Down On The Farm
In Hogtown
(1970–1973)

"You couldn't ever have planned it, or dreamed it up: just two of the best musicians in the world walked right into my life and completely grasped what I wanted to do."

— T.P.

In 1970 Tom Petty had come to the conclusion that The Epics just weren't serious enough about the music business. His horizons extended much further than the limited Gainesville music scene, towards rock'n'roll's world stage, and bandmate Tom Leadon shared Tom's frustrations. Together, they set out to form a new group.

Tom knew that if his band had any chance of being noticed by the mainstream, they had to perform their own material. "We realized that, if we wanted to truly make a living doing this, we were going to have to play original music," he says. "I was playing the bass. Tom [Leadon] was playing the guitar. Jim Lenahan was singing lead. We were looking for another guitarist and a drummer." While this is the story that's often told these days, some local Gainesvillians say that The Epics actually changed their name to Mudcrutch prior to the Rucker brothers leaving the band. When they did depart, that's when Tom and Tom sought out replacements. Either way, changes were afoot for them both.

The duo tacked a flyer to the community corkboard at Lipham Music to let area musicians know they were holding auditions. Local drummer Randall Marsh answered that call and the two Toms went to Marsh's place – a house on a farm just outside town – to audition him. Guitarist Mike Campbell, now affectionately known by Tom as the "Co-Captain" of The Heartbreakers, was Randall's roommate at the time.

Randall's audition was going well and when the musicians took a break from playing they mentioned that they were also looking for a second guitarist. Randall was quick to say, "Well, my friend is in the back room here. He plays guitar." So the guys coaxed shy Mike Campbell out of his bedroom for an impromptu audition. Tom is fond of recounting his first meeting with Mike: "He's carrying this $80 Japanese guitar. At that point, we all kind of looked at the ground like, 'Oh, no. This guy's bound to be terrible.' Mike kicks off 'Johnny B. Goode', and we aren't looking at the floor any more. The song ended and I just said, 'Hey, you're in our band.' He's like, 'Oh, I don't know.' I said, "*I* know. You're in the band,' and we were fast friends right away."

Mike was hesitant because he was enrolled for the upcoming semester at the University of Florida. Tom emphatically told him, "You *don't* want to do that." He actually lobbied for Mike to quit school. He was sure that Mike's fortunes would be much richer in the music world than in any academic setting.

"I can't believe now that I had that much gumption," laughs Tom, "but I talked him into quitting school." Tom may have only been 20 years old at the time but he was charismatic even back then and *very* convincing. These traits have only strengthened in the years since.

Quitting college brought a new obstacle, though. This was 1970 and the conflict in Vietnam was far from over. In fact, fighting peaked in 1968 during the Tet Offensive and even though the Paris Peace Accords were signed in January of 1973, fighting went on until 1975. Young men who enrolled in college during this time period got a draft deferment, but the Army was calling up others who were of sound mind and body. Many men of that era made the choice to enlist in the hopes of getting better (and somewhat safer) assignments overseas instead of taking their chances and being drafted.

Mike was beginning to think that perhaps he should join up before the Army came calling. Tom reassured him, "Aw, we'll handle that." In actuality, Tom had no idea how they'd "get around the Army" but he was sure they'd find a way. Knowing Tom, they would have. Luckily, their draft cards were never drawn and that crisis was averted.

Mike quickly learned that Tom Petty was not like other guys his age. "I thought that he had something on the ball with the songwriting," admits Mike "because not too many people around the college were really writing their own songs."

Mike Campbell was born eight months before Tom, on February 1, 1950, in Panama City, Florida, and later moved to Jacksonville. He came from a humble, working-class background and back then no fortune-teller could have predicted that he was destined to become one of the most acclaimed rock guitarists of his generation. He was a quiet kid whose passion for guitar came in his mid-teens. "I got my first guitar kind of late as we were kind of poor," Mike recently told Tom Guerra of *Tone Quest Report*. "I was about 16, I think, when I started fiddling around with it and it was like everything else in my life became unimportant at that point. It was all about the guitar."

Before 1966, Mike had to be content with simply listening to records and even rode out the beginning of the British Invasion without a guitar. He says, "My dad was a big Elvis and Johnny Cash fan, and he always played those records and I always seemed to key in to the guitar playing, either Scotty Moore or Luther Perkins. I just loved that stuff. And then, like most kids my age, when The Beatles happened in '64, I was mesmerised by the whole thing, and picked up the guitar and started learning off of records."

Mike never had any formal guitar training but he does remember taking some accordion lessons in school in sixth grade. From that he picked up a little theory and learned the rudiments of how to read music. Like Tom, Mike was given his first guitar by his mother. It was

36

"a Harmony acoustic for $30 that was unplayable", he recounts. "The strings were so high and I would struggle like crazy and my fingers would bleed trying to play the damn thing. Then I went to a friend's house one day and he had a Gibson SG and I could not believe how easy it was to push the strings down. So I started on that Harmony acoustic and later my dad got me my first electric guitar, a Guyatone."

Mike's first amp was his record player. "My dad was an electrician and he had a record player that was all in pieces, so I just plugged my guitar into that," he says.

Like Tom, Mike figured things out by trial and error. "Back then we didn't have cassette players or anything," Mike says, "but I would sometimes slow the records down and listen real close and try to figure out how the guitar player was doing certain things. I had a couple of guitar books, too. I got a couple of ideas on how to finger certain chords from that, but most of it I just picked up by ear, off the records.

"I was just trying to learn how to play," Mike admits. "I'd get together in the garage with friends occasionally and try to play 'Louie, Louie' or something like that."

In June of 1968 Mike graduated from Jean Ribault High School in Jacksonville and set out for Gainesville, enrolling for the next semester at the University of Florida. In the meantime, he was enjoying the rich music scene. According to Mike, "I didn't really get a group together until I went to college; then I met Tom and joined his group."

Benmont Tench, a keyboardist on the Gainesville music scene at the time, was in awe of Mike's guitar playing from the beginning, saying, "It was very strange. Mike would just stand there and play beautifully and he wouldn't show off and he wouldn't try to sound like Duane Allman. You could hear some [Jerry] Garcia in him. You could hear some country in him. He was really, really good and he wasn't flash. Even on the long instrumental pieces, it was never about flash. It might be about excitement but it certainly wasn't about 'Look how fast I can play.' It was just about fun."

Tom Leadon recalls those early days with Mike in the band. "We tried to get him to sing harmonies, but he was so shy," Tom remembers. "We put a mic in front of him, turned it up as loud as we could, and you still couldn't hear him. He was such a fantastic guitarist. His fingers did his talking for him, I guess."

Mike brought equal parts raw talent and dedication to the craft. He plays the guitar for hours on end each day. He always has. That's how he's honed his trademark sound that Tom Petty couldn't live without.

★ ★ ★

With the line-up in place – Jim Lenahan on vocals, Tom Petty on bass, Tom Leadon and Mike Campbell on guitar and Randall Marsh on drums – it was time to name the band. Tom had always hated the name "The Epics" because he felt it sounded so "corny". The moniker for his new band had to grab listeners. They came up with Mudcrutch. "We all liked it," said Tom Leadon, "because it kind of sounded dirty and decrepit. It sounded like something adults and straight people would not understand or wouldn't approve of. We liked that."

Before progressing much further, though, vocalist Jim Lenahan departed, leaving a void in the lead singer slot that Tom Petty filled by stepping into the role as singer-songwriter and consummate bandleader. (In time Jim Lenahan would make a name for himself in the field of concert lighting, and he works with Tom to this day.)

With Tom at the helm, each member of the group was energised by the formation of Mudcrutch. It wasn't long before they were playing all over town, including the University of Florida. They also scored a coveted gig as the house band at Dub's Steer Room, a dive bar on US Route 441 that boasted a special feature: topless dancers. Tom recounts this particular gig fondly. "I had never played in a bar. The Epics played teen dances and things like that, but we were all too young to work in a bar. You worked five sets a night, six days a week, but you all got 100 bucks at the end of the week. The real feature of Dub's was six topless dancers. You know, we got down to the club and it hadn't really registered to me what topless dancing really was."

Tom Leadon followed up on that thought in the *Runnin' Down A Dream* documentary: "We played two or three songs and they [the go-go girls] came walking up. They started dancing and removing their tops and everyone in the band was just getting all blush-faced." That's when Tom Petty realized something: "I'm going to like this professional musician thing."

The band soon became accustomed to the new venue, but its patrons weren't always receptive to the music Mudcrutch wanted to play. The club owner was adamant that the guys play only Top 40 material. Randall Marsh explained how the band got around that little rule. "We'd just play a Neil Young song and say it was a number one hit or something. Or, we'd do one of our own songs and say that it was by Santana. They didn't know the difference."

★ ★ ★

Next to join the band was keyboard player Benmont Tench III, born in Gainesville on September 7, 1953. His unusual Christian name was adopted from the first few letters of each of his given names, Benjamin and Montmorency. His father, Benjamin M. Tench Jr., was a well-respected circuit court judge in Gainesville, and his mother, Mary Catherine "Katie" McInnis Tench, was an airline stewardess before becoming a homemaker.

In an interview Benmont's father gave to historian Nancy Steigner in 1986, he explained how his son began his musical education. "I started him with my music teacher. At that point, I was playing the piano. I was working on a little Beethoven sonata in two movements, a sonata G, not very good," he recalled. "I came home one afternoon and I heard it just being ripped off. I wondered who in the hell was playing the piano. It was my six-year-old son. So I said, 'Wait a minute. This little boy has got more going for him than I realized.'" From that day on, Benmont would continue piano lessons – first with Professor Danberg in Gainesville and then at the National Conservatory of Music in Panama from 1960 to 1962 when his father was in the Foreign Services. The family returned to Gainesville in 1962 and Benmont picked up where he left off with Professor Danberg.

Benmont's parents were proud of his training in classical music but all that went out the window in 1964 when The Beatles arrived in America. Like it did for Tom and Mike – and thousands of other American kids – rock'n'roll took hold of Benmont from that point forward. It was also in 1964 that Benmont would first meet Tom Petty. "Benmont, I knew, when he was just a little guy. He couldn't have been more than 11 or 12," reminisces Tom. "He came into Lipham Music. He began to play a Beatles album on the organ, and he played the entire album. Certainly, the best keyboardist I've ever heard." Tom was impressed at the time but didn't really think much of the chance meeting until years later.

Benmont continued studying the piano and learned the Farfisa. "I played Farfisa [organ] for a while, and then I switched to Wurlitzer [electric piano]," Benmont told Jon Regen of *Keyboard* magazine. "I didn't like the sound of Hammonds. I loved Matthew Fisher and Booker T. Jones, but I didn't like the 'big Hammond with a lot of tremolo' sound. It seemed like it was trying too hard. So I didn't want to play Hammond."

In 1967 Benmont's parents sent him to Phillips Exeter Academy, a prestigious private boarding school in Exeter, New Hampshire. He continued piano classes there while he prepared for college. He still spent as much time as he could on Gainesville's music scene, though, and he made it a point to check out the hottest band around, Mudcrutch. "On a break from boarding school, I went to see them play at a bar," says Benmont. "I was underage. They were great. When they came off the stage – if there even was a stage, there was probably just a corner of the bar, I don't remember – you could see Tom had something going on. He had some kind of vibe, even at the time, just playing some bar.

"Mudcrutch was a real interesting band," he contends. "There was a good deal of the Burritos [Flying Burrito Brothers] in it, a good deal of country. It was a rock'n'roll band but there were also these beautiful pieces of instrumental music that would go maybe 10 minutes that were orchestrated and largely worked out that were pretty wild. My friend Sandy [Stringfellow] would call me and say, 'Come down, Mudcrutch is playing this fraternity party tonight.' And I'd go down and they would play something just out of this world that sounded very strange – not an instrumental along the lines of [the Allmans'] 'In Memory Of Elizabeth Reed', but somewhere between The Beatles' 'And Your Bird Can Sing' and the Grateful Dead."

One of the first bands Benmont was ever in was with his childhood friend Sandy Stringfellow who recalls the good old days in Gainesville when Mudcrutch was the hottest band on the scene. "Nobody I knew of was writing songs or even interested in trying, except for Tom Petty," Sandy says. "The thing about Tom was that his songwriting was so exceptionally good, even back then, that it was somewhat intimidating to engage in musical discourse with him. Not that he was condescending or anything like that. He simply had a remarkable and intuitive sense of how songs were put together. I'd never been around anyone who seemed to know much about songwriting, and here was this local cat writing better songs than most of what was being played on the radio."

Sandy explains on his website SandyStringfellow.com, "In my senior year of high school I used to hang out at the infamous farm house just to listen to Mudcrutch practise sessions. It was obvious to me that Mudcrutch was a band that had something special. There was a definite musical synergy born of talented musicians, excellent songs and a common creative direction." That is probably why he always encouraged his pal Benmont to check out the band whenever he was home from boarding school.

In 1971 Benmont graduated from high school and matriculated to Tulane University in New Orleans that fall. The Tenches were still holding out hope that their son would follow a traditional career path and pick a profession that would keep him close to home. That wasn't meant to be.

One night when he was in town during a college break he sat in with Mudcrutch. "I played Farfisa the first time I played with Mudcrutch," Benmont recalls, "and then I played Wurlitzer. I had a Wurlitzer with a Marshall stack. It was fantastic – 100 watts of a Wurlitzer. It got loud. We played some high school auditorium and cracked the ceiling."

Tom was knocked out by Benmont's musicianship: "He got up, and he didn't have any rehearsal and he out-played all of us for five hours." Mike Campbell concurred: "He was so good and he had so much musical training that none of us have." Everyone in Mudcrutch agreed: Benmont had to join the band.

His piano prowess may have impressed the band but Benmont says they were still on a steep learning curve when he joined. "There was one long piece that was absolutely gorgeous and when I joined the band it was a bitch for me to learn how to play Tom Leadon's part on the piano and work out the harmonies with Mike. Mike was pretty impressive. Mike was scary."

With Benmont now in the band, everyone was motivated to take their craft to the next level and they spent much of their time offstage practising at Mudcrutch Farm, as Randall and Mike's place of residence became known.

Tom recalls that at this point Mudcrutch was strongly influenced by the British Invasion, the slew of bands from the UK that followed The Beatles across the Atlantic and virtually monopolised the *Billboard* charts in 1964 and '65. Manning the barricades in the US was The Byrds, another influence on Tom and Mudcrutch, as well as their country-rock spin-off band, The Flying Burrito Brothers. "I think we were trying to kind of be the Southern version of The Flying Burrito Brothers," says Tom. "We stuck a lot of country and fifties rock into our stuff and tried to blend it all together." The band didn't really sound like any other group in the area. They had their own unique vibe. "I think Mudcrutch was a pretty interesting band for a bunch of kids that didn't know what they were doing," Benmont says. "It was all over the map but it was trying to find some kind of ground and we finally found it: Let Tommy take the ball and run with it!"

Gainesville's rich music scene also influenced Mudcrutch and there was a never-ending supply of musicians to watch and learn from. "I think the Allman Brothers was one of the first bands I ever saw at the American Legion when they were The Escorts or some band like that playing Beatles songs," says Tom. "And [Lynyrd] Skynyrd were around; they used to open for Mudcrutch, but they were more like a heavy metal group than a boogie band in those days. There are probably a lot of people who surfaced out of that... But there wasn't anybody doing what we were doing. We were kinda outside things because we didn't play long solos, and I never really copped to the blues. We dug R&B, but it was more like Wilson Pickett stuff and Stax.

"I think it really helped in some way where we grew up. It was a real musical place. You have lots of good musicians and lots of places to play because of the college," says Tom. "And you had to be good there, too. If you weren't pretty good you wouldn't get a gig, because there were too many people who *were* good. So when we were really little boys, we had to practise and get pretty good."

Gainesville was also the type of place where musicians could create their own opportunities, as evidenced by the Mudcrutch Farm Festivals. These memorable gigs are a hallmark of the band's years in Gainesville. Held at the band's place of residence at 2203 N.W. 45th Avenue in 1971 and 1972, the multi-band festivals drew large crowds of music lovers who turned up to see Mudcrutch and a line-up of other local bands. The first free concert was held on December 13, 1971.

Tom Leadon recalls how it all got started: "We were sitting around the Mudcrutch Farm and we wanted to play for the kids. We wanted to play some of these outdoor shows that are so much fun. Mike had the idea: 'Let's invite them all out here.'

"We cleared an area at the side of the house, and we invited a couple of other bands, on a Sunday. We had the local health food co-op bring some free food. We just put posters around town, and there were hundreds of people, maybe 1,500 people," Leadon recalls.

Randall explains what happened next. "The police came the first time we had it and said, 'What the hell's going on here? Do you guys have a license and everything?' Luckily, back then, it was a simpler time and they said, 'Next time...' Next time, we got the license."

Even though the band's landlord served them with an eviction notice after the first festival, the band had time to sneak another performance in under the wire. "The second time," says Leadon, "we must have had 15 bands, and from all over the south. It became quite a famous thing."

Sadly, like so many other cool events, it got too big and too difficult to control. "We had to quit because people were coming from other states," says Randall. "That was really, in some ways, some of the best times. We were our own little entity. We didn't have any controllers. We did everything ourselves. It was just a really good time."

The Mudcrutch Farm Festivals proved what the band already knew: the locals and college kids had an insatiable thirst for live music. Gainesville was a true proving ground for the band. Playing live on a near-constant basis, they were often referred to as "Gainesville's No. 1 Boogie Band". On February 13, 1971, they played the Rat in Gainesville. The cover was 75 cents; 50 cents for single girls. My, how things have changed!

They played out constantly during this time period and often teamed up with other local bands, like Road Turkey and Cowboy.

As 1972 rolled around, Mudcrutch was still going strong in terms of live gigs. A May date at the Rat was a success and they returned there later in the year in August. It's worth noting that ticket prices jumped from a mere 50 cents in May to a whopping $1.50 in August. The band's popularity certainly outpaced inflation, which was about 3.4 percent in the United States in 1972.

Although they were able to get the crème de la crème gigs across the state, Mudcrutch was nearing a crossroads. A record deal was obviously the next goal, and they decided to hit up Phil Walden's Capricorn Records in Macon, Georgia, the home base for many Southern rock bands of the era, including The Allman Brothers Band. "I remember hanging around the studio with this band called The Marshall Tucker Band," says Tom. "They were making their first record, and they invited us in, and we sat around all day and waited for someone to listen to our tape. And the answer was, 'It's too British. It sounds too English.' So we decided then we were going to California."

First, though, they needed a demo. It was crucial that Mudcrutch have some of its songs professionally recorded so Tom could properly "sell" the band to record company execs when he hit Los Angeles, the epicenter of the record business on the West Coast. They were fortunate that a friend of the band, who earned a living off his pepper farm, was able to front the money for an excursion to Miami's Criteria Studios where producer Mack Emerman, who owned the facility, assigned producer/engineer Ron Albert to the session. This was an incredible break since Albert had tracked the sessions for Eric Clapton that resulted in his acclaimed 1970 album *Layla And Other Assorted Love Songs*, recorded as Derek & The Dominos, on which Duane Allman was a guest guitarist. Ron was the real deal and the sessions yielded two singles, 'Up In Mississippi (Tonight)' and 'Cause Is Understood'.*

Around the same time an altercation at Dub's bar led to the band being summarily fired from their mainstay gig and Tom Leadon leaving the group, his place taken by guitarist Danny Roberts. Leadon headed to Los Angeles on his own, following in the footsteps of his brother Bernie who had joined the newly formed Eagles. Tom Leadon ended up playing bass in Linda Ronstadt's band for a while.

His replacement, Danny Roberts, is barely mentioned in biographies of Mudcrutch today. Truth be told, he was a member of the very short-lived Mudcrutch 2.0 and most music historians are more likely to wax nostalgic about the original line-up. Still, Danny was an official member of the band and shared Tom's dream of leaving Gainesville behind and heading to Los Angeles.

Danny recalls how Tom recruited him after he'd played a gig in Gainesville with another band. "I was getting my stuff off the stage," he recalled on an online message board recently, "and this guy named Tom Petty walked up to me and asked if I'd be interested in joining Mudcrutch. I told them I'd stick around and check 'em out. We immediately started rehearsing several times a week, so I made the move to Gainesville and joined the band."

While Mudcrutch did have two demo songs recorded, Tom felt they needed more material to convince a record company to give them a deal. "We had become the biggest thing Gainesville had ever seen," Tom remembers. "But we felt we had to break out of there."

At the time, Mudcrutch had a roadie named Keith McAllister who was a regular customer at Marvin Kay's Music Center. The manager, Rick Reed, also owned a mobile recording van and made his living not only from the music store but by the fees he collected from high school bands and choirs that paid him to make recordings of their live performances.

---

* Fans can still occasionally find these 7-inch vinyl gems at used record stores and on eBay. Look for #9449 on the Red Pepper label.

Rick recalls how no-nonsense his approach was: "The recording technique was fairly simple: a two mic setup, trying to capture the sound field of a live acoustic performance. The key was carefully placing the microphones. For location recording I had bought a 1973 Dodge Maxivan and built all the equipment into it except the recorder. The tape deck was in a console with wheels, and I could roll it in and out of the van."

Rick may never have worked with Mudcrutch save for the fact that one of his co-workers, Sandy Stringfellow, knew all the guys in the band and he proposed the idea of a remote location demo recording to Keith and Tom. Professional, affordable recording studios in the Gainesville area were very limited in the early seventies, and having a demo made – even in someone's living room – probably greatly appealed to Tom and the rest of the guys in Mudcrutch.

For Rick, it was the chance to do something new. "The Mudcrutch sessions were the only rock'n'roll multiple-microphone recording I had done," he admits. "Everything else had been just two microphones on tall stands in an auditorium, recording concert bands or choral performances."

After Tom hired Rick, the only question that remained was where they would record the demo. Benmont volunteered the use of his parents' living room. "I pulled into the Tench driveway," says Rick, "and I had this big single cable, known as a 'snake', that I reeled into the living room. It had a terminal box at the end with inputs for 16 microphones. Keith [McAllister] was saying, 'Put eight mics on the drums,' but that wasn't going to be possible with only 16 inputs to work with. I probably used some of Mudcrutch's mics as well as my own.

"We put microphones on the Tench grand piano and guitar amps, and Keith was helping me understand how he would mic them for a concert. Then he and I sat in the truck out in the driveway and tried to get a decent mix as the band played," remembers Rick. "After the first few takes the band would come out to the truck and we'd make a few adjustments. We recorded a few hours a day for two days that way. We left everything set up in the living room after the first day, so the second day we just had to plug the snake back into the truck and start recording again. Then the band came up to my house and we did the editing with everyone's input, in one afternoon, and created a master tape with leader tape between each cut. There's eight songs. Then I made reel-to-reel copies on 7-inch reels for them."

Rick was paid the princely sum of $200 for two days' work; Tom paid the bill himself with a personal check. Rick recalls that even back then Tom was no-nonsense "which really stood out at the time. During the playback and editing he seemed to be real tuned in to making it happen in an organised, efficient way. It was all business."

For all the professionalism that seemed to come naturally to Tom, it was still incredibly hard to make a living. After all, $100 didn't go much further in the early seventies than it does today. Mike Campbell has said in the past that, "Our families were just scraping and barely making ends meet. Tom and I come from a poor, Southern background – you wouldn't believe how poor. Rock'n'roll is your ticket to make something of yourself, if you can do it well. It's the dream." This dream sustained the band throughout the lean times.

"I was really lucky because, from an extremely early age, music was all I wanted to do," says Tom. "I never even considered doing anything else or thought about the consequences if it didn't work out." Tom knew, as if by divine intervention, that music was his salvation. At the time, and many times since, Tom said, "All I want to do is keep playing, even if I don't make a dime."

Still, it was important to him to leave Gainesville behind and see what kind of life he could make for himself – all on his own. He just knew there was so much more to life somewhere else.

"I never bought the idea of having your life laid out for you," he confides, "and I got out, but a lot of them never do. It's hard to understand why, but that tradition is so strong that they don't ever realize that two hours in any direction gets you somewhere else. But I could see the creases in the curtain at a real early age." Music helped Tom break away.

CHAPTER 3

Phone Booths And First Records (1974–1976)

"Out of the blue, here he came."

— Denny Cordell

It was 1974 and Tom Petty was frustrated. All he thought about was relocating to Los Angeles — a veritable Mecca for rock musicians. Yes, it was true that Mudcrutch was one of the most popular bands in Gainesville. And he was truly grateful for that. The band played throughout the region to packed clubs and could even fill University Auditorium with nearly a thousand fans. The band was enjoying local success. That much was certain.

But strategically, what would the band gain from staying in Gainesville? Capricorn Records, the big label in the South, had already turned Tom and the boys down. So, why should they stay any longer?

At this point, Tom figured the only reason the band stuck around Northern Florida was the familiarity and the good feelings that come with being the biggest fish in a very small pond. Was that a good enough reason to stay put? The answer always came back as a resounding, "no".

He knew, deep down, that he had to get out of Gainesville. He'd actually known this fact since he was two years old. He didn't belong in this sleepy town.

Of course, there were a few personal issues that he needed to grapple with. In 1970 his mother had been diagnosed with a brain tumor and while she was fighting to get better, she was struggling. There was really nothing Tom or anyone else could do to make things better for Kitty but he probably felt helpless and sad about moving away while she was ill. Would sticking around Gainesville help his mom? No. And she wouldn't want him to sacrifice his future for hers.

Tom was also in a serious relationship at the time with a girl named Jane Benyo. What would happen when he moved to Los Angeles? Would they break up? Would she move to California, too? These questions probably flitted through his mind but at the end of the day, one way or another, he was going to leave Gainesville. The question was: when?

Where to move was a much easier question to answer. Los Angeles seemed like the logical choice for the band's next home base. After all, Tom said, he "figured it would be better to starve in the sunshine than go to New York and starve in the snow". Fair enough. The fact was that the music scene in New York City was focused more on upcoming new wave acts like Patti Smith and Blondie or punk bands like the Ramones than on straightforward rock acts like Mudcrutch. This band of Southerns would probably have felt out of place with the punks and the hip-hop precursors like Grandmaster Flash and Afrika Bambaataa who were emerging in Manhattan at the time. The Big Apple was gritty and dirty and fast-paced and none of those attributes appealed to Tom. New York City was definitely off the table. The band would move on, but they would head to Los Angeles.

Tom had always felt that the band needed professionally recorded material before striking westward. That problem had been solved with the remote recordings Rick Reed made with them at Benmont's family home. Tom now had everything he needed to try to convince a record company executive to take a chance on his band. How hard could it be to get a record deal, anyway? Tom didn't know the answer to that vital question but he was willing to give everything he had to find out.

Would everyone in the band follow him? After all, he may have been born with deep-seated wanderlust but was the rest of the band? Would Mike be willing to leave or would he be content staying in this small town to eventually marry and raise his own children in the same tight-knit community? Tom Petty knew he was destined to leave Gainesville as soon as he was able and he hoped Mike, Benmont, Randall and Danny would follow him.

"I decided that we should drive to LA," remembers Tom. "None of us had been west of the Mississippi – it was a big deal." With the Mudcrutch tapes in hand, all Tom needed was some money and a car to get him out to Los Angeles. "We started selling anything we owned, of value, which wasn't much," admits Tom. Mike recalls that, "We put all our money together in a pool. I think I had like fifty bucks to my name. I gave him my fifty bucks for gas."

Tom wasn't going solo on this road trip. Mudcrutch's new guitarist, Danny Roberts, volunteered to drive, and roadie Keith McAllister was up for an adventure as well. According to Danny, "Me, Tom and our roadie Keith drove out to Hollywood in my '69 VW bus, looking for a record deal." It sounds so naïve and idealistic now, but the band felt they had something to offer and any record company executive worth his salt would surely see that. The trip out to California was an event in itself and spirits were high. Danny recalls how it felt to be heading toward his own destiny during the drive westward. "As we rolled on through the night, we tuned in some radio station on the AM radio that was in the bus," he says, "listening to this voice that sounded like it was coming from Heaven. It was Dolly Parton singing, 'Jolene, Jolene, Jolene, Jolene...I'm begging of you, please don't take my man.' I remember getting goose-bumps!" Would this journey hold the keys to Mudcrutch's future success? Would someone someday listen to their music on the radio and be inspired? It was a heady time for Tom, Danny and Keith.

The guys were out on their own, hoping to get it right the first time. "We didn't have a manager, we didn't have *nothin'*," says Tom.★

"We drove out in a Volkswagen van. I had $37 and I remember packing sandwiches in bags," grins Tom. "We'd go, 'OK, dinner time,' and everybody'd pull out a sandwich and eat it. We slept on the floor of a friend of a friend who wasn't real happy about us being there."

But Tom, Keith and Danny didn't think they'd need to crash with friends for long. The Mudcrutch demo tapes were terrific – in their humble opinions – and they figured they'd have a deal sewn up in no time. They hit the streets hard on day one.

Tom recounted those first few days in California in the *Runnin' Down A Dream* documentary: "Our first stop was Playboy Records. In those days, it had a big Playboy Bunny emblem on the side. We must have looked pretty funny, I mean, just having driven 3,000 miles. He brings us in the office, 'Look, guys, it's not done this way. You just don't walk in.' We said, 'Well, we're here, and there's the tape deck, and why don't you put it on and listen?' He played not quite 30 seconds when he stopped the tape and said, 'I've heard enough, get out of my office.' We're back on the street thinking, 'This is going to be harder than we thought.'

"The next day, we start out the day at Capitol Records. They send us to the A&R department. The guy says, 'I like what I hear, I'd really like to cut a demo.' Now, we go, 'Well, we've already made a demo.' We left Capitol thinking, 'waste of time', so I'm going to call ahead and try to make an appointment at a record company. While I'm on the phone asking for the number, I look down in the bottom of the booth and there's a piece of paper lying there. I picked it up. On this paper, there are 25 record companies and their phone numbers. That made me feel

---

★ That might have been a bit of an exaggeration. There's at least one image of a business card floating out there on the Internet that touts Mudcrutch's personal manager as being one Michael J. Lembo. There's no other mention of him anywhere else though so it's doubtful that Michael assisted with the band's exodus from Gainesville back in the day.

good *and* bad. Good, because I had the numbers. Bad, because, *Christ!* How many people are doing this?" But Tom's tenacious spirit was not about to let him give up. The guys were determined to meet with as many record companies as possible during their first "business trip".

Tom continues the story: "MGM was there with a big lion [logo], and I said, 'Well, I've heard of them. Let's go in there.' We go in, and the guy says, 'OK, I'll listen to it.' He goes and he listens to the whole tape, and he says, 'I'd like to make a deal for a single.' Our eyes go up, and we said, 'Well, we're really looking for an album deal.' He goes, 'You start out with a single, and if the single goes good, we'll talk about an album.'"

The trio was in shock. That hadn't taken long at all! Tom was ecstatic. "We hit the street, just leaping in the air. 'All right, we got a single, but we've got more places to go.' The next stop was a label called London Records. He plays our tape. He plays the whole thing, and he starts clapping his hands and jumping around going, 'This is fantastic. You've got a deal.' We just looked at him, you know. 'I want to hear the band right away. I want to make a record. This is great.'"

So in one afternoon the guys were able to score not one but *two* record deals. It took talent, tenacity and plain dumb luck to make that happen. Then it was time for Tom to call home with the good news. "I called Mike and said, 'Guess what? We got two record offers.' He goes, 'You're crazy.' 'No, we've really done it,'" recalls Tom. "We made the trip back, and we went up to Ben's place in New Orleans where he was attending college and said, 'Look, this is it with school. We're going to make records.' I do remember having to go to his father, who was a big-time judge, very intimidating. I had to talk him into letting his son quit college. I made a pretty good case."

Things were happening fast. Benmont's dad gave him the green light to quit school (could he really have stopped him?), and the rest of the band started packing their things and saying their goodbyes. Mike Campbell set a date to marry his girlfriend, Marcie, and they tied the knot at the end of March 1974.

Tom also had some unfinished business he had to tend to before heading to LA. First, he proposed to his girlfriend, Jane Benyo. She'd been by his side as he built up Mudcrutch's reputation in their hometown. Two years his junior, Jane would follow Tommy anywhere and having said 'yes' the moment he asked her the couple married in a simple ceremony at a local house of worship on March 31, 1974. Tom, with his seventies-style shoulder-length hair and moustache, wore a brown suit jacket and his bride wore a simple floor-length dress in a floral rose pattern. She carried a simple but tasteful bouquet of spring flowers and spent the happy day looking forward to their life together in California.

Tom Petty fans may be aware of how preciously Tom guards his personal life and the clear boundaries he set early on between his home life and professional one. Those barriers have been intact since the very early days. Tom almost never discusses his family with fans or the media and his family doesn't give interviews to the press either. The family has so closely guarded its privacy that there are only one or two photographs of Jane floating out there on the Internet, quite a feat in this day and age of social media and celebrity overexposure. Starting in the seventies, Tom went out of his way to keep details of his relationship with Jane quiet. It was no one else's business, in his opinion, and he and Jane lived most of their married life without the focus of public attention on them.

After the wedding Tom went to visit his old friend and Mudcrutch alum, Jim Lenahan. "A week after he left for Los Angeles the first time," says Jim, "he comes walking into my 7-Eleven, where I'm behind the counter, and he goes, 'We're leaving next week. You're the stage manager.' I said, 'OK,' and that was it." Jim knew it wouldn't be easy but he was willing to take a chance and see what fate would bring his way in Los Angeles, "We had enough money to pay for gas to get from Gainesville to Hollywood, California, and once we got there we would have 200 dollars left," laughs Jim. "We said, 'We can live for a month on two hundred dollars.' Seven people! Seven, eight, *nine* people." Were they crazy or motivated? Maybe a little bit of both.

Of course all the guys were a bit hesitant. They were Floridians who'd never really lived anywhere else. They wanted Tom to tell them what Los Angeles was like. He sums it up this way: "There's something really magical about it. It just feels like all the people who want to escape their little small town hell and really don't fit into conventional life head for

Los Angeles. I do love Southern California and Los Angeles. It's always been the land of milk and honey to me."

Karma had been good to the band and it would put its force to use one more time before Mudcrutch let the curtain fall on their beloved Gainesville. "We're rehearsing in this little bedroom," remembers Tom. "We had a car for sale for money for the trip. The phone rings and I answer the phone, but they're still kind of playing in the next room. I hear someone saying something, and I think they're calling about the car because it's someone I don't know. I'm saying, 'Well, it's a hundred bucks; it's not that good.' He goes, 'No, no, no! This is Denny Cordell, and I'm calling for Mudcrutch.'"

Tom repeated the name "Denny Cordell" out loud and the band stopped everything. The room was silent. A strange energy field built as Tom continued the conversation and the band listened. They all knew who Denny Cordell was.

Born in Brazil in 1942, Denny Cordell's first involvement in music was as manager of doomed jazz trumpeter Chat Baker but it was as an employee of Seltaeb, a company selling Beatles merchandise, that he came across the song 'Go Now', by Bessie Banks, which he offered to produce for the UK band The Moody Blues, thus helping to create his first, though certainly not his last, memorable recording. After working with Georgie Fame and The Move, he discovered Procol Harum, producing their worldwide surrealistic smash 'A Whiter Shade Of Pale', then moved on to produce Joe Cocker who introduced him to singer-songwriter Leon Russell. Cordell and Russell then created Shelter Records, based in Russell's hometown of Tulsa, Oklahoma.

According to Benmont, "Denny Cordell produced records by bands we really loved, 'A Whiter Shade Of Pale' from Procol Harum to Joe Cocker, great, great early stuff. He co-produced Leon Russell's records. He was the real thing." And he was interested in Mudcrutch. The phone call to Tom made that crystal clear.

The conversation went something like this: "'This is Denny Cordell. I got your tape. I think it's the best thing I've heard in years. I want to sign the group up." Tom politely explained that they'd already promised to sign with London Records. Denny saw his opening and took it. He invited the band to stop in Tulsa, on their way to LA. Denny would host the band in his recording studio there and pay for some test sessions to see how everyone liked working with him. If it went well, they could throw London Records under the bus and sign with him instead. If it didn't go well, no harm, no foul and the band could continue on to California and fulfill their promise to London Records.

During an interview years later Cordell admitted that: "The Tulsa trip was my effort to sort of head him off at the pass, get to him before he came to Hollywood, and go into the studio and try and strike up a sort of bond because I felt, at the end of the day, he wasn't going for the biggest deal that he was possibly going to get, but he was going for the chance to make good records. I hoped if he could do that in Tulsa, maybe when he got to Hollywood, he wouldn't bother with the others."

The band – and an entourage of wives, girlfriends and dogs – left Gainesville on April 1, 1974, with no intention of looking back. Of course, things hardly go as we plan them. "All of us crammed in [to Danny's Volkswagen bus]," remembers Tom. "We had the dogs and everything in the truck, and all our gear. Right at the city limits of Gainesville, the truck breaks down. You know, hours of getting the truck ready. OK, we took off again.

"Well, we got a little further along, the bearings go out on the station wagon. We had to stop and stay there for two or three days while they ordered the parts to fix the station wagon."

The road trip itself was a learning experience for the troupe of southerners. As they headed west, the landscape – and the attitudes of the locals – started to change. Everything was new.

"After a day or two, we got to Oklahoma," says Tom. "It was just a windstorm of dust blowing everywhere and through the clouds, almost, this Englishman stepped through, who was really something to see. He had an earring, which you didn't see a lot of then, and a bandana. We had never met anybody that was English. We immediately hit it off.

"Cordell was a great guy. Really smart. Really talented," says Tom. "I dug him right away. I can say that he gave me a great education in the studio. He always had the right ideas musically. On the business side, I don't agree with anything that he wanted to do, but on the creative end, I have to appreciate that he did all that for us. We said no to the others. 'We're gonna go with Denny because he talks like we do, and to hell with the rest of 'em.'"

Shelter Records owned Church Studio at East Third Street and South Trenton Avenue in Tulsa. At this point in the seventies, Tulsa was lobbying to become "the next Nashville" and, in fact, songwriter and multi-instrumentalist Leon Russell, Denny's partner in Shelter Records, owned a fancy home in the Maple Ridge section of the city.

Tom Russell (no relation to Leon) was the recording engineer at Church Studio. He explained that Denny and Leon liked bringing new bands to town, "giving these guys a chance to have a place where they could bring their ideas together and just see what happened." When it worked and the music and recording fell into place, Shelter Records would sign the band before the crew continued on to Los Angeles to jump-start their West Coast career. Denny was hoping that he'd made a good call by bringing Mudcrutch to T-town, as Tulsa was nicknamed at the time.

When the band arrived, Mudcrutch was astounded at the setup. "We had never seen anything like this studio," notes Tom. "It was just amazing. We went down the next day, played awhile in the studio. He [Denny] clapped his hands and said, 'I'm sold. I'll sign you right now.'"

It might sound improbable but that's exactly what happened. Denny was a consummate producer and a shrewd businessman, and he knew that Tom Petty had something special. "Either the guy is a true artist, and a true poet, and a true rocker, or they're not," said Denny back in the day. "In my judgment, he was."

Denny was not about to let him sign with another label. The band was flattered by his offer. "We spent forty-eight hours in Leon Russell's Church Studio," says guitarist Danny Roberts. "When we were done, Denny offered us a deal and gave us $5,000 to get someplace to live when we got to LA as well as telling us to get an attorney for contract negotiations."

On a euphoric high, the band continued the drive to Los Angeles. Mudcrutch hired attorney Arthur Leeds to handle legal matters. Thomas

Petty, Benjamin M. Tench III, Michael Campbell, Randall Marsh and Daniel Roberts signed the recording agreement on June 24, 1974.

"Within a day or so they [Shelter Records] had rented us a couple of houses, one with a swimming pool," notes Tom. "Now, this is heavy stuff for us, you know? We ain't hardly seen a house with a swimming pool, let alone live in one. Of course, there's no furniture."

Tom may have been looking for a surrogate family when he joined his first band, and Shelter Records would only reinforce that theme. The men and women who worked at Shelter were family who cared as much about each other as they did about the music. They were the cool kids in town as *Creem*'s Stephen Demorest attested to in August of 1978: "Shelter Records may have the coolest offices in America: a ramshackle wooden house nestled under a grove of tall trees set well back from Hollywood Boulevard. There's a genuinely rural flavor about it, a substantial earthiness, which contrasts the surrounding city of electric lights and sky. Los Angeles, the mirage in the desert. Shelter is not just 'casual', which is now a designers' term for expensive clothes – it's totally loose."

Tom admitted years later that Denny was "his guru" during this time period. "I would go to his house in Malibu every Sunday, and every day when the end of the work day came I would sit in his office and out would come the records. The office was closed and we'd sit there until eight or nine o'clock and he'd play me everything in the world. Just everything: Lloyd Price, reggae stuff, Rolling Stones, everything that had ever turned him on, or me. We'd bring them in. I'm forever indebted to Denny Cordell because we couldn't afford that many records. We were so hungry to hear anything. In Gainesville you could only hear what you owned and we didn't have enough money to have stacks of albums. So running into somebody who had just unlimited access to records was incredible. It was just a bonanza of information."

Everyone in the band was appreciative for everything Shelter was doing for them. For Benmont, "It was like a family. It wasn't like some corporation or something."

While Tom and Benmont were taking it all in stride, the move out West was much more difficult for Mike. "It was like going to Mars, for me. I mean, coming from Florida, back then, it was a huge cultural gap. It was overwhelming. Things were moving so fast. In the south, back then, everything was real slow. Everybody talked slow and thought slow. You get to LA, and it's like, 'Yeah, go, go! Do this, do this, do this!' It took us a while to catch on."

At this point in time, the guys were always on the run, doing something. Danny recalls what was on the agenda after the record contract was signed. "When we finally got our record contract done, we set aside a certain amount of money so that we could buy some proper rock star duds," Danny wrote on Mudcrutch.com's online message board. "We went to this really cool shop in Hollyweird called Granny Takes a Trip. They also had one in New York City.

"So, we're in there shopping away, a smallish shop, mind you, when I see a Rolls-Royce or a Bentley pull up out front. Out of the corner of my eye, I see the shop manager go to the door and let two people in, locking the door behind them. When I turned to see who it was, I nearly shat myself – it was Elton John and his manager John Reid. So for the next couple of hours, we were shopping with Elton John! He bought the gaudy outfit that he's wearing on the *Caribou* album cover. I still have the red-wine coloured Kinks-style velvet coat that I bought that day."

The band spent just about all of their time together – either in the studio or at their houses. The music benefitted from so much rehearsal time and Mudcrutch sounded as good as it ever did when playing live.

Time spent in the studio, however, was surprisingly a struggle. "We couldn't make the transition from live group to the studio. It was really hard," admits Tom. "We were always shocked. We'd play and then go into the control room and it didn't sound anything like we thought it was going to sound. And Cordell had to slowly teach us that it didn't really have anything to do with the way you did your gigs. It's another art and you have to learn how to make the mic receive the sound you want it to."

These were tense times for the band as Denny pushed them to focus solely on Tom's songs and sensibilities. Everyone in the band was fine with that except for Danny Roberts who decided to leave the group and go out on his own. Or, at least that's what Tom Petty & The Heartbreakers lore now suggests. However, you'll notice that Danny Roberts is almost never mentioned when it comes to discussions of the early days of Mudcrutch. He wasn't even included in director Peter Bogdanovich's 2007 documentary, *Runnin' Down A Dream*, and there are very few mentions of him in magazine and newspaper articles about the nearly 40-year history of The Heartbreakers. Danny Roberts has turned up on online message boards throughout the years to talk with fans, and even he isn't exactly sure why Tom and the other members of Mudcrutch have airbrushed him out of the history books.

Soon after Danny left/was forced out of Mudcrutch, Denny Cordell sent the remaining band members back to Tulsa for six weeks, hoping that a few weeks sequestered with an engineer would help break their block. The band invited Florida-based bassist Charlie Souza to join them. Souza, a member of The Tropics in the sixties in the Tampa area, recounts at his website CharlieSouza.com how he ended up on those sessions with Tom Petty.

"I had done some recording with a group called White Witch for Capricorn Records in Miami with 'Layla' [Derek And The Dominos] producers Ron and Howie Albert," Charlie explains. "Months went by and we didn't seem to be playing very many concerts. In January of 1975 I received a record in the mail called 'Depot Street' by a band called Mudcrutch and got a call from a Gainesville kid who used to come and watch The Tropics play when he was a kid. The Tropics played for all the fraternity parties up in Gainesville for Gator students. He said his name was Tom and he was calling from California. He asked if I wanted to fly out and play bass on some recordings. I made the long drive out, with the equipment truck and all of my belongings.

"First we headed to Leon Russell's house in Tulsa to record for a while," he continues, "and then out to Leon's house in Encino for a few more months."

Charlie is still playing music these days and has written an interesting book about his experiences working with all sorts of musicians, including Tom Petty. The book, titled *Live Your Dream*, even includes a testimonial from Petty himself: "In 1965 The Tropics were the biggest

59

band in the state of Florida – simple as that. I watched them in awe. Their power was never truly captured on record, but a show beyond belief! No small part of that was bassist Charlie Souza. When my band in 1975 was looking for a bass player, as I was switching from bass to guitar, we asked Charlie to join and he did. Unfortunately the band folded not long after he arrived. But in that short time, I found him to be a great musician and a nice guy. I'm sure his book will be an interesting read for anyone looking for rock'n'roll adventure."

When Charlie met up with Tom and the rest of the band back in the day in Tulsa, they recorded a few tracks including 'I Can't Fight It', an early version of 'Don't Do Me Like That' and Bert Russell's 'Cry To Me', three tracks that can be heard on *Playback*, a box set issued by Tom Petty & The Heartbreakers in 1995. The Tulsa sessions helped a bit, but the dam certainly hadn't broken. Denny was still very concerned about the future when Mudcrutch returned to Los Angeles.

It's important to remember that while Mudcrutch was working day and night to forge a path to success with its music, Tom was a newlywed with equally important responsibilities to his wife, Jane. On November 24, 1974 – just five months after Tom signed his first recording contract – Jane gave birth to the couple's first child: Adria R. Petty. It was a happy occasion for the couple but it wasn't without stress. There never seemed to be enough time to spend as a family and never enough money to make the home that Jane and Tom had dreamed about. These were tense times on several fronts.

As Tom learned his way around fatherhood, Mudcrutch continued refining its craft in the studio. Finally, in February of 1975, Shelter Records released 'Depot Street' as a single with 'Wild Eyes' as the B-side. Denny produced both tracks. Everyone's hopes were high but, in the end, the single failed to make even the tiniest of impressions on the radio waves or charts. It was over before it had even really begun.

Denny didn't want to take another chance on Mudcrutch in its current iteration. He felt some dead weight needed to be jettisoned. "The band had one or two sort of weak links in it," he said to reporters years later, "but because of that sort of brotherhood, 'The Three Musketeers', you know, all together, it was very hard to dislodge the weaknesses." Denny had been telling the band for ages: focus on Tom's songs. That was the key. Benmont and Danny had also been writing songs, and while Benmont was willing to table that part of his work, Danny was not. Danny had walked away already, but now Tom had to sever ties with other members of Mudcrutch.

Randall remembers the fateful day when everything changed for him: "One day, Tom sat down with me and he said, 'The record company told me that they want me and they're kind of not that interested in the band.'" The conversation didn't seem real at first and then the enormity of what that meant hit Randall hard. His dreams of drumming in a top rock'n'roll band were slipping away.

Benmont heard the news next. "I was really devastated. I felt like I'd been hit by a truck or something. These were the people that I knew, that I'd moved out to California with. It's like, 'Oh, dissolution of the family', and what am I going to do? Who am I going to play with?'" It was humiliating for each member that didn't make the cut and it put Tom in an awkward position.

"I went immediately to Mike," recalls Tom, "and said, 'Don't leave me. You gotta stay with me.' I felt really bad about Benmont leaving, but I didn't know what to do. I wanted to be in the band. I didn't want to be a solo guy." Mike did stay with Tom and Benmont understood. "Mike and Tom. You can't split that up," he says.

Everything was in disarray when Mudcrutch disbanded. Danny Roberts went back to Florida, though he did return to Los Angeles at the behest of Denny Cordell to work with musician Phil Seymour later down the road. Danny says that he was still on good terms with Petty on his return to California. Danny wrote the following in a message-board post at Mudcrutch.com: "The first night that I'd flown into LAX to get a room at the Tropicana and meet with Phil Seymour, I got a call about an hour after I check into my room. It was TP, sayin', 'Hey man, whatcha doin'? Wanna go to the Roxie with me?' He told me that it was a band made up of players from Dylan's Rolling Thunder Revue, T-Bone Burnett, David Mansfield and some other dudes [Steve Soles]. They were called The Alpha Band and they were supposed to be great. Tom came by and got me, I think he had a 'Vette or something sharp.

We talked like in the 'old' days, just like everything was just peachy. We hung out with Roger McGuinn....I'll always cherish that night! That was the last time Tom called me and we hung out together with one of The Byrds, one of our biggest influences in Mudcrutch. Tom took me back to the Tropicana, where we hung out for a little while. We talked about doin' it again sometime and shook hands, seeming like everything was cool. But that was the last time I ever saw TP act friendly towards me and I'll probably never know the truth."

After the band break-up, Mike and Benmont stayed in town and started playing with other musicians on a casual basis. Money was hard to come by for each of them and Tom was especially struggling to support his wife and child. Years later, in 1999, Tom reflected on the financial and emotional challenges to Fred Schruers of *Rolling Stone*: "I remember living in a Travelodge when Adria was a baby. We actually used to put her in a drawer for a crib. You don't forget stuff like that. It's a really down-to-nothing way to live. We didn't have any money at all, and then I sent Jane and the baby back to Florida for a while, and then when I got more on my feet, they came back." It's experiences like this that Tom draws upon when he writes about the average man who's struggling for a leg up. He knows what it's like because he started out on the bottom rung himself. You don't forget how difficult it is to claw your way out of these sorts of situations and you don't wish that hardship on anyone else either.

With Jane and Adria back in Florida, Tom was on his own to pick up the pieces. "I was living in Hollywood at the Winona Hotel – kind of a hooker's place. The phone rings and its Leon [Russell]. He'd heard a song ['Lost In Your Eyes'] I'd written – which finally came out on a Don Johnson album – and he wanted to know if he could record it. I didn't know where tomorrow's rent was coming from. He said, 'Do you feel like writing?' and I said, 'Yeah, buddy! I'm ready right now!' He came over to the Winona in a Rolls-Royce.

"He was a pretty cool guy, Leon, and he kept me on salary as a lyric writer. There was a 40-track studio in the house – really advanced – and all these people used to hang out: Gary Busey [actor], Roger Linn ["father" of the drum machine]....and we'd sit around waiting for Leon to make records. If he needed lyrics, I was the guy. I never got credit – I didn't know about that – but it was a great education. For a while he was trying to make each song with a different producer, so George Harrison would be there one night, and then we'd see Brian Wilson, Bobby Womack, Terry Melcher, a long list of people, and I'd watch them work."

With all that experience now behind him, Tom decided to get back in the studio and make a solo album. He'd have to use all session players though and he wasn't crazy about that concept. He loved being in an actual band and working with "day laborers" didn't much appeal to him. He also needed to make a record and start bringing in some money because he desperately wanted his wife and daughter to return to California. He needed to prove to himself and to his wife and child that he had what it takes to make it – both in the music business and as a family man.

Fate was about to help Tom Petty achieve that goal. It just so happened that Benmont had put together a recording session to make a demo. He invited Mike Campbell as well as drummer Stan Lynch and bassist Ron Blair – both fellow Gainesville expats. Jeff Jourard – soon to be the lead guitarist of The Motels – was there, too. If all went well, the demo would be released under the band name, The Drunks.

Benmont invited Tom to sit in on the session and as soon as he heard the band play, he knew this was *his* band. He had to convince Mike and Benmont to give it another go, and to explain to Stan and Ron that he already had a record deal and wanted them to be his backup band on the album – and beyond.

Any hard feelings that might have been hanging in the air soon disappeared. Mike and Benmont loved collaborating with Tom and, hey, he *did* have a record deal. Why work on this demo when this guy's got a deal and he's asking me to play on his record? Likewise, Stan and Ron were willing to give it a go. They remembered Tom from the Mudcrutch days in Gainesville. In fact, Stan's band, Road Turkey, was often billed with Mudcrutch back in the day in North Florida. Stan had even sat in with Mudcrutch a few times when Randall Marsh wasn't available. Stan and Ron said, "What the hell?" They had nothing to lose.

The guys decided to throw in their lot together and were soon thinking up names for the new group. Tom preferred The King Bees but that was not destined to be. The deal was Tom's and he was the frontman so it made sense to name the band "Tom Petty and the somethings". Of course, not everyone might have been very keen on the idea of singling out one band member in the moniker, but the delineation of who's in charge was ironed out from the very early days of the band.

"When Elliot Roberts [the band's first manager] got involved," remembers Tom, "he said, 'Look, you know, Tom writes the songs, he sings the songs, he does this, this and this. Everybody's great, everybody does their thing, but you have to face reality.' We just kinda laid it right on the table, and said we can either accept it or if we can't accept it, we should break up. And everybody accepted it. They're a great band, they're not dumb in ways of letting their ego ruin something good."

The fact of the matter is that Tom leads the band in many ways: through his songwriting prowess, his business savvy and his ability to inspire everyone around him to live up to his or her potential. At the end of the day, it's Tom's band and he'll call the shots as he sees fit. "If I've said it once, I've said it a thousand times," notes Tom. "If we're Kentucky Fried Chicken, I'm the colonel on the bucket. This whole thing has my name on it, and ultimately I'm responsible, so I want things presented the way I see them."

Tom may be aggressive with his points of view but the band understands where he's coming from. "He's got a very powerful opinion," Mike agrees, "and he's usually right. He's a great boss, a great leader, a great force. It's like having Bob Dylan and Keith Richards in one guy. He's stern when he needs to be, but he's also democratic."

With everything out in the open, the band decided on a name: Tom Petty & The Heartbreakers. They certainly didn't think of themselves as Casanovas so the name struck them as a bit comical. A wry sense of humour is shared among all of The Heartbreakers and this name appealed to that sensibility.

Over the next few weeks, the band got together at Shelter Studios in Hollywood to lay down tracks for the eponymously titled album. Tom would write snippets of songs at home and then bring them into the studio where Mike, Benmont, Stan and Ron would work out their parts and help create the arrangement. It wasn't the most efficient way to work, but they were new to making records and this trial-and-error process was part of their evolution as the band further developed its technique for recording new material.

Tom Petty & The Heartbreakers held true to its Mudcrutch roots in many ways, but the addition of Stan and Ron expanded the band's repertoire of rock'n'roll standards and broadened its musical landscape. An incredible array of musicians had influenced the work of all of The Heartbreakers. "We grew up at a time when music was really rich and good," concedes Tom. "All those influences slowly meld into something. We were always trying to do it our own way – we weren't trying to copy people. It all just mixes up and something of your own comes out of that.

"People don't notice that The Beatles were a huge influence on us," Tom laments. "They always go to The Byrds or the Stones, who *were* big influences on us, but The Beatles were enormous. We were particularly into The Beatles. They were just so good. God, they were good. A lot of people miss it. We don't sing like The Beatles but I think we've inherited that sort of melodic sense.

"The Everly Brothers have been a huge influence on us, too," he continues. "It's almost silly to say that because they've been an influence on everybody. Not even speaking of harmonies; melodically, Don Everly had a huge influence on me."

Many of those early influences are evidenced on *Tom Petty & The Heartbreakers,* produced by Denny Cordell. Released on November 9, 1976, the band's debut album clocked in at just 30 minutes and 35 seconds but the 10 tracks – sometimes labeled punk and sometimes classified as power pop – made a sonic impact. The record didn't exactly shoot up the charts though.

Despite the fact that this was the band's first salvo to capture the attention of the record-buying public, not much was done in terms of publicity and only a few gigs were scheduled for the end of 1976. That included the opening slots for Kiss in Columbus, Georgia, on November 30 and for Al Kooper at Paul's Mall in Boston on December 12. The latter set was recorded and Shelter Records released it in December as a four-song EP titled *Official Live 'Leg*. Mid-December found the band headlining at New York City's famous CBGB's but Tom Petty & The Heartbreakers needed even more exposure than that if they hoped to make a dent in the psyche of America's record-buying public.

First records introduce a band to the world so it was important that Tom's initial batch of songs spoke to listeners on a very personal level and that the band found its own unique sound. From their very first album, it was clear that The Heartbreakers had a very distinctive guitar-driven sound.

According to Mike, "Most of the guitar tones on that first record were Tom playing my '64 Stratocaster and me on a fifties Broadcaster through a Tweed Fender Deluxe [tube amplifier] and a [seventies] Fender Super Six, which were in the Shelter Records studio. That Stratocaster was something I had gotten for $200. I didn't have the money, so someone had fronted it to me. I did like the guitar sounds on that record, especially the crunch of that Tweed Deluxe, which is like the one Neil Young uses that has such a beautiful distortion."

The cover of the album pictured a slightly smirking Tom Petty mugging for the camera. He's wearing a black leather jacket with an ammunition belt casually slung across his shoulder. The imagery might have given the wrong impression to the public and the album was soon tagged as punk and New Wave instead of good, old-fashioned rock'n'roll.

Regardless of which record bin the album was placed in – punk or rock – just about everyone could relate to the woes Tom sang about, from daring the woman he loves not to leave him, to unrequited love, love lost and a healthy disrespect for authority. The songs also spoke of loyalty and the desire to get just a little bit more out of life. It was clear after one revolution on the turntable that the album – and Tom Petty & The Heartbreakers – had teen spirit.

Newsweek's Barbara Graustark wrote about the album and its accessibility: "Their 1976 debut LP, which reverently aped The Byrds, was bulldozer-direct music for the working class." Indeed, 'Anything That's Rock 'N' Roll' – the very single that would eventually propel the band to stardom in the UK when it hit #36 on the UK singles chart

– throws punches at parents, bosses and authority figures in general: "Some friends of mine and me stayed up all through the night / Rockin' pretty steady till the sky went light / And I didn't go to bed / Didn't go to work / I picked up the telephone / Told the boss he was a jerk." In an us-against-them world, Tom Petty was one of "us". 'Anything That's Rock 'N' Roll's' got a predictable beat that's incredibly likeable upon first listen. It's the perfect two-minute anti-establishment number – the ideal song to spin over and over at home just to annoy your parents. It's not that the band was "underground" per se, but the music certainly had a sense of authenticity that was lacking in other American rock groups at the time.

Despite buzz building around the band's music in the UK, the venerable US industry trade magazine, *Billboard,* could only be bothered to run a 40-word review of the album: "Petty, another punk rock, black leather jacketed offshoot, delivers an assortment of sullen ballads and up-tempo shriekers. This LP gains impact on its second spin. Petty's laidback vocals become rather infectious. Best cuts: 'Hometown Blues', 'Luna', 'Mystery Man', 'American Girl'.

Americans might not have immediately grasped the beauty of Petty's work but the British Empire did. The band was a near-immediate success in the United Kingdom and the single 'Anything That's Rock 'N' Roll' became an anthem in Britain. It would take more than a year for Americans to warm up to their fellow countrymen.

Rock critic Dave Marsh gave a back-handed compliment to the band in his album review for the *Meriden-Southern Journal*: "No part is particularly special – songs, singing, playing are all kind of primordial L.S. rock, like Love or The Seeds. But, it's such a sixties throwback, you can't help but fall in love."

Critic Don Cope actually downplayed Tom's role on the album in favor of Mike's, writing in his review for *The Technique* that, "The star of The Heartbreakers is guitarist Mike Campbell. While he never gets the chance to step out and solo, his rhythm work is the backbone of the album. Unfortunately, Petty and The Heartbreakers may never get off the ground without a hit single." Time would tell if Cope's prediction was correct or not.

The songs on this freshman album weren't nearly as polished as they could have been but they showed quite a range of songwriting styles on Tom's part. The record opens with the sweet but short – and certainly rushed – 'Rockin' Around With You'. With just 10 lines, this frenetically paced track won't win any poetry competitions but it gets its point across: love and loyalty. Why the band was in such a hurry to race through this tune is unclear but it is definitely a toe-tapper based on call-and-response lyrics, double-tracked vocals and a bright, punchy guitar line. Future songs from Tom Petty would not be nearly as lightweight.

Just as 'Rockin' Around With You' fades out, the snare drum vamp of 'Breakdown' begins. The hypnotic organ part anchors the blues-tinged track with Tom singing in a smug fashion that "It's all right if you love me / It's all right if you don't / I'm not afraid of you running away / Honey, I get the feeling you won't." While the lyrics lead you to assume that the storyteller is an egotistical son-of-a-bitch, Tom's performance of this song in concert turns it on its ear with the storyteller begging his love to stick around. This particular song is the first of many in Tom's career in which he successfully creates a sense of tension by way of both the melody and lyrics. He pushes and pulls his powerful vocal performance in an effort to get the listener emotionally invested. Meanwhile, Mike's sinewy yet simple guitar riff is the perfect complement to the vocal line.

The album certainly consisted of an eclectic mix of songs as the next track on the record, 'Hometown Blues', illustrates. This little number enjoys a solid metre that you can't help but clap to. While the majority of the songs on *Tom Petty & The Heartbreakers* were recorded at Shelter Studios in Hollywood with Denny producing and the engineering team of Noah Shark and Max Reese at the console, 'Hometown Blues' was an outlier. This track was actually recorded in Encino at Leon Russell's house with overdubs done later at Sound City in Van Nuys. The line-up of musicians for this song was a bit different too with several guest players, including Donald "Duck" Dunn of Booker T. & The MGs fame on bass, ex-Mudcrutch member Randall Marsh on drums and Charlie Souza on saxophone. Even Jane Petty helped out by contributing handclaps to the track.

Phil Seymour and Harley Fiala sang background vocals throughout the record and guitarist Jeff Jourard played on several tracks as did bassist Emory Gordy, drummer Jim Gordon and saxophonist Charlie Souza.

In addition to the more radio-friendly three-minute rockers, *Tom Petty & The Heartbreakers* also deftly showcased Tom's sensitive writing style with three gorgeous ballads: 'The Wild One, Forever', 'Luna' and 'Mystery Man', which has an almost Hawaiian slack-key guitar vibe against a Bo Diddley beat.

Bassist Ron Blair recalls recording that one: "At A&M Studios we were cutting the song....We ran through it and Denny Cordell went, 'Fucking ace!' We had cut a track before we even knew what we were doing. Even to this day, somebody had better be rolling tape at our sessions. I felt really at home playing with the band. It must have something to do with our Florida roots. Maybe it's the lifestyle, but if you grew up playing there with so many good bands, you were soulful whether you tried or not."

While the band rarely plays 'The Wild One, Forever' in concert these days, it's a fan favourite that wistfully tells the story of a passionate one-night stand that should have been more – if only the cold-hearted woman could have seen it that way. The affair only lasts a few hours but it's one the singer will remember for a lifetime. Brilliant cymbal rolls swell throughout the song and ratchet up the idea that the likes of this passion may never be experienced again.

Similarly, 'Luna' – the longest song on the record – presents Tom's voice at its silky best as he yearns for the woman he absolutely adores. He begs her to "glide down from the moon" and be with him. Benmont eases the listener into the song with a smooth organ line paired first with a simple drum part before the rest of the band falls in.

Sandwiched in the middle of the album were 'Strangered In The Night' and 'Fooled Again (I Don't Like It)'. 'Strangered' told an in-depth story about rough streets – of Los Angeles or elsewhere, we're never really sure – and interracial violence. Take a listen and you'll hear Shelter label mate Dwight Twilley singing background vocals on this one.

'Fooled Again (I Don't Like It)' was just the first of many songs Tom would write about conflict in a relationship, or to put a finer point on it, about another man trying to hone in on his girl. And he's pissed about being made the fool again by his two-timing girlfriend. Tom's performance pulls off a tone of downright indignation with this woman who's done him wrong.

The album eventually went gold in 1978 after selling more than 500,000 copies in the United States. One song in particular – 'American Girl' – helped make that happen and can be heard across the radio dial to this day. Back at the time of its release though, it didn't gain immediate traction in the United States. Instead, the UK adopted the song and it raced to number 40 on the singles chart in August of 1977.

Guaranteed by its title alone to find a ready audience in his homeland eventually, 'American Girl' established Tom's trademark style of jangly guitars – surely the influence of The Byrds' Roger McGuinn and perhaps 1965-era George Harrison/The Beatles. Tom's sound was more up to date though and captured the energy of the downtown New York City scene, the cradle of punk and new wave music. The introduction sets the scene: eight bars of chiming electric 12-string Rickenbacker over a muted Bo Diddley beat, soon joined by a swooping bass, all paving the way for an urgent, edgy verse that builds to an exuberant, climactic high on the title... 'my Am-eri-can Girl'. After two verses the tempo sits back, idling to regain momentum before the sprint to the finish, a repeat of the intro, this time intensified by a wash of backing vocals, and, finally, an outro solo of piercing top-end clusters that spiral into the fade. At just over three and a half minutes 'American Girl' never outstays its welcome; as timeless as it is memorable, it set a high bar for the future though, scandalously, it was never the hit it deserved to be.

In fact, Tom acknowledges that 'American Girl' is "one of my favourites": "I wrote that in a little apartment I had in Encino. It was right next to the freeway and the cars sometimes sounded like waves from the ocean, which is why there's the line about the waves crashing on the beach. The words just came tumbling out very quickly and it was the start of writing about people who long for something else in life, something better than they have.

"A lot of people think the girl in the song commits suicide, but it's not about suicide. It has also been interpreted as a statement about the country. I was watching the 9/11 concert in New York [an October 20, 2001 benefit show at Madison Square Garden for the victims and first responders of the September 11, 2001 terrorist attacks on New York City, Washington, DC, and Pennsylvania], and The Goo Goo Dolls played 'American Girl'. I could see the crowd cheering in this really patriotic context, but it was just a story when I wrote it. In my mind, the girl was looking for the strength to move on – and she found it." Years after the release of 'American Girl', Tom told *City Limits* reporter Cynthia Rose, "The 'American Girl' is just one example of this character I write about a lot – the small-town kid who knows there's more out there for them but gets fucked up trying to find it. Like the song says, she was raised on promises. I've always felt sympathetic towards her."

'American Girl' was the second single released and it never did chart in America. Years later *Rolling Stone* ranked it as number 76 on its list of The 100 Greatest Guitar Songs of All Time.

Mike remembers first recording 'American Girl' on the Fourth of July. "I don't know if that had anything to do with him writing it about an American girl," he says. "US Route 441 is the Orange Blossom Trail, the highway that goes right through Gainesville, right through the middle of Florida. There is some Gainesville imagery in that sense. To me, it's just a really beautiful love song."

Mike is proud to say that the band came into its own with 'American Girl'. "We found a sound and a vibe that was ours," he says, "and I remember feeling that we had found something really special that no one else could do, and this can be us. This can identify our trip. I could feel it. It hadn't happened yet, but I could sense that, 'We've got something here.'" Mike had no idea how prescient that thought actually was.

CHAPTER 4

High Adventure
(1977)

"The synthesis of English flash, sixties folk-rock and Southern grit that is The Heartbreakers' trademark seems to be coalescing into an identifiable personal style owing little to anyone but themselves."

— Steve Simels, *Stereo Review*

Tom Petty & The Heartbreakers toured almost nonstop throughout 1977 to build their reputation as rock'n'roll artists that deserved a second – and third – look. Nevertheless, momentum was slow to build in the United States and the band was frustrated that radio program directors and DJs hadn't done more to push their two singles: 'American Girl' and 'Breakdown'. There were pockets of America – San Francisco and Boston in particular – that loved the band but other regions just couldn't care less. It became an emotional rollercoaster as they crisscrossed the country evangelizing their music at small clubs and theaters. As they played out more and more across the nation, they ping-ponged between supporting famous rock stars and being a headliner in their own right.

The band opened for the likes of Blondie and the Greg Kihn Band but also headlined the Ivanhoe Theater in Chicago – an important market for rock'n'rollers. But they no sooner walked off the stage in Chicago before being relegated back to a warm-up act for Roger McGuinn and The Runaways. Later, in Ohio, The Heartbreakers were popular enough to stage two headlining shows before reverting once again to opening act status. Schizophrenic is the best way to describe Tom Petty & The Heartbreakers during 1977. They were either complete losers or standing on the very brink of stardom. They just couldn't tell which.

Buzz was slowly, *very* slowly, building across the US. When the band got back to California, they did a KSAN radio broadcast from the Record Plant in Sausalito on April. The next night they headed north to Winterland in San Francisco, where they supported Bob Seger & the Silver Bullet Band. At the end of the month Tom Petty & The Heartbreakers sold out two headlining shows at the influential Whisky A Go Go in Los Angeles. Perhaps they really were inching toward stardom but it would be hard fought.

The harder the band worked, the more the press began to take note. Barbara Charone wrote a particularly effusive review of the band's September 1977 performances at the Whisky A Go Go for UK music paper *Sounds*, saying, in part, "Although their debut album contains excellent slices of the best rock'n'roll to erupt in the seventies, the band truly must be seen live to be fully appreciated. This is an old fashioned, classic band in the truest sense. In short, they are magnificent.... They kicked off with 'Surrender' as Petty became the stage center focal point, as charismatic a figure rock could desire. His phrasing and stage presence is totally overwhelming and completely hypnotic."

While some good reviews were coming in, the band's eponymously titled album still struggled to gain traction in the US charts. Meanwhile, Britain embraced the sinewy lead singer without hesitation. 'Anything That's Rock 'N' Roll' zoomed up the charts and became an anthem for the youth of Great Britain. Probably due to the timing of their arrival, The Heartbreakers were mixed in with all the other punk artists that were climbing the charts at the time. While the band's wariness of authority figures may have resonated with the punk movement, these Southern boys weren't exactly anarchists. It perplexed Tom at the time – still does to this day – but he humbly accepted the accolades of each and every fan. "It was unusual being lumped in [with punk] but it felt better than being lumped in with the other side!" remembers Tom. "We agreed with them in spirit. Music had gotten really bad in our view, and we hated seeing stuff we believed in watered down and crassly commercialised. But we never thought we were [new wave]. And we never tried to embrace it. But it felt pretty cool to be alternative, you know? And it kind of hurt when we got really popular and it felt like, 'They see us as rich people now.' But really, we hadn't changed."

Not everyone on the punk scene was happy to welcome Tom Petty to the fold though – especially Johnny Rotten. "We were walking into our hotel lobby in England," Tom recalled recently. "I hear this snotty voice saying, 'Oh, it's the American *pop* star Tom Petty.' I ignore it, check into the hotel, and Stan [Lynch] and I start walking toward the elevator. We hear the same voice, kind of whining, 'There the hippies go. *Bye-bye* Tom.' At this point, Stan wheels around and starts heading for whoever it is. He wants to kill. Well, it's Johnny Rotten, surrounded by French journalists. Stan has to be restrained. I went over there and said, 'Who the fuck are you talking to?' Rotten immediately went into his wounded punk act, says nothing."

★ ★ ★

One thing was for certain: having Stan Lynch in your corner was always a good thing. Tom knew Stan from Gainesville but they became much closer friends once they hooked up in Los Angeles and formed The Heartbreakers. Stan has a vicious wit and brought a certain zaniness to the band. He could be volatile and had a wild temper but his loyalty to his bandmates was just as fierce. He'd do anything for them and their quest to hit it big.

Stanley Joseph Lynch II was born to Sally and Stanley Lynch Sr. on May 21, 1955 in Cincinnati, Ohio. His father made a living working for UPS and the family, including Stan's sister Jody, were part of a thriving Jewish community.

In his early years, Stan was an average kid just getting by in school but he never lacked energy or enthusiasm for music. "As a kid I had very little opportunity," Lynch told Jayne Moore in a conversation for

Songwriter Universe. "I was a marginal student. I wasn't going to college. My parents didn't have money. I played guitar and piano, and I always thought I was going to be a guitar player," Lynch says. "The drums were sort of a happy accident. I didn't really think that they would be my ticket out of the ghetto. Choosing to be a musician back then was not like choosing a job, but an entire lifestyle. My father looked at me as if I were going to wear a dress and dance in the circus."

By 1960 Stan's father needed a change and became a psychology teacher and moved the family to Florida. From 1960 to 1966, the Lynches moved between Gainesville in the northern part of the state and Miami in the south so Stanley Sr. could pursue various jobs in the education sector. Stan's mom, Sally, was a teacher and librarian and then became an aerobics instructor in later years. The family finally settled permanently in Gainesville.

Stan says now that he was an "unruly" child and his parents arranged for him to take drum lessons, starting when he was 11. They hoped that drumming would help Stan channel his energy in a productive way. His parents, music lovers themselves – his father played the trumpet and his mother played piano – knew that drum lessons would impart a lifelong interest in music to their son.

Stan joined his first band, Styrofoam Soul, when he was 14 and, even then, he felt his future would be tied to music. It got him through tough times, like the divorce of his parents when he was 15 years old. At 17, Stan found a new "home" with popular local band Road Turkey. After graduating from high school, Stan decided to go west to follow his dream of making it big in the music business. He was in the right place at the right time when Benmont called him to play drums on some demo tracks. The stars aligned and Tom Petty, with his solo record deal in place, snapped up the band as his own. Now, The Heartbreakers were in England to make a name for themselves in rock's pantheon.

★ ★ ★

In early 1977, Nils Lofgren – now more famously known as a member of Bruce Springsteen's E Street Band than as a solo artist – reached out to Tom to inquire if he and The Heartbreakers would be interested in joining his tour as the opening band on a three-week jaunt around the UK. Tom enthusiastically agreed to the gigs, which commenced at the beginning of May and continued through the month. They played nearly a dozen cities but London was the most important one.

Nils was out promoting his latest album, *I Came To Dance*. For Tom Petty & The Heartbreakers, it was their opportunity to cement their most-favoured status with the kids of the United Kingdom. It was also the first time Tom and some of the other Heartbreakers had travelled beyond US borders. They were going to enjoy the trip in every way possible. Manager Tony Dimitriades – a partner with Elliot Roberts in Lookout Management – also knew this would be the right time to tack on a headlining tour in Europe after their commitments with Nils were fulfilled.

Even without today's lightning-speed social media outlets, UK music fans learned about the band's visit and news of tour dates spread quickly. By the time the guys landed at London's Heathrow Airport, interest in The Heartbreakers was at a fever pitch. Journalists from *NME* met them at the airport, which must have been a head trip for Tom Petty & The Heartbreakers, a bunch of hardworking southerners who weren't exactly a household name back home in the States.

Tom hadn't yet perfected the art of the interview, but he was gracious with his time to *NME* reporters and the magazine repaid him by naming 'American Girl' on its list of Favourite Singles of 1977 (number 23 on a list that also included the Sex Pistols, Elvis Costello, Ian Dury, the Ramones and Bob Marley & The Wailers).

A few additional shows – including the Pinkpop Festival in Geleen, Netherlands – were sandwiched in between the end of the Lofgren dates and the band's own headlining tour. June 2 brought them to a most unusual venue: Gesellschaftshaus. This was a small hall at the Frankfurt Zoo Society where The Heartbreakers again opened for Lofgren. According to fans that were there, there were only about 50 or 60 people in attendance – despite that the hall could hold 200. It was perhaps one of the more zany locations where The Heartbreakers have ever performed. The band continued on to Amsterdam to play Paradiso and then wound up in Lund, Sweden.

It felt to The Heartbreakers as if each show was a smash – and they were right. European kids were gobbling up their record. In fact, before the tour even began, UK journalists issued warnings to Lofgren, like this one from Russell Kyle of the *Glasgow Evening Times*: "Mr. Lofgren, for whom I have much respect, is in great danger of being blown off the stage if The Heartbreakers can turn in a live show that's half as good as the album. That's how good they are."

Indeed, Tom and company made the most of each and every show and proved their mettle almost immediately as *Melody Maker*'s May 26, 1977, issue stated: "The band's phenomenal rise to headlining status has taken just three weeks. They came to Britain at the beginning of this month to play as support band on the Lofgren tour. Petty and The Heartbreakers, however, are ending the tour as one of the most in-demand bands currently playing in this country."

As band manager Tony Dimitriades had predicted, The Heartbreakers were capable of drawing their own crowds and the Terminal Romance headline tour began in earnest on June 12 in Manchester with Bob Geldof's Boomtown Rats opening many of the shows. The band played nine concerts and taped episodes of television shows like Germany's *Rockpalast* as well as England's *Old Grey Whistle Test* and *Top Of The Pops*.

Music journalists vied for the opportunity to cover the band and write about the American sensation. In just 30 days Tom Petty & The Heartbreakers had become the darlings of Europe. "His live show is consistently excellent, full of chord charisma and no-sweat delirium. Petty seems to have grown up on a stage, a renegade at home among the amps and wires," noted Susin Shapiro in the April 9 issue of *Sounds* magazine. "Why people call him a punk is beyond me. He's not in an adversary space with his audience the way Johnny Rotten is, or all those other depraved no-talents who equate razors, swastikas and hatred with art. Petty and The Heartbreakers push it out with precision and the only thing they're fanatic about is having fun."

The band was ecstatic to finally receive a few props. It felt good to have their music understood by so many people. "The UK seemed to get us immediately, even more than the Americans," notes keyboardist

Benmont Tench. "Maybe because we were a basic rock'n'roll band and weren't wearing white satin trousers; we had really good songs and we were a good band. In the States, for some reason, they found us suspect, maybe because we didn't have punk haircuts. We had long bloody hair. We tried to be entertaining; we didn't take ourselves too seriously. We look a little self-centered in old clips, but I don't think we were pompous."

The band travelled around Europe honing its onstage presence and enjoying the finer things in life – like pretty girls and so-easy-to-score pot. Each Heartbreaker has fond memories of those days, especially Tom. "Of everything we've done, that '77 tour was the most memorable; just the greatest time I ever had," he says. "It was like a rock'n'roll dream, because we weren't of any significance in America yet, and our album had failed to sell at all. We probably would've been dropped if it hadn't been for what happened in England. We did *Top Of The Pops*, we had a record going up the charts and it was unreal. Our faces were on the covers of these weeklies, and the gigs were just fantastic."

Tom wasn't the only one enjoying the band's foray into European culture. Bassist Ron Blair, who – because of his Navy dad – was probably the most travelled of all The Heartbreakers, made sure to explore each city the band visited and had some particularly memorable experiences in Amsterdam, where each band member stocked up on the hashish that was readily available there. As the band transited Amsterdam Airport on its way to Germany to tape a segment of *Rockpalast*, Ron tried to smuggle a block of hash through customs. The entire band was pulled out of line when a customs agent found a small, but empty, hash pipe in Stan's luggage. Ron's luggage would be searched next. He had a decision to make. He shoved the chunk of hash in his mouth and started chewing. The band was detained for a few hours but made it to Cologne just in time for the taping. They played an inspired 40-minute set and Ron somehow made it through the show despite very hazy recollections of the evening.

★ ★ ★

Ronald Edward Blair was born in San Diego, California, on September 16, 1948. His father was in the Navy and the family never stayed in one place for more than a few years.

"I was a military brat; my dad worked for the Navy," Ron told Ken Sharp of *Bass Player* magazine in 2013. "I lived in Jacksonville, Florida, and surf music was the big thing – this was pre-Beatles." Ron got interested in playing music while still living in Jacksonville and started out on guitar – a Guyatone his dad had brought him back from one of his tours in Japan.

"Then sometime in 1964, my dad got stationed overseas. Next thing I knew, we were on a boat headed for Japan. When I got there it was like going back in time; it took a long time for music to get over to Japan, so they were somewhat behind."

Ron started playing in a local blues band that played all of the military bases. "Around 1968 my dad got stationed in Hong Kong, but I stayed and lived with the family of one of my band members, a group called The Mojos," Ron remembers. "Then I needed to go to university, so I chose the University of Florida in Gainesville, Florida. There was such a good music scene there.

"After I got back to Gainesville, I started jamming with a few bands," he says. "I had some friends in a band, two brothers who didn't get along, and one of the brothers had to go. So my friend asked me, 'Would you be into playing bass?' I went down to Lipham Music store – where we used to hang out – and I borrowed a bass…. Back in those days the bass wasn't a romantic instrument. You really had to talk someone into playing bass."

Ron eventually ended up in a band called RGF. A few years later, he met Tom Petty but not through his music contacts. "Around that time I met a great girl who turned out to be Tom's wife's best friend," he says. [Jane Benyo was still just Tom's girlfriend while the pair lived in Gainesville.] "We used to go over to his little apartment above a Laundromat, so I became acquainted with Tom then. I liked him as a friend before we ever started playing together."

While Mudcrutch and RGF's paths crossed in Gainesville, Ron didn't play in a band with Tom Petty until long after Ron had quit the University of Florida after his sophomore year and moved to Los Angeles in search of a long-term career in the rock'n'roll business.

Ron gigged around Los Angeles and kept in touch with other Gainesville expats that were now living in the area. Drummer Stan Lynch called him one day and invited him to Benmont's demo session. This was after the breakup of Mudcrutch and Benmont was intent on making a songwriting demo of his own. Tom Petty dropped by that session and it was there that he heard the trio of Benmont on piano, Stan on drums and Ron on bass. He knew that this was *his* band and he immediately asked them to come work with him. The Heartbreakers were born.

This group of musicians clicked in a way that the last iteration of Mudcrutch had not. If Benmont hadn't put together that demo session, The Heartbreakers might never have been formed.

Benmont loved playing with their new bassist. "Ron is such a sweet, relaxed and giving person in how he relates to the people around him," says Benmont. "His bass playing is just another integral part of that. As a musician, he's thoughtful and he listens. This is a band, and we all have to listen to each other. When we first started playing together, I listened mainly to Tom and Ron; I would play off the vocal melody and whatever Ron was doing. There are great bass players who are less subtle, and then there are [players like] Duck Dunn [Booker T. & The MGs] and Berry Oakley [Allman Brothers Band]. I've always associated Ron with them, particularly Berry Oakley."

Ron was an important part of finding The Heartbreakers' trademark sound. His self-effacing personality doesn't let him take all the credit though: "A lot of bass players have a certain sound that's great by itself, but that doesn't mean much. How it blends with the song, how it's sitting against the rhythm guitar, is more important," he says. The Heartbreakers, from the very beginning, just fit together. Now they needed the public to appreciate their efforts.

★ ★ ★

In the June 30, 1977, issue of *Rolling Stone*, critic Mikal Gilmore commented on the success the band was finally enjoying: "Petty and

The Heartbreakers have been generating a modest but steady wave of such zealous responses since the release last winter of their good-time rock'n'roll debut LP, *Tom Petty & The Heartbreakers*. Critics have been especially kind to them, comparing the band's melodic hard rock to that of Van Morrison and Roger McGuinn." Still, the band needed mainstream popularity in America to remain a viable asset to the record company. The clock was ticking, and Tom knew it.

By July of 1977 the band was back at home in California and it was almost as if nothing had changed. As Stan Lynch has said, they were famous in Europe and taking out the trash back at home. Tom would not be deterred, however. He and manager Tony Dimitriades made plans for more tour dates in the United States from August through the beginning of December. Some dates, like those at the Old Waldorf in San Francisco and the Whisky A Go Go in Los Angeles, were headliners. The band spent other nights opening for Be Bop Deluxe, J. Geils Band, Nektar, Meat Loaf, The Dingoes and even Rush, truly an odd musical pairing.

Around this time Americans started to hear about the band's successful stint in Europe and radio stations were giving the tracks on *Tom Petty & The Heartbreakers* a second listen. Finally, 10 months after its initial release, the band's debut album appeared in *Billboard*'s Top LPs & Tapes chart on September 24. This was all the ammunition Tom and Tony needed. Tony went to ABC, which had recently acquired Shelter Records, and convinced it to put some more weight behind the promotion of the album. 'Breakdown' was re-released with 'Fooled Again' as its B-side and, this time, the song debuted on *Billboard*'s Hot 100 chart on November 5.

The band's fortunes were beginning to change and critics were now not so fast to skim over their music. Some critics, like *Rolling Stone*'s Mikal Gilmore, already knew that there was something unique about the band and, especially, its frontman, saying that "Petty's commitment to rock'n'roll approaches religious fervor." And the congregants were just beginning to gather for services.

CHAPTER 5

At War With The Big Dogs
(1978–1979)

"Then the sharks started to circle."

$-$T.P.

Tom didn't see the thunderclouds in the distance. To his eyes, 1978 looked like it was finally going to be *his* year. The band's first album had seen a modicum of success and last year's European tour was an absolute triumph. A fanbase, a rather devoted fanbase at that, was growing both in Europe and at home in the United States. Tom was cautiously optimistic that this year, with a planned second studio album, would finally bring the band the spoils it deserved. He wasn't the only one predicting that his fortunes were about to change. The record company could sense that Tom was about to reach new heights in his career and they were more than happy to keep their boot on his neck by way of tight control on his recording contract. A contract that frankly did not compensate the musician nearly enough for his efforts.

During the European tour, Tom did some math on the back of a napkin and began to realize just how inequitable his deal with Shelter really was. Of course, the record company didn't agree. A confrontation was inevitable. But, those bumps in the road weren't yet on the horizon as the band rang in the New Year.

Once the holidays were over, Tom and Tony Dimitriades sat down to map out a strategy for 1978 and for the band's second album. The success The Heartbreakers enjoyed in Europe made it clear that they actually *could* sell some records. Tony began to scrutinise the contract Tom had signed with Shelter Records and decided it was a raw deal. Before the band could possibly embark on work for the follow-up album, he insisted that a new contract be negotiated. The record company was none too happy to discuss the terms but, in the end, Tom and Tony calmly explained that the band would put off recording until the record company agreed to restructure the terms of the deal.

The record company acquiesced – not wanting to squander the momentum the band had built in Europe – and the new terms were an improvement, but only slightly and the need to revisit the issue would crop up again within the year.

In the meantime, though, Tom was anxious to get back into the studio and Shelter, for its part, was anxious to start promoting new music from The Heartbreakers. Ads touting *Terminal Romance*, the original title of the second album, were placed in the music trades but somewhere along the line the band cooled on that name and instead went for something more visceral: *You're Gonna Get It!*

The album made its debut on May 2, 1978. Fans snapped up the record and it charted higher than its predecessor, peaking at number 23 on *Billboard*'s Top LPs & Tapes chart in 1978 and ultimately earning the boys their first gold record. (Their debut album went gold later that year.)

Even the usually harsh critic Robert Christgau had something nice to say about *You're Gonna Get It!* on its release: "Tuneful, straight-ahead rock'n'roll dominates the disc, and 'I Need To Know', which kicks off side two, is as peachy-tough as power pop gets."

Tom wrote all 10 of the songs on the album with the exception of 'Hurt' and 'Baby's A Rock 'N' Roller', which were co-written with Mike Campbell. This songwriting partnership would soon blossom into an integral key to the band's longevity.

The themes on this record are similar to those found on the band's earlier album. Loyalty is a recurring element in many of Tom's songs and the opening track of *You're Gonna Get It*, 'When The Time Comes', illustrates that absolute devotion and faithfulness to another. In this song the singer promises to stand by his girl and hopes she will do the same "when the time comes". The driving guitars at the tune's opening and the sing-song-y chorus are especially infectious.

Unlike other rock bands of the era that wrote songs in which women were always the weak ones, Tom Petty often pens songs that show the vulnerability of men. Four songs on his sophomore effort – 'You're Gonna Get It', 'Hurt', 'I Need To Know' and 'Magnolia' – all portray women who hold the upper hand in the relationship.

The women in both 'You're Gonna Get It' ("I can't crawl any further / You never crawled for me") and 'Hurt' ("Cut down the middle / Face down in the dirt / And we both know it's too late to save it / Betcha feel proud about it baby / You taught me how to hurt") have already done their men wrong by walking out on them. On record and when sung live, Tom spits out the lyrics to 'You're Gonna Get It', trying to tell his ex that she'll get her just deserts for leaving him. The only problem is, he doesn't sound all that sure. The character feels betrayed by his lover but still clearly has feelings for her.

On the other hand, the male character portrayed in 'Hurt' has accepted defeat and is heading back home to start all over again. He's been pushed aside and marginalised and he's accepted the pain – albeit he doesn't like it one bit. This one starts out with a bit of random instrument tuning from the band before a beautiful, ringing guitar part emerges to set the stage for the singer.

The fourth track on the record is the lush and hypnotic ballad 'Magnolia', Tom's second song about a one-night stand controlled by the woman. (The first was 'The Wild One, Forever' – "I'll never get over how good it felt / When you finally held me / I will never regret baby / Those few hours linger on in my head forever".) The singer reflects on the perfect night he spent with a girl who never did tell him her name. Does he feel a little bit used? Perhaps disappointed not to have the chance to see where a relationship with her would have led?

Tom sings the song with a very palpable sense of wistfulness. It'
tale of what could have been.

The band pulls out a blues-tinged rocker – 'Too Much Ain't
Enough' – at the midpoint of the album. AllMusic record reviewer
Matthew Greenwald calls this song "one of Petty's lost masterpieces".
The band played this often in concert in the early days before retiring
it for decades. The rollicking guitar and bass parts roll along as Tom's
lyrics powerfully punch through the dense instrument bed.

The jury is still out regarding the subject of 'I Need To Know'.
Is she two-timing her boyfriend? Will she leave him? That's all the
singer wants to know. 'I Need To Know' was the first single released
to promote *You're Gonna Get It!* The track peaked at number 41 on
the *Billboard* Hot 100 chart in the United States. The song – which
is all about impending loss – is balanced by the absolute triumph of
love in 'Listen To Her Heart'. Some dude is trying to steal away the
singer's girl but he knows that won't happen. A story Jane Petty told
her husband actually inspired him to write 'Listen To Her Heart'. She
was at a raucous party at Ike Turner's house one night and things got
a bit weird with everyone being locked inside by the host who didn't
want the party to end. Such shenanigans were foreign to the Pettys who
never adopted LA's party culture. Tom found the tale curious and built
a song around it. 'Listen To Her Heart' made it to number 59 on the
US charts.

The song would have perhaps ranked higher on the charts if Tom
had given in to the wants of some radio programmers. It seemed many
were disturbed by Tom's mention of cocaine in the lyrics. They wanted
him to substitute that word with "champagne". Tom thought the
idea was ludicrous and told that to *Trouser Press'* Gary Sperrazza in the
December 1978 issue of the magazine: "I've heard reservations already
about the word 'cocaine' – they [corporate radio] want me to change it
to 'champagne'. Now tell me: what girl would leave someone for a guy
with money and *champagne?!?* I mean, champagne is only $4 a bottle!"

While 'I Need To Know' became a classic, the sleeper 'No Second
Thoughts' is a fan favourite to this day. The ballad is interesting from
a songwriting point of view. Tom wrote it when he was 28, but the

patina of regret painted in the lyrics seems more like something one would write in his twilight years – after they've lived, loved, been hurt and found the strength to start all over again. Tom's insight into the emotions of love and regret – even at 28 – was striking.

The last two tracks on the album are 'Restless' and 'Baby's A Rock 'N' Roller'. The singer in 'Restless' is looking for a kindred spirit to help him find whatever it is he's looking for. 'Baby's A Rock 'N' Roller' is an exuberant celebration of the girl the singer did find – a girl who lives for rock'n'roll just like he does. These songs may be weaker than those on the rest of the album from a songwriting point of view but they are no less interesting musically.

You're Gonna Get It! was a cohesive album of rock songs that reinforced the innate sound of The Heartbreakers, which is so often punctuated by jangling guitars, melodic organ lines and aggressive percussion parts.

The music press made a point to follow Tom closely during this period and wrote about his music at length. In September of 1978, *Rolling Stone's* Tom Carson wrote about the album and the future as he saw it for Tom Petty: "He's got too much determination and integrity to be contained within a cult, and *You're Gonna Get It!* is a bid to break him loose."

Steve Simels of *Stereo Review* notably wrote at that time that, "He seems truly to believe in all this stuff with the same fervor and intensity you find in all the great ones, from Chuck Berry to Bruce Springsteen." The ethos of rock'n'roll was important to Tom Petty and his second album was cementing his reputation as someone who understood the angst of the younger generation while writing music in a style that borrowed from his elders, like Elvis and the Everly Brothers.

As the months wore on, it really did look like 1978 would be the year of Tom Petty. In June, just one month after the release of *You're Gonna Get It!*, *Los Angeles Times* music critic Robert Hilburn wrote, "Predictions are hazardous in any field where success depends on something as fickle as public taste, but there's enough evidence available to take a stab at one: Tom Petty's going to be a superstar in rock."

It was clear to almost everyone that the band's trajectory pointed skyward. Hilburn tried to pinpoint why the band worked: "Rather than deal in a narrow jazz-rock, classical-rock, pop-rock fusion, Tom and The Heartbreakers band deal in a classic rock style so powerful and pure you'd think they'd stumbled across some long-lost formula. Most importantly, Petty connects with his audiences."

Tom and The Heartbreakers were enjoying their newfound success and as more rock papers touted their music, the offers came rolling in. Tom played live in the John A. Alonzo-directed movie *FM*, which was released in the spring of 1978 and on June 24 the band headed back to England to play Knebworth. These open-air events took place on the grounds of Knebworth House near the village of Knebworth in Hertfordshire, England. The concert was dubbed A Midsummer Night's Dream and also featured Genesis, Jefferson Starship, Devo and the Atlanta Rhythm Section.

While Knebworth turned out to be a fantastic show, one on July 29 back in Miami in the States wasn't as successful. The double bill consisted of Tom Petty & The Heartbreakers and Patti Smith at the Jai Alai Fronton. During the show Tom was badly shocked due to faulty electrical wiring onstage. He was able to finish the set but did postpone the next night's gig in Dayton, Ohio. These little setbacks were par for the course, considering the band was almost always on the road.

It's also at this point in his career that other musicians began asking Tom to write music for them or produce their projects. He'd already collaborated with Roger McGuinn on his *Thunderbyrd* album. It was Roger's fifth solo album and included a version of 'American Girl'. Tom points out now, though, that he actually wrote 'Magnolia' for McGuinn. "He wanted to do 'American Girl' and I taught him that," recalls Tom, "and then I made a little demo of this ['Magnolia'] and sent it over. Roger dug it, but they couldn't make it happen to where they were pleased with it." Tom decided to take the song back and that's how it ended up on 1978's *You're Gonna Get It!*

Also around this time The Searchers released a self-titled album on Sire Records and included a song that Tom wrote: 'Lost In Your Eyes'. The Merseybeat band had roots in sixties Liverpool and their chart-topping covers – like The Clovers' 'Love Potion No. 9' and Jackie DeShannon's 'Needles And Pins' – inspired a young Tom Petty to pick up a guitar and learn how to play. In fact, 'Love Potion No. 9' was one of the first songs he ever learned on guitar. Tom was humbled by the fact that one of his musical heroes came to him for a song. It was the highest form of compliment anyone could have given him.

The band closed out the year with a few memorable concerts, most notably the December 30 show at Winterland in San Francisco. They played 18 songs that night, including the now rarely heard 'Surrender', 'Strangered In The Night' and 'Too Much Ain't Enough' before lunging into an encore set featuring, among other songs, the Isley Brothers' 'Shout'. The Heartbreakers would end up playing this song often during their decades-long career.

The event was memorable – especially for Tom – because the audience pulled him into the crowd during his performance of 'Shout' and proceeded to rough him up quite badly (although unintentionally). Tom recalls that evening: "I think it was in '78 that it dawned on me about the audience. We had only been playing big rooms a little while and we went into Winterland. I think Bruce [Springsteen] had been there two nights before, and he built a lower stage across the front and it was still there. We weren't using it because the kids had all their jackets and everything piled up. So by the end of the night, I was just getting a little bit playful and went out, jumped down, just leaned over the crowd. We thought at the time they'd gotten me by the hand, but on the videotape you can see they get me almost by the waist. And take me into the audience and try to kill me. I mean, they were going take my life. It was very violent in the sense that they were all going take a finger and a leg. On the tape, I have on a real heavy vest and they ripped that, my whole shirt went, I had a neckerchief tied real tight around my neck and on the tape, it's hanging down to my chest because it had been so pulled and twisted. I lost handfuls of hair and my whole lip was busted. It was this weird sensation of falling and never hitting the ground and people diving in. They're crazy people when they're that worked up. I remember that night was when it dawned on us: we *can't* go down there. I didn't intend to go down there in the first place, but it was like, 'Hey, watch it, if they get ahold of you. They'll just get you down... it took a *lotta* guys to get me out."

This troubling incident didn't stop Tom from playing the band's New Year's Eve show the next night at the Santa Monica Civic Auditorium. Del Shannon joined the band onstage for an electrifying version of his 1961 hit 'Runaway'. As the champagne corks popped at midnight, Tom may have felt a bit bruised and battered but he had no idea that things were about to get a whole lot worse.

Something happened in March of 1979 that would radically alter the fortunes of Tom Petty & The Heartbreakers. MCA Records acquired ABC Records, the distributor for Shelter Records, and while it may have simply looked like an organizational flow chart on paper, this change of ownership absolutely enraged Tom. He maintained that he wasn't a piece of meat that could be bought and sold on a whim. His contract was nontransferable without his express permission. He didn't know the guys at MCA. He had no way of knowing if the new regime would support the band in the ways they needed – both in the studio and on the road. It was a pivotal time for the band and Tom felt his very career was in jeopardy. He was not going to leave his future in the hands of strangers. He was going to fight this.

Tom commented on the issue at the time: "I've got nothing personally against MCA – except they tried to buy me without asking. When we negotiated the deal with ABC, we put in a clause that they couldn't sell the contract without my consent. I don't think the fact that you've got $35 million means you should be able to buy my business, or my music or my life. So I decided to fight to the wall even though it's important to have another record out there now."

Tom understood that the music industry was in a time of flux, and had been evolving since the day his band made its way from Gainesville to Los Angeles. "When we came up in '77, we couldn't even get an agency to represent us. People thought our sound was uncommercial," he said. "But the success of 'Breakdown' and the success of bands like The Cars and Blondie and Cheap Trick shows there's a market for this kind of rock'n'roll. I just hope I can get it out there and participate in it again. The only thing I want from a record company is assurances that they believe in my music and will give it a real shot." He was sending signals to everyone in the business that he considered himself a free agent and was willing to be courted.

Their savvy manager Tony Dimitriades reinforced that message by letting the press know where the band stood: "We don't consider ourselves affiliated with MCA because there is no provision in our contract for our transfer to MCA. We're not affiliated with any company. We're talking to various people."

This is when other record companies began to come calling. If Tom really was free of his contract with ABC, he was a free agent: a very in-demand free agent. Deals worth millions of dollars were being offered while Tom was veritably handcuffed to MCA. The situation was untenable.

Tom decided that he'd embark on his third album with no help from MCA. He self-financed the recording while working through the legal system to free himself from MCA. Tom went into debt – some calculate the figure just north of half a million dollars – and proceeded to file for bankruptcy protection under Chapter XI on May 23, 1979. Simultaneously, Tom sued MCA to be released from his recording contract. A hearing was set for August of 1979. If the court favored Tom's position, he'd be free of all contractual bindings and would become a free agent. He wanted nothing more than the opportunity to decide his own fate with the record company partner of *his* choosing.

Of course, the downside of going to court was the fact that the third studio album would be held up indefinitely. MCA's lawyers began firing off injunctions, including one that stopped Tom from playing his music in front of live audiences. This affront was probably just one of the reasons why he later titled the third album *Damn The Torpedoes*, in homage to American Civil War-era Admiral David Farragut who ordered his men into the Battle of Mobile Bay in Alabama with the call, "Damn the torpedoes, full speed ahead!" Tom was determined to flatten MCA and every lawyer it had in its arsenal.

In the past, Tom has talked about how difficult this time period was for him, the band and everyone around them. He felt that the sharks were circling and that the executives of MCA would rather squash his career than let him gracefully out of his contract to continue making music. Tom couldn't fathom a world that would let a faceless corporation silence a simple songwriter. He was not going to let that happen, but the fight would take a huge toll on his health and well-being. He admits that the lawsuits "almost finished me off, mentally and financially.

"I remember telling the lawyers for the other side, 'Screw you. I will go to Florida; I'll sell peanuts if I have to. But I will *never* give you this goddamned record.' At least I'll have the satisfaction of knowing that you want this and you'll never get it," Tom asserted during the debacle.

MCA desperately wanted to release Tom's next album. It wasn't stupid. It had heard all the rumors going around the Los Angeles recording community. The band's work with producer Jimmy Iovine and engineer Shelly Yakus at Sound City in Van Nuys was unprecedented. There was a fire in the new music that wasn't detectable in either *Tom Petty & The Heartbreakers* or *You're Gonna Get It!* MCA wanted to get its grubby paws on the tapes from the *Damn The Torpedoes* sessions – at any cost. The company began filing motions to force the court to seize the tapes.

"We'd be working in the studio," remembers Tom, "and then they'd say, 'You gotta look out for the marshals, the marshals are gonna come in tonight and grab the tapes.' It got to where poor Bugs [Alan Weidel, Tom's longtime guitar tech and roadie] was just carrying all these tapes around in his car, and moving 'em, so on the stand I could honestly say, 'I don't know where the tapes are.' 'Cause these guys would have released the album in whatever condition it was in."

All this legal wrangling was fodder for not only the music trades, but also for venerable newspapers like the *Wall Street Journal* and *New York Times*. Many in the industry understood that the ruling in this case could reverberate throughout the business and set a precedent that would allow other musicians to contest their recording contracts.

The court of public opinion was certainly on Tom's side. In 1979 the economy was sagging and blue-collar workers were tired of being at "the man's" beck and call. MCA disgusted the masses that felt the company was trying to silence a musician. Tom certainly felt the same way: "I couldn't believe I was so valuable to people that they'd rather destroy me than see me on another label. I felt pinned to the wall."

MCA was getting nervous. It was possible that the court would rule in favor of Tom Petty and the label would lose out on all future proceeds of his albums. In the end, they worked out an agreement that released Tom from his existing contract. MCA then offered him a revised deal worth $3 million. Tom still wasn't convinced. MCA was tarnished in his eyes and he really wanted a break from anyone tied to the company. To solve this problem, Danny Bramson, a music executive that Tom trusted – who's now a music supervisor for the film industry – was allowed to set up a new subsidiary label under MCA called Backstreet Records. Tom says now that Danny came in as the peacemaker and allowed both sides to save face.

The band was elated and incredibly relieved that the legal battle was over. They were proud of Tom for standing up for what he believed in but they always knew he'd prevail. According to Mike Campbell, "Tom is just a natural leader. He has the vision and he's mentally dominant. He's like Dylan. He can walk into a room full of strangers and nail them all on their bullshit. Like the lawyers. They thought they were dealing with a bunch of dummies. And we didn't know much legal language, but Tom could cut to the heart of the issue better than anybody."

Tom says that winning the case gave him a lot of faith in the country. "I don't see too many countries where you could go to court and say, 'Your Honor, I have a little band here and these guys have come in and done this to me, and I would like to get rid of it. What do you think? I'll give all the money back, and everything. I just want out. I quit.' And they took it dead serious."

Backstreet Records released *Damn The Torpedoes* on October 19, 1979. At the time, Steve Simels of *Stereo Review* wrote, "The title of this one, if I may venture a guess, seems to be a response to the little legal hassles that prompted Petty to launch what he referred to as his Bankruptcy Tour. I like the attitude that demonstrated, and I like the attitude this album demonstrates even more: justifiable cockiness."

There was just 36 minutes of music on the album but the public drank in every second of it. The album peaked at number two on the *Billboard* 200 album chart, where it stayed for seven weeks. (Pink Floyd's *The Wall* kept *Torpedoes* from ever making it to the number one spot.) What was the secret? What did everyone find so compelling about Tom's third record?

Mitch Cohen of *Creem* tried to answer that question: "*Damn The Torpedoes* takes the American Stand: 'Don't tread on me.' When you've been 'raised on promises' like the heroine of Tom Petty's bicentennial debut, you have a birthright to try and make those promises hold up. Petty and The Heartbreakers have turned out an ace third LP that simply crackles with the spirit of defiance and energy, though being who he is – a rock'n'roll bantam to the core – Petty can't help but throw down his gauntlet with an air of teen rockabilly cockiness, with a swagger and a wink, and some mixed-up confusion."

Tom asserts that he never intended to come off in an adversarial way on tape. "I wanted to present *Torpedoes* as a collection of love songs – not lawsuit songs – and if there's one thing I know about music theory, it's that if you don't believe the singer, you won't believe the song. But I guess that sense of persecution was inescapable. I'm still bitter about some of that stuff. All those sleepless nights, sitting up in my house wondering, '*what is life?*' Going a little nuts. I never got into one of those places before, and I refuse to ever go back there."

Tom co-produced the album with Jimmy Iovine though Tom had originally only hired him to engineer the record. In Dave Grohl's 2013 *Sound City* documentary, Tom says, "I hired Jimmy as an engineer to do *Damn The Torpedoes* there [Sound City] but he showed up with an engineer without telling me that. He manipulated his way into being the producer of the record along with me."

That probably wasn't too surprising. Jimmy was a no-nonsense Italian from Brooklyn, New York, who had the same type of dogged determination as Tom did. The pair became fast friends. Jimmy was an unfailing cheerleader throughout the grueling sessions and legal woes. The band worked out of Sound City in Van Nuys as well as Cherokee Studios in Hollywood.

Jimmy looked forward to working with Tom because he knew of his reputation for speaking his mind. Jimmy felt the two had harmonious work styles. There was no need to tiptoe around Tom Petty. According to Jimmy, "Some artists you have to walk around the block. Tom wants total honesty at all times." Tom's songwriting itself was another draw. "He doesn't write his songs because he heard something similar on the radio. He writes those songs out of commitment and courage," says Jimmy. "There's nothing calculated about Tom Petty."

The sessions were tense and difficult from the beginning though it didn't seem that way to onlookers. Paula Salvatore, who was studio manager of Sound City at the time, says, "Tom was great. His whole approach. Low key. He'd come in like it was his own garage studio."

Despite appearances, the pressure on Tom really was enormous; the pressure to create the album that would break the band as superstars, the pressure to finance the album without record company involvement, and the pressure of filing for bankruptcy and challenging one of the largest record labels on the planet. If this all went wrong, his career would be over and the fallout might even irrevocably damage his friendship with the members of the band. For all these reasons, Tom was absolutely uncompromising in the studio. He became a veritable taskmaster and Jimmy only reinforced that drive for perfection. Most members of the band weathered the storm fairly well but drummer Stan Lynch was growing increasingly edgy, especially when his drumming prowess was being questioned from the control room.

It's not that the pressure came out of the blue. Everyone knew Tom was single-minded in his pursuit of success. Stan understood where Tom was coming from. "Tom was very demanding. He was very professional without knowing that he was. Tom was driven. He would tell things to people… promoters, managers…heavy. I mean, he would talk to people that we were all supposed to be cowering from and he would flatten them," Stan recalls.

These days, Tom admits he was harsh during the *Torpedoes* sessions, especially in regards to Stan. "Being a drummer in a session is like being a pitcher on a baseball team – it's always his fault. Whatever's wrong, it's the rhythm section, right? And I tell you, there aren't that many people who could live through an album with me and Jimmy, because we tend to push people very hard, and we're not always what you'd call polite. We will say exactly what's on our mind. It's not meant to be rude, it's just meant to get on with things.

"I think I like the studio a little too much," Tom admits. "I could stay there endlessly. I wear everyone out. Nobody wants to stay. They always want to go before I do." It was that sort of bullishness that made the sessions difficult for Stan and other members of the band. Even the normally laid-back Mike Campbell reached his breaking point during these session, leaving the studio to take off for a few days when the pressure was too intense. He returned a few days later, recharged and able to make peace with the process.

For Mike, these sessions were vitally important to his future – not only as a rock guitarist but also as a songwriter, producer and arranger in his own right. It's at this point that Tom and Mike began collaborating and writing music together on a regular basis. In fact, Mike wrote the music for the stirring anthem 'Refugee' with Tom contributing the iconic lyrics.

"That ['Refugee'] was a hard record to make," Mike says now. "It was a four-track that I made at my house. Tom wrote over the music as it was, no changes, but it took us forever to actually cut the track. We just had a hard time getting the feel right. We must have recorded that 100 times."

When it was released, 'Refugee' was embraced as an anthem that validated the very spirit of America: despite any adversity, we will get back up and fight. The message was clear to fans: yes, life is hard, toughen up and fight back. Tom had fought MCA and won and that lesson of underdog triumphing over a huge corporation was something to celebrate.

'Here Comes My Girl' – written the same week as 'Refugee' – also had a celebratory tone but this time it was all about a relationship gone right. Mike had made a dozen demos of different songs for the Sound City sessions and Tom liked 'Refugee' and 'Here Comes My Girl' best. Mike says, "'Here Comes My Girl' was interesting because we had the chorus and Tom wasn't sure how to do the verse. He kept trying to sing it different ways and he finally came across sort of half-talking it, and that's when the song seemed to come to life."

Fans identified with the character in the song who toils in a town that "seems so hopeless" but he can "somehow rise above it" because of the love of his woman. After the quasi-spoken verse and the adrenalin rush of its escalating final line, Tom and the band surge in with a killer chorus that lifts the song to anthem-like proportions before he takes the mood down again. 'Watch her walk,' he says, almost off-handedly, conjuring up the perfect image of the girl he adores strolling towards him and making everything all right again.

The tracks the pair co-wrote for this album fueled Mike's interest in songwriting and future albums would include even more collaborations. Mike has always approached guitar playing with economy in mind and that's the same approach he takes to songwriting. It's interesting to hear Mike talk about his approach since he has co-written so many rock'n'roll standards with Tom over the years as well as for Don Henley and other artists. Mike says this about how he gets inspiration: "Sometimes if I'm stuck, I will play a song that I like, a Beatles or Stones song, to get me in the state of mind to just open up, to have a pivotal point that I can key from. Other times, I might put on a song I've heard a million times and listen. Or I might hear something on the radio, and think, 'Wow, that's a great chord or sequence,' and I'll sit down and learn it, and as I'm learning it, I might get an idea to do something like it but different. I might play the chords backwards, or take a lick and stick it over a different chord, and that will lead me into something that's mine, which was inspired by something that turned me on. Sometimes you'll just hear a chord, you'll sit down and learn it, and you think, this is a great chord, and you can just write a whole different song starting with that as your foundation. That's the beauty of writing. You can tap the soul of the thing that inspired you and find a way to make it your own. It's hard to talk about it because it's very mysterious.

"I'm always writing," adds Mike, "even when I don't have a guitar in front of me. I'm always trying to keep the antenna open to any idea that might come, at any time…. Writing is a gift, and it's a sort of channeling. Sometimes it's not even coming from you, you are just sort of open and things come to you. A lot of times, it will just happen if you are in the right state of mind. The ideas just come."

That's most certainly what happened with the tracks on *Damn The Torpedoes*. Despite the legal battles, Tom and Mike were able to write some of the band's most enduring songs during this time period.

Other standouts on the record written by Petty include 'Even The Losers', in which the songwriter laments of a time gone by with a

By the time Petty headed to Los Angeles to land a record deal in 1975, he'd already earned his stripes as a consummate musician and bandleader. IAN DICKSON/REDFERNS

The Epics. Petty joined The Epics on his sixteenth birthday in 1966, from left: Petty, Rodney Rucker, Dickie Underwood, Ricky Rucker, and Tom Leadon.

Mudcrutch in the mid-seventies, immediately after singer Tom Leadon was axed from the band for torpedoing their mainstay gig at Dub's in Gainesville, from left: Mike Campbell, Petty, Benmont Tench and Randall Marsh. JIM MCCRARY/REDFERNS

An early portrait of Tom Petty & The Heartbreakers, mid-1976, from left: Mike Campbell, Benmont Tench, Petty, Jeff Jourard, Ron Blair and Stan Lynch. While never an official member of the band, Jeff was around for early Heartbreakers' sessions and then went on to join The Motels. ED CARAEFF/GETTY IMAGES

The early eighties found Petty playing his Flying V in concert around the world. MICHAEL OCHS ARCHIVES/GETTY IMAGES

Spring 1977 found The Heartbreakers playing London's Hammersmith Odeon. Mike Campbell trades guitar licks with Petty onstage. IAN DICKSON/REDFERNS

Tom Petty & The Heartbreakers toured Europe in 1977 to back Nils Lofgren and then – at the behest of fans in England and Germany – launched their own wildly successful headline tour.

Suffering from a painful case of tonsillitis, Petty, struggled through this spirited concert at New York City's Palladium on November 11, 1979, one of fewer than 20 shows the band performed that year because an injunction prevented them from playing live until the case was resolved. RICHARD E. AARON/REDFERNS

The first of many photo shoots for Tom in 1976. It's unclear exactly why Tom is using a cane as a prop in this one.
RICHARD E. AARON/REDFERNS

Britain embraced Tom Petty & The Heartbreakers early on and the 1976 single 'Anything That's Rock 'N' Roll' raced up the charts. The band found an eager audience waiting for them when they toured the United Kingdom in 1977.
IAN DICKSON/THE HELL GATE/CORBIS

Petty with Roger McGuinn after opening for him with The Heartbreakers at Manhattan's Bottom Line on November 19-20, 1977.
CHUCK PULIN/SPLASH NEWS/CORBIS

As The Heartbreakers cemented their place as one of rock 'n' roll's pre-eminent bands, Petty was in demand for his production sensibilities. Sixties star Del Shannon drafted Petty to help him produce his comeback record, *Drop Down And Get Me*, in 1981.

Petty's popularity only grew after the breakout success of *Damn The Torpedoes*. The band's 1981 tour backing the follow-up record, *Hard Promises*, was a victory lap around America. Here Petty shares a moment backstage in Chicago with publicist Paul Wasserman.

The Heartbreakers grow up circa 1981, from left: Mike Campbell, Ron Blair, Benmont Tench, Petty, and Stan Lynch. CORBIS

woman he loved, 'Shadow Of A Doubt' about a woman who keeps him guessing and 'Don't Do Me Like That' – a warning to his girl not to dump him for some other guy. Tom's father actually coined the phrase 'don't do me like that' and it always stuck with Tom. The sentiment resonated with fans that helped push it to number 10 on the *Billboard* Hot 100 singles chart. The song actually charted higher than 'Refugee', which only made it to number 15.

A little more than halfway into the album, listeners are treated to 'Century City', a song Tom wrote about all the lawyers housed in that neighbourhood of Los Angeles. Tom's strong delivery of the vocals pushes the driving guitars forward in this song that was no doubt inspired by all the legal hassles he'd enduring throughout the previous year.

The two ballads on the record – 'You Tell Me' and 'Louisiana Rain' – soften the harder edge of the rest of the tracks. 'You Tell Me' is about a couple who have to decide if they're going to stay together or split. That tune really didn't stand the test of time and hasn't been in the band's live set for decades. The nostalgic 'Louisiana Rain', however, had a resurgence of popularity in 2010 when the band released an expanded and remastered "deluxe edition" of *Damn The Torpedoes*. Finally, you have to wonder if 'What Are You Doin' In My Life?' is autobiographical. The singer tries to push away a hanger-on who thinks she can muscle her way into his world. Benmont offers up a terrific and angry piano part on that track.

In 1979 and early 1980 you couldn't twirl the radio dial without hearing one or more of the songs from *Damn The Torpedoes*. Critic Fred Mills phrased it best in *Harp* magazine, "Imagine a world without 'Refugee' in FM radio's DNA. Every song here adds nuance to defiance, from the jangly optimism of 'Even The Losers' to the R&B-flavored entreaties of 'Don't Do Me Like That' to the pop swagger of 'Here Comes My Girl'. In the latter's unapologetic appreciation of feminine pulchritude, Petty marvels 'watch her walk', an aside as memorable as Roy Orbison's famous 'Mercy!' in 'Pretty Woman.'"

Damn The Torpedos was on fire and rock critics tried to divine Petty's secret for connecting with the audience. *Newsweek*'s Barbara Graustark might have hit upon something in her review of the album: "There's nothing complicated about The Heartbreakers' spirited sound: they've taken the kicking electric guitars of the British mid-sixties rockers, the soulful harmonies of The Byrds and streamlined the sound for the eighties with clever, melodic twists and lean, snapping rhythms. Petty's raspy delivery at times evokes Jagger's menace and Dylan's twang, but despite the obvious influences, the songs work on their own because of Petty's straightforward lyrics."

★ ★ ★

1979 ended up being a blur for Tom and the band. The making of *Damn The Torpedoes* and the lawsuits took up three quarters of the year. Once the album was finally released, they could get back on the road. They kicked off a series of live shows with an appearance on *Saturday Night Live* in early November. That evening Tom's tonsils became inflamed and he struggled through a gig the following night at New York City's Palladium. He finally lost his voice the next evening during a concert at Philadelphia's Tower Theater. The timing couldn't have been worse. Under doctor's orders, the band postponed the next date on the tour so Tom could rest his vocal cords. His physician cautioned that rest alone wouldn't resolve the problem and what Tom really needed was surgery. Checking into the hospital during a tour – one so eagerly awaited by fans – wasn't practical so Tom decided to surge forward and make it to the end of the year before seeking further medical attention. He was tired, in pain and irritable, but he was also thankful to be back out on the road singing for people who understood his message. Three months ago he wasn't sure if he'd ever have an audience again. Despite the hardships, Tom wouldn't think of packing up and going home. He was a fighter and he'd get back up as many times as he was knocked down – not unlike the character in *Damn The Torpedoes'* 'Even The Losers'.

"The guy in those songs *isn't* a loser," Tom contends. "I've been through things where I thought it just couldn't get no bleaker. It was a bad stretch, but I had to bring myself out of it. If you can't take the attitude that even losers get lucky, I don't see how you can face life. I figure you either lose your girl or your job – sometimes both. But why let anyone know they've beat you?"

And so, with that sort of determination, tonsillitis didn't scuttle the tour. Before the year's end the band played to packed theaters across the United States as well as playing a few gigs further north in Canada.

To be sure, 1979 was a rocky one for Tom Petty but the phenomenal success of *Damn The Torpedoes* and the subsequent tour was a redemption of sorts. "I don't think there will ever be a feeling like when that record was a hit. It was such a total victory," he smiles. "I think you've got to be careful not to discount the things that come easy – but there is a certain satisfaction in struggling for something and getting it. That's the American way," Tom concludes. The band had gone through so much and came out the other side seemingly unscathed – at least for the moment.

Rock critic Bill Flanagan – now editorial director of MTV – pondered Tom's resolve as it related to his successes over the year: "Petty is tenacious, straight-ahead, impatient with fools and able to fight to the death for a cause he believes in." Tom was proud of sticking up for what he believed was his innate right and he fervently hoped 1980 would be much less dramatic. All he wanted was to write songs and play rock'n'roll to an appreciative audience. 1979 proved that he would be able to do that for a long time. As Steve Simels wrote in his *Stereo Review* column as he closed out the year, *Damn The Torpedoes* is "clearly the work of one of the handful of truly vital mainstream rock bands currently working". Tom had plans to keep his band busy for decades to come.

CHAPTER 6

Success And Its Fallout
(1980–1985)

"Most of the last few years, I was ready to throw up my dukes at anything."
— T.P.

A new decade may have dawned but Tom Petty & The Heartbreakers were still in the midst of their US tour promoting *Damn The Torpedoes*. Tom was driven to perform at his peak each night, but he was restless. They had wasted precious time last year fighting with MCA before finally releasing the third album. The tracks were now exploding on the charts and you couldn't turn the radio dial without hearing 'Refugee' or 'Don't Do Me Like That'. Success – true get-all-the-chicks, earn-zillions-of-dollars success – had visited the band and it looked like just the beginning of the fairy tale. Still, Tom felt like he had so much work to do to evangelise his music and so little time to play catch-up with his audience. Tom was determined to stay out on the road as much as possible in 1980. In January alone the band blew through 10 dates in Oklahoma, Missouri, California and Arizona. Fans and critics alike greeted each concert enthusiastically. *Sounds* critic Sylvie Simmons' led her review of the band's February 2 date at the Los

Angeles Forum this way, "Lighters come on round the arena, a couple of firecrackers go off, then on strides Petty with his rockstar lope, leans into the microphone with his rockstar stoop, pouts the pout (invisible past the twelfth row but you know it's there), sneers the sneer, surveys the 18,000-strong cocktail party below and dives into 'Shadow Of A Doubt', 'Anything That's Rock 'N' Roll' and 'Fooled Again', without coming up for air." The band was definitely on fire.

Tom's singing remained fairly strong throughout concerts in January and early February of 1980, though Simmons did note in her review that his voice was giving out by the encore set at the Forum. He still needed that tonsillectomy. A date for surgery was set in February during a break in tour dates. The procedure went well and the following month found the band in England, where they jump-started a brief visit that called on Birmingham, London and Oxford as well as a side trip to the Empire in Paris.

Japan was next up on The Heartbreakers' agenda with three dates in April at Tokyo's Yomiuri Hall. Australia followed, where they played in Sydney on April 26, Brisbane on the 29th, Melbourne on May 1–2 and Adelaide on the third. Two dates in New Zealand (in Christchurch and Wellington) were also tagged on. Never being the type of guys to waste an opportunity, the band even stopped off for a gig in Honolulu, Hawaii, on May 11, as they made their way back home to California for an appearance on ABC-TV's late-night comedy show, *Fridays*.

The 1980 world tour was pivotal in cementing a fervent fanbase. The many, many tour dates and near-constant radio airplay helped ensure that *Damn The Torpedoes* would become one of the best-selling albums of the year. Success didn't exactly feel like Tom expected it to, though. While he enjoyed the accolades, life – and all its disappointments – plodded along just as it always had. "Having a successful album doesn't solve all your personal problems," Tom acknowledges. "It creates problems of its own. It can confuse you. You want to think that when you become successful you'll wake up one day and all your problems will have been cleaned up. But *you've* got to clean them up."

Those of us who aren't rock gods may be incredulous. What kinds of problems do rock stars have? Frankly, the same ones we all do: worries about caring for ill or aging parents, knock-down-drag-out arguments with a spouse, wrangling rebellious kids and never quite living up to the expectations we set for ourselves.

For newly minted rock superstars, the pressures of everyday life *and* stardom can take its toll. Tom Petty & The Heartbreakers weren't any more imaginative than the rest of us when it came to dealing with their anxieties. They went for booze and drugs. "We'd never really done a tour like we were doing then and we were just kind of nuts," admits Tom. He told *Musician*'s Dave Marsh that, "In those days, I think, we'd just discovered cocaine or just come to where we could really afford to have cocaine. It just caused a lot of friction and disorientation; we were more caught up with putting another line out and talking about what we were doing than doing it. So we go through that; no real *Enquirer* stuff there, it was just disorientation."

When Tom was first coming up in the music business he noted many peculiar aspects of stardom. One thing boggled his mind: "You know when you're broke, nobody gives you nothin' – *nothin*'. But as soon as you can afford it, it's, 'Sure, go ahead, take whatever you want.' It's *absolutely* backwards." As the band's reputation grew it was easier to get the best tables in restaurants, meet the prettiest girls and gain access to other famous people. It was truly perplexing to these Southern boys but they soon learned that this is how the world works – whether it makes sense or not.

Controversy entered the picture once again in May of 1980 when the *No Nukes* VHS was released. Tom was adamant that the organisers delete his band's performance from the movie. Tom felt the gig wasn't up to their exacting standards and he did not want it memorialised on film for all to see. Producers Jackson Browne, Graham Nash, John Hall and Bonnie Raitt understood Tom's position and acquiesced. (While Tom Petty & The Heartbreakers are absent from the film, the record released in 1979 – *No Nukes: The Muse Concerts for a Non-Nuclear Future* – did include their stirring rendition of 'Cry To Me', written by Bert Berns and made popular by R&B legend Solomon Burke.)

The summer of 1980 raced by with more concert dates in the US supported by Tommy Tutone, including a three-night stand at Manhattan's Palladium.

By mid-July the band was ready to exchange their tour bus for the recording studio, and set to work on the album that would become *Hard Promises*. Almost everyone in the band was looking forward to making new music, but bassist Ron Blair was less than enthusiastic. The pace of the past two years was frenetic and he was totally and absolutely burned out. He hadn't lost his interest in Tom Petty & The Heartbreakers; he'd lost his taste for the music business entirely. At this point he would have been grateful for a few weeks of vacation but the schedule forced them back into the studio almost immediately after the summer tour came to a close. He struggled to keep his commitment to the band strong, but he was floundering.

Meanwhile, Tom's personal life was in complete turmoil. His lovely mother, Kitty, was gravely ill and she passed away on October 21, 1980. She is buried at Forest Meadows Memorial Park East in Gainesville. Tom, who had a very special bond with his mom, was blindsided. He tumbled into a deep and lasting depression after avoiding her funeral. At this point in his career, Tom couldn't walk down the street without fans chasing him for an autograph or handshake. If he showed up in his hometown, he worried that he'd turn his own mother's funeral into a mob scene. He purposely stayed away and mourned privately at his home in California. The untimely death of his mother at a relatively young age plagued him, but he found comfort in knowing, "She lived long enough to know I was all right."

The fact was that Kitty Petty has been very ill for many years. She was diagnosed with a brain tumor in the early seventies and endured grueling chemotherapy treatments. Epileptic seizures were a side effect of her illness and it got to the point that she could not always communicate with those around her. It was terribly difficult for Tom, his brother Bruce and their father. Tom missed talking with her. "She was sitting there but no longer available to me," he says. "She had one period when she seemed to be getting better, then completely relapsed. From the time I was 20, there was no mom, really." So while Kitty Petty passed away when Tom was 31, he'd actually been mourning her absence for more than 10 years.

After her death Tom found solace in working on the band's fourth album and spent many hours writing new songs, bouncing ideas off

Mike – his now-regular writing partner – and getting ready for his next foray into the studio with producer Jimmy Iovine. Tom and Jimmy both knew one thing: they did not want to make *Damn The Torpedoes 2*. If Tom felt the pressure of writing relevant songs for *Damn The Torpedoes*, it was tenfold when it came to creating music for the follow-up. This record would signal whether or not Petty had staying power. Critics questioned whether he had the right stuff and he wanted to prove that he did.

Sessions commenced at Sound City, Cherokee Studios and Goodnight LA, and Tom gave Ron Blair a bit of leeway. He sensed that the bassist was struggling and he wanted to give him the space he needed to recharge. To that end, Tom actually brought in a session player to help out when Ron was absent. Duck Dunn – who'd done sessions with the band in the past – played the bass line on the now classic 'A Woman In Love (It's Not Me)'.

Work progressed through 1980 and, in November, the band heard that Beatle John Lennon would record at the same studio where they were camped out. Tom was thrilled and was looking forward to meeting someone who so greatly influenced his own career. Tragically, in an act that shocked the world and continues to distress rock fans everywhere, Lennon was murdered before he was able to get to his session in Los Angeles.

1980 ended on a somber note with Tom looking back not just on the band's meteoric success but also on the hard battles won as well as everything he'd lost.

★ ★ ★

Sessions for *Hard Promises* continued into the early months of 1981 and it was clear that this record would definitely land far afield from *Torpedoes*. While tracks like 'The Waiting' and 'Kings Road' were quintessential rock songs, the sessions were more notable for introspective ballads like 'Insider' – a duet cut with Fleetwood Mac's Stevie Nicks – and 'You Can Still Change Your Mind', co-written by Mike. Those songs were certainly different – both in terms of lyrical content and musical style – from anything on the previous album.

Expectations on the street held that Tom would release more a
in the style of 'Refugee'. The band had to wonder if there was space on
the radio dial for something gentler than that. "I had to constantly talk
myself out of wondering whether people would accept this or that," Tom
recalls of the *Hard Promises* sessions. He had to have faith in his audience.

Radio stations couldn't wait to get their hands on the album and
KLOS in Los Angeles actually ignored the official release date and
began spinning 'The Waiting' days in advance of the official drop. This
riled rival station KMET enough to also begin playing songs from *Hard
Promises* early. Tom Petty & The Heartbreakers only benefitted because
by the time the album was on sale, fans were waiting in line at record
stores to buy a copy having already fallen in love with several tracks they
heard on the radio.

The album opened with 'The Waiting' and one has to wonder
whether Petty and his crew understood at the time that this song would
become one of their calling cards for the rest of their lives. At concerts
today, 'The Waiting' inevitably transforms into a group sing-along with
the crowd emotionally all-in by the first chorus.

The song might not have had the same steel as 1979's 'Refugee'
but it was as anthemic as its predecessor. The beauty of the song is
its simplicity. Fans adopted the tune as their personal theme. Maybe
someone was toughing out a divorce. Someone else was just trying to
get through high school. Another fan was hatching a plan to get ahead
in life at a new job. 'The Waiting' could inspire hope on so many
different levels. It's not surprising that this single made it to number one
on *Billboard*'s Rock chart.

NME's Cynthia Rose felt that the album shone in ways that Tom's
previous songs hadn't. "Instead of finding glory in pure assertion, *Hard
Promises* finds a dignity in acceptance. That's the theme of its most
powerful cut, 'The Waiting', which kicks off the album in that optimistic
vein of Byrds homage (here, 'Turn Turn Turn'), by now somewhat
synonymous with Petty's band. From the dazzle of an initial swoop,
punch drunk on the pure ecstasy of love, into a cheeky confessional
verse only Petty would have written through Mike Campbell's stinging
bridges, The Heartbreakers drive their hard bargain of holding out for

the genuine over the facsimile. And Petty ignites the whole package with a new vocal authority evident throughout the album."

Rolling Stone's Debra Rae Cohen's extensive review of the album for *Rolling Stone* provided this insight into the album's second track, 'A Woman In Love (It's Not Me)', which peaked at number five in the United States: "This taste of loneliness is clearest in the album's masterpiece: 'A Woman In Love (It's Not Me)'. Petty's aching, murmured vocal – leaping for and missing a falsetto in a move that sums up dashed hopes and heartbreak – is the finest thing he's ever done. The tune's stirring dynamics underline the contrast between the high-flying illusions of the past and hard-boiled present-day reality. A Byrds-style guitar break works like a nostalgic glimpse backward, while the chorus harmonies sweep the singer off into romantic dreams until he thuds back to earth with the words: 'She's a woman in love, but it's not me.'"

Another interesting song on *Hard Promises* that points to Tom's state of mind in the early eighties is 'Nightwatchman'. He says that the track "actually started out as a joke on the whole thing of security. I have a guard on my house now, a guy who sits outside the door and keeps people back. So I wrote a song for him. It got so amusing to me. 'You mean, there's gonna be a *guy* outside the *door* – all the time?' I went as long as I could without doing it. For a long time, I just said, 'No, I will *not* do that.' And then it got where, yeah, I'm gonna do it now, because I don't want people standing in the middle of my living room. And worse." The murder of John Lennon no doubt made Tom re-evaluate his personal security and the safety of his family as he grew more and more famous in the rock stratosphere.

While *Damn The Torpedoes* was an album full of singles, *Hard Promises* was much more introspective and the songs – many ballads – spoke to fans in a different way. Tracks like 'Something Big' and 'Kings Road' were story-songs. The focal point of 'Something Big' is a loser looking for the next "big thing" that could transform his life into something just a bit more fulfilling. Sadly, this guy is always looking for the easy way out though. He never does get where he wants to be.

'Kings Road' on the other hand looks at a man who's already taken the leap into a strange new world to see where his fortunes may lie. He's not sure where the road will lead him but he knows it's the only way to move forward.

Tom devoted much of the last half of the 10-track album to beautifully crafted ballads like 'Letting You Go', 'You Can Still Change Your Mind' and 'Insider'. 'Letting You Go', about a man grappling with the departure of the one he loves, is something we can all relate to on a certain level. Tom was double-tracked in the studio so he could harmonize with himself on this number. The result creates a lush counterpoint to Benmont's organ part. 'The Criminal Kind' revisits a topic that often recurs in Tom Petty's lyrics: the sometimes misfit – maybe the guy from 'Something Big' – that may be tempted to take the easy and somewhat illegal way out of certain predicaments.

The *Hard Promises* sessions were notable for something else too: the appearance of Stevie Nicks on The Heartbreakers' radar. In 2011 Stevie told *Rolling Stone* magazine that she was a Tom Petty fan from the very first record. "In 1976, I'd been in Fleetwood Mac for about a year when I heard Tom Petty's debut. I became a fan right then. I loved the way Tom's Florida swamp-dog voice sounded in cahoots with Mike Campbell's guitar and Benmont Tench's keyboards. Tom had the same influences we had – The Byrds, Neil Young, Crosby, Stills & Nash – but he dropped in lots of serious old blues. And Tom is such a great singer and so charismatic onstage."

In 1981 she was collaborating with Jimmy Iovine on her own solo album, *Bella Donna*, and was completely enamored by Tom's songwriting prowess and his gravelly vocal style. She had been a permanent fixture at Sound City in Van Nuys for many years and she systematically maneuvered her way into the band's hemisphere – bit by bit. At first, they didn't know what to make of this free spirit who was so gung-ho on hanging out with them in the studio. Then she began her hard sell to Tom: write me a song.

At first Tom begged off, saying he was too busy prepping his own album. Stevie wouldn't be deterred, however, and Tom eventually broke down and gave her 'Insider'. He recalls that he originally wrote the song for *Hard Promises*. "Then she decided to sing harmony, not lead," he says, "so we tried it, and it came out great."

"I got really excited about it, because I'd always wanted to record a song like that. I'd always loved duets like Gram Parsons and Emmylou Harris on *Grievous Angel*, or George Jones and Tammy Wynette. Those things kill me. Finally, Stevie said, 'I can tell you're excited about it; why don't you keep it and we'll do another song for *my* album.' I'm happy that she let me steal it back, because it's one of my favourite songs I've written and it ended up fitting the album perfectly."

'You Can Still Change Your Mind' – with background vocals by Stevie – closes the album and the lyrics inspire all of us to keep putting one foot in front of the other to get through the adversity that will inevitably visit our lives.

Tom then penned 'Stop Draggin' My Heart Around' for Stevie and it became one of the singles for her *Bella Donna* album. The duet between the pair is backed by The Heartbreakers (minus Ron Blair and plus Duck Dunn). When she sat down to program the tracks on her forthcoming record, she almost decided against including the duet at all. She told *Rolling Stone*, "I thought, 'Is this the right thing to do? I only get 11 songs and one of them won't be mine.' And both Tom and Jimmy said to me, in a brutally honest way, 'You don't have a single on this record. And here's a single for you.'" She humbly accepted that criticism and included the song, which went on to hit number three on *Billboard*'s Hot 100. It was also nominated for a Grammy in 1981 in the Best Rock Performance By a Duo or Group With Vocal category.

Although Stevie was enjoying superstardom as a member of Fleetwood Mac and for her own solo efforts, she says now that what she really wanted was to be a Heartbreaker. "In 1978, if Tom Petty had said, 'Leave Fleetwood Mac and come and join us,' I would probably have joined Tom Petty & The Heartbreakers."

The album proved one thing: Tom Petty & The Heartbreakers were growing up. Journalist Cynthia Rose said as much in the March 23, 1981 issue of *NME*. "As formidable a success as *Torpedoes* proved commercially, its thinking suggested something beyond even the goods on display and *Hard Promises'* darkness on the edge develops, rather than merely continues, the story."

Hard Promises wasn't all about the band's musical progression though. It also signaled another first for The Heartbreakers: their music video debut. The band rented a soundstage for the day and filmed five videos: 'The Waiting', 'A Woman In Love (It's Not Me)', 'Letting You Go', 'Insider' and 'Stop Draggin' My Heart Around'. The staging was simple for 'The Waiting': a white backdrop and band platform splattered with paint and triangles of primary colours painted behind the drum riser. The band simply performed the song, much as they do in concert. The set for 'A Woman In Love' looked like the band was playing in an abandoned airplane hangar in the middle of the night. Tom looked dapper in his black suit with Mandarin collar and white trainers. Future videos would depart from this performance style in favor of storytelling. Still, this was an important first step for the band to learn the craft of making a good music video.

★ ★ ★

Tom was just finishing the song sequence for *Hard Promises* when he heard a rumor about plans his record label, Backstreet/MCA, had for the fourth record. The "man" planned to raise the retail price of the album by one dollar, making it the first rock album to list for $9.98. Tom went ballistic and flatly refused to deliver the record unless it was listed at the usual price of $8.98. "I didn't want to be the guy that brought the price up – I didn't want that hung on The Heartbreakers, because we had no part of it," he told David Gans of *Hit Parader*. Tom got so angry about this that he went as far as threatening to title the album *$8.98* if Backstreet didn't give in to his demands on the pricing issue.

"I naively thought I could keep our record prices down so the average person could afford them," Tom explains. "Once again we were at war with the big dogs… this along with the band thinking I've just gone crazy… the death of my mother and in general too much responsibility was affecting greatly the tone of my music."

Tom took the issue to the people and voiced his displeasure to magazines like *Rolling Stone* and *Musician*, whose reporters hyped the stalemate between Tom and Backstreet and suggested a write-in campaign to stop the company from raising record prices. To everyone's

109

surprise, fans wrote to Backstreet/MCA and it worked. The label backed down. Tom said at the time, "A lot of our fans have been with us for a long time, and I think they trust us. MCA has done a great job selling our records, but they couldn't see the reality of what it's like on the street. They couldn't see that raising the album's price wouldn't be fair.

"My beef with MCA was that they originally told us *Hard Promises* would be $8.98, and then changed their minds. But it would be wrong to single them out; every other company would like to push record prices right on up there. I'm not usually as concerned with record company business as you might think; I like to devote my time and energy to being a musician. But sometimes there's a communications breakdown and, when that happens, you just have to stand up for yourself.

"It's a great example of what can be done," Tom went on. "The kids responded and something happened. But I hope people don't get the impression that I hate this industry. There are some good people in the business, and I'm relieved that for once the record company was big enough to accept public opinion. I've got to thank all the fans who wrote in, because they're the ones who really helped me out.

"I'm glad I pulled it off," he says. "There's no reason that a kid who works after school to pay for what he wants in life should have to pay those kind of prices."

At the time, Tom had hoped that other artists would join on to his campaign but no one stepped up to the plate. No one. "It's really hard to get artists to do anything together for the collective good," Tom notes. "When I was out there fighting my battle, it was very lonely. The fact is once you decide to try to set a precedent you're no longer just fighting the company that hired you. You're fighting *all* of them. This kind of thing could end up costing some very powerful people a whole bunch of money. And these aren't the kind of guys who just roll over. They keep an entire legal team on staff and attorneys on retainer just to scare folks like us off."

The crisis was averted though, and the *Hard Promises* LP shipped to stores at the usual price of $8.98. In one last quiet message to MCA, the cover of the album pictures Tom browsing in a record store – no doubt looking to pick up a few choice albums at the $8.98 price point.

When *Hard Promises* was released on May 5, 1981, the vinyl record held a special inscription – WE LOVE YOU JL – etched in the master. All first issue vinyl copies of *Hard Promises* in the United States carried this message. It was just a small way in which the band could say goodbye to one of the most beloved musicians – and soulful pacifists – of our time.

While *Damn The Torpedoes* hit number two on the *Billboard* 200, *Hard Promises* only made it to number five. Still, the record garnered plenty of attention and songs like 'The Waiting' and 'A Woman In Love' are staples in Petty's live set even today – more than 30 years after their release.

Accolades ran in rock magazines throughout the United States: *High Fidelity*'s Mitch Cohen said, "*Hard Promises* is a passionate kind of mainstream rock, more ruled by the heart than by the mind," and Dave Marsh of *Musician* summed up the album's mood perfectly when he said, "It's as if, on *Torpedoes*, all you could see was how much there was to win. On *Promises*, what you see is how much there is to lose." The stakes had certainly changed and Tom Petty was wisely learning what really mattered to him most. Songwriting was the core of everything and he vowed to take it as seriously as possible, which is perhaps why *Hard Promises* is the first Heartbreakers record to include a lyric sheet. The songs mattered... pure and simple.

Blair Jackson of *Trouser Press* agreed that the songs were the entire point of Petty's latest work: "Petty has emerged as one of the most striking personalities in music – a figure with the charisma of Mick Jagger, some of Bob Dylan's dark mystique and lyrical insights that rival Bruce Springsteen's."

Mitch Cohen of *High Fidelity* distilled the essence of *Hard Promises* in this way in the August 1981 issue of the magazine: "Petty is playing the displaced soul on *Hard Promises*, battered and embittered by romance, out of his element as 'a new world boy on the old 'Kings Road'. He's 'the broken-hearted fool' on one cut ('Insider'), and 'your bleeding heart, your crying fool' on another ('The Waiting'). There's probably a limit to how far he can take this character, and it may not be true that 'there's no one as honest as those in pain' ('Letting You Go'), but the honesty of *Hard Promises* is undeniable. Its emotional uncertainty is matched by an artistic confidence that makes the album another hard-won victory for Tom Petty & The Heartbreakers."

Tom couldn't fully enjoy the compliments from the press and fans, though, because right around this time his good friend and band bassist, Ron Blair, decided that he wanted out. It wasn't that he didn't love being part of this band of brothers, it was just that he couldn't accept the rock star lifestyle. It wasn't how he wanted to spend his life. He wanted something simpler. He wasn't walking out on the band; he was giving up the music industry entirely.

"I was married by then," says Ron, "and my wife's family manufactured swimwear. We wanted to do something different and went from thinking about opening up a store, to just doing it. It was quite an experience and seems a little surreal looking back on it. I sold the store sometime around 1996."

"There wasn't any argument or fight – he just didn't want to tour anymore," Tom reported at the time. "Ron said, 'I just can't get on that bus again. I just want to get out of the music business.' He was very nice about it. Emotionally it was a blow, because we all really loved him. But musically, he'd been drifting away for so long that it wasn't a big change. He'd lost interest. It didn't change a lot of the sessions, because a lot of times Ron wasn't there and Michael or I would play the bass. But, emotionally, it was a little sad because we missed him." Ron stayed away from the music business for several decades, but he always remained close with each Heartbreaker.

Now the search was on for a replacement bass player. The tour supporting *Hard Promises* was slated to commence on June 14, so a line-up had to be in place soon. The new bassist had to be a musician with impeccable skills, an easy-going attitude and a resilient sense of humour. At the time Tom was producing *Drop Down And Get Me*, the comeback record for Del Shannon who'd been a star in the sixties and in 1961 had a number one hit with 'Runaway'. Back in 1982, Del told Mitchell Cohen of *Creem* magazine what it was like working with Tom. "The key to the whole project was Tom Petty and The Heartbreakers. When I met him in the office and he said, 'What are you doing going down to Nashville? You're a rocker, man!,' that's all I really had to hear. His confidence. So I said, OK," recalled Del. "He let me be Del Shannon. He didn't try to change this much or that much. Here's how we worked: he called me up and said, 'I'm ready.' I said, 'You're kidding. I'm going to England in three days.' He says, 'So what?' And I thought, 'Yeah, so what? I don't need 10 hundred years to lay down these rock'n'roll songs.' That's the way I used to cut."

Tom had always appreciated Del's music and was thrilled to work with him and his band, which included talented bassist Howie Epstein. Tom felt that Howie would fit right in with The Heartbreakers. Del wasn't happy to hear that Tom was poaching Howie, his bandleader, but he really couldn't protest or hold Howie back from this opportunity. Del was angry but Tom says, "He eventually got over it. I think."

★ ★ ★

If Stan Lynch was the wild man of the group, Howie was the quiet and soulful one. In all the years The Heartbreakers played together, no one can remember a time when Howie raised his voice to anyone. He was a gentle soul and a musical genius. Howard Norman Epstein was born on July 21, 1955 in Milwaukee, Wisconsin. He grew up surrounded by music. His father, Sam, was a record producer with expertise in the rock and soul categories. His dad let Howie tag along to recording sessions and he learned so much about music theory and performance from watching the players assembled to perform.

Howie was a quiet kid who picked up guitar and bass at an early age. He also had a beautiful voice and instinctively knew how to sing harmony. He was a highly sought-after musician in Milwaukee as a teenager and played in bands like MHB Experience, Winks and The Craze. Howie took off for Los Angeles after graduating from Glendale's Nicolet High School in 1973. He had a gig waiting for him in LA: playing bass for singer-songwriter John Hiatt. He spent two years with Hiatt before joining Del Shannon's band. Maybe it was fate? If Howie hadn't been in Shannon's band at the time, Tom may never have found him.

After just a few sessions with The Heartbreakers it was clear that Howie was the right addition. "He's a good bass player," Tom said at the time, "but the main difference is that now we sing a little better because he's got a real good high harmony. We never really gave him much of a shot to rehearse or anything. We'd just say, 'Howie, we're going to play 'Listen To Her Heart', and then we'd run through the song – and he'd know it better than we did. He knew all the changes from the records."

That's not to say that Howie didn't take the brunt of some vicious hazing. According to producer Jimmy Iovine, "He got his head taken off the minute he walked in. He was real nervous at first and I wanted him to play like he'd been in the band for a long time, so I came on like a tornado. We had no time for him to be nervous. It was basically a confrontation. 'Here's this wonderful job. How you handle it is up to you. Win or lose, it's your decision.' And Howie came through with flying colours."

Tom was pleased by how easily Howie got into The Heartbreakers' groove. "By the time we played the US Festival [September 4, 1982], Howie had been with us for a year playing in the studio," Tom says. "He's smart, too, because he's not the kind of person who came in and tried to push his views on us. He was just kind of quiet for a while, checking us out before he opened up much. Sometimes when you meet a new group of people you try to prove yourself again and again, out of insecurity. And for diving right into this mess, Howie did OK."

★ ★ ★

The band broke Howie in during the *Hard Promises* tour. Tom and The Heartbreakers played 56 shows in the United States and Canada between June 14 and December 10 of 1981. (The tour was originally slated to begin on June 1, but Tom injured himself while exercising on a trampoline, so the tour was postponed by two weeks.)

By mid-June the band was out on the road but controversy, of course, hit before they were barely out of the gate for the summer leg. Program directors at Chicago's WLUP "The Loop" radio station cooked up an idea to promote the new album and concert tour. They'd purchase all of the tickets to the band's Chicago area appearance to give away to fans that called in to the station. Tom thought it was a brilliant idea.

Who wouldn't want to give kids the chance to see their band for free? What Tom didn't count on was the blowback from rival radio station WMET, which threatened to either not play *Hard Promises* at all or play it over and over again to give people the opportunity to record it. "I can't believe what a mess it turned into! I wanted to do this show, which will let in something like 18,000 kids for *free*, and the fuckers on a rival radio station are saying they don't want to play my record." Tom was incredulous. "I'm not doing it for The Loop. I'm doing it for the 18,000 kids. The last thing I want to do is take sides with one station and kill myself on another," he says.

Careful politicking lessened tensions between rival stations and both ended up putting *Hard Promises* into heavy rotation throughout 1981.

The tour was a boon to fans who also loved Stevie Nicks. She showed up at 14 of The Heartbreakers' gigs and joined the band onstage to duet on numbers like 'Needles And Pins', the Searchers hit that was written by Jack Nitzsche and Sonny Bono, 'Insider' and 'Stop Draggin' My Heart Around'. Around this time the press occasionally bandied about the idea that Tom and Stevie were an item, but that was pure fiction. The two were friends and musical collaborators – nothing more.

While the pace of the tour was absolutely grueling, Tom cherished each and every opportunity to step onstage. He especially enjoyed a homecoming show on October 8, at the O'Connell Center at the University of Florida in Gainesville.

As the holidays approached, the tour wound down and The Heartbreakers all headed home to California. They'd spent nearly three years on the road and recording new music and had amassed a huge number of fans in the States and abroad. It seemed as if everything Petty touched sparkled, but how long could that last?

★ ★ ★

Most of 1982 was spent in the studio preparing for the release of the band's fifth studio album, *Long After Dark,* in November. As such, the band didn't really play live a whole lot with the exception of a few dates like Peace Sunday on June 6, two dates in September at Santa Cruz's Civic Auditorium that acted as a warm-up for the fall's European tour and the US Festival on September 4. Staying off the road was designed, in part, to make sure that Tom also had some time at home as he and Jane readied for the birth of their second daughter, Annakim.

One of the few dates the band agreed to play, Peace Sunday, was an attempt to promote a world without nuclear weapons. It took place at Pasadena's Rose Bowl and more than 85,000 people attended the show. Tom played two Buddy Holly numbers, 'Well Alright' and 'Not Fade Away', and was backed by Jackson Browne and Joe Lala. Other musicians on the bill included Bob Dylan, Bonnie Raitt, Donovan and Linda Ronstadt – among others.

The US Festival in San Bernadino was the other big stadium show and it featured artists like the Ramones, The English Beat, The B-52s, Talking Heads, The Police, Santana, The Cars, The Kinks, Pat Benatar, Jimmy Buffett, Jackson Browne and Fleetwood Mac. Apple co-founder and millionaire Steve Wozniak organized the event, which did not go particularly well. Temperatures were searing – over 100 degrees – during that weekend, and drug arrests and overdoses marred the event, which lost $12 million.

Besides those few gigs, the band sequestered themselves in the studio. They were on the merry-go-round to release another commercial success. *Long After Dark* – released on November 2, 1982 – fell short of that mark. Despite the single 'You Got Lucky' hitting number one on *Billboard*'s Mainstream Rock chart, the album as a whole was not critically acclaimed and it only briefly peaked at number nine on *Billboard*'s Top Pop Albums in 1983. It's easy to look back on *Long After Dark* now as Tom's first musical failure, but that wouldn't be an entirely fair statement.

The 10-song album still held some gems, like 'Change Of Heart', the only song on the album to hit the US charts, 'Straight Into Darkness' and 'Deliver Me'. The mainstream also particularly enjoyed 'You Got Lucky', especially after seeing the quirky music video on MTV a million times.

It's true that none of those songs became long-running staples of the band's live set, although many fans would welcome the resurrection of 'Change Of Heart' and 'Straight Into Darkness'.

Several things were at play during the writing and recording of the songs, which took place between 1981 and 1982 at the Record Plant and Rumbo Studios. Tom once again selected Jimmy Iovine as the album's producer and in hindsight that was a mistake. There was a certain level of familiarity between them that transformed from an easy-going work relationship to boredom. The two also didn't explicitly agree on the tone of the album and were often at odds when it came to determining which tracks would make the album's final cut. Iovine was pushing the album in the direction of 1979's *Damn The Torpedoes,* while Tom was perfectly happy noodling on more acoustic numbers à la *Hard Promises.* The two would duke it out in the studio to determine which songs would make the cut and Iovine was very persuasive. He nixed the incredibly likeable 'Keeping Me Alive' and 'Turning Point' – both of which can be heard on the band's 1995 *Playback* box set. To this day, Tom feels *Long After Dark* would have benefitted from a track list that included those tunes. This record reinforced to Tom that he had to stay true to his instincts and not be swayed in these types of situations in the future. It would greatly influence his choice of producers down the road.

Despite all that, the album did enjoy one number one hit: 'You Got Lucky'. Its popularity was no doubt thanks to the music video. The movie-style clip to promote the song was inspired by the *Mad Max* films. It features the band in a futuristic desert landscape, dressed as bikers/cowboys. Tom and Mike arrive on the scene in the hover car that was used in the 1977–1978 television show *Logan's Run* while Stan, Howie and Benmont follow up in a motorcycle with sidecar. The dusty motley crew has stumbled on an abandoned tent filled with banks of old TVs, reel-to-reel players, one-arm bandit slot machines and video arcade games. You get the feeling it's been a long time since anyone's been here. Stan finds and throws the power lever to launch the music – a full minute into the video. The video went into heavy rotation on MTV and solidified the band's reputation for inventive visuals to accompany its songs.

The music itself is unusual for Petty and was built on drum loops and a surf-style guitar solo with tremolo arm in homage to the theme

117

music for Clint Eastwood's *The Good, The Bad And The Ugly*. While some may interpret the lyrics as egotistical, Tom sings it as if he's trying to convince himself of his greatness in order to avoid feeling the sting of being walked out on. ("You better watch what you say / You better watch what you do to me / Don't get carried away / Girl, if you can do better than me, go / Yeah go/ But remember / Good love is hard to find....You got lucky babe....When I found you")

Long After Dark was also one of the few times a synthesizer was used on any Heartbreaker tracks. (Listen for a Prophet-5 on 'We Stand A Chance'.) The instrumentation was less earthy than on previous records and while *Long After Dark* certainly sounded of its time, it feels dated now.

Why did this record flounder? It's possible that by this point Tom was simply exhausted by everything that had transpired between the recording of *Damn The Torpedoes* and *Long After Dark*. Critic Stephen Thomas Erlewine agrees with that hypothesis and wrote this in his review of the album for AllMusic: "Petty & The Heartbreakers sounded tired. Even if there are a few new wave flourishes here and there, the band hasn't really changed its style at all – it's still Stonesy, Byrdsian heartland rock. As their first four albums illustrated, that isn't a problem in itself, since they've found numerous variations within their signature sound, providing they have the right songs. Unfortunately, Petty had a dry spell on *Long After Dark*. With its swirling, minor key guitars, 'You Got Lucky' is a classic and 'Change Of Heart' comes close to matching those peaks, but the remaining songs rarely rise above agreeable filler."

Tom himself was not happy with that record for a long time but he's since had a change of heart himself: "When I hear *Long After Dark* now, I say, 'This is great. Why was I so down on it?' It's just a record of pop songs, but I was feeling pressure, people saying that, 'You didn't send us a message!' Well, I didn't *have* any message to send. That's a hard expectation to live with; it's flattering in one way, but I've never been able to look at myself well in that light. I get too self-conscious. It's hard to complain – what you're really striving for is to inspire someone. But it does seem in the last few years there's a certain great expectation of us and that can cause a certain amount of pressure."

The high point on the record was the appearance of new bass player Howie Epstein. His playing was solid and he also contributed beautiful harmony lines that reinforced Tom's lead vocal. That aspect was a glimpse of what was to come for the band as a whole once Howie was fully integrated as a Heartbreaker.

In January of 1982 there was an event in Tom's life that was even more important than the music though: the birth of his second daughter, Annakim. You'd think that he might have taken some time off to bond with the new family member but that didn't happen as the road was calling once again.

★ ★ ★

Promotion for *Long After Dark* continued throughout 1983 and that meant the band spent most of its time on a tour bus crisscrossing America. Despite Tom's current stance against corporate sponsorship, Tecate Beer underwrote this particular outing. The Heartbreakers toured America from January through April and took a one-month break in May. They picked up again for a handful of dates in June.

After the tour Tom and the rest of the band needed a break from the road, the studio and – frankly – each other. They agreed to go their separate ways for a little while and try to figure out what normal people do at home all day. The holidays were spent with their friends and families and 1984 presented myriad opportunities for each band member. All of The Heartbreakers were in demand at this point in their careers as session players, songwriters and producers.

Each Heartbreaker fell into his own groove. Mike began collaborating with Don Henley and co-wrote the hits 'Boys Of Summer' and 'Heart Of The Matter' with him for his album *Building The Perfect Beast*. Mike and Don would continue working together for years to come. Benmont worked with Stevie Nicks and Lone Justice, and all of The Heartbreakers sans Tom recorded with both Bob Dylan and Eurythmics during this time period.

Tom found it hard to believe that his band wouldn't step foot onstage once in 1984, but he liked that idea. Everyone needed some time away. "I think I started to take it all too seriously. I really wanted to part the

Red Sea every night. I felt I had to. If we hadn't taken the break, I think we might have split up because I was bored," Tom says in retrospect. "When we started, there was an idealism to what we were doing but it had been beaten up pretty bad by the music business and probably by success over the years. There was also that problem of being on the road so long there is very little chance to live. I think that stifles a writer. I just needed time off."

Tom started his siesta with a construction project. He wanted a state-of-the-art recording studio in his own home so he could get his ideas down on tape anytime – day or night – without schlepping across Los Angeles. He oversaw the installation of Gone Gator One in his home.

Not long after that, Tom wrote what would become one of the most beautiful ballads and tributes to the American South: 'Southern Accents'.

"That may be my favourite among my songs – just in terms of a piece of pure writing," says Tom. "I remember writing it very vividly. It was in the middle of the night and I was playing it on the piano at home in Encino. I was just singing into my cassette recorder and suddenly these words came out. I was at the point in my career where I was very much trying to find some new ground. I had thought I had used up what I had started with and I wanted a new direction. We had lived in California for about 10 years at that point and I started thinking about growing up in Northern Florida, which is a lot different from Miami Beach. It's close to Georgia and I came from a real Southern family, and I wanted to address that world. Once I came up with this song, I decided to write an entire album about the theme."

For inspiration Tom visited his vacation home in Crescent Beach, Florida (near St. Augustine). Being back "home" seemed to break loose the floodgates. "All of a sudden," remembers Tom, "I was writing things without even thinking about them. It felt natural again."

The trip to Florida with his wife and girls gave Tom the chance to just live life and observe – something that's absolutely necessary for any writer. He was recharging and finding plenty of stories he wanted to explore through his songs. In fact, he knew he'd found the theme for his next album: the duality of the American South.

"I grew up there and I was back there after the *Long After Dark* tour," he says. "For some reason it just hit me that there was a real wealth of material there. There was so much that I'd still be writing if I tried to cover everything. I wanted to deal with an album where I could assume characters rather than just write, 'Here's what I have to say about life.'"

He began writing a series of songs that he was incredibly proud of, including 'Rebels', ' Trailer', 'The Image Of Me' and 'The Apartment Song'. (In the end, only 'Rebels' would make it on to the concept album although the other songs were all released later: 'Trailers' and 'The Image Of Me' on *Playback* and 'The Apartment Song' on *Full Moon Fever*.)

Some of Tom's new songs touched on what it was like to grow up in the South while others, like 'Rebels', were written from the character's point of view. Tom left Florida with dozens of solid demos and the newfound path to The Heartbreakers' evolution. "At that time The Heartbreakers were looking for something new," says Tom. "We felt like we'd taken the Big Jangle as far as we could."

When he arrived at home in Encino, things didn't progress the way he thought they would. He worked diligently in his home studio to get his new songs beyond the demo phase. The problem was, nothing was working. The demos all sounded better than the tracks he had labored on for weeks in the studio.

After a particularly gruesome session, Tom decided to call it quits at 4 a.m. He headed up the stairwell that connected his studio to the rest of the house. Out of pure frustration he slapped the wall with his left hand. He put a lot more energy into it than he realized and his hand immediately hurt like hell. He knew something was wrong. Very, *very* wrong. Within minutes his hand swelled to twice its normal size. He was treated at Cedars-Sinai, where doctors weren't particularly optimistic about his prognosis. He required surgery during which metal pins were inserted into his hand. He underwent physical therapy three times a week after that as well as painful electroshock therapy for months.

"I nearly blew it there," he admits. "I almost didn't play anymore. That had a huge effect on my brain. People remember the fact that I hit the wall back then but at that time in my life, my marriage and just about everything else was on the rocks. I was just overindulging more than I should – the brandy was coming around more often. I was hitting all sorts of walls," Petty confides.

So, did The Heartbreakers gather round him in support during those uncertain days when it was unclear if he'd ever play guitar again? "They came in and said, 'Well, Brian Setzer's looking for a band.' No sympathy ever from them! That's the way they are. They never said, 'Oh God, it's terrible!' They just made jokes about it all the time. They never thought I wouldn't play again, so that helped me think about it," says Tom. "But it was nine months before I could even strum a chord. You don't think how many times you just reach for the guitar and pick it up without thinking. It's just part of what you do, like smoking a cigarette. That was the hardest thing for me. I think that had an effect on me. The way I was living at the time was rowdy. I was getting ready to rowdy myself off the end of a cliff."

It just seemed as if Tom and the entire band were in the throes of turmoil. The record wasn't going well and nearly each Heartbreaker was living closer to the edge than he ever had before. Drummer Stan Lynch remembers that it was around this point in time that the band's tight circle began to expand. Previously, sessions were closed events and even their social occasions were closely guarded. However, in the mid-eighties the dam seemed to split open and there were always a ton of people around – many of whom brought around plenty of booze and drugs. Were these dark days for the band? "Everybody goes through dark times," shrugs keyboardist Benmont Tench. "The band went through dark times. I went through very dark times."

"I think that everybody that gets successful goes through a period of extreme disorientation," says Tom. "It's a scary thing when all of a sudden it's really happening and every door is open. Usually that's when the group survives or doesn't, depending on how well they handle that. But after a year, or however long, all of this isn't such a big deal. The only thing that matters is records and shows and music. If you want to fall over drunk and you can play great, then fine."

Mike Campbell says that the guys quickly figured out that they needed to rein in the situation. "If you don't watch it," he warns, "you won't hang around very long. We were lucky to get through that period of our lives without short-circuiting. And we're still here."

Tom reflected on those days to *Q*'s Tom Hibbert in 1989. "In therapy and in the hospital I started to realize that I had taken intensity about as far as it could go in my personal life and with the guys in the band and business people and everybody," says Tom. "I realized I couldn't go on living so intense and revved up and stuff. Because, with some kind of flash of realization, I realized that I had actually never really *enjoyed* myself. I'd done partying and I'd done work but I'd never *genuinely* enjoyed myself. I'd been very reclusive and I didn't know a lot of people and I didn't ever *see* many people. I wasn't very social at all because I was revved up all the time. And I just was not very happy. It was time to calm down. And I made this great discovery; people are quite *fun* you know. And I'm really warm-hearted these days, I think, and more healthy in mind *and* body."

★ ★ ★

By early 1985 the band needed to hit the reset button and get their next record back on track. That's when another incredibly talented – and quirky – musician came on the scene: Dave Stewart of Eurythmics. As unlikely as it may seem, Dave was exactly what The Heartbreakers needed to refocus and finish their sixth studio album.

How did Dave meet Tom? "It happened more or less by accident," Dave says now. "It was through Jimmy Iovine. Jimmy met me backstage at the Wilshire Theater in Los Angeles when Eurythmics played there, and he was really interested in our songwriting. I came down to one of his sessions in the studio and while I was there, he rang up Tom to come down. I remember we had this bottle of Jack Daniel's or some American whiskey, and while Jimmy was doing something else, Tom and I went into the studio where the piano was. We started writing this song together, messing around and it came out really good."

The song Dave is referring to is 'Don't Come Around Here No More'. He had already been playing with the track when he met Petty but wanted fresh ears on it. Tom remembers that day clearly: "Dave had done a little cassette and had the sitar sound. He showed me that and we sat down on a bench and in about an hour the song was done. I only did one take of that vocal. I'm not very good at doing them after I've sung them once or twice. And it's the same way with the band. It's either the first or second take and if it don't happen then we have to change songs or come back another day. They're real good players, these guys, and they start improving it immediately and I like it best... the real fire is there before they know exactly what's coming next. Feel is really all there is to it."

In 1987 Dave told Adam Sweeting of Q magazine that he thought Tom needed a change in order to get *Southern Accents* back on track when the pair met in 1985. "I think Tom got a bit sick of that original idea," Stewart asserted. "He suddenly thought, 'Why am I making a concept album? Why don't I just make music I like?' So I ended up doing these new songs with Tom and that was really a fun time, because that was really the first time I had been to Los Angeles or California without flying in to do two gigs and flying out again. I got completely absorbed in driving Thunderbird cars and 'hanging out' – I'd never known what 'hanging out' was, or 'cruising.'"

The two musicians – albeit from very different circles – got along famously and it was clear that the all-American rocker and the British new wave darling were on the same wavelength. "I liked Dave because he just had no reverence for anything, which helped me shake out of what I was doing and go somewhere else," recalls Tom. Likewise, Dave appreciated Tom's dry humour: "I think he's a very astute comedian." There was more to it though as Dave continues, "These mishmashes or hybrids of influences is something I've always been interested in. Because I think the world is like that now, all mixed up. But Tom and I found it really, really easy to write together. We didn't even have to think about it."

The men began spending more and more time together in the studio. When all was said and done, the pair had written three songs that would end up on the next record, *Southern Accents*: 'It Ain't Nothin' To Me', 'Make It Better (Forget About Me)' and the now classic 'Don't Come Around Here No More'.

Everyone that visited the Petty home got a chance to hear the newest batch of songs and agreed that he certainly went somewhere new and different musically. The tracks were so different that there was strife among certain factions of The Heartbreakers who just didn't feel the new work resonated with the concept album devoted to their shared Southern heritage that they had set out to make.

No one could deny the fact that the newly formed friendship with Dave Stewart was helping Tom immensely. He was centered again, recovering from his hand injury and writing more and more. The theme of the album may have weakened but this natural progression was important for Tom and the entire band.

Southern Accents was released on March 26, 1985, and the album cover art – an 1865 painting by Winslow Homer titled "The Veteran In A New Field" – certainly underscored the theme that fans were expecting. Many were surprised when they put this record on their turntables for the first time though. While the South did inspire some songs, the album didn't feel of a piece. Still, the record hung together surprisingly well considering the concept of the album was loosely applied track to track.

While the band's last effort – *Long After Dark* – netted only one song on the charts, four tunes from *Southern Accents* charted within the top 20 on *Billboard*'s Mainstream Rock chart.

If the band had been nervous about how the record would be greeted, the apprehension disappeared once singles like 'Don't Come Around Here No More', 'Make It Better' and 'Rebels' started to climb the charts. 'Don't Come Around Here No More' charted at number two on *Billboard*'s US Mainstream Rock Tracks chart while 'Rebels' made it to number five on *Billboard*'s Modern Rock Tracks list. The album as a whole peaked at number seven in the United States and at 23 on the UK charts. Rock critic Fred Mills wrote about the album release for *Harp* magazine, asserting that, "Petty reached a storytelling peak on the thematic rockers 'Rebels' and 'Dogs On The Run' and the orchestral title track."

The public seemed intrigued to hear Tom's take on the South and the music papers offered a string of commentary. Bill Flanagan of *Musician* magazine wrote at the time, "Not that Petty hasn't always displayed the rock'n'roll equivalent of traditional Southern values: appreciation for hard work, a mistrust of silliness, an inclination toward understatement.

These qualities have helped the musician produce solid work for a decade."

Slavery and the civil rights movement of the fifties and sixties still reverberated in the South and Tom wanted to shed some light on that. Songs like 'Rebels' painted the picture of throwbacks who still embraced ideals from long ago. "If you go to some places in the South, the Civil War is still very present," says Tom. "You can go into a 7-Eleven and buy stickers that say, 'Hell no, we ain't forgettin'!' and 'Lee surrendered – I didn't!' There's a million phrases: 'Rebel by birth, American by choice'. Since that album people send me things all the time. I could really be taken wrong if somebody walked into some rooms in my house – 'cause there's some real horrific things." But Tom wanted to write an album that showed all the facets of the South – even if the portrait wasn't altogether positive.

Because of the album's theme, Tom was often seen with the Confederate flag during these days – a flag that many in America see as a symbol of slavery and racism. For some Southerners like Tom, the flag was more a symbol of the essence of the South and not of that ugly period in American history when another race was enslaved. The issue was dealt with publicly when Mike Mills, bassist of R.E.M., – a Southern gentlemen himself – made a point of telling a reporter that he thought Tom's use of the flag was ill advised. Tom took up the issue with Bud Scoppa in an interview for *Creem* magazine in 1987. "I hate to say bad things about a band, but I will about that one…. One of those guys in R.E.M. criticised me for using the Confederate flag; he said it was stupid. I didn't mean it in any racist sense at all; I just used it to represent the character of the song. So I'll criticize them. I just was really irritated by what was said. I don't think it's a good policy in general to criticize other artists in the paper, 'cause we're all guitar players and we're all on the bus. It's just not done. I thought it was real tacky.

"But maybe it's good they said that," Petty reflected. "It made me question it. And I'm not gonna use the flag anymore anyway, because now I see all these white power Klan-type people using it as a symbol, so maybe there's a point there. But at the time it was, 'This guy's callin' me *stupid* here!' Wondering if I've got racist values. Well, no, I don't."

A winter tour had been planned but it was ultimately cancelled to allow Tom's hand more time to heal. As summer approached, the band gathered in St. Petersburg, Florida, for pre-tour practise sessions and it felt good to play as one complete unit again. The band was staying at Don CeSar Hotel on St. Pete Beach and staged an impromptu 30-minute gig on the roof. Hotel security and local police shut it down, but not before beachgoers were treated to live renditions of the songs from *Southern Accents*.

Tom Petty & The Heartbreakers took to the road in June of 1985 and this time they brought along some guest musicians. A three-piece horn section, dubbed Soul Lips Horns, toured with the band and included Jimmy Vavala on sax and harmonica; Lee Thornburg on trumpet, flugel horn and flugel bone; and Nick Land on trombone and euphonium. Two female backup singers were also drafted. The Rebelettes were Pat Peterson and Carroll Sue Hill. It was a typical summer tour of the United States, hitting sheds and civic centers from east to west, and places in between.

Sandwiched in the middle of all this was the band's appearance at JFK Stadium in Philadelphia on July 13 as part of the dual-concert Live Aid benefit. Organized by Bob Geldof of The Boomtown Rats and Midge Ure of Ultravox, the simultaneous concerts – one at JFK Stadium and one at Wembley Stadium in London – raised funds to alleviate the famine in Ethiopia. One hundred thousand fans attended the show in Philly and the entire event was televised all over the world. The crowd was especially enthusiastic about Petty's set, which included 'American Girl', 'The Waiting', 'Rebels' and the always-rousing 'Refugee'.

The last gig of the year was Farm Aid. After the success of Live Aid earlier in the year, musicians Willie Nelson, Neil Young and John Mellencamp decided that they would spearhead an event to help individuals much closer to home: family-based farmers in America. Tom Petty & The Heartbreakers agreed to appear and to act as Bob Dylan's backup band for his set. Dylan hadn't been out on the road for four years and didn't have his own band at the ready. Like Tom, Dylan was looking for a new direction. When he and The Heartbreakers took to the stage at Farm Aid for a six-song set, it was like a thunderbolt. The band was incredibly attuned to Dylan and it appeared to the audience as if these gentlemen had spent a lifetime working with each other. The group blazed through 'Clean Cut Kid', 'Shake', 'I'll Remember You', 'Trust Yourself' and 'That Lucky Old Sun'. Then, Willie Nelson joined the band onstage for the set-closing 'Maggie's Farm'.

Tom, Mike, Benmont, Howie and Stan went home that night feeling as if they'd reached a pinnacle in their careers. They had no idea then that their association with Dylan was only just beginning.

As the holidays came around, the band released its first live album, *Pack Up The Plantation: Live!*, on November 26. Most of the material for the double album was culled from songs recorded during a two-night stand at the Wiltern Theater in Los Angeles in August 1985, although a few tracks were sourced from previous tours.

The record included a variety of hits like 'The Waiting', 'Breakdown' and 'American Girl' as well as covers like Chris Hillman and Roger McGuinn's 'So You Want To Be A Rock 'N' Roll Star', 'Don't Bring Me Down' (written by Gerry Goffin and Carole King), 'Shout' (written by O'Kelly Isley, Ronald Isley and Rudolph Isley) and John Sebastian's 'Stories We Could Tell'. Duets with Stevie Nicks – 'Needles And Pins' and 'Insider' – were also included along with favourites from *Southern Accents* like the album's title track, 'Rebels' and 'You Got Lucky'.

The Wiltern Theater gigs were filmed and ultimately released on home video with the same title as the live album and included some material not on the record, like 'Don't Do Me Like That', 'Don't Come Around Here No More' and covers like Bobby Troup's 'Route 66', and 'Little Bit O' Soul', which was written by John Carter and Ken Lewis.

Looking back on the year, Tom couldn't help but be pleased by what his band had accomplished. Yes, it's true that *Southern Accents* wasn't quite the album he set out to make, but the twists in the road helped him break new ground as a musician and songwriter. The music he released was a bit unexpected, yet the fans still adored the album – and Tom reveled in that fact. The audience *was* willing to follow and that was incredibly reassuring.

Each member of The Heartbreakers had refocused his energies and the Southern Accents tour was hugely successful – both musically and monetarily. The band had been together for nine years now and Tom finally felt that their futures were assured. He realized that he didn't have to go looking for a fight anymore. Despite being a rock'n'roll musician, maybe it was time to mature and mellow just a bit?

"'Mellowed' is such a frightening word," says Tom, "but, yes, I suppose I have. I don't hit things as much now. That was a turning point in my life. I didn't have the use of my hand for nine months, and it scared me pretty bad, because I suddenly realized I might never play again." Tom understood what was important now – his family and music – and he was concentrating on upholding his responsibilities in both arenas. He vowed to spend more quality time with his wife, Jane, and their little girls, Adria and Annakim. And, he promised himself to let the future of his songwriting style unfold naturally – no matter where it might take the band. He was open to all possibilities and wondered where The Heartbreakers would go next. All that was important was the music and the close relationships he shared with his bandmates, friends and family. Despite the popularity of The Heartbreakers and the intense media coverage throughout the year, Tom was still pretty much the same person he'd been back in Gainesville all those years ago. Hollywood hadn't taken him in and he eschewed the entire concept of being famous. "Tom's not much different from the guy I first met," says Benmont. "He's just a lot more famous. I was over at his house a few weeks ago, sitting around the kitchen table talking about whatever was going on, and it felt pretty much the same as sitting around the kitchen table in their old apartment in Gainesville. Of course, it's a *much* bigger kitchen."

"I can honestly sit here and say that I've avoided celebrity most of my life," Tom says. "I have no desire to be a celebrity. Never did. I'd rather just be a working musician and songwriter. As humble as it sounds, it really is true." Tom Petty's authenticity can't be denied and fans have always sensed his honesty. It comes across in everything he says and in all the songs he writes and that's perhaps why so many of his songs – from 'American Girl' to 'Refugee' – have become anthems for people who view themselves as underdogs fighting for a shot at a better life.

"I never look at it as fighting the world, but I guess the songs convey that," Tom admits. "It's good to have something in the songs that inspires people. That's our aim with this music – the highest it can achieve is to inspire people, to lift people up."

CHAPTER 7

The Hurricane
(1986–1987)

"Dylan hooks up with one of America's last great rock'n'roll bands."
— True Confessions tour book

Band manager Tony Dimitriades took the call not long after The Heartbreakers backed Bob Dylan at Farm Aid. Would Tom Petty & The Heartbreakers consider touring Australasia with Dylan in 1986? The idea was intriguing. "It's an outgrowth of the Farm Aid rehearsals," Tom confirmed at the time. "We spent a week rehearsing, and we would play a lot every night. Hours and hours and hours. We did Hank Williams songs, Motown songs ['I Second That Emotion']. We even played 'Louie Louie' one night and 'Then He Kissed Me', the old Crystals song. When we went to the gig, we only did 20 minutes, so everyone was saying, 'Boy, it's a shame we can't really play for a while.'" A double-bill tour made an incredible amount of sense.

Music critics were downright giddy on hearing the news. The Farm Aid set was powerful and fans around the world would pay good money to see Dylan and Petty on the same stage.

Tom understood Dylan's need for a reliable backup band. Building one is something of an art and something that Tom had grappled with himself many years ago, having been out in the cold without a band during that short period between the dissolution of Mudcrutch and the launch of Tom Petty & The Heartbreakers. While there are plenty of talented session players, it's often preferable to use a group that is already comfortable with one another. The Heartbreakers excel in that regard.

"I think Bob's attracted to the idea of working with a group," agreed Tom in 1986. "A handpicked band of good players doesn't always make a great band. Somebody like him needs a sympathetic unit that understands music. He told me, 'This band is like talking to one guy.'"

The powers that be designed a short "teaser" tour across New Zealand, Australia and Japan. The 20 dates were dubbed the True Confessions: Alone and Together tour. The band arrived in the Land of the Long White Cloud on February 3, and spent a few days warming up. The opening show was set for the outdoor Athletic Park in Wellington on February 5. The band's soundcheck there turned into a full-fledged rehearsal, annoying residents, and local officials nearly pulled the permit for the concert. In the end, management smoothed the ruffled Kiwi feathers and the show went on.

The first concert wasn't as warmly received as Dylan had hoped. In fact, the audience didn't really come to life until halfway through the set when Tom launched into a soaring version of 'Refugee'. Dylan decided the band needed a bit more practise so on February 6 they got together at the Park Royal Hotel. Benmont took over the piano in the lounge and led a sing-along that included Dylan, Petty and all The Heartbreakers, Stevie Nicks (who was travelling with the band) and backup singers Queens of Rhythm. The "Queens" were a quartet that included Debra Byrd, Queen Esther Marrow, Madelyn Quebec and Elisecia Wright.

The supergroup sang nearly two-dozen songs. Those in attendance were particularly wowed by renditions of 'Sincerely', 'What Becomes Of The Broken Hearted', 'Crying In The Rain' and 'Not Fade Away'.

After the New Zealand dates, the troupe headed to Australia for gigs across the country. Two Sydney shows at the Entertainment Center stand out because Stevie Nicks made guest appearances on February 11 and 12, joining the band for a few numbers including the finale, 'Knockin' On Heaven's Door'. The tour closed in Japan with concerts in Tokyo, Osaka and Nagoya.

Dylan and The Heartbreakers did more Down Under than just perform. They spent several of their days off in the studio and invited Australian director Gillian Armstrong to shoot the Sydney shows, the footage of which was eventually released on HBO as a one-hour special called *Hard To Handle*. The video included performances of nearly a dozen songs but 'Like A Rolling Stone', 'It's Alright Ma (I'm Only Bleeding)' and 'Girl From The North Country' were the standouts.

The mini-tour lit a spark for all of The Heartbreakers and they wanted more. Management worked out a deal for an American leg of the tour, which began on June 6 at The Forum in Los Angeles. Tom Petty & The Heartbreakers and Bob Dylan roared across the United States but Canada only got one date of its own.

Tom found it liberating to back Dylan. He was finally able to experience what it was like to be a band member and not the star of the show. While he still led The Heartbreakers onstage and was the conduit between them and Dylan, the pressure of having the focus on him all night had disappeared.

At the time, Tom commented on what it was like to work with Dylan. "It's a real good experience because after this many years you can forget exactly what it's like to have somebody else out front," he said. "It's easy for me because I can understand exactly the little insecurities that creep in, and why a singer gets frustrated. It's also kind of fun – in that the heat isn't always on me. I'm getting a lot better on guitar. I get to play a lot more guitar than I ever get to play with The Heartbreakers where I have to sing all the time. There are very few people we'd do this for. Musically it's the most satisfying thing I've done in a long time.

"I learned so much from Bob Dylan," continues Tom. "He gave us a kind of courage that we never had, to learn something quickly and go out onstage and play it. You had to be pretty versatile because arrangements could change, keys might change, there's just no way of knowing exactly what he wants to do each night. You really learn the value of spontaneity, of how a moment that is real in a concert is worth so much more than one you plan out."

That's not to say that it was always easy working with Dylan. In 1989 Tom talked with Tom Hibbert of Q magazine and reflected about being onstage with Bob. "He's *extremely* spontaneous, I always felt he taxed us to the limit every night when we came off stage because he does throw you some curves up there," he said. "You'll get a lot of songs up there that you've never rehearsed – and you'll get some songs that you not only have not rehearsed but you've never even *heard* and that's a real test. It's quite a challenge. All of a sudden he'd just ignore the song list and creep up to me, nose to nose and blink at me and say, 'OK, get a D chord, here, we're going to do this sort of thing' and he'd go through some song under his breath in my ear and he'd go, 'Have you got it?' and I'd go, 'Uh, I *guess* I've got it,' and I'd turn round and he'd start off playing something entirely different *again*. It was *terrifying* but after a while we got pretty good at it and started to enjoy it."

For Tom, working with Dylan was about more than just the music though. "When Bob came into my life, I think that was good for me and good for Bob. For me, it was the start of a long process of getting all my plugs firing again. And maybe for him, too, if I can be so bold as to say that," Tom says. "Bob is such a wonderful performer, a real showman. Just being around the guy and getting to know him as a friend was a great experience and the start of finding some higher ground. Good things seem to follow bad. It's always been that way, for me, anyway."

Dylan was quite happy with the way things had worked out on the road with The Heartbreakers and said at the time, "Tom's an excellent songwriter, an excellent musician. People talk about how he sounds a little like Roger McGuinn, but playing with him and seeing what he does to a crowd, I think he's more in the Bob Marley area. He's *real* good. I've got a lot of respect for Tom – he's a deep, soulful cat. Tom is a heroic character in his own kind of way."

Meanwhile, back home as the tour wound down, Tom's management company had a bit of legal wrangling to do. Grey Advertising, the agency for tire company B.F. Goodrich, had approached the band previously to ask permission to use 'Mary's New Car' from *Southern Accents* in a new televised tire campaign. Tom turned the offer down. He didn't care how much money was being offered; he just wasn't interested in his music being used to sell tires, or anything else for that matter.

A few weeks later, manager Tony Dimitriades was watching a Lakers basketball game on TV and saw a B.F. Goodrich ad that featured a Tom Petty sound-alike singing a song that sounded conspicuously like 'Mary's New Car'. Dimitriades was disgusted. "They've used a Tom Petty sound-alike to do the song. The melody is almost identical and the voice is practically the same too. Tom's made up his mind to stop these guys. It's unconscionable for these people to try to fool the public into believing that this commercial is something that it's not."

Petty took legal action and a US District Court judge issued a temporary restraining order. That meant B.F. Goodrich had to pull the commercial off the air while the court set to work to make a permanent ruling. In the end, Judge Spencer Letts awarded Petty $1 million in damages and said of the song similarity: "They are very, very much alike... in a number of ways. The words are alike. The music is alike. The tempo is alike."

Looking back on it now, it's shocking that Grey Advertising and B.F. Goodrich took such a chance copying the work of someone with as high a profile as Petty.

Dimitriades summed up the case when talking with the media at the time, "The artist's copyright is one of the few things he has which has any tangible worth. We feel Tom's been wronged here. We just don't think that B.F. Goodrich, or any other company, should be able to get away with it." And, they didn't.

Fighting in court wasn't the only thing on Tom's mind at this time. In between tour dates with Dylan, the band recorded its seventh studio album, *Let Me Up (I've Had Enough),* in just five weeks at Mike's home studio as well as at Sound City in Van Nuys. The record was released on April 21, 1987 – a full two years since the band's last album.. It was a bit of a letdown to some fans and Tom does admit that, "It's kind of a mongrel, this album."

"It wasn't a formal project," defends Tom. "There was no producer, there was nobody in the booth except good ol' Don Smith [engineer], trying to get everything on tape." Tom wanted the record to be as freewheeling as possible. "The only rule of the sessions," Tom says, "was the tape had to roll from the time the first guy got here until the last guy was gone.

"We were hot when we hooked up with Bob," Tom remembers. "Then, he opened up avenues we hadn't explored before. We became more confident and relaxed behind him, and the new album was made when we were still in that state of mind."

Unlike *Southern Accents*, which featured musicians outside of The Heartbreakers fold, this album is solely Tom, Mike, Benmont, Stan and Howie. Five of the 11 songs were co-written by Mike. The record netted the band its first number one hit – 'Jammin' Me' (written by Petty, Campbell and Dylan) – since 1982's 'You Got Lucky'.

For casual fans, the only song that redeemed the album was 'Jammin' Me,' which spent four weeks at number one on *Billboard*'s Mainstream Rock Tracks chart. The song itself was about the ways in which we're all inundated with news, information and entertainment at every turn. In a world filled with disjointed information, how do we process what's important? That's the question Tom, Mike and Bob were pondering. In the song, they name-check a few current day celebrities that were overexposed at the time: actress Vanessa Redgrave and comedians Joe Piscopo and Eddie Murphy. Murphy did not take kindly to being mentioned in the song and his rant against Petty just kept him in the limelight even longer. It was a feud Petty probably should have expected, but didn't. There was no ill will or malice meant in those lyrics. They were a simple reflection on what was going on in the world at the time.

Many rock journalists liked the album though, including *Rolling Stone*'s Anthony DeCurtis who wrote, "Despite the desperate surrender implied in the title, Tom Petty & The Heartbreakers come out standing tough and triumphant on *Let Me Up (I've Had Enough)*. The songs on the album chronicle characters that are reeling from media assaults and shattered relationships. But anger and the urgent need to make sense of a world spinning out of control are strong reasons for survival – and they are powerfully rendered in the muscular, guitar-charged rock The Heartbreakers hammer out."

Tom talked about the album with *Creem*'s Bud Scoppa on its release, saying, "I had booked some time at Sound City for something Dylan wanted to do – he was making a record. Then it turned out he wasn't gonna be ready at that time. And so we had about three songs – I had one or two and I think Campbell had one. And we said, 'Well, let's just go in and try these songs out.' We wound up staying there a month at least, right up until we left again [to tour with Dylan]. And when I left again, not only had we gone on tour we had a *double album*. Nobody could believe us. It could've been a lot like *Exile On Main Street*, but it was gonna be too vast a job to try to get the two albums done. I knew I could get one done."

It was a tough decision to jettison nearly an album's worth of songs. The band felt there were a lot of credible outtakes that could have turned into amazing songs, given the time. Time they didn't have, so *Let Me Up* was released as a single album.

The fact is, though, that none of the songs on the final record stayed in the band's live set very long. It was a very musical album albeit one without the punch of *Damn The Torpedoes* or the emotional heft of *Hard Promises*. Why this album felt lesser than Tom's other work is a matter for discussion. It's possible that at this point, The Heartbreakers were simply tired and were rushed in the studio to put songs down on tape that weren't as developed as they could have been. Still, wistful rockers like 'Runaway Trains' and 'How Many More Days' are worth the listen.

Like so many of Petty's other songs, 'Runaway Trains' – co-written with Mike – focuses on a woman that's eluded the singer. She's gone from his life and he knows he just needs some time to get her out of his mind. The song is haunting in its own way and leaves the listener wondering what went so wrong in the couple's relationship that led them here.

The next track on the record, 'The Damage You've Done', is more of a rocker and finds the singer taking a woman to task. He asks her what in the world he's done to deserve her scorn. He never does find out and he's a bit bitter about how things ended. That song is in sharp contrast to the ballad, 'It'll All Work Out'. Perhaps one of the most beautiful songs on the record and certainly worthy to stay in the band's repertoire, this all too short song paints the picture of a woman that the singer loved but let down. He wasn't there for her – even though he wished he had been in hindsight – but now he feels she's better off with her new boyfriend. He misses her deeply and thinks of her always, but knows everything worked out the way it was supposed to.

The Heartbreakers have probably never played 'My Life/Your World' in concert. It's an odd little number that's got the singer puzzling what the world is all about. He sees all these things happening around him, but doesn't relate one bit.

'Think About Me' reprises another theme Tom often sings about… convincing a woman that she is, in fact, interested in him. The up-tempo number finds the singer admitting that while he doesn't have the money – and all that brings – that her boyfriend has, he knows he could make her happy if she'd just give him a chance.

'All Mixed Up' is a showcase for Benmont's musicianship. "On 'All Mixed Up', we were all knocked out by Benmont's magic fingers," Tom told Bud Scoppa during a 1987 interview for *Creem* magazine. "Benmont had this thing that sampled horns on his keyboard…. Benmont played like five things at once. He'd have everything on – his organ, his piano, just a circle of stuff. All through the tracks he was just changin' around. He's got this hotel key that he can stick in the organ and hold a note down, turn around and play somethin' else. The engineer'd be goin', 'Where's all this shit *comin'* from?!'"

Despite the musicianship on the album, the band itself didn't really embrace the songs for the long haul. While the album is still a good listen – even decades later – it didn't gain traction at the time of its release and the band never plays these songs while out on tour. Some tunes, like 'A Self-Made Man', might just have been too short to consider slating on a set list. In that one, the singer warns his friends to leave the "self-made man" alone as he struggles with the loss of a woman he loved.

'Ain't Love Strange' is certainly a song that's worthy for resurrection all these years after its release. It's a happy little song that states the obvious: how incredibly weird love can be. It can be the most fantastic feeling you've ever had or it can make you go crazy. There's nothing deeper here but it's an accurate reflection of how the same emotion can cause multiple outcomes: both good and bad.

'How Many More Days' finds the singer wishing he could spend more time with his new girl. He wants to but she's eluding him for reasons that aren't entirely clear. Again, it's a pleasing song but there's not much more to it than face value. The album closes with the searing 'Let Me Up (I've Had Enough)' in which the singer questions all the things in life that we do because it's expected of us. At the end of the line, was it worth it? Is there more to life than working for a faceless corporation or spending your life with a spouse who may not have always been faithful? It's a look at all the second guesses everyone has from time to time. Of all the songs presented, this one is perhaps the tune that people can most relate to. The album was a fine addition to Tom's lexicon but fans hoped the next album would have a little more depth and range.

★ ★ ★

The red, whirling lights of a dozen fire trucks pierced the dark May night in 1987 as dozens of water hoses took aim at the house, but it was hopeless. Someone had set Tom Petty's Encino home afire and it was nearly a complete loss. Thankfully, everyone got out OK, but they were shaken.

The day was just beginning when the family discovered the fire. Tom and his wife, Jane, were home with their housekeeper and daughter Annakim. Their eldest daughter, Adria, happened to be at a sleepover at a friend's house. Everyone raced out the door with only the clothes on their backs. They soon realized how bad it was as firefighters wrapped them in blankets as they watched their home burn to the ground. They lost nearly everything – guitars, clothes, family photos, gold records – *everything*. The only area of the house that wasn't a total loss was Tom's basement recording studio. The family huddled in the driveway, dazed by what had happened.

The house itself was an incredible showplace with Frank Lloyd Wright-inspired Big Bear cabin architecture. The five-bedroom home sat on nearly an acre of property in Encino and was outfitted with just about everything you could possibly want, including a pool, sauna, spa, two-story fireplace, gym, and three-car garage.

The family had planned to host a barbeque that very afternoon to celebrate Jane's birthday. With all the commotion, they completely forgot to call it off. The house was still smoldering as guests began to arrive. Eurythmics' Annie Lennox was one of the first on the scene. Having offered her condolences she then took her leave but was back within a few hours after a shopping spree. She'd bought each member of the Petty household some clothes, shoes and basics like toothpaste and toothbrushes. She'd come to their aid in such a kind and essential way and it blew Tom away.

Benmont came to the rescue of Adria. She'd called home to ask her mom and dad to come pick her up after the sleepover and no one answered. She got worried and called Benmont. He lived nearby and went to pick her up. He carefully explained what happened as he drove her home.

The next day the fire chief came round to talk with Tom. It was arson. Someone had tried to murder Tom Petty and his entire family. *No.* Tom wasn't willing to believe that was true, but the fire chief had more to tell him. "The police discovered that somebody had been staking the place out," Tom recounts. "He'd cut a hole in the fence and was on a hill behind the house just watching."

This information shook Tom to the core. It felt unreal... like it couldn't really be happening to him. "I still don't know why it happened. It's a very weird feeling," he contends. "It's one of those things that's very hard to accept. I still can't accept it.

"It was so vicious and angry that it completely scared all of that out of me. I didn't want to do anything except sing really light, happy music after that. In retrospect, I wanted to go to some much lighter place. I was really glad to be alive. I was like someone who had survived a plane crash. You are just really glad that they didn't get you. If you've ever had anybody try to kill you, it really makes you re-evaluate everything.

"I came away with the realization that stuff is temporary. It can be replaced. We found a new house and stashed the family... and I took off on the road. I was traumatized but I didn't deal with it for a long time." The house was eventually rebuilt and was still owned by Jane as of August 2013, when she put the property up for sale with an asking price of $3.5 million.

At the time of the arson, the press covered it extensively as a lead-in to the fact that Tom Petty & The Heartbreakers were about to leave on their own tour and then the next leg of Bob Dylan's tour. Critics were incensed that one of rock'n'roll's royalty would have been violated in this way. Mike Hammer of *RockBill* wrote, "Here's a guy who's given us some of the best hard-nosed rock'n'roll of the last 10 years and somebody turns his private life into a charred black patch on a Southern California field."

Fans worried that the tragedy might stop the band from hitting the road, but that didn't happen. Tom tried to assure fans via comments he made in the press, saying, "I think I'm going to be all right. I'm the kind of person who presses on." That statement couldn't have been more true to his character. So much had happened throughout his career that would have made lesser men crumble, but not Tom Petty. He kept getting back up again because what other choice did he have? He was not the type to surrender and this arsonist would not win.

Tom's friends helped him through this time period as well. "I talked with Roy [Orbison] about it and Roy was great because Roy, well, *he* had a fire and he lost his children in it and he talked to me a lot about it," says Tom. "I asked him if he felt unlucky and stuff and he said, 'You have to remember that it happens *to* you but it's not directed *at* you.' You can't believe that at the time but he was right and what Roy said touched me. And there were positive aspects to the fire in a way because it made us a mobile family and in a lot of ways that pulled us closer together. We had to cling together to get over it."

It was probably a blessing that a tour was set to begin in just a few days' time in Tucson, Arizona. The Del Fuegos and Georgia Satellites would join Tom Petty & The Heartbreakers on the road from May 26 – July 26.

Tom used the shows as a vehicle for talk therapy and often commented during the concerts, "I had kind of a weird week last week. Somebody

141

came and burned my house to the ground. It's all right, though. They didn't burn this," and then he'd triumphantly hold up his 12-string Rickenbacker. It might have been part shtick but it was just one more of those completely honest statements Tom's been known for throughout his career.

The band took the month of August off, allowing Tom to visit his new temporary home in Beverly Hills. Then, it was off on the road again. They hosted a contest with MTV and two winners got to join them on a tour of Egypt that included a Nile River cruise and was capped off with the Dylan-Petty show in Tel Aviv, Israel, to kick off the Temples In Flames tour. This time The Heartbreakers joined Dylan and Roger McGuinn for shows across Europe.

Throughout Tom Petty's life, so many good things started with a simple act of happenstance: meeting Elvis Presley on the set of *Follow That Dream*; miraculously finding his musical soul mate – Mike Campbell – living in an apartment not far from him in Gainesville; fielding a call from producer Denny Cordell that would land him the record deal of his dreams; agreeing to back Dylan for a few songs during Farm Aid. Petty believed that if he kept himself open to possibilities, opportunities would present themselves. Good karma visited Tom Petty many times during his career, and it did so again in October of 1987 when the band closed out the Temples In Flames tour with four nights at Wembley Arena in London.

"England has always been Mecca to me," Tom admits. "That's where it all came from, for me, at least. I was just thinking about how Jeff [Lynne] and George [Harrison] and Derek [Taylor, Beatles publicist] used to come to our shows. I remember we were having such a good time after the [October 14, 1987] Wembley show with Dylan that I stayed back there for hours. I felt really inspired by it all. I went back to the [hotel] room, and a hurricane hit the middle of London the same night. I didn't know they had them. The rain was hitting the windows so hard it woke me. It ripped huge oaks out of the ground, and I got up the next day and thought, 'Holy cow! This is something.' I always thought that hurricane had to do with something. My life was different after that."

Indeed, Tom had lived through the Great Storm of 1987 that ravaged southern England and northern France on October 15 and 16. It was the most powerful storm to hit the region since the Great Storm of 1703. Was the hurricane symbolic for something in Tom's life? It's hard to say, but his life *was* different after that in many ways. The most important of which was his newfound friendship with ex-Beatle George Harrison. George had just released his tenth studio album, *Cloud Nine,* on November 2, and was enjoying the fact that his single 'Got My Mind Set On You' was a hit. He had produced the record with Jeff Lynne, formerly of Electric Light Orchestra.

George was in town throughout the period of the Wembley shows – as was Jeff Lynne – and went to see the band play. Although Tom and George had met briefly on other occasions, this was the first time they truly clicked.

After the last show on October 17, lots of people gathered backstage. Tom's birthday was just a few days away (October 20) and someone had arranged for a cake. Bob, The Heartbreakers, Roger McGuinn, Jeff and George gathered round to sing a rendition of 'Happy Birthday' to their esteemed colleague.

Tom was humbled by the affection he felt from all of his friends. He says now that it was one of the best nights of his life. He knew that night that he and George would be forever friends. "Me and George have something somewhere where we're connected," Tom said at the time. "Some past life or something. I don't understand it." But, George's friendship – and that hurricane – signaled that Petty was at the threshold of an important period in his life.

"I knew that hurricane meant my life was going to change," says Tom. "My little coupling with Jeff and George was so cosmic. It was so damn strange when I ran into Jeff [later upon returning to the States]. I didn't live in that neighbourhood when I left on tour, and neither did Jeff. He moved into it when I was gone. We had spent almost every night together along with George [Harrison] when I was in England a few weeks before so I didn't expect to see him stopped at a light in Los Angeles. We pulled over and talked, and decided to meet the next day. But that's not nearly as odd as when I was Christmas shopping with my daughter about a week later and we decided to eat at this French restaurant that she loved for lunch – something we never ever did. I went in and sat down and the waiter said that there was a friend of mine in a private room and he would like to see me and it was George. He said, 'This is so strange, I was writing your number down from Jeff and they told me you were in the next room.' He came home with me and we spent the holiday together and became good friends."

Musically, George and Tom were kindred spirits. "George knew every obscure Elvis solo; his initial influences were rockabilly – Carl Perkins, Eddie Cochran, Chet Atkins, Scotty Moore – but he always added something to it," says Tom. "Even going way back, I used to just swoon over that solo in 'I Saw Her Standing There'. You just can't imagine anything else there. He had that knack. And how many Rickenbacker 12-strings did that guy sell? That was a whole new sound too – Roger McGuinn got the idea from George, and then Roger took it to his own place with The Byrds.

"When he moved over to the slide guitar later in The Beatles' career, it was a really beautiful thing to hear him play that. He once said to me, 'I think modern guitar players are forgetting about pitch,' and that was something he really cared about. He was very in tune when he played, the slide was very precise, and just a beautiful vibrato on it. It really sounded like a voice, like a very distinct, signature voice that came out of him. Just listen to those records. They're so immaculate, so inventive. He was a guy who could just add so much."

While Tom was an accomplished musician himself, he found that he learned a lot from George whenever they spent time together. It was George who actually taught Tom how to play the ukulele. "He came in with two ukuleles and gave me one. 'You gotta play this thing. It's great! Let's jam.' I have no idea how to play a ukulele. 'Oh, it's no problem, I'll show you.' So we spent the rest of the day playing ukuleles, strolling around the yard. My wrist hurt the next day. But he taught me how to play it, and a lot of the chord formations. When he was going I walked out to the car and he said, 'Well, wait... I want to leave some ukuleles here.' He'd already given me one, so I said, 'Well, I've got this.' 'No, we may need more!' He opened his trunk and he had a lot of ukuleles in there, and I think he left four at my house. He said, 'Well, you never know when we might need them, because not everybody carries one around.'"

★ ★ ★

In 1987 Tom was also making friends with people in the neighborhood, people like offbeat comedian Garry Shandling. The two became so close that Garry asked Tom to be a recurring guest on his Showtime television series, *It's Garry Shandling's Show*. The show it itself was interesting since it was not quite a sitcom and not quite a talk show. Featuring Garry Shandling playing himself, the twist is that he and all the other actors in the show are aware that they are mere characters in a sitcom. It was the first program in the United States that broke down the "fourth wall" of television – the imaginary line at the front of the stage between the actors and the audience. In *It's Garry Shandling's Show*, Garry – and the other actors in the cast – would speak directly to the audience and even sometimes deputize an audience member to become an impromptu character in the episode being taped. Garry began each show with a monologue and finished the program with a synopsis à la *The Burns And Allen Show* that was popular in the fifties. Garry Shandling's destruction of the fourth wall actually inspired Irish stand-up comedian Sean Hughes to create *Sean's Show* in the UK in 1992.

It's Garry Shandling's Show revolves around the Happy Pilgrim Estates, where Garry and the rest of the cast reside. Most episodes took place in Garry's condo, which was set-designed and decorated to look just like where he lived in real life. In the fictional show, Tom Petty lived right next door. In the hilarious Season Two episode 'No Baby, No Show', Garry announces that the audience will witness the birth of a baby. His neighbors Jackie Schumacher (played by Bernadette Birkett) and husband Pete (played by Michael Tucci) are expecting and Jackie has agreed to have her baby on Garry's TV show. There's a hitch though, the baby isn't cooperating and Garry has to find some way to string out his time on air while entertaining the audience. Just as he's getting nervous, the doorbell rings. It's his neighbor Tom Petty, who is returning some hedge clippers that he borrowed from Garry earlier.

145

Tom also happens to be carrying a guitar so Garry convinces him to step inside and play a song for the audience. The musician agrees and plays a beautiful acoustic rendition of 'The Waiting'.

After the performance, Tom steps into the living room with all of Garry's other guests – additional neighbors – and the scene morphs into a slightly awkward talk show that plods along until Jackie announces that she's ready to have the baby. Tom helps lower the woman to the floor as she goes into labor. Petty went on to guest star in several other episodes, including 'It's Garry Shandling's Christmas Show' and 'Vegas', in which the cast heads to Las Vegas to attend a friend's wedding. In the show, Tom tells Jackie and Pete's older son, Grant, that he thought he'd be a clerk at Thom McAn forever until he went to rock star school.

The show ran for 72 episodes before Garry Shandling moved on to HBO with a new show called *The Larry Sanders Show*, a much more traditional talk show. Tom was a guest on that series several times as well.

★ ★ ★

These were indeed Tom Petty's halcyon days. Perhaps for the first time in his life, he was actually *enjoying* time off from the studio and the road and was forging many close friendships with those around him. He was also enjoying new heights of creativity and the songs he channeled during this time period – really meaningful songs – were exactly the sort his fans could relate to. It was clear that Tom's artistic journey was nowhere near its final destination.

CHAPTER 8

I Heard It On The Street That You Might Go Solo (1988–1990)

"I'm still continually amazed by the power a little three-minute song has."
— T.P.

For many reasons, 1988 was one of the happiest and most rewarding years of Tom Petty's life. He'd spent two years on the road with Bob Dylan and had finally built strong friendships with musicians outside of The Heartbreakers, including Dylan, Jeff Lynne and George Harrison. Now, with The Heartbreakers taking a break, Tom was left to his own devices to fill his time. It didn't take long before George drafted him for a pet project he'd been dreaming about: a supergroup he'd name the Traveling Wilburys.

George first discussed the band in public with DJ Bob Coburn on a *Rockline* radio interview on Los Angeles' KLOS on February 10, 1988. George and Jeff Lynne had decided to do the show on the spur of the moment. They took calls from listeners and played a few songs on acoustic guitars.

The idea may have sounded a bit crazy at first. George wanted to be in yet another supergroup? But it wasn't that he was trying to recapture his early days with The Beatles; instead, he was keen to become part of a band of guys who were friends and who all loved music. George had high standards so the only people who could run his gauntlet would have to be rock legends in their own rights, musicians like Tom Petty, Bob Dylan, Roy Orbison and Jeff Lynne.

The idea hadn't come out of nowhere though. George needed a B-side for the *Cloud Nine* single 'This Is Love', so he and Jeff invited Roy to join them in the studio. Jeff was also in the midst of producing Roy's "comeback album", *Mystery Girl*. They arranged to use Bob Dylan's recording studio in his Malibu home, and on the way over they had to make a quick stop at Tom Petty's house, because George had left one of his guitars there during a recent jam session.

When all was said and done, it was actually George, Jeff, Roy, Bob and Tom that ended up in the studio that day to create a B-side. Instead of a throwaway tune, the session yielded the incredibly likable 'Handle With Care'. Warner Bros – George's record label at the time – saw dollar signs when it heard the track. Why not get the band together to record an entire album? Writing songs and recording as a team was a breeze for this group and they looked forward to spending time on a side project in which none of them had to take center stage. The Traveling Wilburys were born.

Cutting wit was a trait all of the musicians shared, so they dreamed up a story to go along with the funny band name. The musicians were actually half-brothers, all fathered by the same man. Each took a "stage name". George was "Nelson Wilbury" while Jeff took the name "Otis". Orbison was "Lefty" in homage to Lefty Frizzell and Tom was "Charlie T. Wilbury, Jr.". Bob was dubbed "Lucky Wilbury". And, while not an official Wilbury, session drummer Jim Keltner won the title of "Buster Sidebury". Other musicians who also played on *Traveling Wilburys: Vol. 1* include Jim Horn on sax, Ray Cooper on percussion and Ian Wallace on tom-toms.

The record was recorded at the home of Dave Stewart, Annie Lennox's partner in Eurythmics. The band camped out there for a 10-

day stint during May 1988, sitting outside under a grove of trees or around the kitchen table with notepads to write lyrics. Then, they'd run through the tunes and get everything down on tape. The process was so live and organic, and the recordings all had a sense of vitality to them.

"The songwriting process was unusual in that each song had the input of five different people. I don't think any of us had written that way before," says Tom, "and it was a very enjoyable experience. Usually one person would start with an idea, then everybody would add lines and make suggestions and criticisms. The sessions began in the afternoon. We started every song with five acoustic guitars and drums. We may be the only group in the world with five rhythm guitar players."

As the youngest member of the group Tom couldn't help but feel humbled to be considered in the league of some of his mentors. "I never dreamed that I'd get to work with anybody," chuckles Tom. "I never dreamed that anyone would give me the time of day so I'm way ahead of what I wanted. I always felt like the kid in the band. I was the one who was really lucky to be there. But they never treated me that way."

The draw wasn't just the music though. "See, I'm not exactly a guy who makes new friends easily," Tom comments. "And here I was making all these great new pals. And we were making this music – and the fact that there were some people who liked it just made it all the better.

"We'd sit down together and write lyrics. What a privilege. I remember he [Bob Dylan] said to me, 'If you are stuck on a line, just say what it is you want to say, and don't worry about the meter or the rhyme or anything. Just write down the sentence, and then find the key words and, wallop, you've got the line.' He tended to write many more verses than we needed, and sometimes maybe in the seventh verse something would pop up that was better than anything in the first three…. Bob is so far above the rest of us. He is the wandering minstrel, the travelling troubadour – and his gift is so great."

Roy was especially respected among his friends in the group, and commented on the work process at the time. "Everybody pitched in – it was really wonderful. There was no leader as such – we would all play rhythm guitar on everything. So there are five rhythm-guitar players on every song. Songwriting for the album was also more or less of a group effort, though each member of the Wilburys takes the lead vocals on the tracks he's most responsible for." Drummer Jim Keltner reflected on those sessions for Barney Hoskyns of *Mojo* magazine. "I remember showing up at Dave Stewart's house in Encino, and there was a bunch of guys sitting out on the front porch together. As I got closer, I could see who they were, and it blew my mind. And they were obviously all there because of Roy. They treated him as if he was royalty. When he sang his parts in the studio, the others would all stand around with their mouths open. That incredibly big, intense voice was always done with the least effort. One time we were standing in the dark, catching him from a side view. He was standing with a little light on the music stand, a pencil in his right hand, and this enormous voice was coming out with all this emotion, and yet he was standing perfectly still and it looked like maybe he was just talking to himself. It was just totally effortless for him."

Each musician came to the table as an equal but Tom says it was George who was the true leader of the band. "He'd only ever been in one band. But he was the best bandleader I ever saw. He was really good at organising things, at knowing who was best at what, delegating what to do," says Tom. 'And he was a great record producer and made the process a lot of fun; he instinctively knew when the session's bogging down and it's better to forget that problem and go onto another one and keep the energy going. That's a lot of what a good producer knows how to do: to keep the session on an up. The smallest things can disrupt a good session and you have to learn to go round them."

Traveling Wilburys: Vol. 1 was released on October 18, 1988. (The album was re-released in 2007 with two bonus tracks: 'Maxine' and 'Like A Ship'.) The undeniable hit of the album was 'Handle With Care' in which Roy sings a lilting chorus begging his girl to show him that she cares. In a sly nod to one of his biggest hits Roy sings, "I'm so tired of being lonely…", poking fun at his image as a character for whom romance all too often ends in heartbreak.

For Tom's part, he wrote two songs on the album: 'Last Night', a comical tale about a man who falls in love with a woman in a bar only to have her rob him at knife point, and 'Margarita'.

After recording with the Wilburys, Roy went into the studio to record an album of his own, and a who's-who of rock stars came and went to help, including Bono and The Edge, who wrote 'She's A Mystery To Me' for Orbison. George appeared on the album but the core group of musicians that were in the studio for the duration included Jeff Lynne, drummer Jim Keltner and most of The Heartbreakers (Tom, Mike, Howie and Benmont). Virgin would release *Mystery Girl* on February 7, 1989.

The Orbison sessions got The Heartbreakers back in the studio – albeit not to record their own music. It was a welcome project since Tom and the band hadn't spent much time together lately. Tom hadn't toured at all in 1988 – with The Heartbreakers or the Traveling Wilburys – though he and The Heartbreakers did play the Annual Bridge School Benefit Concert on December 4, 1988, at the Oakland Coliseum in California. The Heartbreakers hoped they'd win a bit more of Tom's attention in 1989.

★ ★ ★

With a new year dawning and the Traveling Wilburys sessions all buttoned up, it was time for Tom to look around for another project. He and The Heartbreakers were still officially on holiday but Tom was in a very creative space and he wasn't keen on just sitting back and relaxing. He asked Jeff Lynne to collaborate with him on a few songs he was developing.

"I wrote the first two verses of 'Free Fallin'' just trying to make Jeff Lynne laugh," remembers Petty. "A lot of the biggest songs only took minutes to write. It's about waiting for that bolt of lightning." Tom felt he and Jeff were on to something special and he wasn't about to put it on the shelf – Heartbreakers vacation or not. "I wasn't planning on doing a record, but The Heartbreakers were spread out all over the globe, and I thought, 'Shoot, we did these in a day each – we'll just go back and write nine more and put out a solo album.'"

Tom admits that when The Heartbreakers found out he was in the middle of a solo album with the help of Jeff and Mike (who was hanging at home at the time), they weren't overjoyed. "I think they've been as understanding as they can be – probably more understanding than I would've been. And they're busy boys themselves; they've got plenty of work on the side. They just wondered if I was quitting or not, and I tried to reassure them I wasn't. And I'm not," says Tom.

Feelings were hurt and even though guitarist Mike Campbell was working on the new album with Tom and Jeff, he understood the feeling of being sidelined. "When Tom did the Wilburys project, I felt left out," he admits. "Hey, you're doing a record and I'm not there. I would have liked to have been more involved with that so that's probably how they [The Heartbreakers] felt when we did the solo record."

Mike's hurt over being passed over for the Traveling Wilburys was assuaged when he began working with Tom and Jeff on Tom's solo album. "That was an amazing time for me because it was mostly just the three of us – me and Tom and Jeff – working at my house. Jeff Lynne is an amazing record-maker. It was so exciting for a lot of reasons. First of all, our band energy in the studio had gotten into kind of a rut, we were having some issues with our drummer and just kind of at the end of our rope in terms of inspiration. This project came along and really we were just doing it for fun at the beginning, but Jeff would come in and every day he would blow my mind. It was so exciting to have him and Tom come over and go, 'OK, here's this song,' and then Jeff would just say, 'OK, here's what we're going to do: put a drum machine down. Now put up a mic. We're going to do some acoustic guitars. Put up another mic. We're going to do a keyboard. OK, here's an idea for the bass. Mike, let's try some guitar on this. I've got an idea for a background part here...' Sure enough, within five or six hours, the record would be done, and we'd just sit back and go, 'How the fuck did you do that?'

"We were used to being in the studio and like, 'OK, here's how the song goes' and everybody would set up to play, and just laboriously run the song into the ground, and it usually got worse and worse from trying to get the groove and the spirit and trying to get a performance out of five guys at once," Mike concedes. "This guy walked in and he knew exactly how to put the pieces together and he always had little tricks. Tom and I were soaking it up. Pretty amazing. A very exciting time, like going to musical college or something."

With that sort of inspiration happening in the studio, it was no wonder that Tom didn't want to put the brakes on the sessions – whether or not The Heartbreakers were around. "I just wound up in the middle of it, really," says Tom of *Full Moon Fever*, his first solo record. What exactly does "Full Moon Fever" mean? "It's just a little term I use when I'm doing things and I don't quite know why," explains Tom. "I thought the phrase pretty well fit the circumstances behind this album.

"I had written some songs in the studio, just to try them out. They sounded so good that I said, 'I think I'll just keep on doing this.' I was at a period where the band had some time off; we'd been touring for a year straight, plus a year of doing Bob Dylan shows. Once things were under way here, I didn't want to stop. I could have done this album with the band – it was circumstances that made it a solo album."

It was difficult to make that case to Benmont, Howie and Stan at the time though. All of them said they would have dropped what they were doing to race back into the studio with the band as a whole. Benmont and Stan were particularly aggravated and complained to Mike who was sitting in the middle of everything. Howie was probably also ticked off but his laid-back personality prevented him from making a federal case out of it. Stan had been waiting around to begin work on a new record and finally learned about Tom's solo album from someone else. He was enraged that neither Tom nor Mike called to tell him the news personally. "I thought they were shits who were not even man enough to tell me, but about a year later I realized they were embarrassed. We're old friends. How do you call an old friend and say you don't want him at the wedding?

"I don't think it was really that pleasant for any of us. How that started I think was awkward for everyone," asserts Stan. "How it came out was great for everybody. When it really comes down to it, I have nothing to beef about with Tom's solo record," Stan reported to *Musician*'s Bill Flanagan at the time. "I have to be confident that he'll see the value of what we are and bring something else to the trip. I did sessions. Hell, I even toured with other people. Ben's done it. Mike's done a lot of things. Tom was the one who was incredibly loyal for over a decade. He didn't sleep around at all. I feel this is really positive if it stays together.

If you use that as your excuse to break up, I think you're a fool. I don't think anybody wants to be remembered as the one who broke up Tom Petty & The Heartbreakers 'cause it's a cool band."

In the end, Tom invited Benmont and Howie to appear on the album but they were simply told what to play and how to play it, as opposed to the collaborative input that they usually had when working on a record as The Heartbreakers. Howie put down background vocals on 'I Won't Back Down' and 'Love Is A Long Road' while Benmont plinked some keys on 'The Apartment Song'. Stan did take part in a few sessions but those particular tracks didn't make the album cut. (They were later released on the band's *Playback* box set in 1995.) Tensions grew and each member demanded to know what Tom's future intentions were. He'd become a member of a new supergroup and now he was releasing a solo album. Was this the end of Tom Petty & The Heartbreakers?

Absolutely not, Tom told them. "I wanted to remain bonded with the boys, you know. I wanted them to know I'm not leaving. But I don't want to suffocate myself either. I've been in this band 13 or 14 years and I'd like to be interested in it when I'm doing it. So just from time to time I'd like to do something else. They all have that privilege. They play with tons of people all the time; hang out with different bands. I never got to do that.

"I needed to stretch, to try something different, but it doesn't mean that I want a solo career now. I'll always be a Heartbreaker."

Progress continued on *Full Moon Fever* until Tom was ready to play the tracks for the record company. "I carried a tape around and played it for everyone. And everybody liked it *except* the record company. They were quizzical. They were the last ones I was able to convert," he says.

Mike recalls how depressed he and Tom were over the record execs' lack of enthusiasm for *Full Moon Fever*. "We played it for the record company and they said, 'Well, we don't hear any hits on here.' We were very despondent about the whole thing," Mike remembers. "We went back and recorded another track, a song recorded by The Byrds called 'Feel A Whole Lot Better', which was written by Gene Clark, thinking at the time that maybe they'll like this one. Tom had always been fond of the song. "I just love The Byrds so much. I'm their biggest fan, to this day," he admits "It's kind of embarrassing sometimes, 'cause I play these same albums over and over. I went to see them play when they played the Ventura [Theater]. Jeff [Lynne] went with me. And when they played that song, I went, 'Man, that's a good song.' I've played it all my life in bands. So I thought, 'It's a solo record. I can do this.' And it was a lot of fun."

Tom and Mike went back to the A&R department to play the demos again and, in the interim, a changing of the guard had occurred. "We brought the same record back six months later," says Mike, "and they loved it. They said, 'Oh, there are three hits on here.' We were vindicated on that one. It was the same record. We played the same thing for them and they went for it. I guess it's a situation of timing and the right people. At the end of the line, if the songs are good and if the public connects with certain songs, that really is the true test but you've got to get it out there."

MCA released *Full Moon Fever* on April 24, 1989, and it became a true phenomenon, peaking at number three on the *Billboard* 200 and number eight on the UK charts. Three songs – 'I Won't Back Down', 'Runnin' Down A Dream' and 'Free Fallin'' – hit number one on the Mainstream Rock chart and "A Face In The Crowd' made it to number five. If you look at it purely from a chart perspective, this was the most popular Tom's music had ever been – even topping 1979's *Damn The Torpedoes*.

The chiming guitar chords of 'Free Fallin'' open *Full Moon Fever* and the song is, indeed, one of Petty's strongest ever. In his song-as-story fashion he tells the tale of a good American girl who loves Jesus, her family, Elvis, horses and her boyfriend. But, that boyfriend leaves her in the dust and is happily surprised by his new-found sense of freedom: "I'm a bad boy, 'cause I don't even miss her / I'm a bad boy for breaking her heart / And I'm free, I'm free fallin'".

People around the world identified with the album's second track, 'I Won't Back Down', and it became an anthem for the downtrodden who'd loudly sing along with Tom in concert. "That song frightened me when I wrote it," admits Tom. "I didn't embrace it at all. It's so obvious. God, there's nothing to hide behind. There's not a hint of metaphor in this thing. It's just blatantly straightforward. I thought it wasn't that good because it was so naked. So I had a lot of second thoughts about recording that song. But everyone around me liked the song and said it was really good and it turns out everyone was right – more people connect to that song than anything I ever wrote. I've had so many people tell me that it helped them through this or it helped them through that. I'm still continually amazed by the power a little three-minute song has."

The fact is, 'I Won't Back Down' is a simple and straightforward song that captures a feeling we've all experienced at one time or another. It's about that moment when we feel boxed in a corner and decide to fight our way out – no matter what the cost. This song helps all of us steel our resolve to keep on fighting.

After you listen to 'Love Is A Long Road', you'll feel sorry for the singer who continually gives his lover another chance – only to be disappointed again and again. But, then you'll probably feel like a kindred spirit because who among us hasn't been let down by those we love from time to time? Tom's lyrics have a sense of immediacy and are so easy to relate to. Love, indeed, is a long road but we all stick with it in the hopes that we'll receive a just reward at the end of the line.

The next track on *Full Moon Fever* is the short but hypnotic 'Face In The Crowd'. The singer quietly explains about this woman that is simply someone he saw in a crowd. A glimpse of his fate in an alternate universe. Nothing comes of the chance encounter but it's something he thinks of often.

'Runnin' Down A Dream', a quintessential road song, was another tune embraced by radio program directors and fans. The opening lyrics set the scene: It's a gorgeous sun-filled day that's perfect for hopping in the car for a drive. The character turns up the radio as he speeds across the blacktop and sings along to Del Shannon's hit 'Runaway'. The chorus breaks in with "Runnin' down a dream / That never would come to me / Workin' on a mystery / Goin' wherever it leads / Runnin' down a dream".

Listeners just discovering *Full Moon Fever* now, years after its release, will hear something odd directly after the fade-out of 'Runnin' Down

A Dream'. Remember, at the time this record was released, the music industry was in the middle of pushing customers away from LPs and cassettes and toward compact discs. Tom, being an old soul, has always preferred vinyl so he added this funny little audio snippet to the mid-point of his record: "Hello CD listeners. We've come to the point in this album where those listening on cassette or records will have to stand up, or sit down, and turn over the record. Or tape. In fairness to those listeners, we'll now take a few seconds before we begin side two. Thank you. Here's side two." It's odd to hear that admission now. Young music fans probably have no idea that there used to be a side one and two on records and tapes!

The song that would have opened side two on *Full Moon Fever* is the cover of Gene Clark's 'Feel A Whole Lot Better', which was originally released as a B-side to The Byrds' single 'All I Really Want To Do' in June of 1965. Tom had already paid homage to one of his musical inspirations – Del Shannon via 'Runnin' Down A Dream' – and now he gave a nod to Clark, whom he also held in high regard.

In 1989, it had been years since Gene parted ways with The Byrds. His subsequent musical career never reached the heights he had hoped and he'd battled with an addiction to alcohol for years. In 1987 he became gravely ill and a year later underwent extensive surgery to remove ulcers in his stomach and intestines. After the health scare, Gene got clean and sober and stayed that way... until the release of *Full Moon Fever*. The influx of money and notoriety may have been what tipped the scales for Gene and he began drinking in earnest again. That was an unintended consequence of fame and Tom did not realize what was happening until Gene's untimely death at age 46 on May 24, 1991. The official cause of death was a bleeding ulcer.

Tom told *Vox*'s Adam Sweeting in 1991 that, "I only feel good that I made him a hell of a lot of money in the last year of his life. He kept sending me notes saying, 'Thanks, I can really use this.' But I'm not used to people dying around me: I try to remember I'm lucky to have another day to live through."

Tom felt including 'Feel A Whole Lot Better' on *Full Moon Fever* was a good decision and Gene's death probably only reinforced that. Many music fans would have been exposed to Gene's music by way of Tom's version of 'Feel A Whole Lot Better', which he felt was an important way to keep Gene Clark's musical legacy alive.

The record continues with the funny and uptempo 'Yer So Bad' in which the singer compares his good luck in love with the bad luck visited upon his brother-in-law, whose wife dumped him for a singer. It's a bit of lighthearted humour that is very much in context with the rest of *Full Moon Fever*.

'Depending On You' approaches a more serious topic: a young girl who's being seduced by the world to become someone she's not. The singer asks her to trust him and implores her not to give up on who she is.

Many Petty fans will tell you that one of their favorite sleepers is 'The Apartment Song'. Programmed as the ninth track on the album, the song was actually written during the *Southern Accents* sessions. The song didn't make the cut back then but was happily resurrected for placement on *Full Moon Fever* several years later.

While many of the songs on the record were rockers like 'Runnin' Down A Dream', the achingly beautiful 'Alright For Now' is a lullaby of sorts. Tom Petty closed his concerts for many years after the release of *Full Moon Fever* with this number in which he sings, "I've spent my life travelin' / I've spent my life free / I could not repay all you've done for me / So sleep tight baby / Unfurrow your brow / And know I love you / We're alright for now".

Just as the listener is curling up with the last chords of 'Alright For Now', they're blasted awake with 'A Mind With A Heart Of Its Own'. This stream-of-consciousness tale recounts a mysterious woman, a man with a "hurricane business" and a laundry list of the places the singer's traveled to.

The record closes with the incredibly likeable – and strange – 'Zombie Zoo' in which Tom comments on all the young girls who doll themselves up to look like zombies with bald heads or mohawks and make-up and line up to get into the latest hot club. He marvels that they look like Boris Karloff, but don't seem to care.

Full Moon Fever was a runaway success and The Heartbreakers had to go out and support it. The band came together for a reconciliation gig on

May 20 at NBC Studio 8-H, where they would appear live on *Saturday Night Live*. Stan Lynch grumbled loudest, saying he didn't like the music and felt as if he were in a cover band. Despite that, he agreed to play and to join the tour, which would begin in July. The Strange Behavior tour with The Replacements as opening act started on July 5 and rolled across the country. Critics applauded the tour and the group's willingness to play more than just the hits each night – as tempting as that is. Steven P. Wheeler reviewed one of the August concerts for *Music Connection* and honored The Heartbreakers thusly: "They are quite simply the tightest and most versatile American rock'n'roll band since... well, The Band."

While the tour officially came to a close at Dean Smith Center in Chapel Hill, North Carolina, on September 13, the band played the Annual Bridge School Benefit Concert at the Shoreline Amphitheater in Mountain View, California, on October 28. That closed out their live gigs for 1989.

During this time period there was a whisper of a Traveling Wilburys tour, but it was only talk. Before any real serious discussion took place, the band suffered a terrible loss. Roy Orbison died of a heart attack at the age of 52 on December 6, 1988 – just two months after the release of *Traveling Wilburys: Vol. 1*.

Tom was devastated. "I... didn't take it real well," Tom told *BAM*'s Dave Zimmer at the time. "Now I think I've come to some place where I can put it in some perspective. All I feel bad about is that I just miss him so much, his physical presence. Because he was so sweet and lovely. He was just such a happy person. He wasn't, like, a lonely guy like he was depicted in his songs. At least I don't think he was. He was always really happy. He always seemed to be living to the max, appreciating every minute. He really did seem to enjoy just about everything he did. He never criticised anybody. Very positive all the time. As a friend, he was just a very fantastic person to know. A very deep man. Very intelligent guy. He wasn't just some cracker. He was a real bright fellow and he loved being a Wilbury. That's why it hurt us so badly, 'cause he was such a big part of the spirit of the group. Among the five of us, we looked to Roy for that encouragement and that spirit. To see Roy being a Wilbury was the greatest thing."

Roy's album *Mystery Girl* was released after his death and went on to be a hit in many countries. The album made it to number five on *Billboard*'s chart in the US and it peaked at number two on the UK Albums Chart. "I think of Roy sometimes," says Tom, "and I wish that I could reach a stage in my life where I was just as good a human as Roy was, you know? He was very influential in that way. The way Roy saw life and just enjoyed it so much, it just brought home to me that you're only given so many heartbeats and you'd better use every one."

Roy's legacy – as well as the legacies of all the Traveling Wilburys – got another boost at the 1989 Grammy Awards for their contributions to *Traveling Wilburys Vol. 1* in the category of Best Rock Performance by a Duo or Group with Vocal. Tom was also nominated for Album of the Year (*Full Moon Fever* and *Traveling Wilburys Vol. 1*), Best Engineered Album, Non-Classical (the nomination actually went to Mike Campbell and the other engineers who worked on the album) and Best Male Rock Vocal Performance for 'Free Fallin''.

Rolling Stone magazine's Readers Poll Award voted *Full Moon Fever* as the Best Album and Tom Petty as the Best Male Singer of 1989.

Despite the Grammy nods, heartbreak wasn't done with Tom. On February 8, 1990, Del Shannon – his friend and a musician he respected immensely, and who had been considered as a replacement for Roy Orbison on a future Wilburys recording – took his own life. Del had been suffering from deep depression and despite taking prescription anti-depressants, he just couldn't see the value of life any longer. He killed himself with a .22-caliber rifle. "Del's death was out of the blue to me," Tom admitted to journalist Adam Sweeting for a *Vox* magazine article in September of 1991. "We loved him, really; he was a great fella, a really talented guy, but I think he had a tragic side to him in that he could never really get his thing going again.

"It never happened to me personally before, but when someone kills themselves you sort of run the gamut of emotions, y'know: the first one being anger, and then frustration, forgiveness, all those things. At least with Roy [Orbison] I could sort of rationalise it, that he had a bad heart and it got him. With Del, there was just no good reason for it to happen. So I wish him well, wherever he is."

160

Tom Petty & The Heartbreakers were still in high demand in 1990 so additional tour dates for the More Strange Behavior tour were programmed with Lenny Kravitz hired to warm up audiences. The tour kicked off at Tampa's USF Sun Dome on January 26 and an appearance at the O'Connell Center in Gainesville on the next night. By February the tour was winding down but the band took a victory lap through California that included a March 1 show at The Forum in Los Angeles with special guests Bruce Springsteen and Bob Dylan. March 3 found the band at the Pacific Amphitheater in Costa Mesa with Roger McGuinn joining them onstage. The tour concluded on March 6 at the Oakland Coliseum.

The phenomenal success of *Traveling Wilburys Vol. 1* and *Full Moon Fever* catapulted Tom Petty to new heights in his career and all the record labels took notice. Tom was in clandestine talks with Warner Bros. in 1989 and secretly signed a $20-million, six-album deal with the company. Everyone involved kept it hush-hush at the time because Tom did not want to anger his current label, MCA. After all, he still owed them two albums. He went on to deliver the studio album *Into The Great Wide Open* and his *Greatest Hits* compilation – thus fulfilling his contractual obligations. The Warner Bros. deal wasn't made public until 1992.

Tom's string of successes continued to blossom and many fellow songwriters began asking him what secret recipe he was following. "It's all in the songs," he'd emphatically reply. "If you've got the songs, it's all very simple. With *Full Moon Fever*, I was lucky in that the songs just kept coming up, and I hit a good period of writing that carried through the Traveling Wilburys."

CHAPTER 9

Into The Great Wide Open
(1991–1993)

"In these days of the muted poet. In these times of the tortured gypsy."

– T.P.

Being in a successful band is, in many ways, like a marriage. Your bandmates know you better than anyone else on the planet. They may even understand your neuroses better than you do yourself. They've seen you at your absolute best and have been there to share in your proudest moments and they've seen you make mistakes – a lot of mistakes. As the leader of the band, it's up to you to project the vision of the group, act as the cheerleader and charge ahead with what you feel is best for yourself and the band as a whole. Tom Petty had led the charge for The Heartbreakers for 16 years. He thought he'd done a pretty damn good job, but in 1991 his bandmates might have disagreed.

Tom's membership in the Traveling Wilburys had stung a bit, but a full-out solo record caused a river of hurt feelings and anger. Those sorts of feelings don't disappear overnight and there was an ever-present shadow over the Strange Behavior tour dates. As much as Tom had hoped being out on the road would be therapeutic for the band, he didn't realize how long grudges could be held. Drummer Stan Lynch says it was the first tour that felt like work to him. "I never want to feel like I'm in a cover band," he said at the time.

Stan was also frustrated by the fact that he and Tom never wrote songs together. After all, Stan was an accomplished songwriter and arranger in his own right and had co-written 'The Last Worthless Evening' and 'Gimme What You Got' with Don Henley for 1989's *The End Of The Innocence* album. "Tom's never asked me to write with him and that's one party you do not invite yourself into," Stan says. "You just don't invite yourself into someone's bedroom, and that's what writing is. He obviously doesn't see me in that light. He says, 'I don't need any more producers and songwriters around here. I need a drummer.'" Long-held feelings like that were just part of the shadow that was cast on The Heartbreakers in the early nineties.

Each band member was still carrying some emotional baggage when work began on their eighth studio album: *Into The Great Wide Open*. They started working on the album in 1990 and finished up the following year. Sessions were held at Rumbo Studios in Canoga Park as well as Mike's home studio.

One has to remember that Tom Petty was at the height of his career at this moment in time. Al Teller, chairman of the MCA Entertainment Group, asserted that, "Tom Petty is not only one of the cornerstone artists of this company, he's one of the cornerstone artists of the whole music business." *Full Moon Fever* was still a runaway success and two years of touring had gained the band thousands of new, younger die-hard fans. "We were beginning to see the same faces for a while there," said Tom of the band's live audiences. "It was incredible to find so many young people who didn't know anything about us, or me, who were discovering the whole trip because they liked 'Free Fallin'' or 'I Won't Back Down'.

Now it was time to follow up that success, so Tom naturally turned to producer Jeff Lynne. Jeff had been integral to the creation of *Full Moon Fever* and Tom hoped he could create something special with a Heartbreakers record. "I didn't want to leave The Heartbreakers behind," Tom says, "because I figured they were the best band I know, and because it just felt like there was a lot of unfinished business. But at the same time, I knew I was on a roll, and I didn't want to just drop what Jeff and I had going." Jeff, Tom and Mike would produce the forthcoming album.

It's important to note that The Heartbreakers didn't dislike Jeff Lynne. On the contrary: they respected him a great deal. They were just a bit mistrustful since he was part of the machine that they perceived as freezing them out of *Full Moon Fever*. Tom wasn't completely unaware of the misgivings of The Heartbreakers, recalling how he felt on the eve of getting Jeff and the band together: "That was scary for me," he said. "There I was taking one of my new friends to meet some of my old ones. And all I can think is, 'Oh, boy, these people had better get along.'"

It's not that the band didn't get along with Jeff. They weren't really getting along with each other. In fact, it got to the point where the band was rarely in the studio together. Each member would come in and put down his track and leave. It was a far cry from the days when the band would stand in a circle to work out a new song and get it down on tape within one or two takes.

When the album was released and Tom did the interview circuit, he didn't mention these band problems and instead gave short, standard-issue answers to evade the question completely. Years later, Tom did admit to journalists that he and all the band members were "moody" during this time period.

The fact of the matter is that there are some solid tracks on *Into The Great Wide Open*, despite that the band wasn't very communicative with each other during the sessions. 'Learning To Fly' would become a standard at their concerts and in 1991 spent six weeks at number one on *Billboard*'s Mainstream Rock Tracks chart.

In a review of the album for *Rolling Stone*'s July 11, 1991, issue, Parke Puterbaugh noted, "In its best moments, the result sounds like a cross between *Full Moon Fever* and *Damn The Torpedoes* and features the most focused and resonant lyrics Petty has ever written."

In fact, most fans could implicitly relate to the 'Learning To Fly' lyrics in which the story begins… "Well I started out down a dirty road /

Started out all alone / And the sun went down as I crossed the hill / And the town lit up the world got still / I'm learning to fly, but I ain't got wings/ Coming down is the hardest thing". Should the lines be taken at face value or is this just another one of Petty's cryptic storylines? Both. One of the miraculous things about Tom's writing style is that he can pen a song that speaks directly to the listener's circumstance. The song is about what you interpret it to be. Tom won't explain his lyrics and he won't ask you to change your mind about what the song means to you. That's the beauty of his songwriting style.

'Kings Highway' – with its driving snare drum part and ringing guitars – presents an optimistic tone as the singer tries to convince his love that things are bound to get better if they just believe that. Good fortune will come their way – eventually.

The title track of the album is now better remembered for its star-studded video than for the song itself. Johnny Depp starred in the role of Eddie, a teenager who left his Midwest home and headed to Hollywood to make it big in the music business. Faye Dunaway appeared in the video as Eddie's manager and *Burn Notice* actress Gabrielle Anwar was cast as his girlfriend, whom he met in a tattoo parlor. Several other celebrities – Terence Trent D'Arby, Chynna Phillips and Matt LeBlanc – all had roles as well. The music video expands the song's storyline and follows Eddie's rise to stardom before succumbing to alcohol and ego. By the end of the video, he's lost everything and has been abandoned by his record company and girlfriend.

The next song on the album, 'Two Gunslingers' never received the attention it should have. The song tells the tale of two old-time gunfighters who meet in the middle of the street for a duel when both realize that it's pointless. What are they fighting for? They decide to take control of their own lives and vow to make better choices in the future – choices that don't include gun violence. The townspeople assembled for the gunfight are none too pleased that they have been cheated out of their entertainment for the afternoon.

'The Dark Of The Sun' follows up on the theme of two people banding together. This time, it's a man following in the path of a woman he considers to be brave. He wants to achieve the same freedom she has.

'All Or Nothin'' represents the midpoint of the record. *Rolling Stone*'s Parke Puterbaugh called this particular tune out in his review. "On 'All or Nothin'', smog-covered Los Angeles becomes a metaphor for a nation of hyperactive overachievers choking on greed and technology. Petty sings, with taunting, apocalyptic undertones, 'So keep one eye on the weather/You had it good, you wanted better.'"

Many tracks on *Into The Great Wide Open* focus on the theme of staying true to one's self or giving in to temptation and taking the easy way out. That's certainly the case in 'All The Wrong Reasons', which talks of how trouble often blows in with no warning and it's how we choose to deal with life's bumps in the road that truly defines our content of character.

In 'Too Good To Be True' we meet a woman who's on the verge of getting everything she wants and fears that it might all just be too good to be real. Still, she won't give in and she wears hope as a shield that will protect her from future disappointment.

The hardest rocking song on the album is definitely 'Out In The Cold', which tells the story of a man who's down on his luck who can't see what will come next for him or how he'll claw his way out of his predicament.

Fans completely embraced the next song on the record: 'You And I Will Meet Again'. The singer assures his lover that the pair will cross paths again someday in the future – when it's least expected. That being the case, goodbyes are not required as they part this time around. They'll go their separate ways and think of each other until they one day find their way back to each other. The song is wistful but uplifting and gives you the feeling that maybe those doors you closed long ago could actually open again one day in the future. Tom double tracked his vocals on this one and the harmonies he created are lush and beautiful.

From the hopeful tone of 'You And I Will Meet Again', the record veers into a celebration of youth with 'Makin' Some Noise', which documents a young man playing nights in a local bar somewhere. He may be an unknown musician but he sings with reckless abandon that he's "makin' some noise".

The record closes with 'Built To Last', co-written with Jeff Lynne. This old-timey number rejoices in the fact that through the ups and downs that is a romantic relationship, this pair has stayed together and will make their way forward in the future. Despite some of the cautious tones of the rest of the album, this song leaves nothing to chance. The couple will stay "on until forever" no matter what happens.

The album resonated with fans and critics like Parke Puterbaugh, who saluted Tom's progression in songwriting and execution, saying, "On this album, Petty seldom falls into the pained yowl so evident on *Let Me Up (I've Had Enough)*, his most recent outing with The Heartbreakers. These songs are rendered for the most part in the calm voice of someone who has emerged from a soulful bout of contemplation with a new perspective."

★ ★ ★

When the 1991 Grammy nominations rolled around, Tom got the nod in two categories: Best Rock Performance By a Duo or Group with Vocal for *Into The Great Wide Open* and Best Rock Song for the single 'Learning To Fly'.

Even with 'Learning To Fly', the album didn't nearly reach the heights that *Full Moon Fever* did. AllMusic's Stephen Thomas Erlewine had this to say about the album in general: "There are a number of minor gems – 'Learning To Fly', 'Kings Highway', 'Into The Great Wide Open' – but there are no knockouts, either… enough for a pleasant listen, but not enough to resonate like his best work."

Much of the media coverage for *Into The Great Wide Open* centered on the fact that the band was still together. That storyline – Tom Petty ready to sever ties and go solo for good – was just too enticing for reporters and they dwelled on it, which didn't help much in terms of cheering up The Heartbreakers. During an interview with *Rolling Stone's* David Wild, Mike Campbell admitted that everyone thought the band could break up at any time but that feeling was predicated from way back in 1979. "All the time, right from day one. It's a miracle that this band stayed together for two weeks. I don't really know why we're still together. There must be a bond that even we're not aware of."

A three-month North American tour, with opening act Chris Whitley, was set for the end of August through the end of November. The obligatory "homecoming" show at the O'Connell Center in Gainesville took place on October 26. Karen Schoemer of the *Gainesville Sun* interviewed Petty prior to the concert and shared her insights with readers. "The Tom Petty you get in person is not all that different from the one you get onstage…. Like his music, Petty is direct, unpretentious. He's not too keen on publicity: 'Being on the cover of *Rolling Stone* terrifies me,' he says. But once he gets going, he's a thorough talker; when he hits on a subject, he likes to get to the bottom of it. And his conversation, like his songs, communicates a sense of conviction. He's easy to believe in."

Schoemer went on to make a bold statement regarding the band's latest record: "*Into The Great Wide Open* uses simple but elegant metaphorical language to look at the promises of adolescence, and what can become of dreams later in life. He is the only rocker over 40 making honest, articulate and non-patronizing music for and about his primary audience: teenagers." It was an interesting statement considering how many older fans attend Heartbreakers concerts. But, it was clear that the songs on *Into The Great Wide Open* as well as the previous album *Full Moon Fever* both look forward as well as reminisce in ways that appeal to the psyche at any age.

November 24 was the last day of the tour, and the concert that evening, at Oakland Arena, was filmed and released later that year under the title *Take The Highway*.

The tour was notable because it did a great deal to bring The Heartbreakers together and mend fences, and they had also drafted in utility player Scott Thurston. Originally from Oregon, Scott is a musician's musician and is an adept guitarist, keyboard player and singer. He joined The Heartbreakers as more of a "sidebreaker" but quickly became indispensable and is now a Heartbreaker in his own right. In 1999, Tom told *Rolling Stone* that, "He's a good buffer between the rest of us. When we're fighting or have some cliquishness, he's good at getting in there and saying, 'Let's look at it this way,' because Duckhead, as we call him, is neutral. He doesn't come from Florida, wasn't there when this or that happened."

As an all-around utility player, Scott was a necessary addition to The Heartbreakers. Onstage and in the studio he sings harmony and plays the guitar, ukulele, bass, harmonica and keyboards. Born in Medford, Oregon, on January 10, 1952, he learned his craft as a session musician and band member, playing with Iggy & The Stooges as well as The Motels, and he spent 10 years backing Jackson Browne. He recorded with many other well-known rockers too, including Bonnie Raitt, The Cult, Melissa Etheridge and Glenn Frey. Once he started gigging with Tom Petty & The Heartbreakers, the band knew they couldn't do without him and invited him to join the band on a full-time basis.

The set for Touring Into The Great Wide Open was also a departure from the simple Persian rug and tasteful lighting the band usually selected. "Mad King Ludwig", otherwise known as Ludwig II of Bavaria, was the inspiration for the 1991 set. (Ludwig reigned from 1864–1886 and was integral in the construction of several stunning palaces and the famous Neuschwanstein Castle in Schwangau, Germany.) The king had a hunting lodge built around a giant living tree that had been inspired by a set for Wagner's opera *Tristan And Isolde*. Set designer Jim Lenahan took this concept and created the Touring Into The Great Wide Open set around a tree and castle-in-the-woods theme. He continued the rustic lodge theme with bearskin rugs, chandeliers and a projected forest in the background.

An original member of Mudcrutch back in Gainesville who stayed close to Tom even after leaving the band, Jim has been designing the sets and lighting for Tom's tours since the very early days. Today Jim is a sought-after lighting and set designer and has worked with many musicians in addition to The Heartbreakers, like Sarah McLachlan, Jennifer Lopez, Bob Dylan, John Mayer, Toby Keith and others. He lectures on production design at the University of Florida, University of Southern California and UCLA. He's also a consultant for Walt Disney Imagineering, for which he created special effects lighting for *Aida* on Broadway and video projection for the renovated Space Mountain theme park ride. He's had an eclectic career and he always strikes the right tone when it comes to the set and lighting for Petty's tours.

The 1991 North American tour was a financial and critical success and a European outing followed in the spring of 1992. Springtime was actually treating Tom Petty quite well. He'd successfully gotten The Heartbreakers back on track and he was enjoying a quiet patch in his home life. While the late eighties were punctuated with frequent rows with – and even a few trial separations from – his wife, Jane, Tom reported that all was well in the first few years of the nineties. "I'm very much in love with Jane," Tom told *Rolling Stone*'s David Wild at the time. "I'm still thrilled about her. She's the most honest, frank person I've ever met. At this point I don't really like to be very far from her for very long. But there were times when we definitely were not getting along, when we fought like fucking Apaches, you know. I'm lucky they still let me live in this neighbourhood."

After the tour, Tom was at home in California spending some quiet time with his family when he heard about the verdict in the Rodney King/police brutality case. On March 3, 1991, Los Angeles police had pursued King – a black man who was on parole for robbery – in a high-speed car chase before catching up to him. King was dragged from his vehicle and beaten by several white officers. A local resident videotaped the incident and the footage was shown all over the world, highlighting the continuing brutality and possible department-accepted racism of the LAPD. The trial was held in nearby Simi Valley and all four police officers involved in the incident were acquitted of assault with a deadly weapon. The verdict caused widespread rioting, looting and arson throughout Los Angeles between April 29 and May 4, 1992.

"I was watching the TV. I was upset by it," recalled Tom. "I could either pace around the room or write a song." He ended up penning 'Peace In LA'. It's one of Petty's most literal songs. Its simplicity makes Tom's intentions clear: he doesn't want his home city of Los Angeles to tear itself apart over this miscarriage of justice. The band put the song down on tape immediately and MCA released it as a single. Tom hoped the song would commiserate with and calm the residents of Los Angeles.

The video for the song featured scenes of the violence and National Guard troops and police, as well as clips from televised news reports covering the King beating and subsequent trial. All proceeds from the single were donated to charities serving the victims of the Los Angeles Riots.

Tom spent the rest of 1992 focusing on his family, with the exception of an October 16 appearance at Madison Square Garden for the Bob Dylan Columbia Records 30th Anniversary Tribute concert. The four-hour concert of all concerts featured musical director G.E. Smith (*Saturday Night Live*'s bandleader) and a house band consisting of the surviving members of Booker T. & The MGs: Booker T. Jones on organ, Donald "Duck" Dunn on bass and Steve Cropper on guitar. Jim Keltner and Anton Fig played drums.

A who's who of rock royalty came together to honor Bob by singing his songs. John Mellencamp sang 'Like A Rolling Stone', Stevie Wonder handled 'Blowin' In The Wind', husband-and-wife team of Johnny Cash and June Carter turned in an incredible performance of 'It Ain't Me Babe'. Tom and The Heartbreakers, with Roger McGuinn, took on 'Mr. Tambourine Man'.

Dylan only took to the stage for the last four numbers, though the highlight was surely 'My Back Pages' with McGuinn, Petty, Neil Young, Eric Clapton and George Harrison.

The event was a happy one that each Heartbreaker revels in to this day. Columbia released a live album based on the concert, *Bob Dylan: The 30th Anniversary Concert Celebration*, on August 24, 1993.

On the whole, 1993 turned out to be quiet for Tom Petty. The band decided to take a bit of a break but some business was tended to. In 1993 the US Supreme Court upheld a previous ruling that Tom Petty's 'Runnin' Down A Dream' did not infringe the copyright of a song written by plaintiff Martin Allen Fine. Fine had named Tom Petty, Jeff Lynne, Mike Campbell, MCA Records, SBK April Music, Warner Bros. and Gone Gator Music in his court filings with the United States Court of Appeals, Ninth Circuit. Fine alleged that he wrote and recorded a song called 'Ascending' in 1976 and that it's identical to 'Runnin' Down A Dream'. The court did not agree.

Towards the end of the year, the band put on two "homecoming" concerts at Bayfront Center Arena in St. Petersburg, Florida, on

November 2, and at the O'Connell Center in Gainesville on the 4th. Carlene Carter opened both shows.

The hour-long documentary *Tom Petty: Going Home* aired on the Disney Channel and, on November 16, MCA Records released *Greatest Hits*, closing out the band's contractual obligation to the label, and adding one new single – 'Mary Jane's Last Dance' – for the album. The song unexpectedly caught fire and went to number one on the *Billboard* Album Rock Tracks chart and number 52 on the UK Singles Chart. Its popularity – was it about marijuana or not? – surprised Tom. Like so many of Tom's other songs, this one told the story of an empowered girl who left home young and never stayed long with any of her paramours. Or, was it just about taking another toke? You'll need to decide for yourself what the song is all about because the downright bizarre music video won't give you a clue. Instead of following the lyrics from the song itself, the video shows Tom as a night-shift mortician and actress Kim Basinger as a "client" that he's taken a liking to. He steals her from the morgue and takes her home for an evening of dinner and dancing. As the sun begins to rise, he drives to the ocean where he commits her to the ocean's spray and waves. (The following year at the MTV Music Awards Tom would win Best Male Video for 'Mary Jane's Last Dance' as well as receive the Video Vanguard Award for lifetime achievement in the field.)

The success of 'Mary Jane's Last Dance' was bittersweet because it turned out to be the last studio recording in which drummer Stan Lynch participated. After the sessions, sources close to the band say that Lynch simply packed up and headed for his home in St. Augustine, Florida. He had several other projects on his plate and he left town quite unceremoniously and with no discussion about what lay ahead for him and the band.

CHAPTER 10

A Time Of Change—
Wildflowers (1994–1995)

"I've become a little less judgmental and critical. I'm more concerned with myself because I've realized that I can't change anybody else, but I can change myself."

$-$ T.P.

O ne of the things that surprised Tom the most about life was the fact that his songwriting could still evolve – even after 18 years in the business. He was in the midst of a stretch of effortless writing, where the songs just came to him like gifts from some unseen admirer. Tom felt that he still had a lot to say through his music and that fans – new and long-term – were willing to listen. His contract with MCA was fulfilled and he was looking forward to his first record release on Warner Bros. He decided that he wanted to go solo this time around and in early 1994 set to work on an album with producer Rick Rubin.

Known as a wunderkind of the recording business, Rick co-founded rap label Def Jam Records with Russell Simmons in 1984 before creating American Recordings. He'd worked with a veritable who's who in genres as varied as metal, rap and rock. His credits are as varied

as Run-DMC, Public Enemy, Beastie Boys, Danzig, Slayer, Red Hot
Chili Peppers, Black Crowes and Jayhawks. Rick was just 31 years old
when he went to work on *Wildflowers* with Petty.

While Tom was adamant that this was a "solo" record, he still wanted
The Heartbreakers' involvement. The difference was, only he, Rick and
Mike would produce the music. While everyone else's input was always
heard, it wasn't particularly sought out in this instance. Stan decided that
he would have nothing to do with the new record. He'd heard a few
of the demo tracks and wasn't impressed. The music wasn't where he
wanted to go and he had no interest in being a session player. He told
Tom as much. He didn't want to play on the album and he wouldn't
go out on tour to support it either. This stance didn't do much to
improve the already tattered relationship that Stan and Tom shared.
Some outsiders felt that Stan was pushing Tom unnecessarily. Others felt
Tom was making Stan feel like an outsider in his own band. One thing
was certain. Neither man was happy about how things were progressing.

The end of a friendship, though, almost always comes as a shock –
even if the relationship has been withering for years. So it was for Stan
Lynch and Tom Petty. It's been said that Stan was fired or quit the
band 20 times during his tenure with The Heartbreakers. Tom and Stan
were often at odds. Case in point was an argument they had onstage in
1986 during one of the concerts they backed for Dylan. Tom told Jaan
Uhelszki of *Mojo* this story in 1999. "Me and Stan got in a big fight, and
I left the stage. Stan was wound-up about something, and he gave me
the finger during the show. I just took my guitar and walked off. Left.
They didn't know what to do," admits Tom. "And I guess Al Kooper
sat in, and they just carried on with Al. I went to my dressing room
really mad, I wouldn't come out. Then Bob came in and said, 'Come
on, come back. John Lee Hooker is here and he's going to play. Come
on. Let's go play with John Lee Hooker.' I was still mad, but I went
back to the stage. Then John Lee Hooker came out and kicked our
asses. He was just transcendental… That was some night." Incidents like
this over the years took their toll on both Tom and Stan.

By the mid-nineties, Stan no longer felt at home in the band. On
the eve of the release of *Wildflowers*, Stan played his last official gig as a

Heartbreaker on October 2, 1994. "Neil Young's Bridge School Benefit in San Francisco was the last time we played together," remembers Tom. "The Heartbreakers very rarely have a terrible gig; it never happens. But the first night of those shows, there was a bad vibe on the stage and we were terrible. In the van going back we had a big argument: is there anybody here who doesn't *care* about what's happening up there. The next day we did another show and by then Stan had pissed everyone off. I think I tried to talk him down after that, but it was irreparable; the marriage had ended."

The pair had butted heads from the very beginning but made it work for the sake of The Heartbreakers as a unit. The turmoil caused by Tom's initial foray into a solo career with *Full Moon Fever* and later with *Wildflowers* – as well as his participation in the Traveling Wilburys – took an emotional toll on the drummer that, in the end, couldn't be denied. It was time for him to move on and he'd known this day was coming for several years. Even so, it was a sad moment for everyone in the band. Mike Campbell conceded at the time that, "Groups are a very complicated thing. It's like a family. It's like a business relationship. It's a very emotional thing. You care about each other, and you tug just like brothers; you're jealous, and then you love each other. It's a very complicated monster."

Looking back, it's hard to say if Lynch left the band or if Tom expressly requested that he leave. The truth probably lies somewhere in between. In a recent interview with Jayne Moore of *Songwriter Universe*, Stan explains, "When I grew up, drummers were explosive, like buckets of bolts rolling downhill. The drums for me were not really a discipline but more of an expression. After a while, drums became relegated to sort of just the timekeeper. It was a different job, and not a job I wanted to have. I began to think I was getting in the way more than anything, and it was time for me to step aside and let everyone get on with their lives and get what they needed. I was making the wrong noise. There's a graceful time to walk away from anything."

Stan second-guessed himself a bit during a November 1995 interview with Bill DeYoung of the *Gainesville Sun,* though. "Am I a fool to let it go? Maybe. But look at what I get. I have this whole life that now is my own. I can do whatever I want with it.

"I don't think I'll ever be around that good a group of musicians in my life again. I'll never have access to that sound. That's the thing I dream about. It's like having a great old horse. I really miss the feeling of being on that horse. For me, the whole Tom Petty & The Heartbreakers experience was so incredibly rich. Out of a thousand dollars there was a nickel's worth of downside. What a life! Tons of dough, tons of women, tons of adulation, tons of miles that you'd never get to see without this. Enough experience for 20 lifetimes and at a time in your life when you're strong enough to take it. And it couldn't have happened to me without those particular players. Great characters to have been onstage with a couple of thousand times. Great guys to jump around with, funny as shit, wackiest of the wacky. They don't get any crazier than those assholes. They're wonderful."

One has to hope that even when things were the most tense between Stan and Tom that they still remembered the amazing times they'd shared together as members of Tom Petty & The Heartbreakers. Tom once reminisced about an event that happened sometime between 1983 and 1985 when he and Stan were in Florida at the same time and decided to shake things up one night. "We....decided to drive up to this club where heavy metal was being played," he recalls. "We just had two acoustic guitars and we strolled out there and started doing country songs. But everybody just started yelling. They wanted to hear me do 'Breakdown'." Those indeed were better times for the men.

Leaving The Heartbreakers was probably the most difficult thing Stan Lynch ever had to do but he felt he had to do it if he wanted to see his own musical goals come to fruition. While he and Tom didn't remain buddy-buddy after the split, Stan still has a healthy admiration for the man who led The Heartbreakers to such success. "When I put myself in Tom's shoes, I get tired. I couldn't be what he is," says Stan. "He's all the time, round–the–clock creative. Always. Tom, if he has four days off he thinks he's lazy. But he gives you this impression that it's all so easy and it's so gentle and I know he works hard."

Stan went on to forge a successful songwriting career of his own and has worked closely with Don Henley for many years. He co-wrote several songs with Henley, including 'Drivin' With Your Eyes Closed' for *Building The Perfect Beast* as well as 'The Last Worthless Evening', 'How Bad Do You Want It' and 'Gimme What You Got' for *The End Of The Innocence*. By the time Henley recorded *Inside Job*, Stan was co-writing the majority of the material. Most famously Stan co-wrote 'Learn To Be Still', which was recorded for The Eagles' reunion album, *Hell Freezes Over*.

In the intervening years, Stan has also penned songs for Tim McGraw, The Mavericks, Sister Hazel, Toto and other musicians.

★ ★ ★

When it was clear that Stan wasn't going to change his mind about playing on the *Wildflowers* sessions, Tom searched for a new drummer. Auditions were held during recording sessions at Sound City and Ocean Way Recording in Los Angeles.

The band tried to keep the auditions on the QT. Needing to be deliberate and selective about whom they invited to audition, they ensured this was not going to be a free-for-all and they certainly didn't want any media attention during the hunt for a new band member. Longtime session drummer Steve Ferrone, who'd played with Average White Band and Eric Clapton, was one of the musicians invited to audition. At that point The Heartbreakers had already seen a few other musicians like Russ Kunkel (Jackson Browne, Neil Young, Stevie Nicks) and Ed Greene (The Jacksons, Steely Dan). The Heartbreakers had also worked with Dave Grohl – the drummer formerly with Nirvana – prior to Ferrone's audition. Grohl had even performed with the band on *Saturday Night Live* in November of 1994. Ultimately though, Dave had other musical endeavors in the works (Foo Fighters) so he wasn't able to fill the full-time role and that meant The Heartbreakers had to continue to search for the right drummer to fill Stan's slot.

At the time of the audition, Ferrone didn't even know who he was meeting. "I got a call to go out for an audition, but I wasn't told who it was for. This was in 1994," Steve recalls. "So my gears were turning… 'Who could it be?' It was all very top secret, you know? But then I showed up at this studio and there's Tom Petty and Mike Campbell sitting there. Well, I figured out pretty quickly who I was auditioning for." Steve knew Mike

Campbell and had worked with him on a George Harrison project not long ago. To this day Steve thinks that it was George who first suggested to Tom that Steve would make a good addition to The Heartbreakers. At the audition Mike and Tom taught Steve a new song they were working on: 'You Don't Know How It Feels'. Tracking went well and, according to Steve, when they listened back, Tom said, "'Wow, what a difference a drummer makes.' Then he turned to me and said, 'Don't worry, Steve, you've won.' And that was it."

Reporter Joe Bosso once asked Steve how it felt to replace so many great drummers and Steve's response was this: "I'm always the second man asked to the dance, but I'm not complaining because I've been to a lot of nice dances. I've replaced Stan Lynch in Tom Petty & The Heartbreakers. I've replaced Phil Collins with Eric Clapton. I've replaced Roger Taylor with Duran Duran. There's a few choice ones right there…. These drummers have played on amazing records, and I have a tremendous amount of respect for their work. To be asked to go in and sit down and play the parts that they established, I'm flattered and honored. Also, I guess it means that, on some level, I'm that good – or at least in somebody's mind I am."

Steve Ferrone was born in Brighton, England, on April 25, 1950. He learned the drums at an early age and, at 12, opened for The Who before they were famous at a tiny venue called Uncle Bunnie's Chinese Jazz Club. He went to school in France at the Conservatoire de Musique in Nice where he developed his signature sound. Since that time he's played with musicians as varied as Clapton, Bee Gees, Peter Frampton, Chaka Khan, Pat Metheny, George Benson and others. He was a member of The Average White Band from 1974 to 1982.

Steve recorded drums on the rest of the *Wildflowers* sessions and has been a staple of The Heartbreakers' sound ever since. When fans first heard that Stan was out and Steve was in, they had some misgivings. Stan was a fan favourite because of his high-energy drumming and crazy off-stage antics. Still, Steve won everyone over with his musicianship during the tour to support the album.

The existing Heartbreakers are often asked to compare their two drummers. This is what Mike Campbell has to say about it. "Stan and Steve are completely different. Stan always played with more of a 'member of the band' mentality. He was always just part of the band and a friend from early on, and there was that kind of bond that is unique to him. He was essential to helping us find our original sound and he was part of that sound. The way he played really complemented that, and you can't take that away from him. He's a great background singer and he was really important on that level early on and for many years. Stan was really great live; he had energy and power and confidence, and was a cheerleader, too. He would get us up when we were down, and he was a real strong and emotional force, especially live where his energy was really powerful. We got to the point in the studio where we got really pissy with each other and it got really uncomfortable for him – it was time for him to go and do the other things that he wanted to do.

"Steve Ferrone came in," Mike continues. "He's more of a session guy, and his approach is very professional and accurate, and his time is really good. He's great in the studio because he's very consistent and he doesn't get emotional or wrapped up in it. He brings sort of a 'studio cat' mentality. He does his job, and you don't have to think about whether the drums are going to speed up or slow down. He just gets his job done and you can focus on the song and not get hung up on that. He's a sweet guy, and he brought a lot of professionalism and accuracy, and Steve is great live, too. But it's hard to compare two different human beings; they are both great in their own way and equally talented in different ways."

With Steve on the drummer's stool, the band could get down to work on *Wildflowers* – something producer Rick Rubin was looking forward to. He'd been a fan of the band for years and appreciated what they are all about. "It's like a lost art, what they do," asserts Rubin. "Great players, great band interaction, great songwriting and it shows. When you go to see their concert …. you could sing along with every song. It's mind-numbing, how many great songs they have."

In an October 2000 interview with *Mix* magazine's Maureen Droney, Rubin talked more about Tom's approach in the studio: "Most artists only hear their own instrument. Not all, of course; Tom Petty is a good example of someone who doesn't. He really is a record-making craftsman.

He hears the whole thing. Some of the things I'm most proud of are things I've done with Tom. Like the *Wildflowers* album. I really like it a lot; it sounds like it was made on a weekend. Of course, it took us two years to make it sound like it was made on a weekend – the right weekend!"

Wildflowers, with its organic sound and live orchestra on some tracks, showcases the maturation of Petty's songwriting. The tracks meander from ballads like 'Wildflowers' and 'Crawling Back To You' to rockers like 'You Wreck Me' and 'You Don't Know How It Feels'.

Warner Bros. was ecstatic the first time executives heard the record. There was just one hitch: 'Girl On LSD', a track in the album's original sequence. They felt it couldn't stay on the album because it was too controversial but they were fine releasing it as the B-side to the single 'You Don't Know How It Feels', which went on to be a hit and reached number 13 on *Billboard*'s Hot 100 chart.

Tom still scratches his head about that one. "I thought the record company made a terrible mistake releasing 'You Don't Know How It Feels' as a single, but I was wrong." Indeed, the song is still beloved among fans and is part of the band's live set even now.

Most music journalists respected the new album and even those who had a few critical things to say about it were generally pleased with the record. Jim Greer reviewed *Wildflowers* for *Spin*'s January 1995 issue and asserted that, "There's no denying the languid grace of Petty's songwriting." *Harp*'s Fred Mills had this to say about the album: "Producer Rick Rubin brought out the best in Petty, who operated without his usual Heartbreakers net but employed many a Heartbreakers-esque turn (e.g., the blazing 'You Wreck Me' and the twanging, bluesy 'Cabin Down Below'). The ballads are exquisitely etched, too, in particular the symphonic 'Wake Up Time', which, like its stylistic predecessor 'Southern Accents', subliminally conjures wistful images of a simpler, bygone antebellum era."

Mike also received critical acclaim for his work on the album, both as co-producer and lead guitarist. At the time, *Mojo* reviewer Ben Edmonds gave him this compliment: "Campbell's style lies somewhere between self-affacement and in-your-facement, a Clapton who chooses to play more like a McGuinn."

The album begins with the song 'Wildflowers'. Like so many other tunes penned by Petty, this one pivots on our innate desire to be free. "You belong among the wildflowers / You belong in a boat out at sea / Sail away, kill off the hours / You belong somewhere you feel free".

The next track opens with the strains of harmonica and a drumbeat that launches 'You Don't Know How It Feels'. The song would become one of the band's calling cards for years to come – mainly because of the call to action: "let's roll another joint". As one may imagine, conservative American radio declined to play the album cut of this song and instead obliged the band to provide a tweaked version in which the word "joint" was obscured (played backwards, to be precise). It was hard to believe that Americans could be so frightened of a discussion about marijuana.

The video for this song features Tom standing at a mic, singing and playing harmonica and guitar as the scene behind him continually shifts between circus acts, a vaudeville show, an old-timey Main Street and a few Alice in Wonderland-type acid trip scenes that show a man watering some huge, brightly colored flowers. The word "joint" is also obscured in the video and the mic covers Tom's mouth whenever the camera is on him for the phrase "let's roll another *tnioj*".

The album segues to the double-time 'Time To Move On', which really does give the listener the impression that it's time to hit the road and make a change. The singer doesn't know where he's headed or what might come next but he does know it's time to do something different.

From there, *Wildflowers* launches into a more raucous number, 'You Wreck Me', which was co-written by Mike. One gets an impression that tonight has to go right for the singer and his lover, or he'll be absolutely devastated. Mike's soaring guitar solo on this track helped make it one of Tom's most-requested songs in concert. Tom actually originally titled the track 'You Rock Me', and that just didn't sit right with The Heartbreakers. There was something clunky about the phrase. Then, one night, it hit Tom. Change "Rock" to "Wreck". That tiny change made the song click for the band.

'It's Good To Be King' is another song from the album that the band loves to play. Tom feels its theme was central to what he was thinking about most often during the recording of *Wildflowers*: "… how people get so obsessed with that desire to be king, to be wealthy or powerful, as if that might solve their problems. But it's nevertheless kind of an instinct that we all seem to have. It's also just a big daydream," says Tom. "Maybe a man's king when he's fallen in love and raised a family. Maybe that's the greatest reward there is in life. And, strangely enough, available to anyone."

The album continues with the achingly beautiful 'Only A Broken Heart' in which the singer seems resigned to the fact that heartbreak is sometimes inevitable. AllMusic critic Matthew Greenwald wrote this in his review of the track: "One of the most graceful and underrated Tom Petty compositions, 'Only A Broken Heart' is driven by one of his finest and most subtle melodies. The sense of melancholy that is framed by the chords is a perfect reflection of the lyric, which is also stunning. Petty's world-weary sentiments – in this case the realization of emotions he knows all too well – are stark and direct, and without a trace of self-pity. An excellently arranged recording, it also features a fabulous, lyrical 12-string acoustic guitar solo from Petty, one of his rare leads."

The record then takes a turn from the gentle heartbreak of 'Only A Broken Heart' to the sheer lasciviousness of the blues-soaked 'Honey Bee'. The singer warns his sweetie not to tell anyone about their illicit affair, which might not be altogether on the up and up. Tom and Mike swap scorching guitar solos on this one.

As we pass the midpoint of the record, the listener encounters the introspective 'Don't Fade On Me'. The singer turns his thoughts to someone he loved once. Someone who's changed and he can't figure out why. What changed? What forced this person to abandon everything that had been important? The song is sweet and sad with just a tiny bit of hope mixed in.

Producer Rick Rubin himself had a favourite track on the album as he told author Jake Brown for this book *In The Studio*: "There's a song on *Wildflowers* that really moves me called 'Hard On Me'. It's one of the very first things we cut together, so it's got some emotional relevance to me personally. Both the song is good – the tone of it is great – and the mood of the performance just captures the song perfectly. It's a perfect moment in time. It sounds really real, really live, personal and intimate and of a moment. It's personally revelatory lyrically, open and honest. It's just a beautiful song."

Nearly everyone sings along to 'Cabin Down Below', a simple song about the singer taking his girl to a hideaway cabin in the woods. It's their secret place to be together. This one rocks in concert but the band rarely adds it to its set list for some reason.

So many of the issues *Wildflowers* tackles revolve around forks in the road and choices made – for good or bad. 'To Find A Friend' tells the story of a man who, in the midst of a midlife crisis, dumps his wife and sets off to create an entirely new life for himself. But, things don't end up quite the way he pictured them. His wife finds a new boyfriend who moves in, making it clear that the old status quo has been torn asunder for good.

As the record enters its home stretch, the listener encounters 'A Higher Place'. The song imparts the idea that trouble can be overcome if we act at the right moment and aren't afraid to get help from others. By the end of the song you aren't quite sure if the singer's predicament has been solved, but your hopeful he's got the tools to make whatever repairs are necessary.

While the singer may have taken his 'Honey Bee' to the 'Cabin Down Below', 'House In the Woods' is about a much more loving and mature relationship – one in which the singer promises to spend the rest of his days and the rest of his nights with the one he loves. The only option is love for all eternity.

Many of the songs on the record tell vivid stories about characters down on their luck and those just looking for a way to survive. A pinnacle achievement of Tom's in that regard is the ballad 'Crawling Back To You', with its wistful refrain of "I'm so tired of being tired / Sure as night will follow day / Most things I worry about / Never happen anyway".

The record closes with the telling 'Wake Up Time'. The message is clear, live your life with conviction. Don't sleepwalk through it. Find your soulmate and he or she will help you get through the inevitable pain that accompanies all of life's greatest joys.

Tom believes he was in the right frame of mind during the *Wildflowers* sessions to create something different and he also took a chance by working with a new producer. Rubin's approach and style are so different from Jeff Lynne's and that took Tom and the entire band to a higher place.

"I think his [Rick Rubin's] contribution to the album can't be underestimated," Tom said at the time. "Rick really pushed me harder than anyone dared push me for years. I mean hard – 'Do it again! You can do better than that!' Initially, he came over and spent an afternoon listening to the songs that I had, and he had some astute observations right off the bat, which really impressed me and Mike, because we'd discussed what was wrong with the songs before he came over. He had a huge impact on the music – he brought us back to where we were when we began."

Since *Wildflowers* was released at the end of 1994, it was clear that most of 1995 would be spent on the road. The band, along with new drummer Steve Ferrone, toured with opening act Pete Drodge from February through October of that year. The North American Dogs With Wings tour visited 34 states. They also played in Vancouver and Toronto, Canada.

This tour was different from previous outings in two ways: the band had a new drummer in Steve Ferrone and Howie had requested his own tour bus – ostensibly to care for his new German shepherd named Dingo.

Benmont recalls the love Howie had for that dog and how cool it was to see a dog on tour. "There's Howie, playing his bass and singing better harmonies than you ever heard in your life, and there's this giant dog at his feet, looking up at him with all the love in the world. I think Howie and Dingo were literally best friends."

Howie was never one to kick back at the hotel bar with the guys after a show but now, with his own tour bus, the band saw him less and less – even when they were spending months at a time out on the road playing gigs across America. Years later Tom reflected on this time period and said, "I think Howie was beginning to fade on us a little bit. He had big problems beginning then." Benmont agreed, saying, "If you have any proclivity to misbehave, it's bad when you start isolating yourself – and I'm speaking entirely from personal experience. Isolation is not good for the addict. It's just more time by yourself to do drugs."

When the tour rolled into Alpine Valley, near where Howie grew up, he reached out to an old friend who put together a party backstage before the show. The invited guests were musicians Howie had played with while growing up in the area, as well as friends. On the day of the gig, however, Howie refused to leave his tour bus for the gathering. After that day, he never had any contact with some of his closest friends in Wisconsin again.

The *Wildflowers* tour wrapped up at the Lakefront Arena in New Orleans, Louisiana, on October 8, but fans still had something to look forward to: the November 20 release of the *Playback* box set of which Andrew Abrahams of *People* magazine said, "For TP devotees, this is the hymnal from which to sing his praises." The six-CD set includes 92 tracks – hits as well as B-sides, unreleased tracks and even some of the early recordings by Mudcrutch. Every Tom Petty & The Heartbreakers fan should have *Playback* in his or her collection. *Mojo*'s Ben Edmonds concurs, saying, "Distilling story, music and magic into three minutes is a manifestation of the miraculous. Finding fresh ways to make the three minute-miracle happen with consistency for 20 years, as Tom Petty & The Heartbreakers have done, is something else again."

★ ★ ★

It just so happened that in 1995 Rick Rubin was also working with country music legend Johnny Cash on his 82nd studio album and he had an inspiration: what if Johnny drafted Tom Petty & The Heartbreakers as his backup band for this record? Cash's gravelly voice was perfectly matched to The Heartbreakers' guitar jangle. The time was right and everyone in the band looked forward to working with Johnny, who was not only an icon of country music but was breaking new ground with the recordings he'd collaborated on with Rick. Other musicians – like Red Hot Chili Peppers' bassist Flea and Fleetwood Mac's Lindsey

Buckingham and Mick Fleetwood – were on hand for some sessions as well.

This record, *Unchained*, in particular, would showcase several new Cash songs as well as unexpected covers. Johnny sang an aching rendition of Tom's own 'Southern Accents' in addition to Soundgarden's 'Rusty Cage' and Beck's 'Rowboat'. At the time of the record's release Cash admitted that he originally didn't think he could pull off 'Rusty Cage' or 'Rowboat' until Rick and Tom intervened. "Well, if a song doesn't feel right, then it isn't communicating. That was the problem I had with 'Rusty Cage'," Cash told Barney Hoskens for a *Mojo* magazine article. "But Rick and Tom came up with an arrangement that was real comfortable for me, and I think it may be one of my favourite songs to perform now. 'Rowboat' was another one I turned down: as it was, it wasn't for me. I couldn't see a way that I could do it."

In an interview with *Uncut*'s Nick Hasted, Tom talks about his friend Johnny: "He was an interesting artist because he's pictured as a country artist, but he wasn't necessarily completely in that bag. I always thought of him as a folk artist because he knew so much about folk music. And the country that he performed wasn't really much like any other country that you'd heard. It was an unusual thing, his bag was pretty wide. I mean he could trace folk music back to early Irish shanties or hymns or whatever you call 'em. And I remember many times on a break he might sing one of them with June [Carter Cash, his wife]."

Tom went on to recount a story from one of the sessions with Johnny: "I remember one thing that I thought was kind of spiritual. The tape-machine broke in the middle of a particularly hot moment in the studio. And instead of freaking out, June came out in the room where everyone was looking pretty low and she said, 'I think if we all sing a hymn, maybe God'll fix the tape-machine.' Not a procedure I had seen before! And John said, 'Yeah, let's sing a hymn.' And June said, 'Yeah, but we've gotta all hold hands', so we did. And I swear within minutes the machine worked. I always thought that was pretty interesting. That that would be their instinct if something was broken, 'We'll sing a hymn.'"

This was the second album Johnny had recorded for Rubin's American Recordings label. Johnny's career had been floundering prior to that and Rick wanted to see this important member of the music community get back on track. "This guy is a true American legend," Rick said at the time to *Rolling Stone*'s Greg Heller, "and it feels like he's in a place where he's not really being taken care of or cared about. It was an ugly thing to me. I felt like he deserved to be treated better than he was being treated."

The American Recordings did much to relaunch Cash's career and *Unchained* and the other albums released on American were all critically acclaimed *and* commercially successful. One reviewer in particular – *Mojo*'s Barney Hoskyns – credited the backing band for making *Unchained* such a joy to listen to. "For *Unchained*, the follow-up to *American Recordings*, Cash has opted for a full-band sound (essentially Tom Petty & The Heartbreakers, with assorted guests) that almost recalls the raw twang of his Sun days. It's a more accessible album than its predecessor, which wasn't so much unplugged as unclothed. It also manages to span fifty years of music – from Jimmie Rodgers' 'The One Rose' to Beck's 'Rowboat' via Dean Martin's 'Memories Are Made Of This' – without anything sounding out of place. It is, in short, one of the year's best records."

★ ★ ★

The mid-nineties had proved one thing to Tom Petty. He needn't be afraid of change. He'd replaced producer/songwriter Jeff Lynne – his collaborator on the wildly successful Traveling Wilburys album as well as *Full Moon Fever* and *Into The Great Wide Open* – with someone who had a completely different production style. And yet, Rick Rubin had done a lot to open new channels of thought for Petty. *Wildflowers* had become a smash despite – or perhaps *because* – it was so different from *Full Moon Fever*.

"It's a funny thing because the whole point of resisting change is where you get into a lot of trouble in life, I think. And I'm trying to learn to not resist change and accept that life is just a spontaneous chain of events," Tom reflects. "I'm not particularly accomplished at it, but I'm trying to go with the flow, because things *are* gonna change. And I'm not talking about music, necessarily, but your point of view, how you present yourself to other people, how serious you take others. It's just an ongoing process, really deep, heady stuff – just trying to be a good person, an honest person. It's very difficult to be honest all the time, ya know? But I think in the end, it's the best way to go, because it does simplify things a lot. That's kinda my theory of life – I'm just trying to go with it wherever it takes me and trying to be as honest as I can be with people. And hopefully, when you're that way with them, they're usually that way with you. So I think, if anything, as I've grown older, I've become a little less judgmental and critical. I'm more concerned with myself because I've realized that I can't change anybody else, but I can change myself. I can do a lot with me."

CHAPTER 11

Knocked Out
(1996–2001)

"I wasn't happy... Even when I was in public, I didn't want to be there, and that's a terrible feeling."

– T.P.

It's funny how the trajectory of personal lives doesn't always match up to that of careers. The year 1995 may have been profoundly creative for Tom Petty, and a successful one with the rising popularity of *Wildflowers*, but his home life was in a shambles. He and Jane, his wife of over 20 years, were not happy – not at all. Marriage is tricky to master for anyone and it's made all the more complicated when fame – and all the responsibilities that come along with being the leader of one of the world's most popular rock'n'roll bands – is thrown into the mix. The way Tom and Jane felt about each other had changed and it had gotten to the point that it just didn't make sense to try and carry on with the marriage.

Divorce was definitely looming but they still had a family to think about. In June of 1996 their eldest daughter, Adria, was graduating from the School of Visual Arts at Sarah Lawrence College just outside

Manhattan. She'd spent the past four years studying filmmaking, screenwriting and media arts. Tom and Jane had to put their own concerns aside to celebrate Adria's completion of her studies and help launch her into adulthood and her profession. The Pettys couldn't keep their differences from their girls though and they were well aware that their family dynamic was going to change. Those days were likely especially difficult for Annakim, who was just 14 years old at the time. The happy times the family used to spend together at their vacation home on the beach of St. Augustine, Florida, seemed very, very far away.

Tom still had work to do though and had to shoulder this emotional burden while working with rockabilly great Carl Perkins on his album *Go Cat Go!*, which would be released later in the year for Dinosaur. While Carl never reached the same heights of super-stardom that his Sun Records label mates – Elvis Presley, Roy Orbison, Jerry Lee Lewis and Johnny Cash – did, he still made some fine recordings that are beloved to this day. Carl wrote and recorded 'Blue Suede Shoes', perhaps his best-known hit, and the tune sold a million copies in 1956.

The recording sessions for *Go Cat Go!* drew dozens of incredibly talented musicians – a who's who in the rock world. In addition to Tom Petty & The Heartbreakers, Carl was collaborating with U2's Bono, Paul Simon, Willie Nelson, Johnny Cash and all of The Beatles – with a recording of 'Blue Suede Shoes' by John Lennon making the track list.

Tom and The Heartbreakers backed Carl on two tracks: 'One More Shot', which Carl wrote himself, and 'Restless', which he co-wrote with Todd Johnston and Carol Laura. Tom also played on the Jim Garland song 'Give Me Back My Job', which featured the all-star cast of Carl Perkins, Bono, Johnny Cash and Willie Nelson.

Tom and all of The Heartbreakers were humbled to work with one of their guitar heroes and years later Tom wrote an essay in tribute to Carl for *Rolling Stone*'s list of *100 Greatest Artists* (Carl was number 99 on the list). In part, Tom wrote, "Carl was the real deal – a true rockabilly cat. He told me about picking cotton when he was a kid and learning the blues from an older black field hand he knew. Carl would go home from the fields, be practising a Roy Acuff country type of thing on his guitar, and then he would start bending the notes. He told me his father would actually get mad, saying, 'Play that thing right, boy, or don't play it at all.' But it was organic with Carl. He took it to the honky-tonks – the real honky-tonks where people would be drinking out of a jug. It sounds like a cliché now, that rock music was born out of cornfields and honky-tonks, but with Carl it was all true."

Tom lamented that Carl "didn't get the breaks he deserved; hard luck seemed to follow him around." Indeed, on his way to play 'Blue Suede Shoes' on *The Ed Sullivan Show*, Carl was in a devastating car crash and broke his back. Elvis subbed for him on the show and missing that opportunity to play for Sullivan's audience cost Carl Perkins more than we'll ever know.

"Carl himself was a very bright guy, and very funny," Tom wrote in his *Rolling Stone* essay. "He once told me, 'Tom, I like you so much – if I lived by you, I'd cut your grass.' That warmth and wit came through in his music. He was not the kind of guy to blow his own horn; he was very humble. When we did a long stand at the Fillmore in the late nineties, I talked Carl into sitting in with us. Backstage, Carl was very nervous about coming out with us. He said, 'They may not know who I am.' I told him, 'Carl, they're going to know you and love you.' When Carl hit the stage, he just ripped the room apart. Neil Young was there that night, and he was shaking his head. Carl was that good."

Working with Carl Perkins was likely the high point of Tom's life that year. His professional life may have been rich but his personal life was a mess and the possibility of a divorce was all but assured.

By September, things between Jane and Tom were untenable and on September 9, attorney Frederick Glassman filed court papers on behalf of Jane Petty. The request for legal separation cited irreconcilable differences. Tom knew this was coming. He'd known it all year, but it still came as a blow. He and Jane had been married for 22 years. Back in Gainesville as teenagers, her support of his dream to become a musician never faltered. She'd rallied behind him in those early days when he first set out for Los Angeles in search of a record deal. She sacrificed spending time with her new husband in the early years as he toured the world to support his band. She raised two young daughters while Tom was out on the road and in the studio. She was his touchstone for so many years and now that special relationship had inexplicably slipped away. Tom was devastated by the loss and his own failure to keep their marriage together.

He went through all the common emotions when faced with a divorce: sadness, anger, guilt and fear of the future. Life was about to change and Tom wasn't sure he could handle it. Jane had been his compass for so long and he admits that she really raised their two daughters, Adria and Annakim, nearly single-handedly. "There were a lot of years when I just wasn't really around," he says. "And fortunately Jane was strong enough to basically run the whole show by herself for a long time." The demands of being a rock'n'roll superhero – spending weeks on end in the studio, touring for months at a time, devoting precious home time to interviews with members of the media – were all the things that took their toll on Tom and Jane's relationship. "I discovered that this is a hard racket to stay married and raise kids in," Tom says.

Outsiders may wonder how the marriage worked for so many years with the constant demands from the studio and the road. Years after Tom's divorce, *Mojo*'s Mat Snow asked Tom if there was room for a committed relationship when he first set out for California back in the late seventies. "Not as much as there should have been," Tom admitted. "We'd all learned to survive with girlfriends. In those days band girlfriends tended to have apartments or some sort of support system, so became very popular. But it was a constant struggle between having a normal life and living with your brothers. We [The Heartbreakers] all lived in one house – it was not normal. It had to be very hard for the girls. I think I was very naïve thinking I could pull it off. Funnily enough, musicians do tend to marry very young. It's odd if you *don't* need that support of someone there waiting for you, but it's not a great idea." It wasn't easy on Tom's kids, Adria and Annakim, either. "My kids tell me the same thing as an open joke: my music and the band meant so much to me that they might have come in second," he said. "They'd take it with a grain of salt and laugh about it, but it's a struggle. It's not an easy profession to grow up in; it doesn't encourage growing up at all."

Some of Petty's happiest days occurred with his fellow Traveling Wilburys. He's pictured here with George Harrison during a 1990 video shoot in Los Angeles. NEAL PRESTON/CORBIS

Throughout the years Tom Petty has taken to the stage for many causes and with many legends of rock 'n' roll. He's pictured here at New York City's Madison Square Garden in 1979 for the No Nukes concert with Bruce Springsteen and Jackson Browne. CORBIS

They were just kids back in 1981: Stevie Nicks onstage with Petty – likely singing the duets 'Insider' or 'Stop Draggin' My Heart Around'. LARRY HULST/MICHAEL OCHS ARCHIVES/GETTY IMAGES

The Heartbreakers on tour in 1981, from left: Stan Lynch, Mike Campbell, Petty, Benmont Tench, and Ron Blair. GEORGE ROSE/GETTY IMAGES

Tom Petty & The Heartbreakers have been the musical guest on *Saturday Night Live* many times throughout the years. Here they are performing during episode 13 on February 19, 1983, one of bassist Howie Epstein's first performances with the band, from left: Mike Campbell, Petty, Stan Lynch, and Howie Epstein. AL LEVINE/NBC/NBCU PHOTO BANK

The Heartbreakers at Farm Aid on September 22, 1985, in Champaign, Illinois, from left: Bob Dylan, Mike Campbell, Willie Nelson and Petty. NEAL PRESTON/CORBIS

After backing Bob Dylan at 1985's Farm Aid, the band went out on tour with Dylan the following year. They played "alone and together" at venues around the world like Poplar Creek Music Theatre in Chicago. PAUL NATKIN/WIREIMAGE

Petty with his first wife and fellow Gainesville expat, Jane Benyo, in October 1986. The pair divorced ten years later.
NEAL PRESTON/CORBIS

The Traveling Wilburys – from left: Roy Orbison, Jeff Lynne, Bob Dylan, George Harrison and Tom Petty – got together every day to write and track songs for 1988's *Traveling Wilburys Vol. 1*. NEAL PRESTON/CORBIS

The Traveling Wilburys super group was the brainchild of George Harrison (right) pictured with (from left) Bob Dylan, Tom Petty, and Jeff Lynne. NEAL PRESTON/CORBIS

Producer Rick Rubin worked with Tom Petty on his solo album *Wildflowers* and also brought Johnny Cash to Rubin's own label, American Recording, in the mid-1990s, from left: Petty, Cash and Rubin working on tracks for Cash's *Unchained* in a Van Nuys, California, studio in 1996. KEVIN ESTRADA/RETNA/CORBIS

Petty catches up with rock'n'roll pioneer Jerry Lee Lewis after a concert at the Palomino in Los Angeles on January 17, 1984. MICHAEL OCHS ARCHIVES/GETTY IMAGES

Petty often pulled out his Rickenbacker jetglo double-neck guitar at concerts during the early eighties. HENRY DILTZ/CORBIS

Present and former members of Tom Petty & The Heartbreakers gather for their induction into the Rock and Roll Hall of Fame at New York City's Waldorf-Astoria on March 18, 2002, from left: Benmont Tench, Mike Campbell, Tom, Howie Epstein, Stan Lynch and Ron Blair. EVAN AGOSTINI/GETTY IMAGES

The late 1990s proved to be a renaissance for Tom Petty. After lying low after his 1996 divorce, Petty took stock of his life and came back on the scene with the nakedly honest album, *Echo*, in 1999. HENRY DILTZ/CORBIS

Throughout 1996, leading up to the official divorce decree, Tom lived in what he now calls "the chicken shack" in Pacific Palisades. Barebones does not even begin to describe the conditions of the run-down cottage and its contingent of wild chickens that lived on the property. Deep-seeded depression crept into Tom's mind and heart. He had never been one to hit the town and attend high-profile events but during this period he spent even less time in public and became somewhat of a recluse.

Tom reflected on that time with Snow. "I just was not happy. I needed more than a hit album in my life," Tom said. "I needed to feel good about myself. And I was in an unhappy marriage and I had to deal with that. Musicians can stay on the road for five years and not deal with your marriage, but it came to a point when I was going to face these demons and deal with them. I got divorced. I'd hit the wall. Oddly, it was in a period of great success musically. But I had to retreat and live completely alone. I didn't go out, didn't do anything but sit in the house most of the time. I was just wounded and crawled off to lick my wounds. I guess a lot of people go through stuff like that; mine was just a little more public."

Tom wasn't the only one hurting though. It was very tough on his girls. "They were very upset. It was very hard on my family," Tom said. "It was around the time I went into therapy and I slowly found my way back, little by little. And when I finally made the transition, I was much better for it… but it was a very rough time, the darkest period of my life."

The Heartbreakers and his other friends worried for him during his stint at the chicken shack but knew he needed time to work through the myriad issues that divorce brings.

Of course celebrities like Tom Petty have one added issue to contend with after a divorce: the media. Entertainment news programs and broadsheets love to dish the dirt on the misfortunes of the famous and even though Tom has always guarded his home life carefully, some gossip columns were still interested in discussing his divorce from Jane. It's around this time that rumors re-emerged that Tom was seeing Stevie Nicks. While the pair has been friends since the late seventies they have never been a couple – although the media would have you believe otherwise. Earlier in their careers – in 1981 in the United States and again during the 1986 tour of Australia with Bob Dylan – the press hinted at a clandestine relationship between Tom and Stevie. Tom, in his usual fashion, wouldn't stoop to address such rumors but Stevie did comment on it once to *Rolling Stone*. "As God is my witness, Tom [Petty] and I are very good friends," she stated. "I just talked to Tom… talked to him on the phone for an hour. He lives very close to here, he lives right down there. So Tom and I are, like, neighbors. And it's great because he really is my good friend. He's my best guy friend… Tom and I have been really good friends since he gave me *Stop Draggin' My Heart Around*. A hundred years ago, the press really kind of messed up our friendship [so when] Tom did all those shows up in San Francisco, he really didn't want me to come up. Because of the press. And I was very hurt because of this. That is what the press does. So the press did manage to get in and destroy my ability to go and see my favourite rock star play at my favourite place, the Fillmore. I didn't get to go because of the press."

The truth is, Tom has been one of Stevie's true friends through everything she's been through – her famous break-ups, her addiction to cocaine and tranquilizers, her diagnosis of the Epstein-Barr virus and her crisis of confidence that stopped her from writing and recording music for a very long time. If it hadn't been for Tom's encouragement, Stevie may have never gone back into the studio to record 2001's *Trouble In Shangri-La* for Reprise Records.

In May of 2001 Stevie talked with *GQ* magazine about her self-doubts and how her friend helped her get back on track. "Epstein-Barr makes you so tired. I was complaining a lot," Stevie admits. "I had dinner with Tom Petty in '95. We're close like a brother and sister, so Tom can say stuff to me that nobody else can. I said, 'Will you help me get started on this – help me write some songs?' And he got angry with me. He said, 'Yeah, you had a couple of bad years, but you need to reinvent yourself. You're one of the best songwriters I know. You don't need help.' I went home that night and told everyone, 'This is it. I'm starting a new record.'"

Luckily in 1996 the press grew tired of the Petty-Nicks rehashed rumor and it was quickly dropped just as springtime blossomed and April brought news of an industry honor: UCLA's George and Ira Gershwin Award for Lifetime Musical Achievement. Perhaps this would cheer up Tom? The list of past winners is eclectic, ranging from Ella Fitzgerald and Mel Tormé to Randy Newman and John Lee Hooker. This was an occasion Tom didn't want to miss and he attended the event. He felt grateful that his contemporaries appreciated the body of his work and he hoped that he'd still be relevant for many more years. This was the vote of confidence he needed during an otherwise unsure time.

Executives in the music industry certainly thought Tom Petty would be an important figure in rock for a long time to come. This was evidenced by the Golden Note Award that was presented to Tom at the Beverly Hilton Hotel in Los Angeles on May 20 as part of ASCAP's 13th Annual Pop Music Awards, which are "presented to songwriters, composers and artists who have achieved extraordinary career milestones". His friend and former producer Jimmy Iovine – now chairman of Interscope-Geffen-A&M – presented the award, along with Marilyn Berman, ASCAP president and chairman of the board. ASCAP could think of no one better to honor for his "enduring place in contemporary American music". Despite generally hating these types of events, Tom decided to attend this soiree as well.

Throughout this period he was working on tracks for the band's ninth studio album, *Songs And Music From The Motion Picture She's The One*. Director Ed Burns had come to Tom to ask him to act as music supervisor for the film. When Tom couldn't really find the right mix of songs from other artists, he suggested that he custom-write music to fit. Burns agreed. From there, Tom, Mike Campbell and Rick Rubin produced the album together.

The resulting 15 tracks – including 'Change The Locks', written by Lucinda Williams, and 'Asshole', written by Beck – offered up nearly 60 minutes of music. Fans didn't quite consider this a new album though since the music was technically written for use in a film. Today, only two tracks from *She's The One* have endured and still feature in Petty's live set: 'Angel Dream' and 'Walls'. Two versions of both songs appear on the record.

Some of the tracks were actually cast-offs from the *Wildflowers* sessions but others, like 'Walls', were brand new. The entire album has a ramshackle, freewheeling tone and the music is looser than any of the band's albums in recent memory. It was scrappy and just a little rough around the edges, but really likeable with lots of little instrumental bridges and songs that ranged from soulful ('Angel Dream') to downright silly ('California' and 'Zero From Outer Space').

All of The Heartbreakers played on this album, as did a few "guest stars", like Ringo Starr (on 'Hung Up And Overdue'), Carl Wilson of The Beach Boys on harmony vocals on several tracks and Fleetwood Mac's Lindsey Buckingham singing background vocals on 'Walls (Circus)'. A string section, featuring Lili Haydn on violin and Michael Severens and Gerri Sutyak on cello, lent a dreamy quality to several of the songs.

Warner Bros. released the album on August 6, 1996, and it was certified Gold by December of the same year. 'Walls (Circus)' cracked the upper echelon of *Billboard*'s Mainstream Rock Tracks chart, peaking at number six (though it only made it to 69 on the *Billboard* Hot 100). 'Climb That Hill' also made it to number six on the Mainstream Rock Tracks chart, and Tom's rendition of Williams' 'Change The Locks' peaked at number 20.

It's ironic that 'Grew Up Fast' is one of the longest songs on the album but the five minutes and nine seconds go by incredibly quickly with the reverb-soaked guitar line that's paired with Tom's incredibly direct and dry vocals. The song is dark and moves from a silky plea to a rocking anthem with the thump of drums and crashing symbols throughout the chorus.

Tom's dry wit comes out in the lyrics of 'Zero From Outer Space', in which he uses self-deprecating humor as his shield against the world. This rockabilly track is reminiscent of early Dylan with a bright harmonica part and handclaps.

'Climb That Hill' could be at home on the sequence of several Tom Petty & The Heartbreakers albums. It's a simple song beseeching each of us to keep up the good fight, swallow a bit of pride when necessary and keep putting one foot in front of the other to move forward – both literally and figuratively. The song is a bit blocky and repetitive but the harmonized background vocals are a highlight.

In the mournful 'Hope You Never', the singer talks directly to the woman that's scorned him and seriously tells her that he hopes she never falls in love "with somebody like you". The lilting melody and Beatles-esque double-tracked vocals are a striking counterpoint to the bitterness of the message. Does he really wish this woman well? It's hard to tell.

After the cryptic 'Supernatural Radio' comes Tom's ode to his adopted state of California. The main lines of the tune – 'California's been good to me/I hope it don't fall into the sea' – are certainly memorable. A really nice harmonica interlude punctuates the track. A lovely instrumental interlude, 'Hope On Board' – with its piano and strings – separates 'California' and the reprise of 'Walls (No. 3)' and 'Angel Dream (No. 2)'. 'Hung Up And Overdue' comes next with its double-tracked vocal and bright piano part, before Benmont closes the album with the instrumental 'Airport', equal parts jazz and honky tonk. It's a shame there isn't room on traditional Heartbreakers records for more of this sort of experimentation.

Rolling Stone's Parke Puterbaugh said of the record: "This is more than your average rock'n'roll soundtrack album" while the *New York Times* noted that it was "an album of troubled love songs". AllMusic's Stephen Thomas Erlewine had a different take: "Petty sounds like he's having a good time throughout the album. It's not a major statement in his catalog, but it's all the more entertaining because of its simple, direct approach." *Salon*'s Cynthia Joyce came to the table with a thought most fans would agree with: "… the album highlights Petty's knack for writing songs that personalise the universal".

This album is rarely mentioned when it comes to Tom Petty's enduring body of work, but it's an important record. If for no other reason, it helped keep Tom occupied during a difficult divorce and it resulted in two of Tom's most beautiful ballads: 'Walls' and 'Angel Dream'.

Rolling Stone critic Puterbaugh took note of the songwriting on the album at the time, saying, "*She's The One* serves to remind how deceptively effortless good songwriting can be. A chiming, Byrds-trademark 12-string guitar decorates 'Walls (Circus)', an evocation of lost California-sunshine innocence heightened by the playfully syncopated backing vocals of Lindsey Buckingham (harking back to his own Cali-pop heyday with Fleetwood Mac). Like a vintage Beach Boys single, the song fades at the end with the golden grandeur of a Pacific Coast sunset."

The second ballad of note, 'Angel Dream', is integral to Tom's story because it signals an incredibly meaningful change in his life. Around this time Tom reconnected with a woman named Dana York. The two had met briefly in 1993 at an after-concert party and Tom remembered thinking highly of her at the time. They both were married then, so it had been just two people meeting and then going their separate ways. When they reconnected by chance in 1996, it was a case of two people being in the right place at the right time. Tom & The Heartbreakers were backing Johnny Cash at a show at the House of Blues in Los Angeles. Dana was in the audience with some friends. Tom was surprised to see her there and the two spent time catching up after the show. When they connected at the House of Blues, there was an instant understanding between them. Something just clicked. They'd both been through divorces and were both mapping out new lives. Tom quickly fell in love with Dana, who was the very inspiration for 'Angel Dream'. According to Tom, "That's one of my all-time favourites. It's about Dana and it's the truth, line for line. That has always been our song."

It's interesting to note that Tom rarely writes about individuals in such a literal way. He so often tries to obfuscate the meaning of his lyrics – intentionally or otherwise – but that didn't hold true for 'Angel Dream'. He sings: "Now I'm walking this street on my own / But she's with me everywhere I go / I found an angel / I found my place / I can only thank God it was not too late."

The pair began spending more and more time together, and slowly, the icy depression that had gripped Tom so fiercely started to melt. Today, Tom says that Dana "… saved me from going down the tubes. She got me to a good place where I did want to rejoin society and keep going. I've got a great girl, and she's strong. It took a strong person to deal with me at that point.

"It got pretty dire. I had a lot of repair work to do with my family and children. I had to grow up in a lot of ways. If you do this all your life, you don't have a normal experience. The rock'n'roll lifestyle does not encourage you to be responsible."

The band did not tour to support *She's The One*, but they did appear on *Saturday Night Live* on September 28. They performed 'Angel Dream' and 'Walls' to a very receptive audience.

As 1996 ended, it looked as if Tom would be able to fight his way through his emotions and return to a happier frame of mind.

★ ★ ★

By early 1997, Tom Petty was feeling much better. The pain of the divorce wasn't quite behind him, but he was slowly constructing a new life and was trying to live in the moment. That's one of the reasons the band decided that it wanted to play out live again. They didn't necessarily want to embark on a full-fledged tour, but they hungered to get in front of an audience and share their brand of American rock'n'roll.

A plan was hatched for an unprecedented 20-night stand at San Francisco's Fillmore. The residency began on January 10 and came to a close on February 3. Why exactly did Tom decide to play an intimate theater instead of simply booking another arena tour? He told *Mojo*'s Joel Selvin that, "I just want to play and get away from the land of video and records for a while. We want to get back to what we understand. We're musicians and it's a life we understand. If we went out on an arena tour right now, I don't think we'd be real inspired. We've made so many records in the past five years, I think the best thing for us to do is just go out and play and it will lead us to our next place, wherever that may be."

The iconic Fillmore shows sold out within hours of going on sale because fans knew something special would happen at this very intimate venue that holds 1,100 people. The band decided to pay homage to all of the artists that inspired them and so the set list looked more like a who's who of rock'n'roll than a Tom Petty & The Heartbreakers concert bill. Additionally, the band lured some terrific opening acts to warm up the crowds. The Wallflowers played, as did Roger McGuinn,

199

Carl Perkins, John Lee Hooker and others. Tom himself introduced the acts onstage each evening.

The nightly set lists of some 40 songs differed from what the band usually plays at arena gigs. For starters, they played a whole lot more covers like Chuck Berry's 'Around And Around', J.J. Cale's 'Call Me The Breeze', 'Green Onions' from Booker T. & The MGs, 'Diddy Wah Diddy' by Willie Dixon and Bo Diddley and – as one of the encores – Van Morrison's 'Gloria'.

The band also mined its own catalog to present a balanced set that included music from its early days ('American Girl' and 'Even The Losers') as well as more recent songs like 'Runnin' Down A Dream' and 'I Won't Back Down'. On many nights of the residency, Tom closed out the set with his lullaby 'Alright For Now'.

Each and every show was a spectacle proving that good rock'n'roll songs never lose their relevance. The band impressed fans and critics that couldn't quite believe how many covers The Heartbreakers could successfully pull off. Years earlier, *Musician* magazine's Charles M. Young commented that, "Whatever the band feels like playing, it seems all Petty has to do is stroke a couple of chords to jog his memory and the complete lyrics to Everything That's Good Since 1955 are at his command."

San Francisco revelled in the nearly month-long celebration of American rock'n'roll and Mayor Willie Brown proclaimed February 7, 1997, "Tom Petty & The Heartbreakers Day". There was one little blip during the Fillmore residency however. One night at the height of the band's set, some jackass set off a can of pepper spray in the middle of the audience. The Heartbreakers were whisked off the stage before succumbing to the fumes but members in the audience weren't so lucky. Venue staffed hurriedly opened all the windows in the theater and attended to fans with water and free drinks. Within 45 minutes the band was able to take to the stage again and finish the show. Viva las Heartbreakers!

The 20-night stand at the Fillmore would have to tide fans over for quite a while, though, because these dates were the only ones the band performed in 1997 and 1998.

Throughout 1997, music channel VH1 collaborated with the band to create an episode of *Behind The Music*. Fans that weren't able to get to the Fillmore shows were happy to at least have some new commentary about their favourite band.

1998 was another quiet year for Tom Petty & The Heartbreakers though Tom did accept the Bill Graham Lifetime Achievement Award at the Bay Area Music Awards (Bammies) on March 7, at the Bill Graham Civic Auditorium in San Francisco.

The rest of the year was spent working out the demons that come with being middle aged and finding that you need to reinvent your entire concept of home life.

★ ★ ★

By 1999, it was time to thank fans for all the support they'd shown over the past few years – despite a lack of new music or full-scale tours. The Heartbreakers had plans to release their tenth studio album, *Echo*, in April but they wanted to reach out to fans before the album dropped.

Around this time, Tom – despite his total lack of interest in computers and the Internet – had been experimenting with various online forums as a way to stay in touch with fans. There's no doubt that his girlfriend, Dana York, advised him on these matters and helped him participate in a few online Q&A sessions. Then, on March 1, Tom decided to give the gift of music to his audience by releasing a single from *Echo*, 'Free Girl Now', on MP3.com. The free download was available for two days before being unceremoniously pulled from the site. It wasn't immediately clear why the song had been yanked, but it was downloaded 150,000 times during its short stint online. Tom later told David Letterman during an interview on the *Late Show With David Letterman* on April 13 that Warner Bros. gave him a "casual elbow in the ribs. 'Maybe you shouldn't do this, Tom.'"

Warners said it never told Tom to take the song off MP3.com, but it's fairly clear what the company's stance on digital downloads was at the time. Unwilling to offer fans such easy access to free music, Warner Bros. felt this was setting a dangerous precedent. The incident didn't cause any harm for Tom, though, and his fans appreciated the chance to hear some gratis new music.

With the record in the offing, The Heartbreakers planned to support the album with an extensive US tour. To warm up for those dates, they reprised their Fillmore residency, albeit with just seven nights instead of the 20 they played in 1997. They booked the venue for March 7, 8, 10, 12, 13, 15 and 16. Once again, the shows sold out quickly.

Tom appreciated the chance to be a house band again – something The Heartbreakers hadn't done since they were starting out in Gainesville, Florida. What exactly appealed to Tom? "To have a place where you leave your amps set up and the material can be anything that comes to you, and you have an intimacy and closeness with the audience," he says. The dates at the Fillmore were special, especially the seventh night. According to Tom, "Things just caught fire right off the bat. It was like we caught a really big wave and you know you're going all the way to the beach with it. I felt free to play whatever I wanted."

In addition to the shows at the Fillmore, the band played three sold out gigs at New York City's Irving Plaza on April 11, 12 and 15. Like the dates in San Francisco, the small venue accommodated about a thousand fans. The day before the first Irving Plaza show, the band was on *Saturday Night Live*, previewing 'Swingin'' and 'Room At The Top' from the new album.

From Manhattan, they set out for England, where they did two intimate shows at Shepherd's Bush Empire on April 19 and 20 and ended their "warm-up" tour at Docks Konzerte in Hamburg, Germany on April 23. Everyone who saw the band play during this period was amazed by the newfound energy and vitality Tom showed. He bounded onstage each night and seemed so much more relaxed than during previous tours. He reached as a performer and played a variety of songs that weren't often on the band's set list. He smiled often into the wings and fans sometimes caught a glimpse of the source of Tom's happiness: girlfriend Dana York. She was travelling with the band now and was a constant source of comfort for Tom. The difference in his outward appearance was striking. He seemed healthier and happier than he had in decades. The same, sadly, couldn't be said for bassist Howie Epstein. When he came out onstage during these shows, longtime fans wondered if he was ill. While he had always had a baby face, he now seemed grizzled and weathered. His nose had been broken and never fully healed – and no one could really get an answer from Howie as to how it had happened in the first place. He also looked dangerously thin. He still played and sang like a pro, but his appearance did make more than a few bystanders wonder about the state of his health. Once the band launched into its set though, these fears were quieted and fans simply enjoyed the music.

Tom was pleased that they booked these warm-up dates and felt it was a boon for the band as a whole. "It really unified us, let us hone our material and try lots of things we wouldn't have been able to do in a hockey rink," he says.

Tickets for the summer Echo tour were already being purchased before the record of the same name arrived in stores on April 13. Upon first listen it was clear that this was not one of the band's strongest albums, but fans were willing to give Tom some slack knowing that he struggled to get through the previous few years as he coped with his divorce from Jane. Fans did have questions though. The cover of *Echo* featured a photo of Tom in the forefront with Mike and Benmont to his left and utility player Scott Thurston in the background on his right. To be honest, most fans of The Heartbreakers didn't even realize that Scott was a full-fledged band member at this point in time. They just thought he was someone that joined up with the band while on tour. Where, however, was bassist Howie Epstein? Why wasn't he pictured on the album cover? While several reporters tried to get to the bottom of the mystery, Tom always deflected the question.

While the album wasn't going to set the world on fire, it was still a Tom Petty & The Heartbreakers record and a certain number of music fans will always embrace that – no matter what. Journalist Tom Sinclair summed it up nicely in a review for *Entertainment Weekly*: "In these post-everything musical times, there's something reassuring about a new Tom Petty & The Heartbreakers album. You know that when you plunk down your money for it, there'll be no misguided attempts to sound modern, no silly trip-hop experiments, computer-generated noise or rap flavoring; you can be confident the songwriting will be dead simple, catchy choruses will abound and solos will be concise and organic. On the aptly titled *Echo*, jointly produced by Petty, Rick Rubin and Heartbreaker Mike Campbell, Petty's patented formula reverberates on every solidly crafted tune with the comforting predictability we've come to expect."

AllMusic's Stephen Thomas Erlewine interpreted the album in a slightly different manner, saying, "To be blunt, much of *Echo* feels like a by-product of Petty's divorce from his wife of over 20 years; even the intoxicating hard rock of 'Free Girl Now' has a layer of sorrow and regret. That weary melancholy is the bond that keeps *Echo* together." Critic Greg Kot said in *Rolling Stone*, "Though one could fault *Echo* for its lack of innovation, that would be missing the point. This isn't the sound of rock'n'roll vigilantes merely rehashing their past. It's Petty & The Heartbreakers standing their ground with wise-ass grins and loud guitars, past the point of caring about what anyone else thinks. This is a band smart enough to know what else is out there and sure enough of itself not to be particularly concerned or threatened by any of it."

The struggle to get through another day comes across in almost every song on the record and the listener gets the feeling that the characters in these stories feel pushed aside and marginalized. There are no sweeping anthems here... just deep sadness and regret. Songs like the album opening 'Room At The Top' – with its warbling guitars and gentle vocal line – are laments about what's gone wrong and if it can ever be put to right.

'Counting On You' sounds as if it could have come from a Traveling Wilburys session and it's perhaps one of the only songs on the record that challenges the woman in the singer's relationship. He warns her that he knows that someone's going to let him down but hopefully not her. He's counting on her and is still holding out hope that they can make it.

The album then segues into its most raucous track: 'Free Girl Now'. In this one, a woman emancipates herself from a bad relationship and a shitty job. She revels in her newfound – and hard won – freedom and independence. The Heartbreakers attack this track with a *joie de vivre* that's not necessarily present throughout the balance of the record. This one is guitar-thrumming, drum-banging and foot-stompingly joyous.

Benmont's subtle piano track is the perfect counterpoint to Mike's tasteful and simple guitar line in the beautiful 'Lonesome Sundown'. Tom's voice warbles with emotion as he tells his girl that he loves her but the path forward will still be difficult.

Many people especially sympathized with the character in 'Swingin', a down-on-her-luck girl who's trying to get out of her situation. She vows to go down "swingin'". The song name-checks Benny Goodman, Glenn Miller, Tommy Dorsey, Sammy Davis and the boxer Sonny Liston – presumably all people that had to fight their way out of their own troubled situations at one time or another.

In the incredibly likeable 'Accused Of Love' Tom double-tracks the vocals so he can harmonize with himself. The result is a lush soundscape that propels the music forward.

The most melancholy song on the record has to be the title track, 'Echo'. It's a lament about relationships ending, feelings shifting and the unease that comes with not immediately knowing what path to take to go forward.

After the quiet nature of 'Echo', the band erupts into the rocker that is 'Won't Last Long' before heading into 'Billy The Kid'. Tom tosses off the lyrics in an off-kilter sort of way. The guitar wobbles in the background as the story of a fighter who keeps getting knocked down unfolds. The important takeaway is that he gets up again and again, no matter what his adversary does to try to keep him down.

As the record breaks into its home stretch, the listener encounters something completely new, a Tom Petty & The Heartbreakers song in which Tom doesn't take the lead. Mike Campbell penned 'I Don't Wanna Fight' and went on to sing the song on the album as well as during the summer tour to promote the record. While Mike has always had his own side projects and garage bands, this is the only time he's ever sung lead on a Heartbreakers record in their 30-plus-year history.

The next three numbers – 'This One's For Me', 'No More' and 'About To Give Out' – are a trio of the strongest tracks on the record. 'This One's For Me' – with its chiming guitars and sing-songy background vocals – sounds like it could have been a *Full Moon Fever* outtake. 'No More' is far more visceral and the singer assures everyone that he is done wallowing in hardship. He is done living this way and will now move forward living up to only his own expectations. 'About To Give Out' ratchets up the record to new heights and is a song that the band really should think about bringing back into its live set. The Heartbreakers build tension in this song until it crescendos and crashes into a full-on, classic rock song.

If 'Echo' is the saddest song on the record, 'Rhino Skin' is the most cautious. In this one, Tom warns all of us that we've got to have skin as tough as a rhino's if we want to be able to deflect all of the hurt and pain that will inevitably be thrust towards us throughout your life. An uplifting message, to be sure.

The album closes with 'One More Day, One More Night' and this one does have a hint of hope around its edges. It's all about taking one more step forward – despite any adversity – and believing that you will come out better on the other side.

Tom admits that the album was difficult to write and record, and to this day he avoids performing these songs in concert. "This record was coming from kind of a rough time for me. I got pretty depressed for a long time," he admits. "I couldn't work, really, when I was that depressed. After the long tour we did for *Wildflowers*, I spent a whole year not doing anything. I kind of came down to earth. You know, that awful period where you have to assess your life. What went wrong and right. I'm kind of over it now. Getting back to work was good therapy in a way."

When Tom did interviews to support *Echo* he was often asked if he set out to write a "divorce album". Hell no. He didn't set out to do that, but it happened anyway. "The depths of despair – if you really want to take the trouble to go there, and I hope you don't – is really debilitating. You're a maimed human," he says. "But I certainly think you remember that afterwards and it informs your work. I certainly didn't want to do an album about my personal problems, but there's no way that some of that wasn't going to seep through. And I wasn't going to try to keep it out either. It is what it is. I think the album is more about my recovery from that period than that period."

AllMusic's Erlewine commented at the time that, "The disc feels a little long, but all the pieces work individually and illustrate that Petty is the rare rocker who knows how to mature gracefully. Although the album is spiked with sadness and regret, nothing feels forced or self-conscious – either lyrically or musically – and he is one of the few rockers of his generation that can make such a claim."

While *Echo* will never be considered the strongest Tom Petty & The Heartbreakers record, it did reach number 10 on the *Billboard* 200. And, on *Billboard*'s Mainstream Rock Tracks chart, 'Free Girl Now' peaked at number five, 'Swingin'' at 17 and 'Room At The Top' reached number 19. There was also an outtake track, 'Sweet William', that appeared as the B-side on the 'Room At The Top' CD single. By July of 1999, *Echo* had already gone Gold in the United States and continues to sell consistently. *Entertainment Weekly*'s Tom Sinclair feels that *Echo* shows that there will always be room on the music scene for Tom: "Part of Petty's charm has always been the apparent ease with which he knocks out instant classics, his ability to project passion seemingly without raising his pulse rate. Preternaturally unruffled as always, the guy shows no signs of creative slippage, no diminution in his belief in the eternal verities (hooks, chops, guitars), no loss of rock'n'roll heart. If the shifting tides of musical trendiness ever threatened his continued relevance, you can be sure that, just like the above-mentioned heroine of 'Swingin'', this consummate traditionalist would go down fighting. Even then, he probably wouldn't break a sweat."

With the release of *Echo*, 1999 was shaping up to be a good year. Tom was relieved that the new album was being received well and the band was looking forward to continuing its tour. First though, the band recorded a live performance on March 31 in Los Angeles for VH1's popular *Storytellers* series. The gig, which showcased a variety of songs interspersed with commentary from Tom, was a highlight for fans. The episode was broadcast on May 16 and featured mostly hits – like 'Mary Jane's Last Dance', 'I Won't Back Down' and 'Free Fallin'' – as well as a song called 'Titanic', cheekily written on the spot.

The following month, on April 28, the band received a star on the Hollywood Walk of Fame and the city declared it "Tom Petty & The Heartbreakers Day". You can see the star for yourself the next time you're in Hollywood. It's located at 7018 Hollywood Boulevard.

The band then kicked off the arena leg of the Echo tour on June 14, at Van Andel Arena in Grand Rapids, Michigan. The 59-date tour powered through North American. The final date of the tour took place at the Hollywood Bowl on October 16.

Milwaukee Magazine later reported in 2011 that The Heartbreakers had encouraged Howie's brothers, Craig and B.J., to join their brother on the road during the 1999 tour. The band was concerned about Howie's drug use and thought having family members present could help their friend get back on track. Craig Epstein told the magazine that he wished the band had contacted him earlier. He felt that perhaps his brother had already slipped beyond the point of no return.

Fans, by and large, remained ignorant of Howie's plight and the band's concern for him. They were just thankful that The Heartbreakers had one final gift to present to them in 1999: a DVD and VHS release of *High Grass Dogs: Live From The Fillmore*. Now fans everywhere could enjoy a little bit of the band's Fillmore residency.

In early December Tom found himself in the nation's capital. He and girlfriend Dana attended a White House dinner to honor the spirit of the Special Olympics on December 4. Throughout the years Tom has been a staunch supporter of the Special Olympics, often contributing tracks to its annual holiday CD. Tom stayed in town to tape a TNT special, *A Very Special Christmas From Washington DC*, which was to air on December 19. The televised concert featured musicians who contributed to *A Very Special Christmas* benefit albums in the past.

Then, on December 13, Tom found himself in a unique position: consoling presidential hopeful Al Gore. One hour after Gore conceded the election to George W. Bush after a contentious court battle over the vote count, Petty sang 'I Won't Back Down' to the would-be world leader at his home. Other musicians like Blues Traveler's John Popper and Jon Bon Jovi were also at the event. (Popper and Bon Jovi were also in town for the Special Olympics concert taping.)

Sadly, Tom was dealt a series of blows later in December. His father, Earl Petty, passed away peacefully at home in Gainesville on December 11 at the age of 75. While Petty had never been close to his dad, the death of a parent is always difficult. Then, on December 30, Michael

Abram broke into George and Olivia Harrison's home, Friar Park, in the Thames-side town of Henley in England. The crazed attacker heaved a garden statue through the patio doors to the kitchen and climbed in. He came at George with a knife and the ex-Beatle tried to disarm him. Abram stabbed George four times and punctured his lung. Olivia went after the lunatic as well and received cuts and bruises during the ordeal that lasted some 15 minutes before the police arrived. George, in keeping with his droll sense of humour, told police on the scene that the intruder "wasn't a burglar, and he certainly wasn't auditioning for the Traveling Wilburys". George recuperated in the hospital but his health never quite rebounded from this troubling incident, which shook Tom. He knew all too well what some people are capable of and the incident made him relive some of the moments in 1987 when an arsonist burned down his home and tried to murder his family.

Tom Petty and all of The Heartbreakers were exhausted but relieved by the end of the year. Their time away from the public eye hadn't diminished the ardor fans held for the band. Tom was climbing out of his long-term depression, but Howie's problems were only deepening.

Tom decided to keep a low profile throughout 2000 and the band only played out once at the Annual Bridge School Benefit Concert at the Shoreline Amphitheater in Mountain View, California. They played sets on October 28 and 29 that included covers like Muddy Waters' 'Baby Please Don't Go' and Howlin' Wolf's 'Little Red Rooster' as well as their own 'A Face In The Crowd', 'To Find A Friend' and 'I Won't Back Down' – among other songs.

On Halloween, the double compilation album, *Anthology: Through The Years,* was released. This trip down memory lane features the band's "greatest hits" and one additional song, 'Surrender'. The song was actually penned during the *You're Gonna Get It!* sessions in 1978 but was re-recorded in 2000 for this occasion. It would take six years before *Anthology* was certified Gold.

★ ★ ★

By 2001 Tom had overcome the grip of depression and was living a happy, new life with his girlfriend, Dana, in their home in Malibu,

California. The Heartbreakers were all in good spirits and decided that they'd tour extensively throughout North American from May through July.

Before they set out on the road though, they decided to contribute a track to the *Timeless: Hank Williams Tribute* that the Lost Highway label was putting together for a September 2001 release. The Heartbreakers pulled off a raucous version of 'You're Gonna Change (Or I'm Gonna Leave)'. It's a must-have for the record collection of any Petty fan. The entire album is actually worth a listen, with other tracks contributed by Bob Dylan ('I Can't Get You Off My Mind'), Beck ('Your Cheatin' Heart') and Johnny Cash ('I Dreamed Of Mama Last Night') among others.

With recording sessions for the tribute out of the way, the band was ready to go out on the road for its own tour. The first leg was dubbed the Way Out West Tour and geared up at Gill Coliseum in Corvallis, Oregon, before the band moved on to Idaho, Washington state, Colorado, Texas and California. The last two nights of the tour were a highlight because the band chose to play the Joint at the Hard Rock Hotel in Las Vegas. The tiny club was packed with fans from all over the world that wanted to hear The Heartbreakers in a small venue. The band was in high spirits and Tom seemed especially exuberant. He closed the June 1 and 2 shows by singing the lullaby 'Alright For Now'. Days later fans discovered just why Tom was in such a fantastic mood. He and Dana York married in Las Vegas on June 3, 2001, in a civil ceremony. Twenty or so friends and family members attended the event and dined at Ruth's Chris Steakhouse afterward. When the couple returned home, they invited a larger group of friends to join them for a spiritual service and reception at their home on June 21. Little Richard, an ordained minister as well as one of the architects of rock'n'roll, presided over the event.

For Tom, this was one of the happiest days in his life. He'd found a soulmate in Dana and was grateful that fate brought her into his life. "My wife is a calming force in my life," Tom says. "Meeting her was one of the most mystical things that ever happened to me."

The band had one month off before heading out again at the end of June on what was dubbed the East Coast Invasion tour. A few days before the tour was set to roll, Howie Epstein and his long-time girlfriend – singer-songwriter Carlene Carter, daughter of June Carter Cash and her first husband, Carl Smith – were taken into police custody in Albuquerque, New Mexico, near where they lived after being stopped in a stolen vehicle. Officers found 2.9 grams of heroin and drug paraphernalia in the car. Carter pleaded with police to let them go and convinced them that the drugs were hers and hers alone and that the heroin was simply for personal use. As Howie and Carlene's mug shots were broadcast on evening entertainment programs, lawyers for The Heartbreakers scrambled. They needed this problem resolved *fast*. The tour couldn't easily go on without Howie. The couple was ultimately released on bond and Howie arrived at the concert hall on the tour's opening night with just minutes to spare.

What in the world had Howie and Carlene been thinking? Was Howie out scoring enough heroin to last him through the upcoming tour dates? Was the pressure of everyday life too much for him to handle? Despite success in the music business, bills were not being paid and the couple's mortgage company was suing to foreclose on their home in Tesuque, New Mexico.

It would be an understatement to say that things were tense between all of The Heartbreakers during the tour. The Heartbreakers were at their wit's end with Howie. When Tom initially heard the news of Howie's arrest, he wasn't sure if he was more angry or sad. The band had been pleading with Howie for several years to get help for his escalating drug problem. Tom was always of the mind that individuals have free will and it wasn't up to him to tell his band members what they could do in their private lives. After all, Tom was no stranger to illicit substances over the years. Still, when drug use began interfering with Howie's ability to do his job, the band had to get involved.

The release of the album *Echo* in 1999 marked the point when Howie's problem started spiraling out of control. He was supposed to fly to Los Angeles for the photo shoot for the cover of the *Echo* album. He'd been at home in New Mexico and promised to get to LA. He missed flight after flight and, finally, the band just couldn't wait any longer for him. As the light began to wane, the photographer posed

Tom, Mike, Benmont and Scott Thurston. Tom was livid and refused to retake the photo – even after Howie arrived in town. He thought that maybe tough love would get Howie to clean up. It didn't.

Now, Tom would not take 'no' for an answer. Tom encouraged Howie to get help and Howie was admitted to a drug rehab program in Miami immediately after the last date of the 2001 tour. Friends say the stint did Howie some good but it didn't stick and he was doing heroin again once he returned home.

Howie's decline wasn't the only thing that saddened Tom at the end of 2001. On November 29 he learned of the death of his close friend and fellow Traveling Wilbury George Harrison. George, who had bravely battled cancer since 1998, succumbed to the disease at the age of 58, dying in Los Angeles at a house that belonged to Paul McCartney. His family said that, "He left this world as he lived it, conscious of God, fearless of death and at peace, surrounded by family and friends."

Tom ended the year grieving for George and hoping that Howie would find a way to regain control over his own fate.

CHAPTER 12

To Everything There Is A Season
(2002–2005)

"What's rare with Tom Petty is after 25 years, his next song might be his best one yet."

– Jakob Dylan

Stan Lynch did a double take when he saw his old friend Howie Epstein walk in to the rehearsal for the band's performance at the 17th annual Rock and Roll Hall of Fame Induction Ceremony. "The Howie I remembered," Stan told Tom Matthews of *Milwaukee Magazine* in 2011, "would beat my ass at arm wrestling. He was a tough kid. But when I saw him at rehearsals, he was almost emaciated. He didn't look 100 pounds soaking wet."

Tom Petty & The Heartbreakers were being inducted into the Rock and Roll Hall of Fame on March 18, 2002, and Stan had been invited to drum on one song during the show as part of the original Heartbreakers line-up. He'd arrived to the rehearsal early and was enjoying catching up with his old bandmates.

The rest of The Heartbreakers had been in town for a few days. Just yesterday they'd rehearsed 'American Girl' with original bassist Ron

Blair. It had been a joyous occasion and the band ended up playing anything and everything for two hours straight. Today's rehearsal with Howie was not going nearly as well. "At the time you could tell he was really trying to keep it together, but he was sort of falling apart," Tom said in an interview for the band's *Runnin' Down A Dream* documentary.

It was clear that Howie was still indulging in drugs and it was now affecting his physical and emotional well-being as well as his ability to be an integral member of The Heartbreakers.

Stan was downright shocked by the state Howie was in and was dumbfounded as to why Tom and the other Heartbreakers hadn't done anything about it. Truth be told, the band *had* tried just about everything possible – from arranging stays at reputable rehab facilities to trying to spend more time with him outside of The Heartbreakers to tough-love arguments and snubs. Nothing, absolutely *nothing*, made Howie veer from the course he was on.

The group assembled for rehearsal plodded along as best they could but one thing was on everyone's mind: 'What are we going to do about Howie?'

★ ★ ★

It was a chilly winter's night in New York City and the Waldorf Astoria was the place to be. Guests were arriving for the Rock and Roll Hall of Fame Induction Ceremony. An incredible range of musicians – the Ramones, Talking Heads, Isaac Hayes, Brenda Lee and Gene Pitney – were being inducted into the Hall along with The Heartbreakers.

The mood in the Petty camp was high. Tom and all of The Heartbreakers were feeling grateful that their little band had found an audience all those years back and the fans stuck by them year after year. The band had been making music together for more than a quarter century and their prospects looked better and better as each year passed. The band was in a good place.

Bob Dylan's son Jakob, of Wallflowers fame, inducted Tom Petty & The Heartbreakers into the Hall. In prepared remarks, Jakob spoke of his own appreciation of the band as well as the importance their music held in American culture: "Two guitars, bass, drums, keyboard player; a lot of people might call that a retro line-up. To me that was where rock'n'roll started, and that's where it gets back to," Jakob said in his speech. "They truly are one of the great American rock groups. They picked up the torch and held it proudly for a long time and when they're done, they'll pass the music along stronger for having been there. Tom's written songs we'll never forget. From 'American Girl' to 'Refugee' to 'Free Fallin''. What's rare with Petty is after 25 years, his next song might be his best one yet."

Tom was downright humbled by the accolades from his peers and went to the podium to thank the music industry moguls assembled. "It's almost unthinkable to join such a sophisticated list of artists. I'm very proud that we're being inducted as a group, because this is the best fucking band in America. They are my family." Despite all of the struggles, legal battles and tug-of-war between his band of brothers, Tom Petty & The Heartbreakers had travelled the long road and came out the other side as relevant as they'd been when their fortunes changed with the breakthrough success of 1979's *Damn The Torpedoes*.

Benmont spoke about the fact that the band is as relevant today as it ever was. "We've become ourselves more as individuals, and we've become way more confident as a band over the years," he said. "We love each other like a family, with all of its ups and downs and complications and simple answers and unanswerable questions. But I would say that the reason the band is still together is we really love the sound we make. I have a ton of great friends who are spectacular musicians who I play with, but nobody makes the sound that this band makes. If I want to get that fed, there's nowhere else I can go." It was clear to everyone at the induction ceremony that all of The Heartbreakers shared that sentiment.

The band performed two songs at the ceremony: 'Mary Jane's Last Dance' and 'American Girl'. Current band member Steve Ferrone stepped away for 'Mary Jane's Last Dance' so original drummer Stan Lynch could take the stool. Original bassist Ron Blair took over from Howie when the band played 'American Girl'. Ron says playing 'American Girl' was one of the most poignant moments of his entire career. "It had so many dimensions to it for me," he admits. "And interestingly enough, I had a great time with Howie that night. We helped each other with the bass changeover."

Many of the band's friends were in attendance, and that included Stevie Nicks. After the show, she was spending time with Tom and the rest of the band when she noticed that Howie wasn't in the room. "She insisted that we call him," says Tom. "So I think it was Dana, my wife, got on the phone and said, 'Howie, your presence is required. You have to come.' He came and he was in a really good mood, and he was very sweet. He sat with us for a while, and then when he got up to go he stood in the door and waved goodbye."

After the rehearsal incident in New York, it was clear to Tom that Howie could not be counted on to work on the band's next album. He just couldn't be relied upon any longer and Tom was beginning to think that allowing Howie to stay in the band was tacitly giving him permission to keep doing drugs. It was a difficult decision but The Heartbreakers would make the next album without Howie and his services were no longer needed on tour. Tom had hoped it wouldn't come to this but he didn't see any other options. It's true that Tom did not break this news to Howie himself. Instead, he delegated that responsibility to long-time manager Tony Dimitriades (who was the one that gave Stan Lynch the official heave-ho when it was time for his departure from the band). It couldn't have been an easy conversation for Tony or for Howie. All of The Heartbreakers shared one hope though, that Howie would get the help he needed to put his life back on track.

The Heartbreakers started work on *The Last DJ*, the band's eleventh studio album, in 2001 and were finishing up tracks and mixing in the first few months of 2002 at Cello Studios in Hollywood. Tom and Mike split bass duties on most songs, and then invited their old friend and original bass player Ron Blair to play on two songs: 'Lost Children' and 'Can't Stop The Sun'. When it came time to officially replace Howie, there was only one choice: Ron. The fact that he was willing to rejoin the band after all of these years was a blessing for him, Tom and the rest of The Heartbreakers.

"Ron was a founding member and was very instrumental to us finding our original groove, sound and vibe, and that's irreplaceable; it was sad when he left," recalls Mike. "Howie came in and was a great harmony singer, which was the main thing he brought to us. Howie played the bass more like a guitar player or a singer who was accompanying his voice, and Ron was more like a bass player in terms of his groove and feel. And they're both valid in their own way. I don't prefer one over the other – they are both equally talented. We were pleased to bring Ron, who was part of our original soul, back. Ron and I stayed in touch for many years, played in the studio and were very close. When Howie's leaving left a void, and it was like, 'Oh, now we have to audition some guys,' and if that didn't feel good, we probably would have disbanded rather than do that."

Tom absolutely agreed that the very future of The Heartbreakers rested on Ron's decision to return to the fold. "It was kind of cosmic, in a way," notes Tom. "Had we looked into putting a new person in The Heartbreakers, I would have just walked away. It wouldn't have been a band to me. I think we all knew that this is the end of it. And Ron stepped in and had this huge enthusiasm through the whole thing. When he first quit, he didn't quit the band, he quit the whole music thing. He was fed up. But we were all young boys then. When he got interested in music again, he started playing with Mike quite a bit, and so he was just there when we needed a bass player for the last two tracks we did for *The Last DJ*."

Returning to the band after all of those years could have been a difficult undertaking for Ron, but he was up for the challenge. "Coming back to the band was like surfing a tidal wave and I don't even surf," says Ron. "Really though, it connected a lot of dots in my mind and I feel like I'm living the 'right life' now."

Today, Tom says The Heartbreakers are stronger since Ron's return. "The band has a good family atmosphere that wasn't there for a while," he admits. "I think when Ron returned, it really bonded us back together in a weird way."

While most bands tour in support of an album that's already been released, Tom Petty & The Heartbreakers never felt constrained by that industry standard. Even though *The Last DJ* wouldn't be available until later in the year, on October 8, 2002, the band set out on a two-legged summer tour. Part one started off at Van Andel Arena in Grand Rapids, Michigan, on June 27 and then sped through the United States through September 1.

After *The Last DJ* dropped in October, the band set out on part two, the official Last DJ tour. This time they began with two shows at the Grand Olympic Auditorium in Los Angeles before heading eastward.

Fans took to the new record immediately and identified with the theme of corporate greed. The song titles themselves are quite visceral. In the album's title track, the story follows the last free-form DJ as his voice gets snuffed out by the conglomerate that controls the airwaves: "The top brass don't like him talking so much / And he won't play what they say to play / And he don't want to change what don't need to change." The song is loosely based on Jim Ladd, who is considered to be one of the last and best free-form DJs on the planet. Jim was forced out of Los Angeles' KLOS in late 2011, but now hosts a nightly show on SiriusXM Satellite Radio's Deep Tracks channel.

Tom wrote *The Last DJ* to document his own frustration at radio conglomerates that offer narrowly focused play lists that don't allow DJs to curate their own shows. "It would be great if DJs were actually hired on a sense of musical taste and knowledge," notes Tom. "There was a time when the DJ was selecting records and was interested in it and hunted down good records to play to his audience. Radio at its best is an art form, and in America, it has really been treated badly."

In the next track on the album, 'Money Becomes King', the storyteller reminisces about the days money wasn't the only motivating factor in the music industry. In the old days, anyone could go see a show – concerts weren't all that expensive. Then things changed with entertainment conglomerates and more middlemen entering the picture who all wanted to take a cut. Ticket prices have risen to obscene amounts in recent years. This song laments that in today's world, it's often only the rich that can attend these events. The result is the passion for the music – that magical spark – has somehow disappeared.

With the focus on the songs that may or may not have been a finger in the eye to the record business, some people missed the gorgeous and soulful ballads on the *The Last DJ* like 'Dreamville'. Here, Tom – accompanied by piano and acoustic guitar – revisits the town of his birth and thinks back to days spent visiting local establishments like Lillian's Music Store and other spots: "Ridin' with my mamma / To

Glen Springs Pool / The water was cold / My lips were blue / There was rock and roll / Across the dial / When I think of her / It makes me smile." It's hard not to think back on one's own childhood when listening to this poignant song.

The hard-edged 'Joe' finds Tom commenting on the sad state of manufactured celebrity in America these days. Talent isn't as important as good looks and a willingness to do whatever you're told. In the song, Tom spits out a sneering vocal line as he apes the point of view of a seedy record company CEO: "I'm the man makes the big wheel roll / I'm the hand on the green-light switch / You get to be famous, I get to be rich."

'When A Kid Goes Bad' is peppered with some horn tracks and a vocal that sounds as if the song could have been recorded for 1982's *Long After Dark*. From wondering about the ill-advised turns in life people sometimes make the album then shifts into a more reflective mood with the Beatles-esque 'Like A Diamond'. The album then segues into 'Lost Children', which really should see the light of day on one of the band's set lists in the future.

From the regretful 'Blue Sunday' ("When it's time to leave you go") to the ebullient 'You And Me' ("Wherever that wind might blow / Wherever that river rolls / You know I will go with you"), *The Last DJ* spoke to listeners on many different levels.

Tom's now departed friend George Harrison's love of the ukulele clearly influenced the arrangement of the next song, 'The Man Who Loves Women', with the instrument opening the tune. A glorious, circular vocal call-and-response signals the end of the track.

On first listen of 'Have Love Will Travel', you'll feel like you've known the song your entire life. Its sentiment – enduring love – is a comforting thought for any of us.

Despite the angst and sadness that's present on some songs on *The Last DJ*, the record actually closes with the very strong and hopeful 'Can't Stop The Sun' in which the storyteller asserts, "You may take my money / You may turn off my microphone / But you can't steal / What you can't feel. Can't stop the sun from shining. And you may think it's over / But there'll be more just like me / Who won't give in / Who'll rise again. Can't stop a man from dreamin'." Mike builds a force field of energy with a scorching guitar solo that closes the song and album. Listen to this track on headphones and you will be blown away by his guitar-playing prowess.

These songs, along with other tracks, convinced listeners that the album was an indictment of the greed present in today's music industry. While Tom felt he was commenting on the issue of American greed in general, music industry executives took it personally. They felt he was thumbing his nose directly at them and they were none too happy about it.

Tom couldn't see their point. He was clearly talking about a much broader field than simply the music business. "I left nobody out," Tom says of *The Last DJ*. "I pick on the artist, the audience, everyone. And not just in the music industry. It could be any business. The problem is greed, pure and simple. Never mind a healthy profit; the idea is: 'We want all the money we can get. We want every damn dime out there, and our computers can show us where every dime is.' The mom-and-pop store has to care about its customers and its products to survive. These giant corporations don't care about anything but profit."

The US economy had tanked in 2001 and 2002 after the country rode a wave of prosperity and excess. By 2002 the average worker was pretty exasperated with the way corporate America works and Tom was commenting on that frustration in *The Last DJ*. "We're all working for the man, whether we like it or not," he says. "It's hard to know who you work for. You climb the ladder and look around, and nobody's there. That instills in people a kind of apathy. They don't really care about much beyond getting off work at six, because they're not going to change anything and nobody notices if they do something good or bad."

Some radio stations misguidedly boycotted the album so sales weren't as brisk as the band would have hoped. The album peaked at number nine on the *Billboard* 200 while 'The Last DJ' single went to 22 on *Billboard*'s Mainstream Rock Tracks chart.

Though the album's reception was a bit of a letdown, one highlight of the year for Tom came on November 10 when he voiced himself on an episode of *The Simpsons* ('How I Spent My Strummer Vacation'). Then in its fourteenth season, this animated series had become a beloved staple of American television. "My family went ape when I was asked to do an episode," says Tom. "It's as if I'd never accomplished anything in my life. For them, this is the absolute pinnacle of my career."

★ ★ ★

The most emotion-packed show that Tom & The Heartbreakers performed during 2002 was unquestionably the memorial concert for his friend and fellow-Wilbury George Harrison, staged at London's Royal Albert Hall on November 29. At Olivia Harrison's behest, Eric Clapton had gathered together a host of George's musician friends to celebrate his life with an evening of music that stretched back to his early Beatles compositions, through his many solo records and including a generous measure of the Indian music that had so inspired George when he first heard it in the mid-sixties.

Tom's arrival midway through the show – after a set by Anoushka Shankar, daughter of Ravi, some Monty Python tomfoolery and Harrison songs performed by Jeff Lynne and Eric Clapton – certainly raised the mood of the evening. The Heartbreakers stormed through 'Taxman' and 'I Need You', both songs executed tightly with a welcome mixture of reverence and affection, before Tom raised a cheer by announcing the first and only Traveling Wilburys song of the night, 'Handle With Care', on which he shared the vocals with Jeff Lynne, and The Heartbreakers were joined on stage by George's son Dhani. Regrettably, the only other surviving Wilbury – Bob Dylan – was detained elsewhere.

Thereafter the Georgefest got better and better as Ringo Starr and Paul McCartney joined the all-star band, the crowded stage resembling rock's own Royal Court as the assembled musicians performed all of George's best-known songs. At the climax, with everyone who'd played now on stage, Joe Brown brought proceedings to a close with Hoagy Carmichael's 'See You In My Dreams', performed – as George would have done – on ukulele. Many in the crowd were reaching for tissues when rose petals dropped from the ceiling of the great hall as Olivia and

Dhani joined Rock's Royal Court in this final, touching tribute not just to a dearly loved musician but also to a husband and father.

★ ★ ★

Tom Petty & The Heartbreakers planned to take it easy in 2003 and there were no public appearances on their schedule for the near future. The Heartbreakers went their own ways at the beginning of the year but as they were enjoying a bit of a break, former band member Howie Epstein suffered a sad loss at his home in Tesuque, near Santa Fe in New Mexico. In late February, his best friend – a 16-year-old German shepherd named Dingo – passed away. He and Dingo had been just about inseparable for years and Howie grieved fiercely for his friend. The emotional blow was made more difficult because Howie was dealing with the flu as well as a nasty abscess on his leg that just wasn't going away. He'd finally gone to the doctor and was taking an oral antibiotic in the hopes that his leg would heal more quickly.

Howie decided to accept the moral support of a friend and was staying at her house the day after Dingo's death. He'd been scarce that afternoon, however, and when his friend went looking for him, she found Howie passed out on the floor of her bathroom. Despite the panic that swept over her, she burst into action, calling 911 and rushing him to St. Vincent's Hospital.

He was breathing when he was admitted to the hospital but, according to the facility, he never regained consciousness. He passed away due to complications from heroin use that very day at the age of 47.

Major Ron Madrid of the Santa Fe Sheriff's Department said at the time that there was "physical evidence that he [Howie] had been doing heroin".

Tom issued a statement after Howie's death that read, "We are deeply saddened at the news of Howie's passing. It's difficult to put into words how much we loved him and will miss him. The world has lost a great talent and a kind and gentle soul. We can only take solace in knowing he is now at peace. Our thoughts and prayers are with his family and his many friends." A daughter, Jamie, and two brothers – Craig and B.J. – survived Howie.

The news tore Tom to pieces. He understood that Howie was in trouble. He knew that his friend had been struggling with a drug addiction. He knew an outcome like this was entirely possible, but he was not remotely prepared when it actually happened. Tom and all of The Heartbreakers were absolutely heartsick over Howie's passing. He was such a gentle person and an incredible musician, and it was hard to believe he'd left this earth.

Carlene Carter, Howie's former girlfriend, was shocked to learn of his passing. "I'm devastated. I loved him very much," she said at the time. "My kids thought of Howie as their father." John Hiatt, who'd struggled with his own addiction to alcohol and had worked with Howie in the late seventies and early eighties, spoke fondly of his old friend: "He was just a sweetheart, and he loved to rock'n'roll." Hiatt was actually surprised that Howie succumbed to drugs, saying, "Howie was the sane one. He was the least likely to have wound up the way he wound up. I remember feeling no matter how crazy everybody else got, I could always look to Howie and think, 'Well, Howie's got *his* shit together.'"

Dealing with the untimely loss of a friend due to drugs is incredibly difficult but it's made even more heart-wrenching when the matter is in the public eye. Newspapers and magazines picked up the story about another musician who had been felled by drugs.

Howie's remains were flown to Wisconsin and the funeral was held at Temple Menorah in Brown Deer. Benmont Tench and Stan Lynch were the only Heartbreakers – past or present – who attended the service. At the time, Tom received some flack from fans because he did not pay his respects in Wisconsin. Instead, he organised a memorial for his friend at McCabe's Guitar Shop in Los Angeles and wrote a piece about the loss for *Rolling Stone* magazine.

Friends like Carlene Carter, Stevie Nicks, drummer Jim Keltner, engineer Don Smith and the late Roy Orbison's wife, Barbara, and son Roy Kelton Orbison, Jr., attended the memorial at McCabe's. After the event Barbara Orbison posted a note to her husband's website saying, "We needed to find peace within ourselves to justify the sudden loss of Howie. We all agreed that there was not a sweeter, more talented, funny guy than Howie. It was wonderful for Roy Kelton and I to have reconnected with part of the gang that was so close to us during the making of *Mystery Girl*... Howie sang and played on *Mystery Girl* and was with us in the studio at all times. He was an intricate part of making the album." There was no doubt that many musicians were deeply touched by the loss of Howie Epstein.

Tom tried to explain to the public that he and the band loved Howie dearly but were never able to help him overcome his drug addiction. "I want people to know we did care about Howie and really tried hard to do everything we could," Tom said at the time, "but heroin's just such a powerful, ugly drug that it was even bigger than us and Howie. Howie should be remembered as a kind, wonderful guy, as an extremely talented musician."

Tom fervently wished that things had turned out differently. "The thing is, Howie never played bad, but then he'd fall apart as soon as the show was over. It drove us crazy. You'd get angry, you'd get sad, you'd get indifferent, you'd get passionately involved, but none of it was enough and I don't know why.

"There's a great sadness, because Howie was never not a Heartbreaker. He just got to where he couldn't do it anymore... It's like you got a tree dying in the backyard. And you're kind of used to the idea that it's dying. But you look out there one day and they cut it down. And you just can't imagine that beautiful tree isn't there anymore."

Mat Snow of *Mojo* magazine once asked Tom if drugs ever worked for him on any level. "No," Tom replied emphatically, going on to say, "They finally killed one of us. Drugs don't work. There's the old saying that when you take drugs, things happen. I'm not one to tell people how to live, but I've never seen it work out for anybody. You never see somebody and say, the cocaine is really looking good on you, really helping you out."

After Howie's death, Tom retreated to his home to try to come to terms with the death of his friend. By April, The Heartbreakers were ready to come together again and set up shop at the Vic Theater in Chicago for a series of five dates on April 13, 14, 16, 17 and 19. The theater, with a capacity of just 1,400, is a favourite in Chicago and fans across America vied for tickets as soon as they went on sale. All five shows sold out in minutes.

Like the band's two previous residencies at the Fillmore, the stand at the intimate Vic Theater allowed Tom to freshen the song list. A set consisting of hits made famous by the band was peppered with their favourite songs from other artists. The Heartbreakers tipped their hats to Chicago musicians who came before them and played 'Baby Please Don't Go', first recorded by Big Jo Williams in 1935 and likely handed down from slaves on America's plantations. It has since been recorded by many blues greats like John Lee Hooker, Muddy Waters and B.B. King. The band also tore through Howlin' Wolf's 'Commit A Crime', The Rolling Stones' 'Down Home Girl', Buddy Holly's 'Peggy Sue' and an impressive array of additional cover songs.

Each show lasted nearly three hours and consisted of both electric and acoustic sets. The local music press buzzed with praise. The *Chicago Tribune*'s music critic, Greg Kot, said the Vic concerts were "Petty's most adventurous set of music on a Chicago stage in more than a decade… It's about Petty and The Heartbreakers taking their time, digging deep and mining their pasts as musical appreciators for inspiration. It's a rare opportunity to see Petty not just as a star, which he is, but as a musician and a fan… this week, his roots are showing, and it's a fascinating glimpse into the mind, soul and inspiration of one of the rock'n'roll greats." Across town at the *Chicago Sun-Times*, critic Jim DeRogatis asserted that "Petty's secret weapons were the amazingly versatile keyboardist Benmont Tench and longstanding lead guitarist Mike Campbell, who was as impressive firing off leads on his Les Paul during the louder numbers as he was while finger-picking an electric mandolin during the 12-song acoustic set… an inspired, energetic, revealing and consistently thrilling performance – a gift from one of rock's greats."

For Petty, perhaps the highest praise for the Vic shows came from Mark Guarino at the *Daily Herald* who wrote, "Petty is at an age when most of his peers have creatively peaked and are downshifting to take advantage of fan loyalty with through-the-roof ticket prices for nostalgia tours void of adventure but rich in formula…he is continuing a rich career whose legacy is still in the present, not past tense."

The trip to Chicago wasn't all about the Vic residency, though. The Heartbreakers were in town to tape an episode of *Soundstage* for PBS. The performance is available on DVD and is definitely worth picking up; it includes some of thost fantastic covers as well as their own hits like 'I Won't Back Down' and 'You Don't Know How It Feels'. They even throw in the Traveling Wilburys' classic 'Handle With Care' for good measure.

The Vic residency ensured that there would be buzz about the band's upcoming Lost Cities arena tour. The short, 21-concert summer tour only featured US states.

The Heartbreakers had barely returned home when they got word that yet another friend had passed away. On September 12, 2003, Johnny Cash died of complications of diabetes at the age of 71 in Nashville, Tennessee. Tom and all of The Heartbreakers had worked with Johnny extensively on his *Unchained* album and other projects, and it was difficult to stay goodbye to another friend and legendary singer-songwriter.

October brought happier news to The Heartbreakers. The band was to be honored with the Legend Award at the Radio Music Awards at the Aladdin Hotel in Las Vegas on October 27. While Tom was never crazy about attending these sorts of events, he did with the entire band and was tickled that his friend Stevie Nicks presented the award to them. During her presentation speech, she had this to say about Tom Petty: "He not only started out as my greatest musical influence, but today he's *still* my greatest musical influence." The band played two songs for the crowd assembled: their rendition of The Animals' classic 'I'm Crying' and their own 'Runnin' Down A Dream'.

The year had been a strange amalgamation of terrible personal loss and continued career success. Tom wanted to spend 2004 reflecting and getting back on track. He had been fighting depression again ever since George Harrison's death in 2001, and the loss of Howie was now taking its toll. He knew he had to devote some time to repairing his psyche and focusing on something that could take him out of his own doldrums.

He found that special project when his dermatologist Arnold Klein asked him to help out with a charity benefit. Known as the "dermatologist to the stars", Klein is also the founder of the Orange County nonprofit, Art for AIDS. "Dana [Tom's wife] started crying at last year's event – her brother died from AIDS and was totally abandoned," Klein said. "She was really involved in his care. I was so touched by it. She is such an amazing woman."

The event at the St. Regis Monarch Beach Resort in Laguna Beach had hit home for Dana. She had lost her brother to the disease in 1993 when he was just 30 years old, and though 10 years had passed, the hurt was still very fresh. Going to the benefit brought back so many memories of things she still hadn't fully dealt with.

Arnold had an idea. What if Tom Petty & The Heartbreakers performed a concert in memory of Dana's brother? Tom readily agreed. It would give him the opportunity to give something back to the community and it would hopefully help Dana find some closure after the passing of her brother.

Arnold was thrilled when Tom told him that he and The Heartbreakers would love to headline Art for AIDS III: A Concert for Stephen Cy Costick. "This one involves my family, and I'm glad to be able to do it," Tom told Ann Conway of the *Los Angeles Times*. "It's not a lot of trouble for a good cause," he said. "And it will help my wife work through her loss."

"He's really excited about doing it," noted Jack Kenefick, president of Laguna Art Museum and one of Art for AIDS' sponsors. "It's a big deal; his wife's family is flying in. It's bringing his family together, a reunion concert for Stephen – it makes it a special event."

The gala dinner, auction and concert were held on February 7, 2004. Other celebrities in attendance included Jackson Browne, Barry Manilow, Carrie Fisher and Stephen Stills.

For Dana and her family, the event gave them a chance to remember how special Stephen was and to share that with everyone in attendance. "He was my brother and my best friend," Dana confided to the *Los Angeles Times* on the day of the concert. "He lived with the disease for a long time. It was horrible, and I'd buried all of that. Tonight is going to bring back a lot of memories."

The gala was a huge success for Art for AIDS and, more importantly, it strengthened the already strong bond between Tom and Dana. They were there for each other – for better or for worse. Truth be told, 2004 would test their bond. Tom was still struggling with the loss of his friends George and Howie and perhaps was even suffering from misplaced guilt over Howie's death. Dana was his strength and constant companion throughout this period. She made sure that Tom would not fall into the abyss. She never wanted him to sink as low as he'd been when he was living at the chicken shack in Pacific Palisades, when she reconnected with him while he was recording *Songs And Music From She's The One*.

There were, of course, bright spots on the horizon. Tom and his friend Jeff Lynne had the important duty of inducting George Harrison into the Rock and Roll Hall of Fame on March 15, 2004, in New York City. George's wife, Olivia, had personally asked if they'd do the honors and there was no way they could refuse. The event – which also honored Prince, Jackson Browne, Bob Seger, ZZ Top, Traffic and The Dells – was bittersweet for the pair who'd worked so closely with George during the last years of his life. The musical performances were the highlight of the night, especially 'While My Guitar Gently Weeps', which was played in tribute to George by an all-star band consisting of Tom, Jeff Lynne, Steve Ferrone, Marc Mann, Harrison's son Dhani, Steve Winwood and Prince. Prince's guitar solo has become legendary and the performance can be viewed on YouTube.

The rest of the year passed quietly for Tom and he wouldn't re-emerge into the public eye again until he began hosting his own radio show, *Buried Treasure*, on XM Radio (now SiriusXM Satellite Radio). The concept was simple: he'd rifle through his own record collection and share gems with fans. While Tom may have thought that this project would be a short-lived sideline, he turned out to be a natural-born DJ. The program flourished and he continues to bring the best music – old and new – to his fanbase. "Even when The Heartbreakers are really busy, I'm up all night putting this together," he told Steve Appleford for *Rolling Stone* magazine. "I play a lot of that stuff because I'm so emotionally attached to it. It was a great time for music, and I'm lucky I was born when I was born, I guess." (The appendix of this book contains a list of songs Tom has played on *Buried Treasure*, which airs on SiriusXM's Deep Tracks channel.)

At this point in Tom's career, he wasn't so worried about pumping out new music of his own on a regimented schedule. He waited almost three and a half years after releasing *Echo* in 1999 before dropping *The Last DJ* in 2002. It shouldn't have been a surprise then that he wouldn't offer any new songs to fans in 2005, but the band did stage a fairly extensive 41-date summer tour. Of course, The Heartbreakers were once again – much to the dismay of fans overseas – focusing on the United States. Europeans were beginning to wonder if they'd ever see Tom Petty & The Heartbreakers play live again.

CHAPTER 13

A Return To Songwriting
(2006–2008)

"Lately I've been concerned with what I'll leave behind artistically."

– T.P.

The many trials Tom Petty endured in the early 2000s shaped his outlook for the latter part of the decade. The loss of so many friends and musical collaborators hit him hard. George Harrison was gone. Howie Epstein was gone. His one-time mentor and industry champion Denny Cordell had long since passed. These losses made Tom re-examine his own life and he became very aware of time – or the tenuous grasp we have on it. None of us knows the hour of our own death. For Tom, it started to become more and more important to focus on songwriting. He was conscious of the fact that he wanted to leave behind music that meant something – something to him and something to the music community at large.

He hunkered down throughout 2005 and the beginning of 2006 to work on his third solo album, *Highway Companion*. "Lately I've been concerned with what I'll leave behind artistically," says Tom. "The biggest priority with the new record now is that I know this is here longer than me and that's more important than [it] being a hit record. Years ago you'd have to make sure you had one that was a single. I don't think that pops up in my mind anymore. I'm a little more into the poetry and the lyrical images than I used to be. I don't want to waste a line. I want it to mean something and I want it to be the right line." Petty was writing for the future and hoping that he'd contribute something lasting to his already respectable legacy. Of course, it helped that the pressure to generate hit singles was off. In today's single-song download society, "hit singles" just aren't all that important anymore. Tom simply focused on writing songs and let fate take him where it would.

So what is Tom Petty's songwriting process? How does he set out to write a song in the first place? "I don't have any set formula," he admitted to Iain Blair in a *New Music Express* interview. "I wish I did because that'd make the whole process much easier, but you just have to take what you're given. Sometimes I might get a phrase and that'll trigger something, but usually I'm just sitting around strumming my guitar and a song emerges."

Tom often talks this way about songwriting. He feels that songs are sent to him and he simply "receives" them. An idea or a complete song just appears, almost as if by magic. According to Tom, "Sometimes it's the middle of the night and it's like, 'Something's comin' in! Oh boy! Here it comes!' Building from that kernel of an idea is an organic process that seems to evolve of its own accord.

"Writing songs can be a hard thing at times, so it's always a thrill when one comes in," he says. "And that's kind of what keeps us going – just waiting for the next song. I'm so glad when a song shows up that I really embrace it. I don't question it much. I don't do nearly as much rewriting and proofing as I used to do. Unless something's really terrible, I let the song lay there just the way it came in. I don't labor anymore. I don't think you're supposed to at my stage of life. I think I've really honed what I do. If I sit and sweat over a song these days, I usually don't get a good result. It feels overworked."

Tom Petty is far more prolific than his record releases would suggest. The fact is, many more songs come to Tom than he has the opportunity to release. "In my old age, I've become a very fast writer," he admits. "I've got the craft part down really well. I can write a song any time. I don't know if it will be any good. I'm only interested in the ones that come really fast. These days I'm just interested in what falls out."

Other songwriters respect Tom's ability to grab songs seemingly from thin air. Roger McGuinn has said this about his long-time friend: "Tom's really great when he writes songs. He kind of flies up there into the stratosphere and gets an idea and comes back down and puts it on paper and then he'll fly back up there and get another idea and come back down. He's an amazing songwriter."

The other thing that may set Tom apart from other writers is that he doesn't set out to write a song about a specific topic. "I'm not one of those people who says, 'I just wrote a song about this or that subject.' Usually, when somebody says that, it's a bad song," asserts Tom. "I'm really wary of anyone who discusses their writing with me or tells me they wrote about this or that. That should be apparent when I hear the song, rather than them trying to help me out."

So what counts when writing a song? According to Tom, "Getting what you feel across and then having other people grab that feeling. I've never been one to say, 'I'm going to bare my soul on this one.' But I think you eventually do. My rule is to let the music dictate the lyric – don't try to hammer two things together that don't like each other. There have been times when I wrote a lyric in advance, and it took forever to find music that felt right."

That's not to say that Tom's songs aren't based on things that have happened to him or someone he knows. "There's usually a character that appeals to me," Tom says of his songs. "It's like getting a film script and thinking, 'I can play that guy.' The plot has to come from some experience but you still use your imagination.

"I believe people fall in love or lose their jobs or money. I don't believe they've been to outer space. And if I don't believe it, I ain't singing it," he says.

"The most important thing to me about a song," he continues, "beyond the subject matter, is that I believe the singer. And the quickest way to attain that is simply to sing the truth. A lot of singers go years without figuring that out. They have this great tool, but can't figure out how to be honest."

For Tom Petty, it's almost as if he's a mere commentator sitting on the sidelines and communicating the plot to others. He doesn't feel he's invested in making judgment calls one way or the other. "I'm certainly not trying to preach or tell anyone what's right or wrong," he says of his lyrics. "I see myself as an observer, a reporter. I try to use what's happened to me or people in my immediate vicinity – and the better I get at expressing that and getting it across, the more meaningful the tunes are to people."

One thing that's always set Tom's lyrics apart from many of his contemporaries is how he portrays women. Many rock'n'roll songs treat women as playthings. That's not the case in Tom's work. The females in his songs are strong and often have the upper hand in the situation. It's a welcome change and perhaps why this rock'n'roll band has an equal number of male and female fans.

When Tom was growing up, he certainly spent more time with women than men. His primary caretakers included his mother, Kitty, and grandmother Troas Hale. Kitty also had two sisters that lived in Gainesville and Tom was close to both his aunts, Evelyn and Lottie. That is, perhaps, why women weren't entirely a mystery to Tom and how he learned to respect the fairer sex. "I know that I admire independent women," Tom affirms.

"Female characters are fascinating to me because as much as they talk they don't necessarily say everything that's on their minds," Tom told Jim Faber for a *New York Daily News* article. "You don't see all the cards, whereas men often throw all theirs down. My dad wasn't around a lot when I was growing up. I was raised by my grandmother and I had a lot of women around me. So I've always been sympathetic to them."

Tom knows one thing for certain: "I have this reoccurring character who always comes back in different forms – this escaping woman kind of thing. I can't write her out. I keep trying, but she always comes back in. Sometimes I wonder if it's me. I wonder if I'm singing about me in some way, and don't want to do it, so I transfer it over to a woman.

"I've always loved girls. And I found they were interesting characters to write about, maybe more so than men. It's easier, for me, to write about female characters. It just comes to me easier. And when The Heartbreakers were starting out you didn't hear many positive songs about girls. There were a lot of songs about girls, but a lot of times they kind of put them down. They didn't come off too strong. And somewhere along the line, on the first and second album, I started to write songs that gave them a positive image. I still enjoy doing that. Although I got a little tired of the theme. I don't know why it keeps coming back. It does, though."

★ ★ ★

With Tom's renewed focus on songwriting in 2005 and 2006, it was perhaps not much of a surprise when ASCAP – the American Society of Composers, Authors and Publishers – named Tom as the keynote speaker of its first ever ASCAP "I Create Music" Expo. The event, which took place in Los Angeles on April 22, 2006, was dedicated to songwriting and composing and was designed specifically for songwriters, composers and producers. The event was unique in that it wasn't restricted to its own membership but welcomed anyone interested in the art of writing music.

Erik Philbrook, AVP of Communications & Media and Editor in Chief of ASCAP, interviewed Tom onstage during the event. Many walked out of that session inspired by Petty's words and his forthright approach to his craft.

His path forward also included the question of what record company would be the best partner to achieve his goal of producing finely crafted records for the rest of his life. His deal with Warner Bros. was coming due and he had to make a decision. He could continue with Warners, look for a new company or go the independent route. On June 6, 2006, he signed a deal with Rick Rubin's American Recordings. This was perhaps a perfect compromise. He'd have the weight of a major record company behind him since American was part of the Warner Bros. family but he'd also benefit from Rubin's laser-sharp sensibilities. Tom had enjoyed working with Rick on *Wildflowers* and *Songs And Music From She's The One* so this seemed the logical way forward.

At the time, Rick said that, "Having Tom on American is a dream come true for me. Tom is the consummate craftsman when it comes to recording, and has written great songs consistently for 30 years. Tom Petty & The Heartbreakers is the quintessential American rock band and being a great rock'n'roll band has become a lost art."

The move to American Recordings made sense for Tom but despite *Wildflowers'* critical acclaim and success at record store cash registers, Tom didn't look to Rick for production assistance when it came to his next album, *Highway Companion*. Instead, he went back to his award-winning *Full Moon Fever* formula and asked Jeff Lynne and Mike Campbell to co-produce with him. In fact, the three of them are the only musicians that appear on the album. In a strange twist, Tom decided to lay down lead and backing vocals, rhythm and 12-string guitar, harmonica, electric piano and keyboards, bass and drum tracks himself. Ryan Ulyate recorded and mixed the album with long-time Petty guitar tech, Alan "Bugs" Weidel, acting as session supervisor.

With the exception of Mike, none of The Heartbreakers played on *Highway Companion*. "We started on the Christmas holiday," Tom explains, "and I just wanted the three of us to make a solo record. I probably hurt Benmont's feelings, but I think the world of Benmont. He is really the best piano player there is anywhere. I just thought for this record, I'd rather bang it out myself and make a different kind of record. And I am really proud of the record. I think it's one of my better ones in a long time."

The 12-track *Highway Companion* album was released on July 25, 2006. The songs presented here are much more retrospective than Tom's previous work and they build an enjoyable album albeit one with no discernible "hits". The songs are rustic in their tonality and emotions are laid bare in the lyrics. This is a traveling album, not the type of CD you pop in when heading out on the road with friends but instead what you play when you're driving down the lonely highway, all alone, in the dead of night. This isn't a passive album. It makes you think about where you're going in life.

The first single, 'Saving Grace', was streamed from TomPetty.com starting at the end of July. The theme harkens back to so many other Petty tunes in which the need to keep moving is at its core.

The songs on this record are some of Tom's most lyrical in years. He's telling complex stories here. Some, like 'Square One', are easy to understand: someone who's made mistakes and disappointed himself and others finally comes to terms with who he is and fights to get back to square one again. "I think it's one of my best songs ever," says Tom of 'Square One'. "I mean, you always like your new record. But I really think that one is particularly good." In it, the main character says, "Had to find some higher ground / Had some fear to get around .... Last time through I had my tracks / So well I could not get back / Yeah my way was hard to find / Can't sell your soul for peace of mind." But the protagonist works hard to figure out where he went wrong and struggles to regain control of his life: "Square one, my slate is clear / Rest your head on me my dear / Took a world of trouble, took a world of tears / It took a long time to get back here."

The humility and regret are palpable in 'Square One' and the sentiment hits home – hard – for many people who've had to rebuild their lives for one reason or another, while 'Flirting With Time' discusses what's been on Tom's mind for quite a while now. Our use of time and pondering the eternal question: are we making the most of it?

The acoustic numbers on *Highway Companion*, like 'Down South', are of special note. 'Down South' was inspired by Warren Zanes. Formerly of the Del Fuegos, Zanes now works for Steven Van Zandt's Rock and Roll Forever Foundation and recently told this story to Gwen Orel of the *Montclair Times*. "Thirteen years after my band opened for him, Tom Petty's manager called and said, 'Tom Petty wants to have dinner.' He told me that my book, *Dusty Springfield In Memphis*, inspired him to write a song, and he wanted me to come back to the house and hear it. The song was 'Down South', from the *Highway Companion* record."

The balance of the album concerns itself with life's challenges, like trying to win back a girl ('Jack'), revisiting old decisions ('Turn This Car Around') and the need to blow off some steam when the world is pressing down on you ('Big Weekend').

Some of the other songs on the record – 'Night Driver' and 'Ankle Deep' – are a little more cryptic. Love and responsibility round out the themes here. 'Damaged By Love' is about the beginning of the road while the album-closing 'The Golden Rose' is all about love lost. 'This Old Town' discusses how it feels to be hamstrung by all of life's myriad obligations.

Two other songs – 'Home' and 'Around The Roses' – were released during this period on a special edition of the album that also included and demo versions of 'Big Weekend' and 'This Old Town'.

The title of the album itself invokes the theme Tom was most interested in exploring: heading off on a journey. "With this record I knew that I wanted to have a sound that was cohesive," he says. "I didn't want to make a concept album but I wanted it to fit together sonically. The space is everything in a record. It's not anthemic at all. I'm real bored with anthemic. I did that and I am not trying to do it again."

Rolling Stone gave the album three and a half stars. Critic Alan Light wrote, "Tom Petty was always slightly hard to peg. When he first emerged from the Florida swamps, it wasn't clear if he was a classic-rock stoner or an edgy New Waver. *Highway Companion* comes out of the gate with this versatility intact – the opening ZZ Top/John Lee Hooker boogie of 'Saving Grace', the first single, is followed by the spare, delicate 'Square One'. His songs are filled with images of motion, travel and the road; the sharpest writing appears in the cryptic, evocative 'Down South', describing a journey that includes plans to 'see my daddy's mistress,' 'sell the family headstones' and 'pretend I'm Samuel Clemens/Wear seersuckers and white linens.'"

The album peaked at number four on the *Billboard* 200 album chart but didn't gain the support of critics in the same way *Wildflowers*, his last solo album, had done. It's also possible that younger fans weren't ready to follow Petty when it came to so many introspective songs that either looked wistfully into the rear-view mirror or peered into the murky future. Blogcritics album reviewer Josh Hathaway said this at the time the album was released: "After 30 years, it has become clear Tom Petty is incapable of making a truly bad record."

Despite the fact that *Highway Companion* is Tom's solo album, the entire Heartbreakers crew toured to back the record between June 9 and October 28 of 2006. There was a bit of a snag with the initial sale of concert tickets, however. It appeared that scalpers had joined Tom Petty's fan club at the last minute to gain access to the best seats in the house during presales. These unscrupulous individuals then immediately resold prime tickets online, commanding much higher prices. Tom and his management company instructed Ticketmaster to cancel almost 500 tickets. Manager Tony Dimitriades said at the time, "We don't claim to have completely eliminated all reselling activity on these or any other shows. But this is definitely a step in the right direction and a major strike on behalf of the good guys."

This is exactly what fans expect of Tom Petty, who is known to always care about what's fair in every situation. The band went on to play 40-plus shows throughout the United States. One of the standouts was their September 21 appearance at the O'Connell Center at the University of Florida in Gainesville.

The band was tickled to receive the keys to the city and their families thought it was pretty cool that Gainesville Mayor Pegeen Hanrahan proclaimed September 21 Tom Petty & The Heartbreakers Day. During their short stay in town, Tom was also presented with the University of Florida's Distinguished Achievement Award, which is given to individuals for exceptional achievements in their chosen profession.

The other thing that set this tour apart from others was the fact that Stevie Nicks was a "surprise" guest on the first eight shows as well as select dates later that summer and fall. She joined Tom onstage for the duet 'Stop Draggin' My Heart Around'. Stevie later told the press that the shows were "the best time I've ever had". In fact, she shared a sweet story about Tom with *Rolling Stone* magazine regarding that tour: "In 2006 I did 27 shows with him. Tom made me a little platinum sheriff's badge that had 24-karat gold and diamonds across the top and said, 'To Our Honorary Heartbreaker, Stevie Nicks.' On the back it says. 'To the Only Girl in Our Band.' I keep it on my black velvet top hat. It goes with me everywhere. It's probably the most beautiful piece of jewelry a man has ever given me, *ever*." It's stories like this that help illustrate Tom's commitment and loyalty to all of his friends.

As 2007 rolled around, fans had no idea that Tom would be working on three cool projects throughout the year: a tribute to boogie-woogie great Fats Domino, a new album that involved only some of The Heartbreakers as well as a band documentary with director Peter Bogdanovich.

With The Heartbreakers in tow, Tom headed into the studio to contribute a track to *Goin' Home: A Tribute To Fats Domino*. The band played its rendition of Domino's 1957 number one hit, 'I'm Walkin',' which he co-wrote with Dave Bartholomew. An incredible list of musicians turned out to participate on Vanguard Records' double CD, including Elton John, Buddy Guy, Bonnie Raitt, Randy Newman, Norah Jones and many others.

Of course industry insiders would want to pay tribute to a man who had influenced the very direction popular music took in the fifties but there was an even more compelling reason for musicians to join on to this project. Fats Domino's home in New Orleans was severely damaged when Hurricane Katrina flattened the area in August of 2005. Prior to the storm, he and his wife, Rosemary, had decided to try to ride it out at home. She wasn't well at the time and the pair really wanted to stay in familiar surroundings. They quickly realized their mistake as the floodwaters rose. In the confusion that was the aftermath of the poorly managed hurricane clean-up, someone erroneously thought Fats had died and spray-painted "RIP Fats" on the side of his home. In actuality, a Coast Guard helicopter team rescued Fats and his wife, who were taken to a Baton Rouge shelter before family could track them down. To add insult to injury, while they were away, looters ransacked the house and left them with nothing.

Bill Taylor of the Tipitina's Foundation and Adam Shipley set out to produce a tribute album that would provide funds to accomplish three things: the rebuilding of the Dominos' home, the creation of a community center in the Lower 9th Ward and payment for musical instruments for children attending New Orleans' public schools. At the time Taylor explained why it was so important to get someone of Fats' stature back to New Orleans during the rebuilding efforts. "Fats Domino is the cornerstone of New Orleans music, which in turn became the bedrock for R&B, soul, country, reggae and rock'n'roll," he said. "Getting him back to his Lower 9th Ward house will send a clear message to his friends, neighbors and fans that we in New Orleans are coming back and Fats is leading the way."

Tom had long been a fan of Fats Domino's work and often programs a Domino song or two on his Buried Treasure radio show, most often playing hits like 'All By Myself', 'I'm In Love Again' and 'Let The Four Winds Blow'. He and The Heartbreakers were glad to help the Domino family – and the people of New Orleans – in whatever small way they could.

★ ★ ★

Later that year in August, Tom thought it would be a hoot to reunite with the original members of Mudcrutch. The kernel of the idea to get back together – albeit temporarily – had been planted a while ago but starting work on the documentary and recalling those early days with his Mudcrutch brethren may have been the push Tom needed to actually set a date to get together with his old friends and bandmates. He called drummer Randall Marsh and guitarist Tom Leadon and invited them out to California for a visit with him, Benmont and Mike.

What might have started out as a chance to wax nostalgic turned into a full-fledged recording session at the Clubhouse, The Heartbreakers' private rehearsal/recording space in the San Fernando Valley.

Rolling Stone's Andy Greene talked with Tom about Mudcrutch's "comeback" album in December of 2007. "It was weird. It was one of those lightning bolts to the brain," confided Tom. "A few years ago I just started thinking about how I missed those guys, Tom Leadon and Randall Marsh. We've stayed in contact over the years and we've all stayed good friends. I brought it up to Mike and everybody was up for it. We had a ball doing it... I moved over to bass, like I used to be. Everybody sings at least one song on it, though I did the majority of the singing. It has kind of a country/rock feel, but not as you think of it today. Maybe a little edgier country kind of feel."

After the first day of recording Tom said, "It was like we never left. We're actually a lot better than we were then." The album wouldn't be released until the spring of 2008.

But, of course, before the Mudcrutch album release came the premier of *Runnin' Down A Dream*. This four-hour documentary from director Peter Bogdanovich honed in on The Heartbreakers' long and illustrious career. Even casual Tom Petty & The Heartbreakers fans should see this film. As much as it is about this band, it's about what it takes to break through and rise to the top in an incredibly competitive industry.

The film includes a variety of interviews with Tom and The Heartbreakers as well as Rick Rubin, Stevie Nicks, Jeff Lynne, Jackson Browne, Eddie Vedder, Dave Grohl, Johnny Depp and George Harrison. In addition to the documentary, the four-disc DVD set includes footage of the band's 30th anniversary concert in Gainesville as well as a CD soundtrack with some rare takes like the recording of 'Anything That's Rock 'N' Roll' from the band's performance on *Top Of The Pops* in the UK in June 1977 and 'Keeping Me Alive', recorded at the Record Plant in Hollywood in 1982.

These sorts of films can be a tricky business to pull off effectively but Bogdanovich did so with aplomb. *Slant* magazine's Nick Schager agrees and felt the film only underscored why so many people are enamored with The Heartbreakers' lead singer. "Petty, through a series of simultaneously jovial and frank reflections on his past, comes across as thoughtful and inherently likeable, and even more than that, as the type of musician all-too-rarely found these days: one wholly dedicated to both his craft and his principles, regardless of the personal or commercial ramifications."

Tom and the band had a lot to be proud of at the release of *Runnin' Down A Dream*. It's not easy to keep a relationship going for so long and they've done it successfully for nearly 40 years. Mike commented at the time that, "We stuck together through a lot of hard times because we really have strong feelings for the music we make together." The band members also really love one another. "That's what hit me when I saw the film," says Mike. "It was like, 'God, we really like each other!' I mean, guys don't sit around saying, 'Hey, I love you, man,' but when I saw the film I thought, 'Hey, there really is love here. And it's not an act; it's true love.'"

★ ★ ★

The New Year brought an unexpected but welcome invitation. The NFL came knocking on Petty's door to find out if he and The Heartbreakers would perform during half-time at Super Bowl LXII. Tom was surprised by the invitation but readily said, 'yes'. In December of 2007 he joked with *Rolling Stone*'s Andy Greene, saying that this would be his first Super Bowl since "This is the only way I could get tickets."

The February 3 half-time show in Glendale, Arizona, during a showdown between the New York Giants and New England Patriots, eschewed pyrotechnics and dancing girls in favor of a straightforward rock set featuring 'American Girl', 'I Won't Back Down', 'Free Fallin'' and 'Runnin' Down A Dream'.

As springtime approached, Tom was finalizing the track list for the much-anticipated release from the Mudcrutch reunion sessions of 2007. The album, simply titled *Mudcrutch*, was released on April 29, 2008, and included 14 tunes written by Tom, Benmont and Tom Leadon; a collaboration between Tom and Mike; 'Six Days On The Road' written by Earl Green and Carl Montgomery; and 'Lover Of The Bayou' from Roger McGuinn and Jacques Levy. Two traditional songs, 'Shady Grove' and 'June Apple', also made it on the record.

Despite the fact that the old band was back together, some critics contended that the new music wasn't so much Mudcrutch as it was Mudcrutch 2.0. Stephen Thomas Erlewine of AllMusic put it this way: "Mudcrutch ramble and roll, sometimes stretching out for upwards of 10 minutes, sometimes stopping off for a circular circus instrumental, but they never quite ramp up the rock'n'roll, never lock into a thick swamp groove that would bring them back to their Southern roots. This is thoroughly a Californian album, all sun-bleached riffs and mellow grooves, so unhurried that it never breaks a sweat, more interested in the journey than the destination."

Entertainment Weekly gave the record a B+ with Clark Collis saying, in part, "Some tracks are surprisingly loose, such as the jammy 'Crystal River'. But midtempo rockers 'The Wrong Thing To Do' and 'Scare Easy' could have appeared on Petty's great last CD, *Highway Companion*. And his vocals have rarely sounded more quaveringly beautiful than they do on honky-tonk lament 'Orphan Of The Storm'.

The album made it onto the *Billboard* 200, at number eight, and music journalist Steven Hyden of A.V. Club said in his review what a lot of fans were thinking, "*Mudcrutch* is the great SoCal country-rock record the band never got to make the first time around."

The former bar band decided it would be nice to play a handful of intimate gigs before Tom Petty & The Heartbreakers headed out on their summer tour. The 13-concert California-centric mini-tour was set for April 12 to May 2, with the first concert, on April 12, a benefit for the Midnight Mission at Malibu's Performing Arts Center. The tour highlight was a six-night residency at West Hollywood's Troubadour.

Each concert was recorded for Tom's personal archives but on playback he felt the material should be released as an EP. "I didn't want to do a live album because I thought it would be too much of a mirror image of what we had done in the studio," Tom asserted at the time. "But when I heard things like the 15-minute version of 'Crystal River' from the Troubadour, my mind was changed." On November 11, Reprise released the four-track *Mudcrutch Live!* The disc included 'The Wrong Thing To Do', 'Bootleg Flyer', 'Crystal River' and the Ron Hargrave/Jerry Lee Lewis classic, 'High School Confidential'.

That same day, VH1 Classic broadcast a charming documentary titled *The Story Of Mudcrutch*, in which Tom says, "I made a commitment at the beginning of this project that I wanted this to be Mudcrutch, done as it was back in the day. I really wanted it to be *that* band." The studio and live albums are a testament that Mudcrutch was a worthy band back in the seventies and provides a bit of closure for Randall Marsh and Tom Leadon. They didn't have to wonder, "What if things had been different?" any longer.

★ ★ ★

As time ticks on, Tom Petty continues to refine his craft and branch into new areas of creativity. With the output of music from 2006 to 2008, it's clear that Tom has no intention of slowing down. Indeed, he feels it's vitally important that he continues to focus on his work in the hope of leaving something that endures. "I think a lot about what time I have left and what kind of mark I want to leave," Tom admits.

"But I know I have to keep doing it or I wouldn't know what to do. I might quit the road. I think I've had enough of that – but I haven't had enough of playing."

CHAPTER 14

What Lies Ahead I Have No Way Of Knowing (2009–Present)

"Time is precious these days."

– T.P.

In 2006, at the height of 30th anniversary celebrations for Tom Petty & The Heartbreakers, the media insisted on printing stories about how Tom was on the brink of retirement. There was a ticket-buying frenzy for The Last DJ tour because fans thought it could just be the last time Tom would step out onstage. He tried to put that talk to rest in an interview with *USA Today* at the time: "There's a rumor that I'm not going to tour anymore. I don't think that's true," he said, "but I'd like to take a long break... I love playing, but it eats up so much of your life. I'm really conscious of wasting time... I'm impatient now with anything that gets in the way of what I want to do." Even with Tom's own assurances that he'd be back, fans and music journalists were nearly convinced that he would draw the curtain on the concert and record-making merry-go-round. Happily, that didn't transpire and the band went on to tour extensively in 2008 as they would again in 2010, 2012 and 2013.

This incident in the late 2000s proved that Tom had an inner conflict. While he wanted to step back and take time away from his craft, he also felt compelled to work and create whenever the songs "appeared". There were sometimes long gaps between records and tours, but Tom never stopped creating music. His work ethic won't ever allow him to retire. He may back away from large-scale arena tours but he'll trade that in for appearing at a limited number of intimate venues and music festivals.

★ ★ ★

Fans greeted 2009 unsure of what to expect from their favourite musician that year. There were rumors that a live box set would be released but a date had not yet been set. The fact of the matter was that Tom, Mike and their trusted engineer Ryan Ulyate had been working on *The Live Anthology* box set since 2008. Tom has always been a savvy businessman and early in his career he had decided to record each and *every* live show. He's worked with the best sound engineers in the world to carefully record every single concert his band has played since the late seventies. The result, after 30 years in the business, is a vault of thousands upon thousands of tracks.

Ryan began this project with stacks of tapes and hundreds of digital files. "It took me months to digitise and convert everything into a common format," he explains. Once everything was digitised, he could audition all of the tracks from an iTunes library. The culling process began with nearly 200 concerts and thousands of songs. Ryan talks a bit about this project at his own website, Ulyate.com: "*Buried Treasure* is the name of Tom Petty's weekly SiriusXM radio show, and that's exactly what we found when we auditioned over 5,000 songs to choose the 62 that ended up on *The Live Anthology* [Deluxe Edition]. Developing a methodology to research, transfer, audition, mix and master this massive amount of material was a real challenge – and a lot of fun!" Ryan admits that, "Searching through all those takes was a big job to be sure and took weeks, but it wasn't quite as daunting as it might seem. Tom is a pretty tough critic and so it was easy to toss any song that was imperfect in any way, and we often knew that 20 seconds in. When we had 169 takes of 'American Girl', we felt pretty comfortable skipping over the blemished ones."

Two versions of *The Live Anthology* were released in November of 2009. The standard version, released on November 23, contains four CDs. The Deluxe Edition includes those four CDs plus two bonus DVDs. The first DVD is 1977's *Live From The Santa Monica Civic Center*. The second DVD is a previously unreleased documentary called *400 Days*, which was created in the *Wildflowers* era. The Deluxe Edition also includes a remastered vinyl version of 1977's *Official Live 'Leg* as well as a Blu-ray disc featuring all 62 songs in the box set in 5.1 surround sound. Artist Shepard Fairey – best known for his Barack Obama "Hope" poster designed for the 2008 presidential campaign – was responsible for *Live Anthology*'s cover design.

If the box set accomplished one thing, it's that it reminded everyone that Tom Petty & The Heartbreakers are, perhaps, the best American rock'n'roll band. Hard-to-please *Entertainment Weekly* gave *The Live Anthology* an A- and journalist Simon Vozick-Levinson had these words of praise: "The performances on this career-spanning four-disc compilation define the term 'ageless': Listening to these concert recordings, which date from four decades, you may have trouble figuring out which are old and which are new without consulting the liner notes. That's how tight Tom Petty & The Heartbreakers' onstage rapport has remained over the years."

The Live Anthology wasn't the only project Tom was working on during this time. He'd felt free in 2008 when Mudcrutch utilised a live-to-tape scheme during the recording of their album and Tom wanted to incorporate that same style into the next Heartbreakers record, *Mojo*. In fact, in November of 2009 Tom told *Rolling Stone*'s David Fricke that his goal was to record *Mojo* live in the studio with no overdubs. In today's world of over-processed music, most bands wouldn't dream of releasing a song that didn't contain hundreds of overdubs. That's not what Tom Petty & The Heartbreakers are all about.

Work began on the band's twelfth studio album at the end of April 2009, although the project wouldn't be finished until mid-January 2010. Once again, they used their own rehearsal/equipment warehouse space, the Clubhouse, as the studio. It had been eight years since The Heartbreakers had been in the studio together. Everyone agreed that this album should focus on the blues and, from the very first session, everything just fell into place. The band completed so many worthy tracks that it was hard for Tom to make the final cuts and sequence the record.

Unlike other albums where Tom kept the songs firmly under wraps, a few tunes were tested prior to the release of the record. In the middle of May the band appeared on the 35th season of *Saturday Night Live*. It was their eighth time on the show and they played two songs from the forthcoming album: the hit-worthy 'I Should Have Known It' and 'Jefferson Jericho Blues'.

Mojo was released on June 15, 2010, and the 15 songs therein had a certain earthiness to them. *New York Daily News'* Jim Faber commented extensively on the record's breadth of material. "Some lyrics make sure to expand the common palette of the blues, never more slyly than in the opening cut, 'Jefferson Jericho Blues'. It's about Thomas Jefferson's famed affair with his black maid. How better to address the contradictions, and conflicts, of race, art and ownership than that? The music in the song, like much of what's here, honors the band's own generation, and milieu, of the blues rather than any earlier incarnation. Essentially, that means its main reference point is The Allman Brothers, a fact made obvious from the twinned lead guitars in the opening track. That connection becomes even clearer in 'First Flash Of Freedom', which lifts the floating bass line and dancing structure of the Allmans' 1969 mind-expanding track 'Dreams'."

The emphasis on the blues was somewhat of a departure for the band but the album rocked harder than any other in their catalog since *Damn The Torpedoes*. Mike Mettler of *Sound + Vision* summed it up best when he explained that, "While you've never quite heard the band play this way before on record, the songs sound like you've known them all your life."

In fact, songs like 'I Should Have Known It' and 'Running Man's Bible' became instant fan favourites. The in-your-face 'I Should Have Known It' thumbs its nose at the girl who spurned the main character: 'I shoulda known it / I shoulda seen / Leave it to you / To treat me mean / Every promise was just a runaround / I shoulda known it / Yeah you're gonna let me down.' The character wins out in the end though as he promises his ex-lover that 'It's the last time you're gonna hurt me.' This song is a torch that just about any of us could pick up and carry.

The song was actually one of the more challenging to pull off for The Heartbreakers. Ron Blair talked with Ken Sharp of *Bass Player* about first learning that song. "'I Should Have Known It' was really trippy. Mike had made a demo for the song, and the demo had a bunch of stops in it and wasn't to an exact meter," he said. "I knew I was in trouble when I saw Ferrone busting out the paper and trying to decipher this thing. I was like, 'Shit, I'm gonna have to take some notes, too.' Somehow we deciphered that tune, but it was tricky just to make it through and nail one good take. Tom walked by and went, 'Wow, impressive.'"

'Runnin' Man's Bible' was especially poignant for Tom since the late Howie Epstein was the inspiration for the song. Tom told *Rolling Stone* that he "always wanted to deal with Howie's death, and there's some of that in there. [The track is] one of those embarrassingly revealing songs. It just crept into my mind one day. I was playing the guitar, and it started falling out." The song starts out "on this dark highway" and lines like the following elude to Howie's fate: "I been next in line / I been next to nothin' / Been next to bystanders / Who shoulda said somethin' / It was not in my vision / It was not in my mind / To return from a mission / A man left behind."

'The Trip To Pirate's Cove' – one of Tom's favourites on the album – is a laconic ballad that tells the story of two losers heading out on the road. One falls in love with a motel maid but leaves her behind and wonders years later what might have become of her. 'She was a part of my heart / Now she's just a line in my face.' Two other ballads – 'No Reason To Cry' and 'Something Good' – speak to the listener in an effective way as well. You just might tear up upon hearing 'No Reason

249

To Cry' as the singer comforts the woman he loves and tells her that it will be OK. He'll always be there for her. In 'Something Good' we empathise with a man who's never quite caught a break – likely because of the choices he's made in the past. Still, we're rooting for him to get it right this one last time.

Not all the songs are quite nearly as serious as those three. Another batch of somewhat light-hearted numbers – 'Candy' (about an aversion to vegetables, which has led the charter to a life devoted to sweets), 'Let Yourself Go' (which advises everyone to let go when life's commitments are getting just a little bit out of control) and the reggae-infused 'Don't Pull Me Over' (in which a man prays the cops don't pull him over for a small infraction he's committed) – can be found here as well.

The record comes to a close with 'Good Enough', which tells the story of a hard-to-love woman who wears out everyone in her life. Still the singer misses her when she leaves him.

Critics listened carefully to the new album and it was immediately apparent that this wasn't a typical Tom Petty & The Heartbreakers record. *Magnet*'s Patrick Berkery went as far as saying, "There's nary a harmony vocal or anything resembling a classic Petty hook on the record. This is something different. It's extremely skilled spontaneity. Something Petty has surely been trying to bring out of The Heartbreakers on record for a long time, perhaps as far back as when they were walking a tightrope nightly behind Bob Dylan in the eighties." Every musician shone on the record but Berkery pointed to one man in particular, "*Mojo* is an electrifying showcase for Campbell's lead guitar, quite possibly the most under-appreciated commodity in the history of rock 'n' roll."

Tom was probably extremely thankful that he'd been able to pull off that sense of spontaneity and that the public was eager to embrace this side of his band. It's clear Berkery certainly had since he closed his review of the record by saying, "By reaching way back to their roots, by doing what they do best – playing as a band – and by making a record that sounds like no record they've made before, Tom Petty & The Heartbreakers have come up with their most vital record in years."

Tom felt particularly inspired during the making of *Mojo* and felt he'd tapped into a good run when it came to songwriting. Everything seemed to align. "You have to set yourself up to receive the signal. You've got to help it along. I have to believe that, because there are too many times something's just gone *wallop* – there it is, and I don't really know why. But I don't like thinking about it. I don't want to analyse it too much, or then it'll be gone."

For those who want to know more about Tom's process in the studio, seek out the 13-minute, Sam Jones-directed documentary about the making of *Mojo*. It's archived at YouTube.

★ ★ ★

It was important to Tom to present an album that was worthy of a listen from top to bottom. "I don't know how many people take the time to sit down and listen to an album straight through anymore – but I do," says Tom. "And I look at it that way when I'm making one, too. It's a piece unto itself. It has a beginning, a middle and an end. That's the art of making an album."

The band started touring to back *Mojo* before the record was even released. A 46-date US tour started on June 1. The extent of the tour was surprising since Tom had spent the last few years telling anyone who'd listen that he planned to cut back when it came to being out on the road.

Each show on the tour was recorded and a live album titled *Mojo Tour 2010* was released on December 14. Anyone who bought a ticket for the summer tour received this album as a free download from TomPetty.com. An expanded edition with six additional tracks was released on the same day for members of Tom's fan club, Highway Companions.

The Mojo tour proved that Tom Petty & The Heartbreakers were still capable of filling large arenas and outdoor sheds, and that the fans ranged from teens as well as retirees who've stuck with the band since its birth in 1976. "It's everybody, man, from five to 50 out there," says Tom proudly. "You can see a 50-year-old hippie next to a 15-year-old kid with a green mohawk. And then there'll be a family who brought their baby." At this point in his career, Tom cherishes every fan and is humbled to see younger people in the crowd.

★ ★ ★

The year 2010 was notable for another reason: the release of an expanded "deluxe edition" of 1979's breakout smash album *Damn The Torpedoes* with previously unreleased tracks. It was perhaps inevitable that the band would begin releasing special edition album packages at this point in its career. With 34 years of music under its collective belt, the band had plenty of material in the vault that fans really wanted to hear. The souped-up version of the album was released in November and included additional tracks: two studio outtakes from the *Damn The Torpedoes* sessions – 'Nowhere' and 'Surrender' – and renditions of a few other songs that were previously unreleased throughout the band's career.

Very few people had ever even heard the song 'Nowhere'. It was lost to the ages back in 1979 when Tom's guitar tech, Bugs, moved session tapes around the city on a daily basis to avoid the chance that the court bailiffs could claim them as part of Tom's assets in his bankruptcy trial at the time. The tapes had gone missing and the band forgot all about the song. That is until recording engineer Ryan Ulyate came across the tape while hunting through the band's archive. Its addition to the deluxe edition of *Damn The Torpedoes* helps close the circle on that very trying time in the band's early career. The new album also contained the original 1979 recording of 'Surrender', which was a mainstay in the band's live set back then.

Highlights of the other new material on the record included live versions of 'Shadow Of A Doubt (Complex Kid)', 'Don't Do Me Like That' and 'Something Else' from a 1980 concert at Hammersmith Odeon. The demo of the B-side 'Casa Dega' was also a real treat as was an alternate take of the smash hit 'Refugee'.

★ ★ ★

Tom planned to keep a low profile in 2011 but in May, he and his wife Dana were honored at the 11th Annual Golden Heart Awards presented by the Midnight Mission, a Los Angeles-based nonprofit organization that helps people who need drug and alcohol rehabilitation. It also assists with transitional programs for the homeless in the area. Tom and Dana have been important supporters of the Mission for years and, in 2008, The Heartbreakers played a benefit for the charity. That concert raised nearly a quarter of a million dollars and helped the Midnight Mission continue its good works.

Tom lent his name to another worthy cause in 2011: publicly funded radio. He and The Heartbreakers staged two benefit shows for KCSN-FM Los Angeles at the Plaza del Sol Performance Hall at California State at Northridge. The intimate concerts on October 29 and 30 gave Tom a platform to stand up for the concept of publicly funded radio that's accessible to everyone. The proceeds from the show helped KCSN increase its signal strength and reach more listeners. It was the only opportunity fans had to see the band live in 2011.

In 2012, however, for the first time in 14 years, Tom Petty & The Heartbreakers planned to visit Europe and stage concerts in Ireland, Germany, Denmark, Sweden, Norway, Great Britain, the Netherlands, France and Italy.

A dozen or so warm-up dates were set for North America before The Heartbreakers flew to Dublin, Ireland, to begin their European odyssey. Fans hadn't seen them live in years and the reception was warm and welcoming. The Heartbreakers played a variety of venues, including arenas, festivals (Isle of Wight and Norwegian Wood), theaters like Paris' Le Grand Rex and intimate outdoor events like the one at Piazza Napoleone in the walled city of Lucca in Tuscany, Italy.

The Heartbreakers brought no new music to the table but fans were ecstatic nonetheless. The performances abroad invigorated Tom and the band so it was easy for them to spend the rest of 2012 and the beginning of 2013 working on new music.

Tom enjoyed a personal milestone on September 5, 2012, when 'I Won't Back Down' was played at the Democratic National Convention immediately after President Bill Clinton formally nominated Barack Obama for a second term as President of the United States of America to the enthusiastic delegates who were present. President Obama walked out on stage as the anthem played in the background. "I got chills," Tom told *Rolling Stone* at the time. "I've been on the wrong side where I've had to tell some candidates to stop using my music," he recalled, but that wasn't the case at the DNC event. "They knew it would be OK. I've had a chance to meet the President and talk to him about the music he listens to."

★ ★ ★

Tom Petty was quiet for the first month of 2013 and then in February announced through his website that Tom Petty & The Heartbreakers would play a few summer festivals, intimate theaters and select arenas and amphitheaters in the United States during the spring and summer. The news elated fans – some of whom thought the band might never tour again. Rumors in recent years indicate that Tom's hand, the one he broke all those years ago in a fit of rage over the initial mixes for *Southern Accents*, is acting up again. And, it didn't help that he injured that arm again in the late nineties. The story came out in an interview with Jaan Uhelszki in 1999. "Two years ago I was learning to kick box, and I fell and broke my arm – the same arm as the hand," Tom explained. "When I went into the hospital they X-rayed it, and every doctor who would walk in, even doctors who weren't treating me, would see the X-rays and go, 'Wow! Look at this!' It was all the metal in my hand. 'Come here. Look at this.' I'd hear it all day long. No one was paying any attention to the arm. It was all the metal in the end of the hand. It's all wires and studs. But I've never set off any alarms at the airport. Better than that, my hand works really good. It was a long operation, and a long recovery, but I always thought it would come back. I was never worried about it." Despite that Tom wasn't worried about the arm, fans were. They had noticed his arm sometimes shook – quite visibly – while he played guitar on the previous tour and they worried that the status of his arm might put a damper on future tours. Luckily, it did not.

Two intimate theater residencies – five nights in New York City at the Beacon Theater and six nights at Los Angeles' Henry Fonda Theater – promised to be the absolute highlight of the 2013 tour. Right after the run at the Beacon, Tom told *Rolling Stone*'s Andy Greene that while he enjoys all the shows, including huge arenas where he has an obligation to play the songs his fans love most, he didn't want to become a hit jukebox. These residencies were certainly the cure for that. It gave the band the freedom to eschew the obvious hits – the ones for which the audience knows all the words – in favor of more obscure numbers, songs from various side projects like the Traveling Wilburys, and songs written by other musicians that inspired The Heartbreakers over the years.

Special fan club presales were held months in advance of the concerts and tickets, including pricey VIP packages, were snapped up quickly. During the residencies themselves, the band's fan club went all out promoting the concerts to fans and the media. Every afternoon, the club would post trivia questions on the band's website, on Twitter, and its Facebook page. Correct answers netted the chance to win tickets to that evening's show. The fan club also staged treasure-hunt-style quests across Manhattan and Los Angeles. The clues would lead fans to a fan club rep who held coveted front row tickets to that night's performance. All you had to do was find the rep and offer up the correct resolution to the puzzle of the day. Fans went wild tracking down those front row seats and armchair contestants had fun answering the trivia questions about the band.

In pre-tour interviews, Tom promised that he'd mine his deep catalog at these shows for rarely played treasures and he didn't disappoint. The band dusted off songs like 'A Woman In Love (It's Not Me)', 'Girl On LSD', 'When The Time Comes', 'Best Of Everything' and 'When The Time Comes' among other tunes. Of course, crowd-pleasing hits like 'American Girl', 'Refugee' and 'Runnin' Down A Dream' were inserted into the set throughout the evening.

The band reveled in playing a range of covers like Paul Revere And The Raiders' '(I'm Not Your) Stepping Stone', Lowell George's 'Willin'' and JJ Cale's '13 Days'. Many in the crowd especially enjoyed hearing the band's take on the Grateful Dead tune 'Friend Of The Devil'. According to Tom, "Mike [Campbell] is a huge Grateful Dead fan. He started playing that one and taught it to the rest of us. That was back in the nineties at the Fillmore. We put it out on the *Live Anthology* record a few years ago. I thought, 'Yeah, that's doable. That's a really good song."

The concerts were well received but the set lists didn't change all that much from night to night. Some long-time fans had wished for slightly more varied set lists, like the band had played in 1999 at New York City's Irving Plaza or at their Fillmore residencies in 1997 and 1999. Still, the shows were unique and so much more special than stadium-style hit-fests that most rockers Petty's age feel compelled to promote.

Tom told *Rolling Stone*'s Greene a bit about the process the band went through to ultimately draft the set lists for the residencies: "The way we've done it is we've gone into rehearsal for, like, three weeks, which is long for us. We would just start to play and at the end of the night they [the band's crew] would have lists of everything we played. And that would go on the next day. We'd be like, 'What do you feel like doing today?' It would usually not be anything we played the day before. When we were done we had all these lists of things we played, and that's basically what I'm using to select the songs."

It was through this process that 'Fooled Again (I Don't Like It)' found its way back into the band's set list. "That was a real flash from the past," says Tom. "We used to play that on the first tour we did where we were going around doing clubs. Then we first went over to England. That was a big part of a show, and for whatever reason, that song just got left behind real early. When we re-addressed that one we were like, 'Wow, this is good.'"

One unfortunate event marred the band's six-night run at the Henry Ford Theater in Los Angeles. Fifteen songs into the performance on June 8, a representative from the Los Angeles Fire Department gave word to Tom that there was a problem. The venue was overcrowded and posed a safety issue to fans. As the band readied to play 'Melinda', Tom relayed the news to fans in this way: "Well, there's an official here beside the stage from the Los Angeles Fire Department that says the venue's too full, so they're asking that 100 people move from the floor to the balcony, or they're gonna shut it down. Ron Blair says he'll volunteer to go if need be. There, I've done my part. Now let me get back to doing what I do best." Tom launched into the song but from his onstage demeanor it was clear that he was worried about what might happen next. After all, tickets to this show were highly coveted. If someone bought a ticket for the floor, why in the world would they move upstairs? The logistics of getting 100 random people to willingly move to a worse location in the venue was challenging at best. As the final chords of 'Melinda' rang out, the fire chief was again at the side of the stage. The plug was being pulled and the show was cut short by about 30 minutes. (The band was about 90 minutes into their set at this point of the evening.)

While fans were incredibly disappointed about being cheated out of the rest of the concert – a particularly expensive concert for some – the scene did not become chaotic. Fans were confused as to what exactly had happened and so was Tom. The band and their management sought answers backstage but it was clear it would take a little time to unravel the issue. The next day the band posted the following announcement on their website: "First and foremost, the safety of our fans is our primary concern and the most important consideration. To those fans who attended last night's show at the Fonda Theater, we are as frustrated as you are! While we are still investigating exactly what happened we do know the following as of right now: 1) The number of tickets sold was *not* above the legal capacity of the building. The venue and Ticketmaster documentation confirms this. 2) The Fire Marshal decided that the number of people on the floor (as opposed to on the upstairs balcony or terrace) was unsafe. Tom Petty & The Heartbreakers and our representatives rely on the concert promoter and venue representatives to give us an accurate breakdown of the legal capacity for every part of the building and to provide security and other staff to enforce this. We are still investigating all details of last night's situation and will keep you informed. The shows at the Fonda tonight and Tuesday will go ahead as planned and we are working with the venue, the promoter and the Fire Marshal to ensure that this problem will not repeat itself. We thank you for your support. —Tom Petty & The Heartbreakers."

In the end, concertgoers were given a refund for the entire purchase price of the tickets, including all fees. It didn't assuage all bad feelings but it went a long way to confirm to fans just how much Tom Petty & The Heartbreakers care about their fans. The last two shows of the run at the theater went on without a hitch on June 9 and 11.

In between the band's stint in New York and their residency at the Henry Fonda Theater, *Rolling Stone*'s Andy Greene asked Tom if he thought the next tour would head back to larger venues. "I haven't got that far in my thinking yet... I would rather develop an audience around the quality of our work more than the popularity of our work. I'm very grateful we've been able to play hours of hits. It's a great thing, but not to the point where people think that's the only songs you ever did."

Prior to the tour Tom had actually performed elsewhere without The Heartbreakers: at the Nokio Theater in Los Angeles on April 18 as part of the 28th Rock and Roll Hall of Fame induction ceremony. It was the first time the event had been held in Tom's adopted hometown since 1993. This shake-up was a big deal to the music community who had become a bit tired of heading to New York City or Cleveland for these annual ceremonies. Tom joined Randy Newman, Jackson Browne and John Fogerty on stage to open the show with Newman's 1983 hit, 'I Love LA'. Later in the evening, Don Henley inducted Newman into the Hall. This was a nice precursor to the tour and definitely raised Tom's spirits.

In July of 2013, The Heartbreakers went back into the studio in July to finalise their thirteenth studio album. Tom had hinted to *Rolling Stone*'s Patrick Doyle in an exclusive interview in August that the new songs were born out of a similar style to the blues-rock of 2010's *Mojo,* but then veered off into a new direction. "One good thing about this point in life is that recording has gotten so much easier for us," Tom admits. "We can really realize what's in our heads pretty quickly without a lot of stress, so it's tremendous fun recording. And Ryan Ulyate, who began as our engineer on *Highway Companion* has become like a member of the band almost, you know? He got promoted to co-producer on *Mojo*. He's been a tremendous help to us. I looked all my life for that engineer partner in the studio that would be perfect, and we found him."

It goes without saying that working with The Heartbreakers definitely puts Tom in his comfort zone. "It's gotten where it's so instinctual," he says. "They're so ridiculously good. If I play them a song that I just wrote, they'll do the first take and it's suddenly a whole different thing than I pictured. And we usually go in and listen after one take and then we'll say, 'OK, you should do more of this and you should do less of that.' And in a few takes, we've usually got an arrangement.

"I've gotten where I don't really give out many instructions or try and write a part for anybody else," Tom confided to Doyle. "I just let them try to find their own way and they're very good. We've all recorded so much, we've spent a lot of time in the studio and they're really good at knowing what's too much and what's not gonna groove. It's all about grooves too, you know. You've got to lay down a groove and – I mean I feel like we've got one of the best drummers there is, you know, and he's just a rock. Like, he's unbelievable. [Steve] Ferrone just gets better and better and better – he's amazing."

The new record will drop at the beginning of 2014, just as this book hits stores. Tom is hopeful that he'll get back out on the road to support the record but first he's thinking about rounding up the guys from Mudcrutch in order to record their sophomore album and possibly even do a few shows on the East Coast. Time will tell if that project becomes a reality.

★ ★ ★

August 2013 brought a small controversy to Petty's doorstep. In a post-tour interview, Patrick Doyle of *Rolling Stone* questioned Tom about a comment he made while onstage at the Beacon Theater in May. Tom had asserted today's country music was "bad rock with fiddle".

During the interview, Tom elaborated on this thought, saying, in part, "I hate to generalize on a whole genre of music, but it does seem to be missing that magic element that it used to have. I'm sure there are people playing country that are doing it well, but they're just not getting the attention that the shittier stuff gets. But that's the way it always is, isn't it? But I hope that kind of swings around back to where it should be. But I don't really see a George Jones or a Buck Owens or anything that fresh coming up." Some may question if Tom, as a traditional rock'n'roll artist, has a right to offer such criticism to musicians in a different genre. However, it's important to remember Tom's roots in the south and his early exposure to all sorts of music, including traditional country artists. He and The Heartbreakers worked extensively with country music legend Johnny Cash in the past and certainly were no strangers to the genre while in the studio. Don't forget about the band's heart-felt version of Hank Williams' 'You're Gonna Change (Or I'm Gonna Leave').

Despite Tom's roots in country music, some individuals in that community took great offense to his remarks. Singer-songwriter Chris Stapleton was especially offended by the criticism. Stapleton is a Grammy-nominated musician with solid credentials under his belt. He wrote the song 'Never Wanted Nothing More', which Kenny Chesney took to number one on the charts. He's also written hits for other artists like Vince Gill, George Strait and Tim McGraw.

After hearing Tom's tirade against today's country music, Stapleton aired his frustration with those comments on Facebook, writing this open letter to Petty:

"Dear Tom Petty,

I think it's safe to say most modern country artists, including me, would list you as an influence. Your recent comments lead me to believe you see room for improvement in modern country music. I, for one, would like to see you put you money where your mouth is in a tangible way.

So, in the interest of making country music less "s—tty" (your words), I suggest a collaboration. I'm extending an open invitation to you to write songs with me, produce recordings on or with me, or otherwise participate in whatever way you see fit in my little corner of music.

In the event that you actually read this and are interested, look me up.

Sincerely,
Chris Stapleton"

It's doubtful that Tom will respond to Stapleton's open letter and even more doubtful that he'll collaborate with him in the future. Tom's got his plate full at the moment finishing up his latest album and pondering the possibility of a second Mudcrutch album. It would be highly surprising if he made time to shift his career temporarily toward the country side of the radio dial.

Stapleton wasn't the only singer offended by Tom's remarks. Country music artist Jake Owen – a fan of Petty's music – was disappointed to hear the critique from his fellow Floridian. "It's unfortunate that he'd make a ridiculous, uneducated comment like that about a format he's not even a part of," Owen said in an interview with SiriusXM Satellite Radio.

The fact of the matter is that Tom has publicly criticised other musical genres in the press in the past. Take his 1989 interview with Dave Zimmer of *BAM* magazine. Tom set his sights on heavy metal bands, saying, "It's really sort of comic book stuff. It's not rock'n'roll, by any stretch of anybody's imagination… I'm not trying to criticize the people who do it or saying I'm better than them. But in my opinion, it's not incredibly original stuff. Most of it's downright bad. If you were to play them on piano and really sing some of those songs, which may be unfair since heavy metal, I guess, is only played real loud. But I don't hear a whole lot going on. There's nothing really wrong with it and some of the odd tracks here and there are pretty good. Like Metallica seems to have something going on. But the other stuff is so silly."

Comments like that have been pretty standard throughout Petty's history. He's an honest guy and in an interview he can sometimes let his guard down and phrase things in a way that some people might take offense to. In the end, it's simply Petty's high standards that lead him to critique music and hold out hope that musicians can always strive to be better.

★ ★ ★

In recent years Tom has also tried to devote as much time as possible to his family. His first daughter, Adria, was born in 1974 when he was just starting out and working hard to launch a career in the music business.

By the time Annakim came along in 1982, his stardom was at a fever pitch. He was absent from the home for many childhood milestones. Lamenting those missed moments wouldn't do any good now, but as a father he's been cognizant to try be a part of his children's lives in the here and now. Adria and Annakim may have once been known because of their famous father but they both have grown into young women with extraordinarily creative lives and interesting professions. Their work stands on its own without any help from their dad, although he was surely a major influence.

Adria is now a prominent film director and cinematographer. After graduating from Sarah Lawrence College in 1996 with a strong background in film studies, she went to work in the field. Her sheer determination – likely inherited from her dad – helped her land several high profile jobs as an assistant to renowned movie directors like Jonathan Demme, Penny Marshall and Jonathan Stack. In 2002 she designed the package design for her dad's album *The Last DJ*. By 2008 she was shepherding her own films and directed the wildly popular documentary *Paris, Not France* about celebrity Paris Hilton.

Two years later Adria directed her second documentary: *Regina Spektor: Live In London*. She may be best known as a music video director though and has done groundbreaking work with Spektor, Beyoncé, Coldplay, Rihanna, Kings Of Leon and Macy Gray. She's also developed smart advertising campaigns for corporations like Volkswagen, Lancôme, Converse and McDonald's.

In 2012 Adria was nominated for five MTV Video Music Awards for her work on Beyoncé's 'Countdown', Coldplay and Rihanna's 'Princess Of China' and Regina Spektor's 'All The Row Boats'. Tom and his wife, Dana, accompanied Adria to the September 6 ceremony at the Staples Center in Los Angeles. You have to wonder if Tom reflected on his own illustrious music video career while sitting in the audience that night. He blazed the trail to create storyboarded music videos like 'You Got Lucky', 'Don't Come Around Here No More' and 'Mary Jane's Last Dance'. He himself won the MTV Video Vanguard award for his lifetime contributions to the field. His daughter's interest and aptitude for taking the genre even further must have made him very proud. In fact, while talking with a reporter at the event, he had a message for another rock'n'roll superstar: "Bono, if you're listening, I think you should make a music video with my daughter."

Adria's younger sister, Annakim Violette, is no less distinguished as an artist in her own right. Tom and Jane's youngest daughter changed her last name from Petty to Violette simply, she's told the press, because ultraviolet is her favourite color. All it takes is a few short minutes in Annakim's presence to know that she sees the world differently from most other people and interprets those differences through her unique fashion sense, her cutting-edge artwork and her music.

She's best known for rocking an androgynous vampire-meets-fairy look. She's seen about town in Los Angeles wearing electric colors, vibrant prints, dazzling vintage dresses and psychedelic pieces from the seventies. She models for a variety of photographers, though Autumn de Wilde – best known for her portraits of heavy hitters in the music industry – is one of Annakim's favourites. And while she's no fan of New York City, she does make the trip east for Fashion Week. The designers she's most intrigued about include Rodarte, Alexander McQueen and Summer Harrison.

As a child, Annakim always had dreams of a creative career. At first she wanted to be a roadie, and then a painter and a musician. Today she does a little bit of everything, including being the frontwoman for a band called Mircalla Glass. The outfit released its first album on October 3, 2012 on Glitter Underage Records. *Wet Princess Lost In Paradise* is a concept album – her dad would be pleased about that! – that tells the tale of a vampire-mermaid who goes on a mad murder spree in Los Angeles.

In addition to her music, Annakim is an artist who works in a variety of mediums, but many of her pieces revolve around the vampire theme and bats figure prominently in her work. She's a person who examines life from all viewpoints and feels there are still unchartered waters in the arts. She recently gave this advice to a reporter from the StyleLikeU blog: "Keep moving like a shark so that you won't get eaten, you can actually make what you want in the world… we are jaded to think there is nothing original anymore… there's so much that hasn't been done, and that doesn't mean regret, that just means you can start anywhere."

Adria and Annakim are Tom's only children from his marriage to Jane Benyo, but he is also father to stepson Dylan York Epperson Petty, Dana Petty's son from her previous marriage. Dylan was born in Bellaire, Texas, in the early nineties and he currently resides in Malibu where he graduated from Malibu High School in 2009.

After his mom married Tom Petty in 2001, Dylan spent plenty of time on the road with The Heartbreakers. His stepdad put him to work and fans often saw Dylan working right alongside the crew, setting up equipment onstage before a show. This early exposure to the rock'n'roll scene only solidified his own desire to become a musician. In 2008 Dylan co-founded a band with guitarist Chase Simpson. At first they called themselves Automatic Slim and then changed the name slightly to Automatik Slim. Dylan was the frontman and by 2010 the band had grown to also include Josh Jove on guitar, Sam Skolfield on bass and Sebastian Harris on drums. In April 2011 the band was named Best New Upcoming Artist at the Malibu Music Awards.

The band's now-abandoned Facebook page says its influences at the time included Dylan's famous stepfather as well as The Beatles, The Who, Muddy Waters, Rage Against The Machine and other eclectic artists. Automatik Slim played some club dates like Molly Malones in Hollywood and the Malibu Inn, but now seem to be inactive on the local music scene. According to Dylan's personal Facebook page, he is now studying Early Childhood Education at a college in Woodland Hills.

These days Tom finally has time to spend with those he loves, including his three children and Dana. It should come as no surprise that Dana is also heavily involved in the creative arts. She is a photographer and fine artist in her own right although she tends to keep a low profile in that regard. She is also involved in many philanthropic activities and goes on the road with The Heartbreakers whenever her husband stages a tour. The couple enjoys spending time in their Malibu home.

Tom is always the first to say that his sole focus is on music but he has been trying to widen his circle of interests in recent years. "Music runs my life. I'm embarrassed that I don't have any hobbies," he says. "I don't collect anything. Well, I collect records and guitars." Even so, there are a few other things that he has a passion for and that includes basketball. He can often be spotted in excellent courtside seats at Los Angeles Lakers games with Dana, stepson Dylan or his brother Bruce, who flies into town every so often for a visit. With the respect of the music industry, the love of his fans and his place assured in rock'n'roll's firmament, Tom Petty can finally take time away from the studio and the road to focus on the important relationships in his life.

★ ★ ★

Some would say that, at 63 years old, Tom Petty is in the twilight of his career. He'd likely admonish that line of thinking and counter it with the idea that rock'n'roll troubadours don't follow a prescribed timeline. Since meeting Elvis all those years ago, Tom was destined to be an artisan who patiently waits for those mystical moments when he's able to – somehow – tune in to a song, pull it from the ether and mark it as his own.

Tom has always taken music seriously. Once he realized the breadth of his gift, he felt he owed a debt to the art form itself that he may never be able to fully repay. This respect for the craft is what sets him apart from so many other musicians who so often take it for granted and then lose their connection to it. Tom feels obligated to write the most meaningful songs that he can – anything less would be an insult to music and to his audience. This gift he has is rare and he has no choice but to continue to create music for as long as he possibly can. "This is a crazy thing to do for a living," Tom says. "I never had any choice about it though, I never thought about it. It must go all the way back to the guy who used to wander from village to village with his guitar. Certain people are inclined that way. The ones that aren't are soon weeded out."

With a body of work that will soon span 40 years, Tom Petty & The Heartbreakers are the stuff of which legends are made. Tom's songs are intimately personal and mean so much to millions of people all over the world. The simplicity of the lyrics cut right to the heart of the matter and that is one reason the music transcends geographical boundaries and cultures. The music stands on its own.

These days Tom often reflects on the music his band has made over the years. "I would like to think that we made some good records that will endure," he says. "It's a nice feeling to know that you've made music that's left a mark. It did save my life. It rescued a troubled child. I owe it a great deal."

Fans would assure him that he's more than repaid that karmic debt with the music he's made. Tom probably never dreamed that kids who heard The Heartbreakers' first album in 1976 would still be fans today. From 'American Girl', the theme song to many a woman's life, to the soaring tracks on *Damn The Torpedoes*, the incredibly likeable album that was *Full Moon Fever* and the more current blues-infused music of *Mojo*, Tom Petty's fans have remained loyal to the core. They've stuck around and have always been eager to see where Tom would go next. Petty has long cherished this loyalty and works hard to keep this bond with his fans strong. "Longevity," Tom says, "comes from offering new things from time to time and taking your audience somewhere – if they're willing to go." Tom has been lucky to have a strong fanbase that definitely wants to forge ahead alongside their favourite musician and band.

While Tom Petty's music can easily stand on its own, there is something magical about what The Heartbreakers bring to the table and Tom readily agrees. "That noise The Heartbreakers make… that God awful racket that they make. They do make a noise, a particular noise when you have the five of them together that I've never really heard anywhere else," he muses. "It's funny because if you take two of us and put us with three other guys, it doesn't make the same noise, but it's a good noise and I've come to cherish it and be grateful for it."

In one of the nicest – and completely true – things a music critic ever wrote about Tom Petty & The Heartbreakers, *Mojo*'s Joe Selvin summed up the band thusly in a 1997 review: "The deceptive simplicity of what Petty and band do, the guileless brand of timeless rock they seem to effortlessly create, may have disguised how great The Heartbreakers truly are. Without doubt, when his enormous catalogue and consistent excellence are weighed, Petty ranks with the best in American rock history."

"We have probably the best rock'n'roll band there is," says Tom. "And with that comes the responsibility of making really good records and doing really good shows." That responsibility is something Tom took on from the moment he formed his first band, The Sundowners. As a natural leader in the mold of China's Sun Tzu – an admired military general and strategist of the Dhou Dynasty – Tom mapped out the trajectory of not only his life's work but that of the other Heartbreakers. He's felt the need to take care of the band and he's done so admirably from the very early days.

Tom's daughter Adria recognized this thread of responsibility in her father. She talked with *Interview* magazine reporter Angela Ledgerwood about this very topic. "I think my dad saw himself as a family man, somebody that had a child the year he got a record deal and moved out to California with 12-plus dependents," she says. "He was 22 and felt a great deal of pressure to support all of the people that believed in him. What he was doing was based on a work ethic and a focus on quality. I wasn't given the sense that celebrity, or fame or any of that, was something to be impressed by, or to seek out. It was always impressed upon me that making something well crafted, something respected, was the most important thing to do with your life, and I've tried to do that where I can in my field." If nothing else, Tom should be incredibly proud that he successfully imparted such an important lesson to his children.

Tom Petty continues to write music and perform in a quest to repay fate for giving him this incredible gift: rock'n'roll. It held his hand through childhood when his world was not always as cosmically harmonic as it should have been. "Music is still a safe place for me," he says. "I had to have something to do with the troubled family I lived in, so I retreated into that world and then it paid off for me in the long run. But music is good that way. It really heals people in many ways, and in my life, it's the only absolute real magic that I've ever come across. It's a higher place and it's always delivered for me. It still does."

Album Discography

Tom Petty & The Heartbreakers • **Tom Petty & The Heartbreakers (1976)**
Rockin' Around (With You), Breakdown, Hometown Blues, The Wild One, Forever, Anything That's Rock 'N' Roll, Strangered In The Night, Fooled Again (I Don't Like It) Mystery Man, Luna, American Girl

You're Gonna Get It! • **Tom Petty & The Heartbreakers (1978)**
When The Time Comes, You're Gonna Get It!, Hurt, Magnolia, Too Much Ain't Enough, I Need To Know, Listen To Her Heart, No Second Thoughts, Restless, Baby's A Rock 'N' Roller

Damn The Torpedoes • **Tom Petty & The Heartbreakers (1979)**
Refugee, Here Comes My Girl, Even The Losers, Shadow Of A Doubt (A Complex Kid), Century City, Don't Do Me Like That, You Tell Me, What Are You Doin' In My Life?, Louisiana Rain

Hard Promises • **Tom Petty & The Heartbreakers (1981)**
The Waiting, A Woman In Love (It's Not Me), Nightwatchman, Something Big, Kings Road, Letting You Go, A Thing About You, Insider, The Criminal Kind, You Can Still Change Your Mind

Long After Dark • **Tom Petty & The Heartbreakers (1982)**
A One Story Town, You Got Lucky, Deliver Me, Change Of Heart, Finding Out, We Stand A Chance, Straight Into Darkness, The Same Old You, Between Two Worlds, A Wasted Life

Southern Accents • **Tom Petty & The Heartbreakers (1985)**
Rebels, It Ain't Nothin' To Me, Don't Come Around Here No More, Southern Accents, Make It Better (Forget About Me), Spike, Dogs On The Run, Mary's New Car, The Best Of Everything

Pack Up The Plantation: Live! • **Tom Petty & The Heartbreakers (1985)**
So You Want To Be A Rock 'N' Roll Star, Needles And Pins, The Waiting, Breakdown, American Girl, It Ain't Nothin' To Me, Insider, Rockin' Around (With You), Refugee, I Need To Know (LP and cassette only), Southern Accents, Rebels, Don't Bring Me Down, You Got Lucky (LP and cassette only), Shout, Stories We Could Tell

Let Me Up (I've Had Enough) • **Tom Petty & The Heartbreakers (1987)**
Jammin' Me, Runaway Trains, The Damage You've Done, It'll All Work Out, My Life/Your World, Think About Me, All Mixed Up, A Self-Made Man, Ain't Love Strange, How Many More Days, Let Me Up (I've Had Enough)

Full Moon Fever • **Tom Petty (1989)★**
Free Fallin', I Won't Back Down, Love Is A Long Road, A Face In The Crowd, Runnin' Down A Dream, Feel A Whole Lot Better, Yer So Bad, Depending On You, The Apartment Song, Alright For Now, A Mind With A Heart Of Its Own, Zombie Zoo

Into the Great Wide Open • **Tom Petty & The Heartbreakers (1991)**
Learning To Fly, Kings Highway, Into The Great Wide Open, Two Gunslingers, The Dark Of The Sun, All Or Nothin', All The Wrong Reasons, Too Good To Be True, Out In The Cold, You And I Will Meet Again, Makin' Some Noise, Built To Last

269

Greatest Hits • Tom Petty & The Heartbreakers (1993)

American Girl, Breakdown, Listen To Her Heart, I Need To Know, Refugee, Don't Do Me Like That, Even The Losers, Here Comes My Girl, The Waiting, You Got Lucky, Don't Come Around Here No More, I Won't Back Down, Runnin' Down A Dream, Free Fallin', Learning To Fly, Into The Great Wide Open, Mary Jane's Last Dance, Something In The Air

Wildflowers • Tom Petty (1994)★

Wildflowers, You Don't Know How It Feels, Time To Move On, You Wreck Me, It's Good To Be King, Only A Broken Heart, Honey Bee, Don't Fade On Me, Hard On Me, Cabin Down Below, To Find A Friend, A Higher Place, House In The Woods, Crawling Back To You, Wake Up Time

Songs And Music From The Motion Picture She's The One • Tom Petty & The Heartbreakers (1996)

Walls (Circus), Grew Up Fast, Zero From Outer Space, Climb That Hill, Change The Locks, Angel Dream (No. 4), Hope You Never, Asshole, Supernatural Radio, California, Hope On Board, Walls (No. 3), Angel Dream (No. 2), Hung Up And Overdue, Airport

Echo • Tom Petty & The Heartbreakers (1999)

Room At The Top, Counting On You, Free Girl Now, Lonesome Sundown, Swingin', Accused Of Love, Echo, Won't Last Long, Billy The Kid, I Don't Wanna Fight, This One's For Me, No More, About To Give Out, Rhino Skin, One More Day, One More Night

Anthology: Through The Years • Tom Petty & The Heartbreakers (2000)

Breakdown, American Girl, Hometown Blues, The Wild One, Forever, I Need To Know, Listen To Her Heart, Too Much Ain't Enough, Refugee, Here Comes My Girl, Don't Do Me Like That, Even The Losers, The Waiting, A Woman In Love (It's Not Me), Stop Draggin' My Heart Around, You Got Lucky, Straight Into Darkness, Change

Of Heart, Rebels, Don't Come Around Here No More, The Best Of Everything, So You Want To Be A Rock 'N' Roll Star, Jammin' Me, It'll All Work Out, Love Is A Long Road, Free Fallin', Yer So Bad, I Won't Back Down, Runnin' Down A Dream, Learning To Fly, Into The Great Wide Open, Two Gunslingers, Mary Jane's Last Dance, Waiting For Tonight, Surrender

The Last DJ • Tom Petty & The Heartbreakers (2002)
The Last DJ, Money Becomes King, Dreamville, Joe, When A Kid Goes Bad, Like A Diamond, Lost Children, Blue Sunday, You And Me, The Man Who Loves Women, Have Love, Will Travel, Can't Stop The Sun

Highway Companion • Tom Petty (2006)★
Saving Grace, Square One, Flirting With Time, Down South, Jack, Turn This Car Around, Big Weekend, Night Driver, Damaged By Love, This Old Town, Ankle Deep, The Golden Rose. Special Edition Bonus Tracks: Home, Around The Roses, Big Weekend (demo version), This Old Town (demo version)

Mudcrutch • Mudcrutch (2008)★★
Shady Grove, Scare Easy, Orphan Of The Storm, Six Days On The Road, Crystal River, Oh Maria, This Is A Good Street, The Wrong Thing To Do, Queen Of The Go-Go Girls, June Apple, Lover Of The Bayou, Topanga Cowgirl, Bootleg Flyer, House Of Stone. iTunes Special Bonus Track: Special Place

Mudcrutch Live! • Mudcrutch (2008)★★
The Wrong Thing To Do, Bootleg Flyer, Crystal River, High School Confidential

The Live Anthology • Tom Petty & The Heartbreakers (2009)
Disc One: Nightwatchman, Even The Losers, Here Comes My Girl, A Thing About You, I'm In Love, I'm A Man, Straight Into Darkness, Breakdown, Something In The Air, I Just Want To Make Love To You, Drivin' Down To Georgia, Lost Without You, Refugee. Disc

Two: Diddy Wah Diddy, I Want You Back Again, Wildflowers, Friend Of The Devil, A Woman In Love (It's Not Me), It's Good To Be King, Angel Dream (No. 2), Learning To Fly, Mary Jane's Last Dance, Mystic Eyes. Disc Three: Jammin' Me, The Wild One, Forever, Green Onions, Louisiana Rain, Melinda, Goldfinger, Surrender, Dreamville, Spike, Any Way You Want It, American Girl. Disc Four: Runnin' Down A Dream, Oh Well, Southern Accents, Crawling Back To You, My Life/Your World, I Won't Back Down, Square One, Have Love Will Travel, Free Fallin', The Waiting, Good, Good Lovin', Century City, Alright For Now

Mojo • **Tom Petty & The Heartbreakers (2010)**

Jefferson Jericho Blues, First Flash Of Freedom, Running Man's Bible, The Trip To Pirate's Cove, Candy, No Reason To Cry, I Should Have Known It, U.S. 41, Takin' My Time, Let Yourself Go, Don't Pull Me Over, Lover's Touch, High In The Morning, Something Good Coming, Good Enough. iTunes Bonus Track: Little Girl Blues.

Mojo Tour 2010 • **Tom Petty & The Heartbreakers (2010)**

Kings Highway, You Don't Know How It Feels, I Won't Back Down, Drivin' Down To Georgia, Breakdown, I Should Have Known It, Good Enough, Runnin' Down A Dream.

Expanded Edition: Listen To Her Heart, Kings Highway, You Don't Know How It Feels, I Won't Back Down, Drivin' Down To Georgia, Breakdown, Jefferson Jericho Blues, First Flash Of Freedom, Running Man's Bible, I Should Have Known It, Good Enough, Refugee, Runnin' Down A Dream, American Girl

*Indicates Tom Petty solo albums.
**Indicates record releases from the Mudcrutch reunion of 2008.

Tom Petty has played in bands with guitarist Mike Campbell for 44 years and each night on stage is a new revelation. The pair is pictured here at Newark, New Jersey's Prudential Center on June 18, 2008. TONY KURDZUK/STAR LEDGER/CORBIS

A trio of soulful musicians, from left: Petty, rockabilly legend Carl Perkins and Brian Setzer of the Stray Cats.

Friends and band mates forever, from left: Ron Blair, Petty, Benmont Tench and Mike Campbell.

A night out with the family in 2007, at Warner Bros. Studios in Burbank, California, to celebrate the premiere of director Peter Bogdanovich's documentary film, *Runnin' Down A Dream*, from left: son Dylan Petty, wife Dana York Petty and Tom.
FRED PROUSER/REUTERS/CORBIS

Tom Petty with friend and musician JJ Cale, one of the father's of the "Tulsa Sound". ROMAN CHO

Pearl Jam's Eddie Vedder grew up with the music of Tom Petty & The Heartbreakers, but now he occasionally takes to the stage with his heroes. Here he sings 'The Waiting' with The Heartbreakers backing him during one of their tours. PAUL WARNER/WIREIMAGE

Tom Petty – with and without The Heartbreakers – has won many high-profile awards throughout the years. Here is accepting an honor from (left to right) Richie Gallo of Universal Music and UME President Bruce Resnikoff. Petty's long-time manager, Tony Dimitriades, is at right. MICHAEL SCHWARTZ/WIREIMAGE

Even when Petty's kicking back he's playing music. He and his high-profile friends enjoy a jam session, from left: Jeff Lynne, Petty, Mike Campbell and actor Johnny Depp. FLICKR.COM/HOSKINSIS

Mudcrutch redux. The original band gets back together for a show at West Hollywood's Troubadour on May 1, 2008 in support of the Mudcrutch's self-titled release, from left: Mike Campbell, Randall Marsh, Petty and Tom Leadon. TIM MOSENFELDER/GETTY IMAGES

Tom Petty celebrates the accomplishments of his daughter, Adria Petty (left) at the 2012 MTV Video Music Awards with his wife Dana (right). Adria, a prominent film director and cinematographer, was nominated for five awards for her work with Beyoncé, Coldplay, Rihanna, and Regina Spektor. SPLASH NEWS/CORBIS

Petty onstage with Stephen Stills. KMAZUR/WIREIMAGE

Tom Petty and Mike Campbell join the Allman Brothers Band and other musicians onstage at the Greek Theatre on May 19, 2009 in Los Angeles, from left: Warren Haynes, Campbell, Derek Trucks, and Petty. ANGELA WEISS/GETTY IMAGES

Band members and director Peter Bogdanovich celebrate the launch of the *Runnin' Down A Dream* documentary and book at Milk Studios in New York City, from left: Scott Thurston, Benmont Tench, Bogdanovich, Petty, and Mike Campbell.

The Foo Fighters' Dave Grohl takes a bow with Tom Petty after performing with The Heartbreakers.

Tom Petty performing with The Heartbreakers at the Bridgestone halftime show during Super Bowl XLII between the New York Giants and New England Patriots on February 3, 2008, at the University of Phoenix Stadium in Arizona. STREETER LECKA/GETTY IMAGES

Videography

Classic Albums: Damn The Torpedoes (2010)★
A documentary on the making of the *Damn The Torpedoes* album.

Runnin' Down A Dream (2007)★
Director Peter Bogdanovich's excellent four-hour documentary about the band.

Soundstage Presents Tom Petty & The Heartbreakers (2003)★
This is the live concert DVD of PBS' *Soundstage* television series, which is produced by WTTW in Chicago. This episode was taped during a series of concerts at the Vic Theatre in April 2003.

Live At The Olympic: The Last DJ And More (2003)★
The Heartbreakers performed *The Last DJ* in its entirety at the Grand Olympic Auditorium on October 16, 2002.

High Grass Dogs: Live From The Fillmore (1999)★
Concert footage from the band's 1999 residency at The Fillmore in San Francisco.

Playback (1995)★

A complication of music videos that was released alongside the *Playback* box set

Take The Highway: Live (1992)★★

Concert footage from the band's 1991 Into the Great Wide Open tour.

Full Moon Fever: The Videos (1990)★★

A collection of music videos that were released to promote the album

A Bunch of Videos and Some Other Stuff (1989)★★

This is a terrific VHS for a Tom Petty memorabilia collection. It archives a handful of The Heartbreakers' first music videos along with interview footage of the band.

Pack Up The Plantation: Live! (1985)★★

This DVD features live concert footage from two shows filmed at the Wiltern Theatre in Los Angeles on August 6–7, 1985.

Hard To Handle: Bob Dylan With Tom Petty & The Heartbreakers (1986)★★

HBO produced the *Hard To Handle* concert special featuring Bob Dylan on stage in Australia with Tom Petty & The Heartbreakers during the 1986 tour.

★*available on DVD and Blu-ray*
★★*VHS only*

Other Videos of Interest

Concert For George (2003)★
Filmed at the Royal Albert Hall, this is a touching concert tribute to George Harrison.

Sound City (2013)★
Dave Grohl's fantastic documentary about the legendary Sound City Studios.

★*available on DVD and Blu-ray*
★★*VHS only*

Tour Dates

1976

November 30, 1976, Municipal Auditorium, Columbus, GA (opening
for Kiss)

December 12, 1976, Paul's Mall, Boston, MA (opening for Al Kooper)

December 14 & 15, 1976, CBGB, New York, NY

1977

February 9–12, 1977, Whisky A Go Go, Los Angeles, CA (opening
for Blondie)

February 14–19, 1977, Keystone Palo Alto, Palo Alto, CA (with the
Greg Kihn Band)

February 23, 1977, Ivanhoe Theater, Chicago, IL

March 5, 1977, Royal Oak Music Theatre, Royal Oak, MI

March 7–9, 1977, Bottom Line, New York, NY (opening for Roger
McGuinn)

March 10, 1977, Agora Ballroom, Cleveland, OH (opening for The
Runaways)

March 13, 1977, Bogart's, Cincinnati, OH

March 14, 1977, The Flying Machine, Akron, OH

April 24, 1977, Winterland, San Francisco, CA (opening for Bob Seger)

April 26 & 27, 1977, Whisky A Go Go, Los Angeles, CA

May 8, 1977, Capitol Theater, Cardiff, Wales

May 9, 1977, Lancaster University, England

May 10, 1977, BBC Studios, London (taping a segment of the *Old Grey Whistle Test* TV program)

May 11, 1977, Birmingham Odeon, England

May 12, 1977, Brighton Dome, England

May 14–16, 1977, Hammersmith Odeon, London, England

May 17, 1977, Bristol Hippodrome, England

May 19, 1977, Manchester Apollo, England

May 20, 1977, Sheffield City Hall, England

May 21, 1977, Leeds University, England

May 22, 1977, Trentham Gardens, Stoke-on-Trent, England

May 23, 1977, Empire Theatre, Liverpool, England

May 24, 1977, Newcastle City Hall, England

May 25, 1977, Edinburgh Playhouse, Scotland

May 26, 1977, Apollo Theatre, Glasgow, Scotland

May 30, 1977, Pinkpop Festival, Geleen, Netherlands

June 1, 1977, Pavillon de Paris, Paris, France (opening for The Kinks with Nils Lofgren)

June 2, 1977, Frankfurt, Germany (opening for Nils Lofgren)

June 4, 1977, Paradiso, Amsterdam, Netherlands

June 6, 1977, Lund, Sweden

June 12, 1977, Manchester Free Trade Hall, England

June 14, 1977, WDR Studio, Cologne, Germany (taping a segment of *Rockpalast* TV program)

June 16, 1977, London, England (taping a segment of *Top Of The Pops* TV program)

June 16, 1977, Birmingham Town Hall, England (with the Boomtown Rats)

June 17, 1977, Cardiff University, Wales (with the Boomtown Rats)

June 18, 1977, Aylesbury Friars Club, Buckinghamshire, England (with the Boomtown Rats)

June 19, 1977, Rainbow Theatre, London, England (with the Boomtown Rats)

June 20, 1977, Club Lafayette, Wolverhampton, England (with the Boomtown Rats)

June 24, 1977, Exeter University, Devon, England

June 25, 1977, Hull University, Yorkshire, England

August 5, 1977, Paramount Theatre, Portland, OR

August 10 & 11, 1977, Old Waldorf, San Francisco, CA

August 12 & 13, 1977, Whisky A Go Go, Los Angeles, CA

September 10, 1977, Winterland, San Francisco, CA (opening for Be Bop Deluxe)

September 11, 1977, Warnors Center for the Performing Arts, Fresno, CA (opening for Be Bop Deluxe)

September 12, 1977, The Catalyst, Santa Cruz, CA

September 14 & 15, 1977, Santa Monica Civic Auditorium, Santa Monica, CA (opening for Be Bop Deluxe)

September 16, 1977, Celebrity Theatre, Phoenix, AZ (opening for Be Bop Deluxe)

October 28, 1977, Paramount Theatre, Portland, OR

October 29, 1977, Yakima Valley Community College, Yakima, WA (opening for the J. Geils Band)

November 7, 1977, Santa Monica Civic Auditorium, Santa Monica, CA (opening for Nektar)

November 14, 1977, Agora Ballroom, Cleveland, OH (opening for Meat Loaf)

November 15, 1977, Painesville Agora, Painesville, OH (opening for Meat Loaf)

November 19, 1977, Bottom Line, New York, NY

November 20, 1977, Bottom Line, New York, NY

November 23, 1977, Civic Arena, Pittsburgh, PA (opening for the J. Geils Band)

November 26, 1977, Tower Theatre, Philadelphia, PA (opening for Rush)

November 29, 1977, My Father's Place, Roslyn, NY

December 2, 1977, Riviera Theatre, Chicago, IL (with Elvis Costello and the Attractions)

1978

May 11, 1978, Montezuma Hall, SDSU, San Diego, CA

May 13, 1978, Freeborn Hall, UC Davis, Davis, CA

May 14, 1978, UC Riverside, Riverside, CA

June 3, 1978, Stanford Memorial Auditorium, Palo Alto, CA

June 5, 1978, Santa Monica Civic Auditorium, Santa Monica, CA

June 9, 1978, Chico State Gym, Chico, CA

June 10, 1978, Winterland, San Francisco, CA

June 11, 1978, Veterans Memorial, Santa Rosa, CA

June 12, 1978, Lane County Fair, Eugene, OR

June 13 & 14, 1978, Paramount Theatre, Portland, OR

June 20, 1978, BBC Studios, London (taping a segment of the *Old Grey Whistle Test* TV program)

June 24, 1978, Knebworth Festival, Hertfordshire, England

June 27, 1978, Marquee Club, London, England

July 6, 1978, Jacksonville, FL (opening for the Patti Smith Group)

July 7, 1978, Curtis Hixon Hall, Tampa FL (opening for the Patti Smith Group)

July 8, 1978, Miami Jai Alai Fronton, Miami, FL (opening for the Patti Smith Group)

July 12, 1978, Cobo Hall, Detroit, MI (opening for Journey)

July 13, 1978, Music Hall, Cleveland, OH

July 14, 1978, Palladium, New York, NY

July 15, 1978, Paramount Theatre, Asbury Park, NJ

July 16, 1978, Paradise Theater, Boston, MA (recording for the *King Biscuit Flower Hour* syndicated radio show)

July 17, 1978, Warner Theater, Washington, DC

July 18, 1978, Tower Theater, Philadelphia, PA

July 22, 1978, Cape Cod Coliseum, South Yarmouth, MA (opening for the J. Geils Band)

July 28, 1978, Calderone Concert Hall, Hempstead, NY (opening for the J. Geils Band)

August 1, 1978, Civic Center, Oklahoma City, OK (opening for The Kinks)

August 3, 1978, The Warehouse, New Orleans, LA (opening for The Kinks)

August 5 & 6, 1978, Fox Theater, Atlanta, GA (opening for The Kinks with Blondie)

September 14, 1978, Kiel Opera House, St. Louis, MO

September 16, 1978, Uptown Theater, Kansas City, MO

September 20, 1978, Memorial Auditorium, Louisville, KY

September 22, 1978, Circle Theater, Indianapolis, IN

September 23, 1978, Riviera Theater, Chicago, IL

December 29, 1978, Redding Civic Auditorium, Redding, CA

December 30, 1978, Winterland, San Francisco, CA

December 31, 1978, Santa Monica Civic Auditorium, Santa Monica, CA

1979

July 23, 1979, Sherwood Hall, Salinas, CA

July 24, 1979, Santa Cruz Civic Auditorium, Santa Cruz, CA

July 25, 1979, Community Theater, Sacramento, CA

July 28, 1979, Universal Amphitheater, Los Angeles, CA

September 22, 1979, Muse concert, Madison Square Garden, New York, NY

November 10, 1979, NBC Studio 8-H, New York, NY (taping a segment of *Saturday Night Live*)

November 11, 1979, The Palladium, New York, NY

November 13, 1979, Tower Theater, Philadelphia, PA

November 17, 1979, Orpheum Theater, Boston, MA

November 19, 1979, Masonic Auditorium, Detroit, MI

November 23, 1979, Aragon Ballroom, Chicago, IL

November 25, 1979, St. Paul Civic Theatre, St. Paul, MN

December 2, 1979, Orpheum Theatre, Memphis, TN

December 6, 1979, Music Hall, Houston, TX

December 23, 1979, Paramount Theatre, Seattle, WA

December 27, 1979, The Gardens, Vancouver, Canada

December 28 & 29, 1979, Paramount Theatre, Portland, OR

December 31, 1979 Oakland Coliseum, Oakland, CA

1980

January 9, 1980, Civic Center, Oklahoma City, OK

January 11, 1980, Memorial Hall, Kansas City, MO

January 12, 1980, Kiel Opera House, St. Louis, MO

January 18, 1980, Golden Hall, San Diego, CA

January 20, 1980, The Forum, Los Angeles, CA

January 21, 1980, Whisky A Go Go, Los Angeles, CA

January 22, 1980, Symphony Hall, Phoenix, AZ

January 26, 1980, Main Auditorium, University of Arizona, Tucson, AZ

January 27, 1980, University of California, Santa Barbara, CA

March 2, 1980, Birmingham Odeon, Birmingham, England

March 6 & 7, 1980, Hammersmith Odeon, London, England (recording for the *King Biscuit Flower Hour* syndicated radio show on the 7th)

March 11, 1980, Empire Theatre, Paris, France

March 24, 1980, Polytechnic, Oxford, England

April 16, 1980, Mainichi Hall, Osaka, Japan

April 17, 1980, Kinrou-Kaikan, Nagoya, Japan

April 19, 21 & 22, 1980, Youmuira Hall, Tokyo, Japan

April 26, 1980, Capitol, Theatre, Sydney, Australia

April 29, 1980, Brisbane, Australia

May 1 & 2, 1980, Palais Theatre, Melbourne, Australia

May 3, 1980, unknown venue, Adelaide, Australia

May 6, 1980, unknown venue, Christchurch, New Zealand

May 8, 1980, unknown venue, Wellington, New Zealand

May 11, 1980, unknown venue, Honolulu, Hawaii

June 9, 1980, Red Rocks Amphitheatre, Denver, CO

June 13, 1980, Market Square Arena, Indianapolis, IN

June 16, 1980, Pine Knob Music Center, Clarkson, MI

June 18, 1980, Poplar Creek Music Theatre, Chicago, IL

June 20, 1980, Blossom Music Center, Cuyahoga Falls, OH

June 21, 1980, Merriweather Post Pavilion, Columbia, MD

June 25, 1980, Saratoga Performing Arts Center, Saratoga Springs, NY

June 27, 1980, Capitol Theatre, Passaic, NJ

July 1, 1980, Performing Arts Center, Providence, RI

July 4–6, 1980, The Palladium, New York, NY

July 9, 1980, The Spectrum, Philadelphia, PA

July 10, 1980, Stanley Theatre, Pittsburgh, PA

July 11, 1980, Mosque Theatre, Richmond, VA

July 15, 1980, Bayfront Center, St. Petersburg, FL

July 19, 1980, Robertson Gym, UC Santa Barbara, Goleta, CA

1981

June 14, 1981, Centennial Hall, University of Toledo, Toledo, OH

June 16, 1981, Richfield Coliseum, Richfield, OH

June 17, 1981, Rosemont Horizon, Chicago, IL

June 18, 1981, Cobo Arena, Detroit, MI

June 21, 1981, Red Rocks Amphitheatre, Denver, CO

June 22, 1981, Hollywood, CA (recording for the *Rockline* syndicated radio show)

June 24, 1981, Aladdin Theater, Las Vegas, NV

June 26, 1981, Cow Palace, San Francisco, CA (guest Stevie Nicks)

June 28–30, 1981, The Forum, Los Angeles, CA (guest Stevie Nicks)

July 4, 1981, Pacific Coliseum, Vancouver, Canada

July 5, 1981, Hec Edmundson Pavilion, Seattle, WA

July 6, 1981, Astor Park, Seattle, WA

July 8, 1981, Portland Memorial Coliseum, Portland, OR

July 18, 1981, Castle Farms, Charlevoix, MI

July 20, 1981, Ottawa Civic Centre, Ottawa, Canada

July 22, 1981, Maple Leaf Gardens, Toronto, Canada

July 24, 1981, New Haven Veterans Memorial Coliseum, New Haven, CT

July 26, 1981, Saratoga Performing Arts Center, Saratoga Springs, NY

July 27, 1981, The Spectrum, Philadelphia, PA (guest Stevie Nicks)

July 28, 1981, Rochester Community War Memorial, Rochester, NY

July 30, 1981, Brendan Byrne Arena, East Rutherford, NJ (guest Stevie Nicks)

July 31, 1981, Merriweather Post Pavilion, Columbia, MD

August 3, 1981, Stabler Arena, Bethlehem, PA

August 6, 1981, Nassau Veterans Memorial Coliseum, Uniondale, NY

August 7, 1981, Boston Garden, Boston, MA

August 8, 1981, Providence Civic Center, Providence, RI

August 10, 1981, Memorial Auditorium, Buffalo, NY

August 11, 1981, Indianapolis, IN

August 12, 1981, Kiel Opera House, St. Louis, MO

August 14, 1981, Metropolitan Sports Center, Bloomington, MN

August 15, 1981, Civic Auditorium, Omaha, NE

August 16, 1981, Alpine Valley Music Theatre, East Troy, WI

September 6, 1981, Cal Expo Grandstands, Sacramento, CA (guest Stevie Nicks)

September 15, 1981, Tucson Convention Center, Tucson, AZ

September 17, 1981, ASU Activity Center, Tempe, AZ

September 18 & 19, 1981, Irvine Meadows, Irvine, CA (guest Stevie Nicks)

September 22, 1981, The Summit, Houston, TX

September 23, 1981, Reunion Arena, Dallas, TX

September 24, 1981, Frank Erwin Center, Austin, TX

September 29, 1981, The Omni, Atlanta, GA (guest Stevie Nicks)

September 30, 1981, Savannah Civic Center, Savannah, GA (guest Stevie Nicks)

October 2, 1981, Lakeland Civic Center, Lakeland, FL (guest Stevie Nicks)

October 3, 1981, Civic Auditorium, Jacksonville, FL (guest Stevie Nicks)

October 6, 1981, Bayfront Arena, St. Petersburg, FL (guest Stevie Nicks)

October 8, 1981, O'Connell Center, Gainesville, FL (guest Stevie Nicks)

1982

June 6, 1982, Peace Sunday, Rose Bowl, Pasadena, CA

September 1 & 2, 1982, Civic Auditorium, Santa Cruz, CA

September 4, 1982, US Festival, Glen Helen Regional Park, Devore, CA

September 19, 1982, Whisky A Go Go, Los Angeles, CA

November 30, 1982, Forest National, Brussels, Belgium

December 3, 1982, Isstadion, Stockholm, Sweden

December 4, 1982, Muziekcentrum Vredenburg, Utrecht, Netherlands

December 8, 1982, Manchester Apollo, Manchester, England

December 9, 1982, Playhouse Theatre, Edinburgh, Scotland
December 10, 1982, Coventry Apollo, Coventry, England
December 12, 1982, Wembley Arena, London, England
December 18, 1982, Westfalenhalle, Dortmund, Germany
December 22, 1982, Statdhalle, Offenbach, Germany

1983
January 22, 1983, Arizona Veterans Memorial Coliseum, Phoenix, AZ
January 23, 1983, Tucson Convention Center, Tucson, AZ
January 24, 1983, Don Haskins Center, University of Texas, El Paso, TX
January 26, 1983, Myriad Arena, Oklahoma City, OK
January 27, 1983, Frank Erwin Center, Austin, TX
January 28, 1983, The Summit, Houston, TX
January 30, 1983, Reunion Arena, Dallas, TX
February 3, 1983, Mid-South Coliseum, Memphis, TN
February 4, 1983, The Omni, Atlanta, GA
February 6, 1983, Charlotte Coliseum, Charlotte NC
February 8, 1983, West Palm Beach Auditorium, West Palm Beach, FL
February 11, 1983, Bayfront Arena, St. Petersburg, FL
February 14, 1983, Grand Ole Opry House, Nashville, TN
February 15, 1983, Louisville Gardens, Louisville, KY
February 17, 1983, Stabler Arena, Bethlehem, PA
February 18, 1983, Pittsburgh Civic Arena, Pittsburgh, PA
February 19, 1983, NBC Studio 8-H, New York, NY (*Saturday Night Live*)
February 25, 1983, Hammons Student Center, Springfield, MO
February 26, 1983, Kiel Opera House, St. Louis, MO
March 2, 1983, Colorado University Events Center, Boulder, CO
March 4, 1983, SIU Arena, Carbondale, IL
March 5, 1983, Municipal Auditorium, Kansas City, MO
March 6, 1983, Omaha Civic Auditorium, Omaha, NE
March 10, 1983, Dane County Coliseum, Madison, WI
March 11, 1983, Met Center, Bloomington, MN
March 12, 1983, Cedar Rapids Coliseum, Cedar Rapids, IA
March 14, 1983, Milwaukee Arena, Milwaukee, WI

March 15, 1983, Rosemont Horizon, Chicago, IL
March 17, 1983, Market Square Arena, Indianapolis, IN
March 18, 1983, Cobo Arena, Detroit, MI
March 19, 1983, Richfield Coliseum, Richfield, OH
March 21, 1983, Memorial Auditorium, Buffalo, NY
March 22, 1983, Broome County Arena, Binghamton, NY
March 24, 1983, Worcester Centrum Center, Worcester, MA
March 25, 1983, Providence Civic Center, Providence, RI
March 26, 1983, New Haven Coliseum, New Haven, CT
March 28, 1983, Civic Arena Theatre, Pittsburgh, PA
March 29, 1983, William and Mary College, Williamsburg, VA
March 31, 1983, Nassau Veterans Memorial Coliseum, Uniondale, NY
April 1, 1983, Brendan Byrne Arena, East Rutherford, NJ
April 2, 1983, The Spectrum, Philadelphia, PA
April 8, 1983, Seattle Center Coliseum, Seattle, WA
April 9, 1983, Paramount Theatre, Portland, OR
April 11, 1983, Paramount Theatre, Portland, OR
April 13, 1983, Cow Palace, San Francisco, CA
April 14, 1983, Kabuki Theatre, San Francisco, CA
April 15, 1983, CSUF Amphitheatre, Fresno, CA
April 19 & 21, 1983, Universal Amphitheater, Los Angeles, CA
April 23, 1983, Jack Murphy Stadium, San Diego, CA
April 25, 1983, Universal Amphitheater, Los Angeles, CA
June 1, 1983, Bakersfield Centennial Garden, Bakersfield, CA
June 4 & 5, 1983, Mountain Aire '83, Calaveras County Fairgrounds, Angels Camp, CA
June 8, 1983, Red Rocks Amphitheatre, Denver, CO
June 10, 1983, Irvine Meadows Amphitheater, Irvine, CA

1984
no concerts

1985
June 6, 1985, Kiel Opera House, St. Louis, MO
June 8, 1985, Ohio Center, Columbus, OH

June 9, 1985, Merriweather Post Pavillion, Columbia, MD

June 11, 1985, Worcester Centrum Center, Worcester, MA

June 14, 1985, Mann Music Center, Philadelphia, PA

June 15, 1985, Meadowlands Arena, East Rutherford, NJ

June 16, 1985, Saratoga Performing Arts Center, Saratoga Springs, NY

June 18, 1985, Blossom Music Center, Cuyahoga Falls, OH

June 19, 1985, Indianapolis Sports Center, Indianapolis, IN

June 21, 1985, Pine Knob Music Center, Clarkson, MI

June 22, 1985, Poplar Creek Music Theatre, Chicago, IL

June 23, 1985, Alpine Valley, East Troy, WI

June 25, 1985, Civic Center, St. Paul, MN

June 26, 1985, Kemper Arena, Kansas City, MO

June 28, 1985, Civic Arena, Omaha, NE

July 3, 1985, Frank Erwin Center, Austin, TX

July 5, 1985, Reunion Arena, Dallas, TX

July 6, 1985, Convention Center, San Antonio, TX

July 7, 1985, The Summit, Houston, TX

July 9, 1985, Nashville Municipal Auditorium, Nashville, TN

July 11, 1985, The Omni, Atlanta, GA

July 12, 1985, USF Sun Dome, Tampa, FL

July 13, 1985, JFK Stadium, Philadelphia, PA (Live Aid)

July 14, 1985, Jones Beach Amphitheater, Wantagh, NY

July 20, 1985, Lawlor Events Center, Reno, NV

July 21, 1985, Cal Expo Amphitheater, Sacramento, CA

July 24, 1985, Seattle Center Coliseum, Seattle, WA

July 26, 1985, Greek Theater, Berkeley, CA

July 27, 1985, Concord Pavilion, Concord, CA

July 30, 1985, Compton Terrace, Phoenix, AZ (guest Stevie Nicks)

August 1, 1985, The Forum, Los Angeles, CA

August 4, 1985, Universal Amphitheater, Los Angeles, CA

August 5, 1985, Costa Mesa, CA

August 6, 1985, Wiltern Theater, Los Angeles, CA

August 7, 1985, Wiltern Theater, Los Angeles, CA

August 9, 1985, Sports Arena, San Diego, CA

September 17, 1985, Mulholland Tomorrow Benefit, Universal Amphitheater, Los Angeles, CA

September 19, 1985, Sanctuary Benefit, Tucson, AZ

September 22, 1985, Farm Aid, Memorial Stadium, Champaign, IL

1986

February 5, 1986, Athletic Park, Wellington, New Zealand

February 7, 1986, Mt. Smart Stadium, Auckland, New Zealand

February 10–13, 1986, Entertainment Centre, Sydney, Australia (guest Stevie Nicks on 11 and 12)

February 15, 1986, Memorial Drive, Adelaide, Australia

February 17, 1986, Perth Entertainment Centre, Perth, Australia

February 18, 1986, Perth Entertainment Centre, Perth, Australia

February 20–22, 1986, Kooyong Stadium, Melbourne, Australia

February 24 & 25, 1986, Entertainment Centre, Sydney, Australia

February 28, 1986, Lang Park, Brisbane, Australia

March 1, 1986, Lang Park, Brisbane, Australia

March 5, 1986, Nippon Budokan Hall, Tokyo, Japan

March 6, 1986, Osaka-Jou Hall, Osaka, Japan

March 8, 1986, Nagoya-Taiikukan, Nagoya, Japan

March 10, 1986, Nippon Budokan Hall, Tokyo, Japan

June 6, 1986, Conspiracy of Hope Benefit, The Forum, Los Angeles, CA

June 9, 1986, San Diego Sports Arena, San Diego, CA

June 11, 1986, Lawlor Events Center, Reno, NV

June 12, 1986, Cal Expo Amphitheater, Sacramento, CA

June 13 & 14, 1986, Greek Theater, Berkeley, CA

June 16 & 17, 1986, Pacific Amphitheater, Costa Mesa, CA

June 18, 1986, Veterans Memorial Coliseum, Phoenix, AZ

June 20, 1986, Southern Star Amphitheater, Houston, TX

June 21, 1986, Erwin Center, Austin, TX

June 22, 1986, Reunion Arena, Dallas, TX

June 24, 1986, Market Square Arena, Indianapolis, IN

June 26, 1986, Hubert H. Humphrey Metrodome, Minneapolis, MN

June 27, 1986, Alpine Valley Amphitheater, East Troy, WI

June 29, 1986, Poplar Creek Music Theater, Chicago, IL

June 30, 1986, Pine Knob Music Theater, Clarkson, MI
July 1, 1986, Pine Knob Music Theater, Clarkson, MI
July 2, 1986, Rubber Bowl, Akron, OH
July 4, 1986, Rich Stadium, Buffalo, NY
July 6 & 7, 1986, RFK Stadium, Washington, DC
July 8 & 9, 1986, Great Woods Center, Mansfield, MA
July 11, 1986, Civic Center Auditorium, Hartford, CT
July 13, 1986, Saratoga Performing Arts Center, Saratoga Springs, NY
July 15–17, 1986, Madison Square Garden, New York, NY
July 19 & 20, 1986, The Spectrum, Philadelphia, PA
July 21, 1986, Brendan Byrne Arena, East Rutherford, NJ
July 22, 1986, Great Woods Center, Mansfield, MA
July 24, 1986, Sandstone Amphitheater, Bonner Springs, KS
July 26 & 27, 1986, Red Rocks Amphitheater, Morrison, CO
July 29, 1986, Memorial Coliseum, Portland, OR
July 31, 1986, Tacoma Dome, Tacoma, WA
August 1, 1986, The B.C. Place, Vancouver, Canada
August 3, 1986, The Forum, Los Angeles, CA
August 5, 1986, Shoreline Amphitheatre, Mountain View, CA
August 6, 1986, Mid-State Fairground, Paso Robles, CA
October 5, 1986, Beverly Theatre, Los Angeles, CA (Tom guests with
    Elvis Costello & The Attractions on 'American Girl' and 'What's So
    Funny 'Bout Peace, Love & Understanding'.)
October 13, 1986, Annual Bridge School Benefit Concert, Shoreline
    Amphitheatre, Mountain View, CA (Tom and Benmont)

1987
May 30, 1987, The Summit, Houston, TX
June 1, 1987, Reunion Arena, Dallas, TX
June 4, 1987, Concord Pavilion, Concord, CA
June 5, 1987, Shoreline Amphitheatre, Mountain View, CA
June 6, 1987, Pacific Amphitheatre, Costa Mesa, CA
June 8, 9, 11 & 12, 1987, Universal Amphitheater, Los Angeles, CA
June 15, 1987, Omaha Civic Auditorium, Omaha, NE
June 16, 1987, Met Center, Bloomington, MN

June 18, 1987, Pine Knob Music Theatre, Clarkson, MI
June 19, 1987, Alpine Valley, East Troy, WI
June 20, 1987, Poplar Creek Music Theater, Hoffman Estates, IL
June 22, 1987, Pittsburgh Civic Arena, Pittsburgh, PA
June 23, 1987, Blossom Music Center, Cuyahoga Falls, OH
June 26, 1987, Saratoga Performing Arts Center, Saratoga Springs, NY
June 27, 1987, Great Woods, Mansfield. MA
July 8, 1987, Madison Square Garden, New York, NY
July 10, 1987, Jones Beach Amphitheater, Wantagh, NY
July 11, 1987, Garden State Arts Center, Holmdel, NJ
July 18, 1987, Lakeside Amphitheatre, Darien Center, NY
July 20, 1987, Merriweather Post Pavilion, Columbia MD
July 22, 1987, The Omni, Atlanta, GA
July 24, 1987, Memorial Coliseum, Jacksonville, FL
July 26, 1987, USF Sun Dome, Tampa, FL
September 5, 1987, Hayarkon Park, Tel Aviv, Israel
September 7, 1987, Sultans Pool, Jerusalem, Israel
September 10, 1987, St. Jacobshalle, Basle, Switzerland
September 12, 1987, Autodromo, Moderna, Italy
September 14, 1987, Eisstadion, Mannheim, Germany
September 15, 1987, Westfalenhalle, Dortmund, Germany
September 16, 1987, Frankenhalle, Nurenburg, Germany
September 17, 1987, Waldbuehne, Berlin, Germany
September 19, 1987, Ahoy, Rotterdam, Netherlands
September 20, 1987, Sportpark, Hannover, Germany
September 21, 1987, Valbyhallen, Copenhagen, Denmark
September 23, 1987, Isshallen, Helsinki, Finland
September 25, 1987, Scandinavium, Gothenburg, Sweden
September 26, 1987, Isstadion, Stockholm, Sweden
September 28, 1987, Festhalle, Frankfurt, Germany
September 29, 1987, Martin Schleyerhalle, Stuttgart, Germany
September 30, 1987, Olympichalle, Munich, Germany
October 1, 1987, Arena di Verona, Verona, Italy
October 3, 1987, Paleur, Rome, Italy
October 4, 1987, Arena Civica, Milan, Italy

October 5, 1987, Piazza Grande, Locarno, Switzerland

October 7, 1987, P.O.P.B. Bercy, Paris, France

October 8, 1987, P.O.P.B. Bercy, Paris, France or Forest National, Brussels, Belgium

October 10–12, 1987, National Exhibition Centre, Birmingham, England

October 14–17, 1987, Wembley Arena, London, England

(guest George Harrison on 17)

1988

December 4, 1988, Annual Bridge School Benefit Concert, Oakland Coliseum, Oakland, CA

1989

July 5, 1989, Miami Arena, Miami, FL

July 6, 1989, Bayfront Center Arena, St. Petersburg, FL (guest Roger McGuinn)

July 8, 1989, Orlando Arena, Orlando, FL

July 9, 1989, Marcus Amphitheater, Milwaukee, WI

July 13, 1989, The Summit, Houston, TX

July 14, 1989, Frank Erwin Center, Austin, TX

July 15, 1989, Starplex Amphitheatre, Dallas, TX

July 17, 1989, Fiddler's Green Amphitheater, Colorado Springs, CO

July 20, 1989, Seattle Center Coliseum, Seattle, WA

July 22, 1989, Shoreline Amphitheatre, Mountain View, CA

July 23, 1989, Cal Expo Amphitheatre, Sacramento, CA

July 25, 1989, SDSU Open Air Theatre, San Diego, CA

July 26, 1989, Wells Fargo Arena, Tempe, AZ

July 27, 1989, Pacific Amphitheatre, Costa Mesa, CA

July 29–31, 1989, Universal Amphitheater, Los Angeles, CA

August 4, 1989, Lakewood Amphitheatre, Atlanta, GA

August 7, 1989, Pine Knob Music Theatre, Clarkson, MI

August 8, 1989, Blossom Music Center, Cuyahoga Falls, OH

August 10, 1989, Poplar Creek, Music Theater, Hoffman Estates, IL

August 15, 1989, Mann Music Center, Philadelphia, PA

August 16, 1989, Jones Beach Theater, Wantagh, NY

August 18, 1989, Orange County Fairgrounds, Middletown, NY
August 19, 1989, Brendan Byrne Arena, East Rutherford, NJ
August 20, 1989, Garden State Arts Center, Holmdel, NJ
August 23, 1989, Merriweather Post Pavilion, Columbia, MD
August 26, 1989, New York State Fair, Syracuse, NY
August 27, 1989, Saratoga Performing Arts Center, Saratoga Springs, NY
August 28, 1989, Great Woods, Mansfield, MA
August 31, 1989, Lake Compounce, Bristol, CT
September 8, 1989, Great Woods, Mansfield, MA
September 9, 1989, War Memorial Arena, Rochester, NY
September 10, 1989, Ohio Center, Columbus, OH
September 13, 1989, Dean Smith Center, Chapel Hill, NC
October 28, 1989, Annual Bridge School Benefit Concert, Shoreline
    Amphitheatre, Mountain View, CA
January 24, 1990, Universal Amphitheater, Los Angeles, CA
(taping of *Late Night with David Letterman* 8th Anniversary Special,
    broadcast February 1, 1990)
January 26, 1990, USF Sun Dome, Tampa, FL
January 27, 1990, O'Connell Center, Gainesville, FL
January 29, 1990, Charlotte Coliseum, Charlotte, NC
January 31, 1990, Nassau Coliseum, Uniondale, NY
February 1, 1990, Providence Civic Center, Providence, RI
February 3, 1990, Knickerbocker Arena, Albany, NY
February 4, 1990, Patriot Center, Fairfax, VA
February 6, 1990, The Spectrum, Philadelphia, PA
February 7, 1990, Worcester's Centrum Centre, Worcester, MA
February 8, 1990, Hartford Civic Center Coliseum, Hartford, CT
February 10, 1990, University of Dayton Arena, Dayton, OH
February 11, 1990, Palace of Auburn Hills, Auburn Hills, MI
February 13, 1990, Richfield Coliseum, Richfield, OH
February 15, 1990, Allstate Arena, Rosemont, IL
February 16, 1990, Redbird Arena, Normal, IL
February 17, 1990, Carver-Hawkeye Arena, Iowa City, IA
February 19, 1990, Hilton Coliseum, Ames, IA
February 20, 1990, Met Center, Bloomington, MN

February 22, 1990, Market Square Arena, Indianapolis, IN

February 23, 1990, SIU Arena, Carbondale, IL

February 25, 1990, Kiel Auditorium, St. Louis, MO

February 26, 1990, Kemper Arena, Kansas City, MO

March 1, 1990, The Forum, Los Angeles, CA (guests Bob Dylan and Bruce Springsteen)

March 3, 1990, Pacific Amphitheatre, Costa Mesa, CA (guest Roger McGuinn)

March 5, 1990, Arco Arena, Sacramento, CA

March 6, 1990, Oakland Coliseum, Oakland, CA

1991

August 29, 1991, Fiddler's Green, Denver, CO

September 1, 1991, Riverport Amphitheatre, Maryland Heights, MO

September 3, 1991, Omaha Civic Auditorium, Omaha, NE

September 4, 1991, Met Center, Bloomington, MN

September 6, 1991, Poplar Creek Music Theatre, Hoffman Estates, IL

September 7, 1991, Marcus Amphitheatre, Milwaukee, WI

September 10, 1991, Deer Creek Music Center, Noblesville, IN

September 12, 1991, Palace of Auburn Hills, Auburn Hills, MI

September 13, 1991, Blossom Music Center, Cuyahoga Falls, OH

September 15, 1991, Post-Gazette Pavilion At Star Lake, Burgettstown, PA

September 16, 1991, First Union Spectrum, Philadelphia, PA

September 19, 1991, Hartford Civic Center Coliseum, Hartford, CT

September 21, 1991, Knickerbocker Arena, Albany, NY

September 22, 1991, Maple Leaf Gardens, Toronto, Canada

September 25, 1991, William & Mary Hall, Williamsburg, VA

October 8, 1991, Nassau Coliseum, Uniondale, NY

October 9, 1991, Continental Airlines Arena, East Rutherford, NJ

October 11, 1991, Broome County Arena, Binghamton, NY

October 14, 1991, Walnut Creek, Raleigh, NC

October 15, 1991, Blockbuster Pavilion, Charlotte, NC

October 19, 1991, Lakewood Amphitheatre, Atlanta, GA

October 20, 1991, Carolina Coliseum, Columbia, SC

October 22, 1991, Miami Arena, Miami, FL

October 23, 1991, USF Sun Dome, Tampa, FL

October 25, 1991, Orlando Arena, Orlando, FL

October 26, 1991, O'Connell Center, Gainesville, FL

October 29, 1991, Kiefer UNO Lakefront Arena, New Orleans, LA

October 30, 1991, Cynthia Woods Mitchell Pavilion, The Woodlands, TX

November 1, 1991, Frank Erwin Center, Austin, TX

November 2, 1991, Smirnoff Music Center, Dallas, TX

November 4, 1991, Myriad Arena, Oklahoma City, OK

November 6, 1991, Pan American Center, Las Cruces, NM

November 8, 1991, Blockbuster Desert Sky Pavilion, Phoenix, AZ

November 9, 1991, Pacific Amphitheatre, Costa Mesa, CA

November 11, 1991, Great Western Forum, Inglewood, CA

November 12, 1991, San Diego Sports Arena, San Diego, CA

November 20, 1991, Key Arena at Seattle Center, Seattle, WA

November 21, 1991, Memorial Coliseum, Portland, OR

November 23, 1991, Lawlor Events Center, Reno, NV

November 24, 1991, Oakland Arena, Oakland, CA

1992

March 4, 1992, Sporthalle, Oslo, Norway

March 6, 1992, Scandinavium Arena, Gothenburgh, Sweden

March 7, 1992, Globe Arena, Stockholm, Sweden

March 9, 1992, Sporthalle, Hamburg, Germany

March 10, 1992, Deutschlandhalle, Berlin, Germany

March 12, 1992, Grugahalle, Essen, Germany

March 15, 1992, SECC, Glasgow, Scotland

March 16, 1992, King's Hall, Belfast, Ireland

March 18 & 19, 1992, Point Depot, Dublin, Ireland

March 21, 1992, National Exhibition Center, Birmingham, England

March 23 & 24, 1992, Wembley Arena, London, England

March 26, 1992, Festhalle, Frankfurt, Germany

March 27, 1992, Olympiahalle, Munich, Germany

March 29, 1992, St. Jakob Sporthalle, Basel, Switzerland

March 30, 1992, Zenith, Paris, France
April 1, 1992, Bruxelles, Brussels, Belgium
April 2, 1992, Isstadion, Malmoe, Sweden
October 16, 1992, Madison Square Garden, New York, NY

1993

November 2, 1993, Bayfront Center Arena, St. Petersburg, FL (with Carlene Carter)
November 4, 1993, O'Connell Center, Gainesville, FL (with Carlene Carter)

1994

October 1–2, 1994, Annual Bridge School Benefit Concert, Shoreline Amphitheatre, Mountain View, CA

1995

February 28, 1995, Louisville Gardens, Louisville, KY
March 1, 1995, Market Square Arena, Indianapolis, IN
March 3, 1995, Joyce ACC Arena, South Bard, IN
March 5, 1995, Milwaukee Arena, Milwaukee, WI
March 6, 1995, Peoria Civic Center Arena, Peoria, IL
March 8, 1995, United Center, Chicago, IL
March 9, 1995, Palace of Auburn Hills, Auburn Hills, MI
March 11, 1995, Battelle Hall, Columbus, OH
March 12, 1995, Cincinnati Gardens, Cincinnati, OH
March 14, 1995, Pittsburgh Civic Arena, Pittsburgh, PA
March 16, 1995, CSU Convocation Center, Cleveland, OH
March 17, 1995, Maple Leaf Gardens, Toronto, Canada
March 20, 1995, Madison Square Garden, New York, NY
March 21, 1995, Knickerbocker Arena, Albany, NY
March 23, 1995, Blue Cross Arena, Rochester, NY
April 1, 1995, New Haven Veterans Memorial Coliseum, New Haven, CT
April 2, 1995, Nassau Coliseum, Uniondale, NY
April 4 & 5, 1995, Boston Garden, Boston, MA

April 7, 1995, First Union Spectrum, Philadelphia, PA

April 9, 1995, Patriot Center, Fairfax, VA

April 11, 1995, Richmond Coliseum, Richmond. VA

April 12, 1995, Walnut Creek, Raleigh, NC

April 14, 1995, Blockbuster Pavilion, Charlotte, NC

April 15, 1995, Lakewood Amphitheatre, Atlanta, GA

April 18, 1995, Cynthia Woods Mitchell Pavilion, The Woodlands, TX

April 19 & 21, 1995, Bass Concert Hall, Austin, TX

April 22, 1995, Smirnoff Music Center, Dallas, TX

April 25, 1995, Blockbuster Desert Sky Pavilion, Phoenix, AZ

April 26, 1995, San Diego Sports Arena, San Diego, CA

April 28, 1995, Glen Helen Blockbuster Pavilion, Devore, CA

April 30, 1995, Shoreline Amphitheatre, Mountain View, CA

May 1, 1995, ARCO Arena, Sacramento, CA

May 3, 1995, Memorial Coliseum, Portland, OR

May 4 & 5, 1995, Gorge Amphitheatre, George, WA

May 6, 1995, Pacific Coliseum, Vancouver, Canada

May 15 & 17, 1995, Miami Arena, Miami, FL

May 19, 1995, USF Sun Dome, Tampa, FL

May 20, 1995, T.D. Waterhouse Center, Orlando, FL

May 23, 1995, Pensacola Civic Center, Pensacola, FL

May 25, 1995, Oak Mountain Amphitheatre, Pelham, AL

May 27, 1995, AmSouth Amphitheatre, Antioch, TN

May 28, 30 & 31, 1995, Orpheum Theatre, Memphis, TN

June 2, 1995, Riverport Amphitheatre, Maryland Heights, MO

June 3, 1995, Sandstone Amphitheatre, Bonner Springs, KS

June 5 & 6, 1995, Music Hall, Oklahoma City, OK

June 9 & 10, 1995, Hollywood Bowl, Los Angeles, CA

June 12, 1995, Lawlor Events Center, Reno, NV

June 13, 1995, Shoreline Amphitheatre, Mountain View, CA

August 10, 1995, Delta Center, Salt Lake City, UT

August 11, 1995, Fiddler's Green Amphitheatre, Englewood, CO

August 14, 1995, Tweeter Center, Mansfield, MA

August 15, 1995, Saratoga Performing Arts Center, Saratoga Springs, NY

August 17, 1995, Jones Beach Amphitheatre, Wantagh, NY

August 18, 1995, Meadows Music Centre, Hartford, CT
August 20, 1995 Garden State Arts Centre, Holmdel, NJ
August 21, 1995, E-Centre, Camden, NJ
August 24, 1995, Merriweather Post Pavilion, Columbia, MD
August 26, 1995, Post-Gazette Pavilion at Star Lake, Burgettstown, PA
August 27, 1995, Blossom Music Center, Cuyahoga Falls, OH
August 29, 1995, Polaris Amphitheatre, Columbus, OH
August 30, 1995, Riverbend Music Center, Cincinnati, OH
September 1, 1995, Pine Knob Music Theatre, Clarkston, MI
September 2, 1995, Pine Knob Music Theatre, Clarkston, MI
September 10, 1995, Target Center, Minneapolis, MN
September 12, 1995, Hilton Coliseum, Ames, IA
September 13, 1995, Mark of the Quad Cities, Moline, IL
September 15, 1995, New World Music Theatre, Tinley Park, IL
September 16, 1995, Alpine Valley Music Theatre, East Troy, WI
September 18, 1995, Allen County War Memorial Coliseum, Fort
  Wayne, IN
September 19, 1995, Deer Creek Music Center, Noblesville, IN
September 21, 1995, Roberts Stadium, Evansville, IN
September 23, 1995, Rupp Arena, Lexington, KY
September 24, 1995, Knoxville Civic Coliseum, Knoxville, TN
September 27, 1995, Alltel Pavilion at Walnut Creek, Raleigh, NC
September 28, 1995 North Charleston Coliseum, North Charleston, SC
September 30, 1995 Lakewood Amphitheatre, Atlanta, GA
October 1, 1995, Von Braun Civic Center Arena, Huntsville, AL
October 3, 1995, BancorpSouth Center, Tupelo, MS
October 4, 1995, Mississippi Coliseum, Jackson, MS
October 6, 1995, Coleman Coliseum, Tuscaloosa, AL
October 8, 1995, Lakefront Arena, New Orleans, LA

1996

no concerts

1997

January 10–12, 14–16, 19–21, 24–26, 28–31, February 1, 3, 4, 6 & 7,
  1997, The Fillmore, San Francisco, CA

1998
no concerts

1999
March 7 & 8, 10, 12, 13, 15 & 16, 1999, The Fillmore, San Francisco, CA
April 11, 12 & 15, 1999, Irving Plaza, New York, NY
April 19 & 20, 1999, Shepherd's Bush Empire, London, England
April 23, 1999, Docks Konzerte, Hamburg, Germany
June 14, 1999, Van Andel Arena, Grand Rapids, MI
June 16, 1999, Gund Arena, Cleveland, OH
June 18 & 19, 1999, Pine Knob Music Theater, Clarkston, MI
June 22, 1999, Darien Lake Performing Arts Center, Darien Center, NY
June 23, 1999, Star Lake Amphitheatre, Burgettstown, PA
June 25, 1999, Nissan Pavilion, Bristow, VA
June 26, 1999, E-Centre, Camden, NJ
June 29, 1999, Meadows Music Theatre, Hartford, CT
June 30, 1999, Garden State Arts Center, Holmdel, NJ
July 2 & 3, 1999, Jones Beach Amphitheatre, Wantagh, NY
July 5, 1999, Hershey Park Stadium, Hershey, PA
July 6, 1999, Air Canada Center, Toronto, Ontario
July 9, 1999, Tweeter Center, Mansfield, MA
July 10, 1999, Tweeter Center, Mansfield, MA
July 12, 1999, Southampton, NY
July 21, 1999, Freedom Hall, Louisville, KY
July 23, 1999, Deer Creek Music Theatre, Noblesville, IN
July 24, 1999, Riverport Amphitheatre, Maryland Heights, MO
July 27, 1999, Riverbend Music Center, Cincinnati, OH
July 28, 1999, Polaris Amphitheatre, Columbus, OH
July 30, 1999, Marcus Amphitheatre, Milwaukee, WI
July 31, 1999, New World Music Theatre, Tinley Park, IL
August 3, 1999, Target Center, Minneapolis, MN
August 4, 1999, Sandstone Amphitheatre, Bonner Springs, KS
August 6, 1999, AmSouth Amphitheatre, Antioch, TN
August 7, 1999, The Pyramid, Memphis, TN
August 13 & 14, 1999, Irvine Meadows Amphitheatre, Irvine, CA

August 18, 1999, Coors Amphitheatre, Chula Vista, CA
August 19, 1999, America West Arena, Phoenix, AZ
August 21, 1999, The Joint, Las Vegas, NV
August 22, 1999, Centennial Garden, Bakersfield, CA
August 25, 1999, Reno Hilton Amphitheatre, Reno, NV
August 27 & 28, 1999, Shoreline Amphitheatre, Mountain View, CA
August 30, 1999, Arco Arena, Sacramento, CA
September 1, 1999, Rose Garden Arena, Portland, OR
September 2, 1999, General Motors Place, Vancouver, BC
September 4 & 5, 1999, Gorge Amphitheatre, George, WA
September 16, 1999, Starplex Amphitheatre, Dallas, TX
September 17, 1999, Frank Erwin Center, Austin, TX
September 19, 1999, C.W. Mitchell Pavilion, The Woodlands, TX
September 21, 1999, Ice Palace, Tampa, FL
September 22, 1999, Coral Sky Amphitheatre, West Palm Beach, FL
September 24, 1999, Lakewood Amphitheatre, Atlanta, GA
September 25, 1999, Blockbuster Pavilion, Charlotte, NC
September 28, 1999, Walnut Creek Amphitheatre, Raleigh, NC
October 1, 1999, First Union Center, Philadelphia, PA
October 2, 1999, Virginia Beach Amphitheatre, Virginia Beach, VA
October 4, 1999, Merriweather Post Pavilion, Columbia, MD
October 6, 1999, Assembly Hall, Bloomington, IN (cancelled)
October 7, 1999, United Center, Chicago, IL
October 9, 1999, Palace of Auburn Hills, Auburn Hills, MI
October 11, 1999, Mark of the Quad Cities, Moline, IL
October 12, 1999, Kohl Center, Madison, WI
October 15, 1999, MGM Grand, Las Vegas, NV
October 16, 1999, Hollywood Bowl, Hollywood, CA

2000
October 28–29, 2000 Annual Bridge School Benefit Concert, Shoreline
   Amphitheatre, Mountain View, CA

2001
May 9, 2001, Gill Coliseum, Corvallis, OR

May 11, 2001, Idaho Center, Nampa, ID

May 12, 2001, The Gorge Amphitheatre, George, WA

May 15 & 16, 2001, Red Rocks Amphitheatre, Morrison, CO

May 18, 2001, Cynthia Woods Mitchell Pavilion, The Woodlands, TX

May 19, 2001, Verizon Wireless Amphitheater, Selma, TX

May 21, 2001, Smirnoff Music Center, Dallas, TX

May 24 & 15, 2001, Santa Barbara Bowl, Santa Barbara, CA

May 27, 2001, Sacramento Valley Amphitheater, Wheatland, CA

May 29, 2001, Chronicle Pavilion, Concord, CA

May 30, 2001, SDSU Open Air Theatre, San Diego, CA

June 1 & 2, 2001, The Joint at Hard Rock Hotel, Las Vegas, NV

June 27, 2001, Coors Light Amphitheatre at Montage Mountain, Scranton, PA

June 28, 2001, Tweeter Center, Camden, NJ

June 30, 2001, Nissan Pavilion, Bristow, VA

July 1, 2001, PNC Bank Arts Center, Holmdel, NJ

July 4, 2001, Summerfest, Marcus Amphitheater, Milwaukee, WI

July 5, 2001, Jones Beach Theater, Wantagh, NY

July 7, 2001, Saratoga Performing Arts Center, Saratoga Springs, NY

July 8, 2001, Tweeter Center, Mansfield, MA

July 10, 2001, Post-Gazette Pavilion, Burgettstown, PA

July 12, 2001, DTE Energy Music Theatre, Clarkston, MI

July 14, 2001, HiFi Buys Amphitheatre, Atlanta, GA

July 15, 2001, AmSouth Amphitheater, Antioch, TN

July 17, 2001, Polaris Amphitheater, Columbus, OH

July 18, 2001, Sandstone Amphitheater, Bonner Springs, KS

July 20, 2001, Tweeter Center Chicago, Tinley Park, IL

July 21, 2001, Verizon Wireless Music Center, Nobelsville, IN

2002

June 27, 2002, Van Andel Arena, Grand Rapids, MI

June 28, 2002, Blossom Music Center, Cuyahoga Falls, OH

June 30, 2002, Summerfest, Marcus Amphitheater, Milwaukee, WI

July 3, 2002, Darien Lake Performing Arts Center, Darien Center, NY

July 5, 2002, Saratoga Performing Arts Center, Saratoga Springs, NY

July 6, 2002, PNC Bank Arts Center, Holmdel, NJ

July 8, 2002, Mohegan Sun Arena, Uncasville, CT

July 10, 2002, Verizon Wireless Arena, Manchester, NH

July 11, 2002, Tweeter Center, Mansfield, MA

July 13, 2002, Montage Mountain, Scranton, PA

July 14, 2002, Star Pavilion at Hersheypark Stadium, Hershey, PA

July 16, 2002, Post-Gazette Pavilion, Burgettstown, PA

July 17, 2002, Nissan Pavilion, Bristow, VA

July 19, 2002, Alltel Pavilion at Walnut Creek, Raleigh, NC

July 20, 2002, Verizon Wireless Amphitheatre, Charlotte, NC

August 6, 2002, Ice Palace, Tampa, FL

August 7, 2002, MARS Music Amphitheatre, West Palm Beach, FL

August 9, 2002, HiFi Buys Amphitheatre, Atlanta, GA

August 10, 2002, Oak Mountain Amphitheatre, Pelham, AL

August 13, 2002, Riverbend Music Center, Cincinnati, OH

August 14, 2002, Sandstone Amphitheater, Bonner Springs, KS

August 17, 2002, UMB Bank Pavilion, Maryland Heights, MO

August 19 & 20, 2002, Red Rocks Amphitheatre, Morrison, CA

August 22, 2002, Journal Pavilion, Albuquerque, NM

August 24, 2002, Blockbuster Pavilion, San Bernardino, CA

August 25, 2002, Coors Amphitheatre, Chula Vista, CA

August 26 & 28, 2002, Idaho Center, Nampa ID

August 29, 2002, Reno-Hilton Amphitheatre, Reno, NV

August 31, 2002, Autowest Amphitheatre, Wheatland, CA

September 1, 2002, Chronicle Pavilion, Concord, CA

October 15 & 16, 2002, Grand Olympic Auditorium, Los Angeles, CA

October 27, 2002, Santa Barbara Bowl, Santa Barbara, CA

October 29, 2002, SDSU Open Air Theatre, San Diego, CA

October 30, 2002, Shoreline Amphitheatre, Mountain View, CA

November 1, 2002, Aladdin Theater, Las Vegas, NV

November 2, 2002, Cricket Pavilion, Phoenix, AZ

November 5, 2002, E Center, West Valley, UT

November 7, 2002, Spokane Arena, Spokane, WA

November 9, 2002, Tacoma Dome, Tacoma, WA

November 10, 2002, Rose Garden Arena, Portland, OR

November 15, 2002, Compaq Center, Houston, TX
November 16, 2002, American Airlines Center, Dallas, TX
November 21, 2002, Frank Erwin Center, Austin, TX
November 23, 2002, Great Western Forum, Inglewood, CA
December 3, 2002, First Union Spectrum, Philadelphia, PA
December 4, 2002, Schottenstein Center, Columbus, OH
December 6, 2002, Rupp Arena, Lexington, KY
December 7, 2002, The Palace of Auburn Hills, Auburn Hills, MI
December 9, 2002, Xcel Energy Center, St. Paul, MN
December 11, 2002, United Center, Chicago, IL
December 13, 2002, Madison Square Garden, New York, NY
December 13, 2002, Fleet Center, Boston, MA

2003
April 13, 14, 16, 17 & 19, 2003, Vic Theatre, Chicago, IL
June 26, 2003, Sioux Falls Arena, Sioux Falls, SD
June 28, 2003, Summerfest, Marcus Amphitheater, Milwaukee, WI
June 30, 2003, US Cellular Center, Cedar Rapids, IA
July 1, 2003, Mid America Center, Council Bluffs, IA
July 3, 2003, Rushmore Plaza Civic Center, Rapid City, SD
July 5, 2003, Brick Breeden Fieldhouse, Bozeman, MT
July 9, 2003, Duluth Entertainment and Convention Center, Duluth, MN
July 11, 2003, Civic Center, Mankato, MN
July 13, 2003 Civic Center, Peoria, IL
August 9, 2003, PNC Bank Arts Center, Holmdel, NJ
August 10, 2003, PNC Bank Arts Center, Holmdel, NJ
August 12, 2003, Knoxville Civic Coliseum, Knoxville, TN
August 13, 2003, The Arena at Gwinnett Center, Duluth, GA
August 15, 2003, North Charleston Coliseum, North Charleston, SC
August 16, 2003, AmSouth Amphitheater, Antioch, TN
August 18, 2003, Orpheum Theatre, Memphis, TN
August 21, 2003, Ocean Center, Daytona Beach, FL
August 22, 2003, Teco Arena, Estero, FL
August 24, 2003, Oak Mountain Amphitheatre, Pelham, AL

August 26, 2003, Kiefer UNO Lakefront Arena, New Orleans, LA
August 29, 2003, Snow King Center Ballroom, Jackson Hole, WY

2004

no concerts

2005

June 7, 2005, Germain Arena, Estero, FL
June 8, 2005, Sound Advice Amphitheatre, West Palm Beach, FL
June 10, 2005, Ford Amphitheatre, Tampa, FL
June 11, 2005, Music Midtown Festival, Atlanta, GA
June 14, 1005, Riverbend Music Center, Cincinnati, OH
June 15, 2005, Post-Gazette Pavilion, Burgettstown, PA
June 17, 2005, Tweeter Center, Camden, NJ
June 18, 2005, Tweeter Center, Mansfield, MA
June 21, 2005, Jones Beach Theater, Wantagh, NY
June 22, 2005, PNC Bank Arts Center, Holmdel, NJ
June 24, 2005, Meadows Music Theater, Hartford, CT
June 25, 2005, Darien Lake Performing Arts Center, Darien Center, NY
June 30, 2005, Blossom Music Center, Cuyahoga Falls, OH
July 1, 2005, Summerfest, Marcus Amphitheater, Milwaukee, WI
July 9, 2005, UMB Bank Pavilion, Maryland Heights, MO
July 10, 2005, Verizon Wireless Amphitheater, Bonner Springs, KS
July 13, 2005, Starwood Amphitheatre, Antioch, TN
July 15, 2005, Tweeter Center, Chicago, IL
July 16, 2005, Rock Fest, Festival Grounds, Cadott, WI
July 18, 2005, Wells Fargo Arena, Des Moines, IA
July 20, 2005, DTE Energy Music Theatre, Clarkston, MI
July 21, 2005, Verizon Wireless Music Center, Noblesville, IN
July 23, 2005, Ford Pavilion at Montage Mountain, Scranton, PA
July 24, 2005, Borgata Events Center, Atlantic City, NJ
July 27, 2005, Merriweather Post Pavilion, Columbia, MD
July 29, 2005, Tweeter Center, Mansfield, MA
July 30, 2005, Saratoga Performing Arts Center, Saratoga Springs, NY
August 4, 2005, California Mid-State Fair, Paso Robles, CA

August 14, 2005, Verizon Wireless Amphitheater, Irvine, CA

August 16, 2005, The Joint at Hard Rock Hotel, Las Vegas, NV

August 18, 2005, Red Rocks Amphitheatre, Morrison, CO

August 20, 2005, Coors Amphitheatre, Chula Vista, CA

August 21, 2005, Hyundai Pavilion, San Bernardino, CA

August 23, 2005, Lawlor Events Center, Reno, NV

August 24, 2005, Sacramento Valley Amphitheater, Wheatland, CA

August 26 & 27, 2005, Greek Theatre, Berkeley, CA

August 30 & 31, 2005, Red Rocks Amphitheatre, Morrison, CA

September 2 & 3, 2005, The Gorge Amphitheatre, George, WA

2006

June 9, 2006, Verizon Wireless Amphitheatre, Charlotte, NC

June 10, 2006, Nissan Pavilion, Bristow, VA

June 12, 2006, nTelos Wireless Pavilion, Portsmouth, VA

June 14, 2006, Germain Amphitheater, Columbus, OH

June 16, 2006, Bonnaroo, Great Stage Park, Manchester, TN

June 17, 2006, UMB Bank Pavilion, Maryland Heights, MO

June 20, 2006, Madison Square Garden, New York, NY

June 21, 2006, Tweeter Center, Mansfield, MA

June 23, 2006, Verizon Wireless Music Center, Noblesville, IN

June 26 & 27, 2006, Xcel Energy Center, St. Paul, MN

June 29 & 30, 2006, Summerfest, Marcus Amphitheater, Milwaukee, WI

July 2 & 3, 2006, Pepsi Center, Denver, CO

July 29, 2006, The Amphitheatre at Clark County, Ridgefield, WA

July 30, 2006, White River Amphitheatre, Auburn, WA

August 1, 2006, Spokane Arena, Spokane, WA

August 4, 2006, Smirnoff Music Center, Dallas, TX

August 5, 2006, Cynthia Woods Mitchell Pavilion, The Woodlands, TX

August 8, 2006, DTE Music Theatre, Clarkston, MI

August 9, 2006, Rock'n The Rally, Sturgis, SD

August 12, 2006, New England Dodge Music Center, Hartford, CT

August 13, 2006, Saratoga Performing Arts Center, Saratoga Springs, NY

August 15, 2006, Darien Lake Performing Arts Center, Darien Center, NY

August 16, 2006, Post-Gazette Pavilion, Burgettstown, PA
August 18, 2006, Tweeter Center, Camden, NJ
August 19, 2006, Amsterjam Randall's Island, New York, NY
September 8, 2006, Molson Amphitheatre, Toronto, Canada
September 10, 2006, Alltel Pavilion at Walnut Creek, Raleigh, NC
September 12, 2006, Alliant Energy Center, Madison, WI
September 14 & 15, 2006, Charter One Pavilion, Chicago, IL
September 17, 2006, Austin City Limits, Zilker Park, Austin, TX
September 21, 2006, O'Connell Center, Gainesville, FL
September 22, 2006, HiFi Buys Amphitheatre, Atlanta, GA
September 26, 2006, Hollywood Bowl, Hollywood, CA
September 27, 2006, Coors Amphitheatre, Chula Vista, CA
September 29 & 30, 2006, Greek Theatre, Berkeley, CA
October 4, 2006, Glendale Arena, Phoenix, AZ
October 20, 2006, Raley Field, West Sacramento, CA
October 21, 2006, Indian Wells Tennis Garden, Indian Wells, CA
October 27, 2006, Greek Theatre, Berkeley, CA
October 28, 2006, Vegoose, Sam Boyd Stadium, Las Vegas, NV

2007
August 25, 2007, The Ross School, East Hampton, NY
September 29, 2007, Greek Theatre, Berkeley, CA

2008
April 12, 2008, Benefit for the Midnight Mission at Malibu PAC, Malibu, CA
April 14, 2008, Santa Cruz Civic Auditorium, Santa Cruz, CA
April 16 & 17, 2008, The Fillmore, San Francisco, CA
April 19, 2008, Arlington Theatre, Santa Barbara, CA
April 20, 2008, Ventura Theater, Ventura, CA
April 22, 2008, Concerts in the Park, Alpine, CA
April 25, 26, 28 & 29, May 1 & 2, 2008, Troubadour, West Hollywood, CA
May 30, 2008, Van Andel Arena, Grand Rapids, MI
May 31, 2008, The Palace of Auburn Hills, Auburn Hills, MI

June 3, 2008, Air Canada Centre, Toronto, ON
June 5 & 6, 2008, Wachovia Center, Philadelphia, PA
June 8, 2008, Nissan Pavilion, Bristow, VA
June 10, 2008, Post-Gazette Pavilion at Star Lake, Burgettstown, PA
June 11, 2008, New England Dodge Music Center, Hartford, CT
June 13, 2008, TD Banknorth Garden, Boston, MA
June 14, 2008, Tweeter Center, Mansfield, MA
June 17, 2008, Madison Square Garden, New York, NY
June 18, 2008, Prudential Center, Newark, NJ
June 21, 2008, Darien Lake Performing Arts Center, Darien Center, NY
June 22, 2008, Blossom Music Center, Cuyahoga Falls, OH
June 25, 2008, Hollywood Bowl, Los Angeles, CA
July 2, 2008, United Center, Chicago, IL
July 3, 2008, Verizon Wireless Music Centre, Noblesville, IN
July 5, 2008, Summerfest, Marcus Amphitheater, Milwaukee, WI
July 8, 2008, Riverbend Music Center, Cincinnati, OH
July 9, 2008, Verizon Wireless Amphitheatre at Encore Park, Atlanta, GA
July 11, 2008, Charlotte Verizon Wireless Amphitheatre, Charlotte, NC
July 12, 2008, Walnut Creek Amphitheatre, Raleigh, NC
July 15, 2008, Bank Atlantic Centre, Sunrise, FL
July 16, 2008, Saint Pete Times Forum, Tampa, FL
July 19, 2008, Outer Fields at Dick's Sporting Goods Park, Denver, CO
July 20, 2008, Qwest Center Omaha, Omaha, NE
July 22, 2008, Sprint Center, Kansas City, MO
July 23, 2008, Target Center, Minneapolis, MN
July 26, 2008, Pemberton Festival, Pemberton, BC
August 7, 2008, Verizon Wireless Amphitheatre, Maryland Heights, MO
August 9, 2008, MTS Centre, Winnipeg, MB
August 11, 2008, Pengrowth Saddledome, Calgary, AB
August 12, 2008, Rexall Place/Northlands Park, Edmonton, AB
August 15 & 16, 2008, Gorge Amphitheatre, George, WA
August 20, 2008, Jobing.com Arena, Glendale, AZ
August 22, 2008, Verizon Wireless Amphitheater, Irvine, CA
August 23, 2008, Golden Gate Park, San Francisco, CA
August 26, 2008, Verizon Wireless Amphitheatre, Selma, TX

August 27, 2008, American Airlines Centre, Dallas, TX
August 29, 2008, Cynthia Woods Mitchell Pavilion, Woodlands, TX

2010

June 1 & 3, 2010, Red Rocks Amphitheater, Denver, CO
June 5, 2010, Oracle Arena, Oakland, CA
June 8, 2010, GM Place, Vancouver, BC
June 11 & 12, 2010, The Gorge, Seattle WA
June 15, 2010, Pengrowth Saddledome, Calgary, AB
June 16, 2010, Rexall Place, Edmonton, AB
June 18, 2010, Credit Union Centre, Saskatoon, SK
June 19, 2010, MTS Centre, Winnipeg, MB
June 22, 2010, Xcel Energy Center, St. Paul, MN
June 23, 2010, Qwest Center, Omaha, NE
June 25 & 26, 2010, Summerfest, Marcus Amphitheater, Milwaukee, WI
July 10, 2010, Verizon Wireless Music Center, Indianapolis, IN
July 13,2 010, Sprint Center, Kansas City, MO
July 15, 2010, Riverbend Music Center, Cincinnati, OH
July 17, 2010, United Center, Chicago, IL
July 18, 2010, Verizon Wireless Amphitheatre, St. Louis, MO
July 22, 2010, Palace of Auburn Hills, Detroit, MI
July 24, 2010, First Niagara Pavilion, Pittsburgh, PA
July 28, 2010, Madison Square Garden
July 31, 2010, Wachovia Center, Philadelphia, PA
August 1, 2010, Wachovia Center, Philadelphia, PA
August 11, 2010, Philips Arena, Atlanta, GA
August 12, 2010, Sommet Center, Nashville, TN
August 14, 2010, Darien Lake Performing Arts Center
August 15, 2010, Jiffy Lube Live, Washington, DC
August 17, 2010, Comcast Theater, Hartford, CT
August 19 & 21, 2010, Comcast Center, Boston, MA
August 24, 2010, Izod Center, East Rutherford, NJ
August 25, 2010, Air Canada Center, Toronto, OH
August 27, 2010, Saratoga Springs Performing Arts Center, Saratoga
   Springs, NY

August 28, 2010, Darien Lake Performing Arts Center, Darien Lake, NY
August 31, 2010, Blossom Music Center, Cleveland, OH
September 16, 2010, St. Pete Times Forum, Tampa, FL
September 18, 2010, Time Warner Cable Music Pavilion at Walnut Creek, Raleigh, NC
September 19, 2010, Charlotte Verizon Wireless Amphitheatre, Charlotte, NC
September 21, 2010, Superpages.com Center, Dallas, TX
September 23, 2010, BOK Center, Tulsa, OH
September 24, 2010, Cynthia Woods Mitchell Pavilion, Houston, TX
October 1, 2010, Hollywood Bowl, Los Angeles, CA
October 2, 2010, Verizon Wireless Amphitheatre, Irvine, CA
October 5, 2010, Cricket Wireless Amphitheatre, San Diego, CA
October 7, 2010, US Airways Center, Phoenix, AZ

2011
October 29–30, 2001, Plaza del Sol Performance Hall, California State at Northridge (benefit for KCSN-FM/Los Angeles)

2012
April 18 & 19, 2012, 1st Bank Center, Broomfield, CO
April 21, 2012, Verizon Arena, North Little Rock, AR
April 24, 2012, Tingley Coliseum, Albuquerque, NM
April 26, 2012, Intrust Bank Arena, Wichita, KS
April 28, 2012, New Orleans Jazz & Heritage Festival, New Orleans, LA
April 29, 2012, Verizon Wireless Amphitheatre, Alpharetta, GA
May 1, 2012, Germain Arena, Estero, FL
May 3, 2012, Amway Center, Orlando, FL
May 5, 2012, Frank Erwin Center, Austin, TX
May 31, 2012, Halifax Metro Centre, Halifax, NS
June 2 & 3, 2012, Mile One Centre, St. Johns, NF
June 7, 2012, 02 Arena, Dublin, Ireland
June 8, 2012, The Marquee, Cork, Ireland
June 10, 2012, 02 World, Hamburg, Germany
June 12, 2012, Open Air, Horsens, Denmark

June 14, 2012, The Globe, Stockholm, Sweden
June 15, 2012, Norwegian Wood Festival, Oslo, Norway
June 18 & 20, 2012, Royal Albert Hall, London, UK
June 22, 2012, Isle of Wight Festival, Newport, GB
June 24, 2012, Heineken Music Hall, Amsterdam, Netherlands
June 25, 2012, Lanxess Arena, Cologne, Germany
June 27, 2012, Grand Rex, Paris, France
June 29, 2012, Piazza Napoleone, Lucca, Italy
June 30, 2012, SAP Arena, Mannheim, Germany

2013
May 16, 2013, The Ford Center, Evansville, IN
May 17–20, 2013, Hangout Music Festival, Gulf Shores, AL
May 20, 21, 23, 25 & 26, 2013, Beacon Theatre, New York, NY
June 3, 4, 6, 8, 9 & 11, 2013, Henry Fonda Theatre, Los Angeles, CA
June 15, 2013, Klipsch Music Center, Noblesville, IN
June 16, 2013, Bonnaroo Music and Arts Festival, Manchester, TN
June 18, 2013, Budweiser Gardens, London, ON, Canada
June 20, 2013, Consol Energy Center, Pittsburgh, PA
June 21–23, 2013, Firefly Music Festival, Dover, DE
June 23, 2013, Saratoga Performing Arts Center, Saratoga Springs, NY
June 28, 2013, Summerfest, Marcus Amphitheater, Milwaukee, WI
June 29, 2013, Target Center, Minneapolis, MN

Recommended Websites

TomPetty.com – Official website
SiriusXM.com/tompetty – Buried Treasure
MudcrutchMusic.com – Official website
Mudcrutch.com – Unofficial fan forum

Beatles.com
BobDylan.com
CityofGainesville.org
DaveStewart.com
DelShannon.com
DirtyKnobs.com
Elvis.com
GeorgeHarrison.com
Facebook.com/OfficialJeffLynne – Jeff Lynne
JLPD.com – Jim Lenahan Production Design
JohnnyCash.com
LeonRussellRecords.com
LiphamMusic.com
NormansRareGuitars.com
RoyOrbison.com

Buy.SoundCityMovie.com – Sound City documentary by Dave Grohl
StanLynchMusic.com
RockALittle.com – Stevie Nicks
TheBeatles.com
TravelingWilburys.com
Ulyate.com

Buried Treasure on SiriusXM Satellite Radio

Al Green	Driving Wheel
	I Can't Get Next To You
	I Want To Hold Your Hand
Alan Price	I Put A Spell On You
Albert Collins	Frosty
Albert King	Born Under A Bad Sign
	Crosscut Saw
	Don't Burn Down The Bridge
	Down Don't Bother Me
	Drowning On Dry Land
	That's What The Blues Is All About
Albert King/Stevie Ray Vaughan	Born Under A Bad Sign
Allman Brothers Band	Don't Want You No More
	Hoochie Coochie Man
	Hot 'Lanta
	It's Not My Cross To Bear
	Leave My Blues At Home
	Trouble No More

Alton Ellis	Praise Jah, It's Christmas
Alvin Robinson	Down Home Girl
	I'm Gonna Put Some Hurt On You
Ann Peebles	99 Pounds
	Come To Mama
	Didn't Take Your Man
	Give Me Some Credit
	I Can't Stand The Rain
	(I Feel Like) Breaking Up Somebody's Home
	I Pity The Fool
	I'm Gonna Tear Your Playhouse Down
	Slipped, Tripped And Fell In Love
	(You Keep Me) Hangin' On
Anna King	If Somebody Told You
Aretha Franklin	Eleanor Rigby
	Jumpin' Jack Flash
	Rock Steady
	Save Me
	(Sweet Sweet Baby) Since You've Been Gone
	The Weight
Arlo Guthrie	Coming Into Los Angeles
Arthur Alexander	A Shot Of Rhythm And Blues
	Anna (Go To Him)
	You Better Move On
Arthur Conley	Funky Street
Arthur "Big Boy" Crudup	My Baby Left Me
	Rock Me Mama
	So Glad You're Mine
	That's All Right
Arthur Gunter	Baby Let's Play House
B.B. King	Sweet Little Angel
	Tired Of Your Jive
	Worry, Worry

Badfinger	Baby Blue
	I'll Be The One
	No Matter What
	Sometimes
	Suitcase
Barbara George	I Know (You Don't Love Me Anymore)
Barbara Lynn	Oh! Baby (We Got A Good Thing Goin')
	You'll Lose A Good Thing
Barrett Strong	Money (That's What I Want)
Beach Boys	Farmer's Daughter
	Heroes and Villains
	I Know There's An Answer
	In My Room
	Let Him Run Wild
	Let The Wind Blow
	Little Bird
	Lonely Sea
	Marcella
	Sail On, Sailor
	Shut Down, Part II
	Student Demonstration Time
	Wild Honey
	You Need A Mess Of Help To Stand Alone
Beau Brummels	Just A Little
	Laugh
Bee Gees	In My Own Time
Ben Waters with The Rolling Stones	Watching The River Flow
Bettye Swann	Make Me Yours
Big Joe Turner	Flip Flop And Fly
	Honey Hush
	Shake Rattle and Roll
Big Mama Thornton	Hound Dog

Bill Withers	Lean On Me
	Use Me
	Who Is He (And What Is He To You)?
Billy J. Kramer & The Dakotas	From A Window
Billy Joe Royal	Down In The Boondocks
Billy Swan	I Can Help
Blind Faith	Can't Find My Way Home
	Presence Of The Lord
	Sea Of Joy
	Well All Right
Blue Cheer	Summertime Blues
Bo Diddley	Before You Accuse Me
	Bo Diddley
	Cadillac
	Diddy Wah Diddy
	Diddley Daddy
	Hey Bo Diddley
	I'm Looking For A Woman
	Pills
	Mona
	Pretty Thing
	Ride On Josephine
	Say Man
	Who Do You Love
	You Can't Judge A Book By Its Cover
	You Don't Love Me (You Don't Care)
Bob & Earl	Harlem Shuffle
Bob Dylan	4th Time Around
	Absolutely Sweet Marie
	All Along The Watchtower
	Cold Irons Bound
	Don't Think Twice, It's All Right
	Girl From The North Country
	It Takes A Lot To Laugh, It Takes A Train to Cry

	I'll Be Your Baby Tonight
	Leopard-Skin Pill-Box Hat
	Love Minus Zero/No Limit
	Most Likely You Go Your Way And I'll Go Mine
	Neighborhood Bully
	One More Night
	Outlaw Blues
	Temporary Like Achilles
	Stuck Inside Of A Mobile With The Memphis Blues Again
	When You Gonna Wake Up
Bob Landers with Willie Joe and His Unitar	Cherokee Dance
Bob Marley & The Wailers	Could You Be Loved
	Iron Lion Zion
	Jamming
	Lively Up Yourself
Bob Seger	2 + 2 = ?
	Ramblin' Gamblin' Man
Bobby "Blue" Bland	Don't Cry No More
	Farther Up The Road
	I Pity The Fool
	That Did It
	Turn On Your Lovelight
Bobby "Borris" Pickett & The Crypt-Kickers	Monster's Holiday
Bobby Charles	See You Later, Alligator
Bobby Comstock	Let's Stomp
Bobby Darin	Queen Of The Hop
Bobby Freeman	C'mon And Swim
Bobby Fuller Four	Let Her Dance
	Love's Made A Fool Of You
	Never To Be Forgotten

Booker T. & The MGs	Boot-Leg
	Born Under A Bad Sign
	Silver Bells
	Soul Dressing
Brenda Lee	Rockin Around The Christmas Tree
	Sweet Nothin's
Brewer & Shipley	One Toke Over The Line
Brook Benton & Dinah Washington	Baby (You've Got What It Takes)
Buddy Holly	Heartbeat
	Listen To Me
	Not Fade Away
	Peggy Sue
	Rave On
	Ready Teddy
	True Love Ways
	Words Of Love
Buffalo Springfield	Everydays
	Four Days Gone
	I Am A Child
	Kind Woman
	Leave
	Mr. Soul
	On The Way Home
	Pretty Girl Why
	Rock & Roll Woman
	Special Care
	Uno Mundo
Burning Sunflower Blues Band	Ride With Your Daddy Tonight
Canned Heat	Goin' Up The Country
	Let's Work Together
	On The Road Again
	Poor Moon
	Time Was

Carl Perkins	Everybody's Trying To Be My Baby
	Glad All Over
	Matchbox
	Right String But The Wrong Yo Yo
Carl Perkins / Tom Petty & The Heartbreakers	Restless
Carl Perkins / Van Morrison	Sittin' On Top Of The World
Carla Thomas	Gee Whiz, It's Christmas
Cat Stevens	Trouble
Champion Jack Dupree	Can't Kick The Habit
	Junker's Blue
	Nasty Boogie
Chan Romero	The Hippy Hippy Shake
Charles Brown	Driftin' Blues
Charlie Rich	Mohair Sam
Chartbusters	She's The One
Chris Kenner	I Like It Like That Pt. 1
Chubby Checker	The Fly
	Pony Time
Chuck Berry	Almost Grown
	Betty Jean
	Bye Bye Johnny
	Brown Eyed Handsome Man
	Come On
	Dear Dad
	Downbound Train
	Down The Road Apiece
	Guitar Boogie
	I Got To Find My Baby
	Jaguar & Thunderbird
	Let It Rock
	Liverpool Drive
	Maybellene
	Nadine (Is It You?)

	No Money Down
	No Particular Place To Go
	Oh Baby Doll
	Promised Land
	Roll Over Beethoven
	Route 66 Blues
	Run Rudolph Run
	Tulane
	Wee Wee Hours
	You Can't Catch Me
	You Never Can Tell
Chuck Willis	Hang Up My Rock and Roll Shoes
	Kansas City Woman
	Stop And Think
	Sugar Sugar
	What'cha Gonna Do When Your Baby Leaves You
Clarence "Frogman" Henry	Ain't Got No Home
Clarence Carter	Back Door Santa
	Slip Away
	Soul Deep
	Too Weak To Fight
Clyde McPhatter	Lover Please
Conway Twitty	Lonely Blue Boy
Cowboy	A Patch And A Painkiller
	Livin' In The Country
Crabby Appleton	Go Back
Cream	Cat's Squirrel
	Crossroads
	I Feel Free
	I'm So Glad
	Outside Woman Blues
	Steppin' Out
Creedence Clearwater Revival	Feelin' Blue
	Hey Tonight

	I Put A Spell On You
	Penthouse Pauper
	Poorboy Shuffle
Curtis Mayfield & The Impressions	I'm So Proud
	People Get Ready
Daddy Cleanhead	Something's Going On In My Room
Daddy Cool	Come Back Again
	Eagle Rock
Dale Hawkins	Susie-Q
Dan Penn	The Dark End Of The Street
Dave "Baby" Cortez	The Happy Organ
Dave Clark Five	Any Way You Want It
	Bits And Pieces
	Do You Love Me
	Don't Let Me Down
	Everybody Knows (I Still Love You)
	Having A Wild Weekend
	Glad All Over
	I'll Be Yours My Love
	Nineteen Days
	Please Tell Me Why
	Try Too Hard
Dave Edmunds	Almost Saturday Night
	Never Been In Love
	Deborah
	Girls Talk
	Thread Your Needle
David Bowie	It Ain't Easy
	Sorrow
David Lindley	Mercury Blues
Del Shannon	Handy Man
Delaney & Bonnie	Comin' Home
	Never Ending Song Of Love
	Soul Shake
Delanie & Bonnie & Friends	Only You Know And I Know

Derek & The Dominos	One More Chance
	Roll It Over
Dick Dale & His Del-Tones	Miserlou Rock
	The Wedge
Dion	Ruby Baby
Dionne Warwick	Jesus Gave Me Water
Don & Dewey	Jungle Hop
	Mammer-Jammer
Don Covay	Mercy, Mercy
	See-Saw
	Sookie, Sookie
	Take This Hurt Off Me
Donovan	Barabajagal
	Hurdy Gurdy Man
Downliners Sect	Baby What's Wrong
Dr. John	Right Place Wrong Time
Dr. John with The Band	Such A Night
Duane Eddy	Dance With The Guitar Man
	Peter Gunn
Dusty Springfield	I Only Want To Be With You
	Just A Little Lovin'
	Little By Little
	Stay Awhile
Dwight Twilley Band	England
	I'm On Fire
	Sincerely
Earl King	Baby You Can Get Your Gun
Eartha Kitt	Santa Baby
Eddie "Cleanhead" Vinson	Hold It Right There
Eddie Cochran	Eddie's Blues
	Nervous Breakdown
	Pretty Girl
	Somethin' Else
	Twenty Flight Rock

Eddie Floyd	Knock On Wood
Eddie Hinton	It's All Wrong But It's All Right
	Something Heavy
Edwin Starr	War
Electric Light Orchestra	Showdown
Elmore James	Done Somebody Wrong
	Early One Morning
	Fine Little Mama
	Hawaiian Boogie
	I Can't Hold Out
	Madison Blues
	Shake Your Moneymaker
	The Sky Is Crying
Elvis Presley	A Big Hunk O' Love
	A Mess Of Blues
	Baby, Let's Play House
	Blue Suede Shoes
	Dirty, Dirty Feeling
	Girl Next Door Went A' Walking
	I Got Stung
	Just Because
	(Marie's The Name) His Latest Flame
	Milkcow Blues Boogie
	One-Sided Love Affair
	Run On
	Santa Claus Is Back In Town
	Shake, Rattle And Roll
	So Glad You're Mine
	Trouble
	Trying To Get To You
	Tutti Frutti
	Working On The Building
Emitt Rhodes	Long Time No See
	Love Will Stone You
	Mother Earth

	Really Wanted You
	Take You Far Away
	With My Face On The Floor
Eric Burdon & The Animals	All Night Long
Eric Burdon & War	Spill The Wine
Eric Clapton	Slunky
Eric Clapton & Steve Winwood	Georgia On My Mind
Eric Clapton & The Powerhouse	I Want To Know
Ernie K-Doe	A Certain Girl
	Mother In Law
Etta James	A Sunday Kind Of Love
	At Last
	Don't Cry Baby
	I'd Rather Go Blind
	In The Basement, Part One
	Something's Got A Hold On Me
	Trust In Me
Eurythmics	Winter Wonderland
Everly Brothers	Be Bop A-Lula
	Dream
	Gone, Gone, Gone
	Love Hurts
	Lucille
	Made To Love
	Poor Jenny
	Since You Broke My Heart
	Stick With Me Baby
	Walk Right Back
Faces	Around The Plynth
	Flying
	Looking Out The Window
	Pool Hall Richard

	Shake, Shudder
	Three Button Hand Me Down
	Wicked Messenger
Fats Domino	Ain't That Just Like a Woman
	All By Myself
	Be My Guest
	Everybody's Got Something To Hide Except Me & My Monkey
	I'm Gonna Be A Wheel Someday
	I'm In Love Again
	I'm Ready
	Lady Madonna
	Let The Four Winds Blow
	One Night
	Sick And Tired
Fleetwood Mac	Albatross
	Black Magic Woman
	Drifting
	I Loved Another Woman
	Jigsaw Puzzle Blues
	Like It This Way
	Man Of The World
	Need Your Love So Bad
	Rollin' Man
	Shake Your Moneymaker
	Station Man
	Tell Me All The Things You Do
Floyd Cramer	On The Rebound
Floyd Newman	Frog Stomp
Flying Burrito Brothers	Juanita
	Sin City
	Wild Horses
Fontella Bass	Rescue Me
Fontella Bass & Bobby McClure	Don't Mess Up A Good Thing

Frankie Miller	Ain't Got No Money
	Be Good To Yourself
	Down The Honkytonk
Freddie King	Going Dow
	Have You Ever Loved A Woman
	Hide Away
	Hi Rise 17
	I'm Tore Down
	In The Open
	Let Me Be (Stay Away From Me)
	Let The Good Times Roll
	Lonesome Whistle Blues
	Onion Rings
	Pulp Wood
	San-Ho-Zay
	That Will Never Do
	You've Got To Love Her With A Feeling
Freddy Cannon	Abigail Beecher
	Tallahassee Lassie
Free	I'll Be Creepin'
	Mr. Big
	The Stealer
Gary U.S. Bonds	Dear Lady Twist
Gene Vincent	Be-Bop-A-Lula
	Woman Love
Gene Vincent & The Blue Caps	Hold Me, Hug Me, Rock Me
	Jump Back Honey, Jump Back
George Harrison	All Things Must Pass
	Awaiting On You All
	Behind That Locked Door
	Between The Devil And The Deep Blue Sea
	Here Comes The Sun
	It Don't Come Easy *(unreleased demo)*

Georgie Flame & The Blue Flames	Yeh Yeh
Gerry & The Pacemakers	It's Gonna Be Alright
Gerry Rafferty	Right Down The Line
Gram Parsons	Ooh Las Vegas
	Return Of The Grievous Angel
Grateful Dead	High Time
Gregg Allman	Don't Mess Up A Good Thing
	These Days
Hank Ballard & The Midnighters	The Hoochie Coochie Coo
Harry Nilsson	At My Front Door
	Jump Into The Fire
	Spaceman
Howlin' Wolf	Back Door Man
	Built For Comfort
	Commit A Crime
	Do The Do
	Down In The Bottom
	Evil
	Goin' Down Slow
	Hidden Charms
	Highway 49
	How Many More Years
	Killing Floor
	Shake For Me
	Smokestack Lightning
	Spoonful
	The Red Rooster
	Wang Dang Doodle
Huey "Piano" Smith & His Clowns	Don't You Just Know It
Humble Pie	30 Days In The Hole
	Hot 'N' Nasty

Iggy Pop	I'm Bored
	Five Foot One
Ike & Tina Turner	Come Together
	Honky Tonk Women
	Nutbush City Limits
	Shake A Tail Feather
Ike Turner & The Kings Of Rhythm	No More Doggin' A Black Man's Soul
Isaac Hayes	Walk On By
Isley Brothers	Respectable
	Shout (Parts 1 and 2)
	Twist And Shout
	Yes, Indeed
Isley Brothers	I'm Gonna Knock On Your Door
J.D. Souther	Faithless Love
J.J. Cale	Anyway The Wind Blows
	Bringing It Back Naturally
	Cajun Moon
	Carry On
	Down To Memphis
	Don't Cry Sister
	Durango
	Everlovin' Woman
	I Got The Same Old Blues
	I'd Like To Love You Baby
	I'll Be There If You Ever Want Me
	I'll Make Love To You Anytime
	I'm A Gypsy Man
	Let Me Do It To You
	Lies
	Oh Mary
	Ride Me High
	Rock And Roll Records
	Thirteen Days
	Travelin' Light

Jackie Brenston & His Delta Cats	Rocket 88
Jackie DeShannon	Needles And Pins
Jackie Lomax	Sour Milk Sea
Jackie Wilson	Baby Workout
Jackson Browne	Cocaine
	Take It Easy
James & Bobby Purify	I Don't Know What It Is You Got
	I Take What I Want
	Shake A Tail Feather
James Brown	Ain't It Funky Now
	Bodyheat
	Fight Drug Abuse *(public service announcement)*
	Give It Up Or Turnit A Loose
	Good Good Lovin'
	I Can't Stand Myself (When You Touch Me)
	I Don't Mind
	I Got The Feelin'
	It's a Man's, Man's, Man's World
	Out Of Sight
	Papa's Got A Brand New Bag
	Santa Claus
	Super Bad
	Think
James Brown & the Famous Flames	I'll Go Crazy
Jan & Dean	Dead Man's Curve
	Drag City
Jeff Beck	A Day In The Life
	Beck's Bolero
	Blues Deluxe
	Cause We've Ended As Lovers
	Going Down

	I Ain't Superstitious
	In My Life
	Let Me Love You
	Rock My Plimsoul
	Shapes Of Things
	You Shook Me
Jeff Beck / Jools Holland & His Rhythm & Blues Orchestra	Drown In My Own Tears
Jeff Beck Group	All Shook Up
	Jailhouse Rock
	Plynth (Water Down the Drain)
	Spanish Boots
Jerry Lee Lewis	Good Golly Miss Molly
	Haunted House
	Highschool Confidential
	Honey Hush
	I Can Help
	Just A Little Bit
	Let's Talk About Us
	Rock And Roll
	Wild One (Real Wild Child)
Jerry Lee Lewis with Jimmy Page	Rock And Roll
Jesse Hill	Ooh-Poo-Pah-Doo
Jesse Taylor-John X Reed	Sin Sa Shun
Jet	Are You Gonna Be My Girl
Jimi Hendrix	Drifting
	In From The Storm
	Mr. Bad Luck
Jimi Hendrix Experience	Ain't No Telling
	Are You Experienced?
	Can You See Me
	Castles Made of Sand

	Come On (Part 1)
	Crosstown Traffic
	Fire
	Gypsy Eyes
	If 6 Was 9
	I Don't Live Today
	Killing Floor
	Little Miss Love
	Long Hot Summer Night
	Manic Depression
	May This Be Love
	Spanish Castle
	Up From The Skies
	You Got Me Floatin'
Jimmy Cliff	You Can Get It If You Really Want
Jimmy McCracklin	The Walk
Jimmy McGriff	All About My Girl
	I've Got A Woman (Parts 1 & 2)
Jimmy Reed	Aw Shucks
	Big Boss Man
	Good Lover
	I Ain't Got You
	I'm Goin' Upside Your Head
	Shame, Shame, Shame
	Take Out Some Insurance
Jimmy Rogers	Act Like You Love Me
	Goin' Away Baby
	Walking By Myself
Jimmy Smith	I Got A Woman
	The Organ Grinder's Swing
	What'd I Say
Joe Cocker	Don't Let Me Be Misunderstood
	Hitchcock Railway
	Lawdy Miss Clawdy
	Sticks And Stones

Joe Ely	Me And Billy The Kid
Joe Strummer & The Mescaleros	Get Down Moses Johnny Appleseed
Joe Tex	Hold What You've Got I Want To (Do Everything For You) I Believe I'm Gonna Make It Show Me Skinny Legs And All The Love You Save (May Be Your Own)
John D. Loudermilk	Tobacco Road
John Lee Hooker	Boogie Chillen' Dimples I Want To Ramble I Wanna Walk I'm In The Mood It Serves You Right To Suffer One Bourbon, One Scotch, One Beer
John Lennon	Ain't That A Shame I Found Out Surprise, Surprise (Sweet Bird of Paradox) Well Well Well
John Mayall	Hide Away Little Girl Steppin' Out What'd I Say
John Mayall & The Bluesbreakers	Curly Double Crossing Time Driving Sideways Greeny Key To Love The Stumble The Super-Natural
John Mayall With Eric Clapton	All Your Love
Johnny Bond	Hot Rod Lincoln

Johnny Burnette Trio	Honey Hush
	The Train Kept A-Rollin'
Johnny Cash	Cocaine Blues
	Cry, Cry, Cry
	Don't Take Your Guns To Town
	Pocahontas
	The Running Kind
	Understand Your Man
Johnny Jenkins With Duane Allman	Rollin' Stone
Johnny Otis Show	Willie And The Hand Jive
Johnny Rivers	Highway 61 Revisited
	Hustled Down In Texas
	I'm Yours And I'm Hers
	Memphis
	Rolllin' and Tumblin'
	Rockin' Pneumonia And The Boogie Woogie Flu
	Secret Agent Man
Jools Holland & His Rhythm & Blues Orchestra w/ Jeff Beck	Drown In My Own Tears
Jorgen Ingmann & His Guitar	Apache
Jr. Walker & The All Stars	Shake And Fingerpop
Junior Wells	Good Morning Schoolgirl
	Hoodoo Man Blues
	Messin' With The Kid
	Snatch It Back And Hold It
	Two Headed Woman
Keith Richards	Talk Is Cheap
	Take It So Hard
	Wicked As It Seems
Kim Wilson	Baby Please Don't Lie To Me

King Curtis	Soul Serenade
	Soul Twist
	The Christmas Song
King Floyd	Groove Me
	I Really Love You
Kings Of Leon	Pistol Of Fire
	Taper Jean Girl
	Velvet Snow
KoKo Taylor	(I Got) All You Need
	Wang Dang Doodle
	What Came First The Egg or The Hen
Larry Williams	Heeby-Jeebies
	Oh Baby
	She Said Yeah
	Short Fat Fannie
	Slow Down
LaVern Baker	Voodoo Voodoo
Lazy Lester	I'm Gonna Leave You Baby
Led Zeppelin	Communication Breakdown
	Good Times Bad Times
	I Can't Quit You Baby
	Your Time Is Gonna Come
Lee Allen & His Band	Walkin' With Mr. Lee
Lee Dorsey	Do-Re-Mi
	Ride Your Pony
	Working In The Coal Mine
	Ya Ya
Lena Horne	Let It Snow! Let It Snow! Let It Snow!
Leon Russell	Beware Of Darkness
	Dixie Lullaby
	Roll Away The Stone
Leon Russell & Marc Benno	Tryin' To Stay 'Live
Leonard Cohen	Everybody Knows
	I'm Your Man

	In My Secret Life
	Tower Of Song
Les Paul & Mary Ford	Dialog & In The Mood
Les Paul Trio	Blue Skies
Levon Helm And The RCO All Stars	Milk Cow Boogie
Lightnin' Hopkins	Business You're Doin'
	Don't Embarrass Me, Baby
	Mojo Hand
Linda Lyndell	What A Man
Link Wray & His Ray Men	Rumble Rock
Link Wray Jack	The Ripper Rumble!
Little Eva	Keep Your Hands Off My Baby
Little Feat	Willin'
Little Junior's	Blue Flames Feelin' Good
Little Richard	Directly From My Heart
	Good Golly, Miss Molly
	Hey Hey Hey Hey
	Keep A Knockin'
	Long Tall Sally
	Lucille
	Miss Ann
	Ready Teddy
	Send Me Some Lovin'
	Slippin' And Slidin' (Peepin' And Hidin')
	True Fine Mama
	Tutti Frutti
Little Richard Medley	Kansas City / Hey Hey Hey Hey
Little Walter	Boogie
	Dead Presidents
	I Hate To See You Go
	It Ain't Right
	Juke
	Mellow Down Easy

	My Babe
	Off The Wall
	Roller Coaster
	Sad Hours
	Tell Me Mama
	Up The Line
	Walkin' On
Little Willie John	Fever
	Let's Rock While The Rockin's Good
Lloyd Price	Lawdy Miss Clawdy
Lonesome Sundown	Don't Go
	I'm A Young Man
	My Home Ain't Here
Long John Baldry	Don't Try To Lay No Boogie-Woogie On
	It Ain't Easy
	I'm Ready
Lonnie Mack	Chicken Pickin'
	Memphis
	Wham!
Lou Reed	Dirty Blvd.
Louis Jordan & His Tympani Five	Let The Good Times Roll
Love	7 & 7 Is
	A House Is Not A Motel
	Alone Again Or
	Bummer In The Summer
	Hey Joe
	Live And Let Live
	My Little Red Book
	My Flash On You
	Old Man
Lowell Fulson	Do Me Right
	Reconsider Baby
Lucinda Williams	Can't Let Go
	Car Wheels On A Gravel Road

	I Lost It
	Joy
Madness	One Step Beyond
Manfred Mann	Bring It To Jerome
	Come Tomorrow
	Don't Ask Me What I Say
	Hubble Bubble (Toil and Trouble)
	If You Gotta Go, Go Now
	I'm Your Kingpin
	I've Got My Mojo Working
	Pretty Flamingo
	Sticks And Stones
	What You Gonna Do?
	Without You
	You're For Me
Marc Bolan & T Rex	20th Century Boy
	Children Of The Revolution
	Hot Love
	I Love To Boogie
	Ride A White Swan
Marvin Gaye	At Last (I Found A Love)
	One More Heartache
	Pride And Joy
	Trouble Man
	You're A Wonderful One
Marvin Gaye & Tami Terrell	Good Lovin' Ain't Easy To Come By
Mary Wells	You Beat Me To The Punch
Maurice & Mac	You Left The Water Running
Maxine Brown	Oh No, Not My Baby
MC5	Baby Won't Ya
	Gotta Keep Movin'
	Over And Over
	Shakin' Street
Mel Torme	Comin' Home Baby

Mick Jagger	Memo From Turner
Mighty Sam	Lovebones
Mike Bloomfield/Al Kooper/Steve Stills	Albert's Shuffle
Mink DeVille	Cadillac Walk
	Mixed Up, Shook Up Girl
	Gunslinger
	Spanish Stroll
	She's So Tough
Mitch Ryder & The Detroit Wheels	Jenny Take A Ride
	Ruby Baby & Peaches On a Cherry Tree
	Wheels
Moby Grape	Hey Grandma
	Omaha
Monsters of Folk	Dear God
Mose Allison	Don't Forget To Smile
	Eyesight To The Blind
	I Don't Worry About A Thing
	I Love The Life I Live
	I'm Not Talking
	I'm The Wild Man
	It Didn't Turn Out That Way
	Parchman Farm
	Seventh Son
	Young Man's Blues
	Your Mind Is On Vacation
	I'm Not Talking
Mountain	Mississippi Queen
	Never In My Life
Mudcrutch	Crystal River
	High School Confidential
	Lover of the Bayou
	Scare Easy Mudcrutch
Muddy Waters	All Aboard
	Blow Wind Blow

	Champagne & Reefer
	Diamonds At Your Feet
	Forty Days And Forty Nights
	Got My Mojo Working
	(I'm Your) Hoochie Coochie Man
	I Can't Be Satisfied
	I Just Want To Make Love To You
	I'm Ready
	I Feel So Good
	Long Distance Call
	Look What You've Done
	Rock Me
	Rollin' Stone
	Rollin' & Tumblin', Part 1
	She Moves Me
	Stuff You Gotta Watch
	The Same Thing
	Trouble No More
	Walking Thru The Park
Nappy Brown	The Right Time
Nashville Teens	Tobacco Road
Nat King Cole	The Christmas Song (Merry Christmas)
Nazz	Forget All About It
	Open My Eyes
Neil Young	Alabama Harvest
	Everybody Knows This Is Nowhere
	Roll Another Number (For The Road)
	The Loner
	The Losing End (When You're On)
	When You Dance You Can Really Love
Neil Young & Crazy Horse	Powderfinger
Nick Lowe	7 Nights To Rock
	Heart Of The City
	(I Love The Sound Of) Breaking Glass

337

Norah Jones	Sunrise
Norman Greenbaum	Spirit In The Sky
NRBQ	Me And The Boys
	Still In School
Otis Redding	Day Tripper
	Love Man
	Merry Christmas, Baby
	These Arms of Mine
	Treat Her Right
Otis Redding	Mr. Pitiful
	That's How Strong My Love Is
Otis Redding With Carla Thomas	Tramp
Otis Rush	All Your Love (I Miss Loving)
	Homework Blues
	I Can't Quit You Baby
Otis Spann	She Needs Some Loving
P.J. Proby	Niki Hoeky
Paul & Linda McCartney	Heart Of The Country
Paul Butterfield Blues Band	Blues With A Feeling
	Born In Chicago
	In My Own Dream
	Lovin' Cup
	Nut Popper #1
	Off The Wall
Paul McCartney	The Pound Is Sinking
Paul Revere & The Raiders	Don't Take It So Hard
	Good Thing
	Him Or Me What's It Gonna Be
	Hungry
	I'm Not Your Stepping Stone
	Just Like Me
	Let Me
	Louie, Go Home
	Peace of Mind

	Steppin' Out
	The Great Airplane Strike
Pete Townshend	Rough Boys
Pete Townshend &	Heart To Hang Onto
Ronnie Lane	My Baby Gives It Away
Peter Green / Fleetwood	Man of the World
Mac	World In Harmony
Peter Tosh	Johnny B. Goode
Peter Wolf	Tragedy
Piano Red	Rockin' With Red
PJ Harvey	Down By The Water
Poco	A Good Feelin' To Know
	Honky Tonk
	You Better Think Twice
Quicksilver Messenger	Dino's Song
Service	Gold And Silver
Radiohead	Bodysnatchers
	Just
Ramsey Lewis Trio	Wade In The Water
Randy Newman	Marie
	Pants
	Sail Away
Ray Charles	Don't Set Me Free
	I Don't Need No Doctor
	Leave My Woman Alone
	Let The Good Times Roll
	Let's Go Get Stoned
	Mess Around
	(Night Time Is) The Right Time
	Rainy Night n Georgia
	Sticks And Stones
	Tell The Truth
	Unchain My Heart
	What Kind of Man Are You
	What'd I Say (Part 1)

	Yes Indeed!
	You Are My Sunshine
Ray Charles With Van Morrison	Crazy Love
Ray Davies	Vietnam Cowboys
Ray Stevens	Harry The Hairy Ape
	Santa Claus Is Watching You
Regina Spektor	Dance Anthem Of The 80s
	Laughing With
Rene Hall's Orchestra	Twitchy
Richard Berry & The Pharaohs	Louie Louie
Richie Barrett	Some Other Guy At The Club
Rick Danko With Ringo Starr & His All Starr Band	Raining In My Heart
Rick Nelson	Fools Rush In
	For You
	If You Can't Rock Me
	She Belongs To Me
	Teenage Idol
	Waitin' In School Greatest Hits
	Young World
Ritchie Valens	Come On, Let's Go
	Ooh! My Head
Robert Parker	Barefootin'
Robert Plant With Alison Krauss	Rich Woman
Rockin' Rebels	Wild Weekend
Rockpile	If Sugar Was As Sweet As You
	Teacher Teacher
	When I Write The Book
	Wrong Again (Let's Face It)
	You Ain't Nothin' But Fine
Rod Stewart	An Old Raincoat Won't Ever Let You Down

	Dirty Old Town
	Gasoline Alley
	Only A Hobo
Roger McGuinn	King Of The Hill
Rolling Stones	2000 Man
	All Down The Line
	Back Of My Hand
	Backstreet Girl
	Before They Make Me Run
	Can I Get A Witness
	Can't You Hear Me Knocking
	Carol
	Casino Boogie
	Cool, Calm & Collected
	Connection
	Connection Between
	Doncha Bother Me
	Don't Lie To Me
	Down Home Girl
	Empty Heart
	Flight 505
	Fortune Teller
	Grown Up Wrong
	I Am Waiting
	I Don't Know Why
	I Just Want To Make Love To You
	I Wanna Be Your Man
	I'm A King Bee
	I'm Free
	I'm Moving On
	It's Not Easy
	Little By Little
	Little T & A
	Look What You've Done
	Long Long While

Loving Cup
Miss Amanda Jones
Money (That's What I Want)
Monkey Man
No Expectations
Miss Amanda Jones
Not Fade Away
Oh Baby (We Got A Good Thing Goin')
Out Of Time
Paint It Black
Parachute Woman
Play With Fire
Please Go Home
Plundered My Soul
Poison Ivy
Prodigal Son
Ride On, Baby
Route 66
Ruby Tuesday
Torn And Frayed
She's So Cold
She Said Yeah
Silver Train
Sittin' On A Fence
Soul Survivor
Stray Cat Blues
Stop Breaking Down
Street Fighting Man
Stupid Girl
Susie Q
Sweet Virginia
Talkin' About You
Tallahassee Lassie
The Spider And The Fly
Think Aftermath

	Under My Thumb
	Under The Boardwalk
	Walking The Dog
	What To Do
	Ventilator Blues
	You Got The Silver
Ron Wood	Seven Days
Ronnie Hawkins & The Hawks	Who Do You Love
Roy Buchanan	Sweet Dreams
Roy Head & The Traits	My Babe Treat Her Right
	Treat Her Right
Roy Montrell	(Every Time I Hear That) Mellow Saxophone
Roy Orbison	Blue Angel
	Candy Man
	Mean Woman Blues
	Uptown
	Working For The Man
Rufus Thomas	Jump Back
	The Memphis Train
	Walking The Dog
Sam & Dave	I Take What I Want
	Soul Sister, Brown Sugar
	You Don't Know Like I Know
	When Something Is Wrong With My Baby
	Wrap It Up
Sam Cooke	A Change Is Gonna Come
	Another Saturday Night
	Jesus Gave Me Water
	Good Times
	Meet Me At Mary's Place
	Soothe Me
Sandy Nelson	Drum Roll 9
	Let There Be Drums

Santo & Johnny	All Night Diner
	Roll Away The Stone
Savoy Brown	She's Got A Ring In His Nose, And A
	Ring On Her Hand
Scotty Draw	Your Breaks
Sepia Tones	Boogie #1
Shirley Ellis	The Nitty Gritty
Shorty Long	Devil With The Blue Dress
Sir Douglas Quintet	Isabella
	Mendocino
	She's About A Mover
Slim Harpo	Baby, Scratch My Back
	Buzz Me Babe
	Don't Start Crying Now
	I Got Love If You Want It
	I'm a King Bee
	Shake Your Hips
	Strange Love
	Tip On In (Part 1)
Sly & The Family Stone	Everybody Is A Star
	Family Affair
	Sing A Simple Song
	You Can Make It If You Try
Small Faces	All Or Nothing
	Grow Your Own
	Itchycoo Park
	Lazy Sunday
	Tin Soldier
	What'cha Gonna Do About It
Smiley Lewis	I Hear You Knocking
	Shame, Shame, Shame
Solomon Burke	Cry To Me
	Got To Get You Off My Mind
Son Volt	Drown
	Windfall

Sonny Boy Williamson	All My Love In Vain
	Bring It On Home
	Checkin' Up On My Baby
	Don't Start Me Talkin'
	Fattening Frogs For Snakes
	Help Me
	Keep It To Yourself
	Let Your Conscience Be Your Guide
	One Way Out
	Sad To Be Alone
	Your Funeral And My Trial
Sonny Burgess	Red Headed Woman
	We Wanna Boogie
Spencer Davis Group	Every Little Bit Hurts
	I'm A Man
	Keep On Running
	Somebody Help Me
	Stevie's Blues
	Trampoline
Spirit	Fresh
	Gramophone Man
	Mechanical World
	Straight Arrow
	The Great Canyon Fire in General
	Water Woman
	Uncle Jack
	Mechanical World
Spooky Tooth	I Am The Walrus
Stephen Stills	Bumblebee (Do You Need A Place To Hide)
	Helplessly Hoping
	Wooden Ships
	Johnny's Garden
Stephen Stills & Manassas	It Doesn't Matter
	So Begins The Task

Steppenwolf	Rock Me
	Sookie Sookie
Steve Cropper With Steve Winwood	Thirty Second Lover
Steve Miller Band	Children Of The Future
	Got Love 'Cause You Need It
	Junior Saw It Happen
	Quicksilver Girl
	Steppin' Stone
Stevie Ray Vaughan & Double Trouble	Pipeline The Real Deal
Stevie Wonder	I Believe (When I Fall In Love It Will Be Forever)
	You Met Your Match
Stills-Young Band	Long May You Run
Sublime	Smoke Two Joints
Sugar Pie DeSanto	A Little Taste of Soul
Syndicate of Sound	Little Girl
T-Bone Walker	Alimony Blues
	Don't Leave Me Baby
	Sail On Boogie
	Shufflin' The Blues
	Strollin' With Bone
	Mean Old World
Taj Mahal	Going Up To The Country, Paint My Mailbox Blue
	Hello Josephine Maestro
	She Caught the Katy (and Left Me A Mule To Ride)
	Six Days On The Road
	You're Gonna Need Somebody
Taj Mahal & the New Orleans Social Club	My Girl Josephine
The Allman Joys	Spoonful
	Crossroads

The Animals	All Night Long
	Around And Around
	Blue Feeling
	Boom Boom
	Bright Lights Big City
	Bring It On Home To Me
	Dimples
	Don't Bring Me Down
	Gotta Find My Baby
	Hey Gyp
	It's My Life
	Inside Looking Out
	I'm Crying
	I'm In Love Again
	Inside Looking Out
	It's My Life
	Mess Around
	Roadrunner
	See See Rider
	Shake
	Talkin' Bout You
	When I Was Young
The Band	Don't Do It
	Don't Ya Tell Henry
	King Harvest (Has Surely Come)
	Life Is A Carnival
	Rag Mama Rag
	See See Rider
	Stage Fright
	The Shape I'm In
	We Can Talk
	When I Paint My Masterpiece
The Band With The Staples Singers	The Weight

The Beatles	All I've Got To Do
	And Your Bird Can Sing
	Another Girl
	Bad Boy
	Cry For A Shadow
	Day Tripper
	Devil In Her Heart
	Doctor Robert
	Eleanor Rigby
	Every Little Thing
	Flying
	Getting Better
	Hey Bulldog
	Honey Don't
	I Don't Want To Spoil The Party
	I'll Cry Instead
	I'm A Loser
	I'm Down
	I'm Looking Through You
	It Won't Be Long
	I've Got A Feeling
	I've Just Seen A Face
	Leave My Kitten Alone
	Love Me Do
	Magical Mystery Tour
	Money (That's What I Want)
	Mr. Moonlight
	No Reply
	Not A Second Time
	Paperback Writer
	Rain
	Revolution
	Roll Over Beethoven
	She Came In Through The Bathroom Window

	She Said She Said
	Sun King
	Tell Me Why
	The Word
	There's A Place
	Things We Said Today
	Think For Yourself
	Two Of Us
	Wait
	When I Get Home
	You Can't Do That
	You're Going To Lose That Girl
	You Really Got A Hold On Me
The Beau Brummels	Don't Talk To Strangers
The Black Keys	Next Girl Brothers
The Box Tops	Soul Deep
The Byrds	Artificial Energy
	Deportee (Plane Wreck At Los Gatos)
	Eight Miles High
	Have You Seen Her Face
	Here Without You
	I See You
	It's No Use
	It Won't Be Wrong
	Jesus Is Just Alright
	Lover of The Bayou
	Natural Harmony
	So You Want To Be A Rock 'N' Roll Star
	The World Turns All Around Her
	Time Between
	Why
	Younger Than Yesterday
The Cadets	Stranded In The Jungle
The Capitols	Cool Jerk

The Chantays	Pipeline Rock
The Clash	Clampdown
	Lost In The Supermarket
	Train In Vain
The Coasters	Little Egypt
	Run Red Run
	Shoppin' For Clothes
The Cobras	Shake Up
The Contours	Do You Love Me
The Cookies	Chains
	Girls Grow Up Faster Than Boys
The Creation	How Does It Feel To Feel
	Making Time
The Dictators	The Savage Beat
The Dixie Cups	Iko Iko
The Dovells	Do The New Continental
	You Can't Sit Down
The Easybeats	Good Times
	Sorry
The Five Americans	I See The Light
The Four Blazes	Mary Jo
The Gants	Little Boy Sad
	Road Runner
The Guess Who	Albert Flasher
	Hang On To Your Life
	It's My Pride
	Shakin' All Over
The Heavy	How You Like Me Now
The High Numbers	I'm The Face
The Hollies	Long Cool Woman (In A Black Dress)
	Look Through Any Window
	Pay You Back With Interest
The Ikettes	I'm Blue (The Gong Gong Song)
The Impressions	It's All Right
	Talking About My Baby

The James Gang	Bluebird
The Jaynettes	Sally Go 'Round The Roses
The Kinks	20th Century Man
	A Gallon of Gas
	Ev'ry Body's Gonna Be Happy
	Father Christmas Misfits
	Get Back In Line
	I Gotta Move
	I Need You
	Keep A Knockin'
	Milk Cow Blues
	See My Friends
	Set Me Free
	Stop Your Sobbin'
	This Time Tomorrow
	Till The End Of The Day
	Waterloo Sunset
	Where Have All The Good Times Gone
	Who'll Be The Next In Line
The Knickerbockers	Lies
The Left Banke	Desiree
	Pretty Ballerina
	Surf Rider
	Walk Away Renee
The Lovin' Spoonful	Coconut Grove
	Darlin' Companion
	Didn't Want To Have To Do It
	Nashville Cats
	There She Is
The Mamas and The Papas	Twelve-Thirty (Young Girls Are Coming To The Canyon)
The Manatees	Blowhole
	Dale's Dick
The Marketts	Out Of Limits

The Marvelettes	Beechwood 4-5789
	Playboy
	Please Mr. Postman
	Too Many Fish In The Sea
	The Hunter Gets Captured By The Game
The McCoys	Fever
	Meet The McCoys
The Merry-Go-Round	Live Listen, Listen
	Time Will Show The Wiser
	You're A Very Lovely Woman
The Midnighters	Annie Had A Baby
The Monkees	Let's Dance On
	Mary, Mary
	Saturday's Child
	Valleri
The Move	California Man
	Do Ya
	Message From The Country
The Music Machine	Talk Talk
The Nightcrawlers	A Basket of Flowers
	The Little Black Egg
The Poets	That's The Way It's Got To Be
The Pretenders	Have Yourself A Merry Little Christmas
	Message Of Love
The Pretty Things	Don't Bring Me Down
	Rosalyn
The Pyramids	Penetration
The Quik	Bert's Apple Crumble
The Rascals	Hold On
	Love Is A Beautiful Thing
	Please Love Me
	Too Many Fish In The Sea
The Rascals	See
The Red Button	Cruel Girl
The Romantics	Out Of My Mind (Into My Head)

The Searchers	Alright
	Bumble Bee
	He's Got No Love
	Needles and Pins
	Sweets For My Sweet
	Take Me For What I'm Worth
	When You Walk In The Room
The Seeds	Can't Seem To Make You Mine
The Shadows	Man Of Mystery
	The Frightened City
	Shadoogie
	The Savage
The Shadows Of Knight	Gloria Gloria
The Shangri-Las	Give Him A Great Big Kiss
	I Can Never Go Home Anymore
	Out In The Streets
The Shirelles	Baby It's You
The Slickers	Johnny Too Bad
The Sorrows	I Don't Wanna Be Free
	You've Got What I Want
	Take A Heart
The Standells	Sometimes Good Guys Don't Wear White
The Staple Singers	If You're Ready (Come Go With Me)
	Respect Yourself
The Stooges	I Wanna Be Your Dog
The Strangeloves	Night Time
	I Want Candy
	Cara-Lin
The Supremes	Nathan Jones
The Sweet Inspirations	Sweet Inspiration
The Swinging Blue Jeans	Hippy Hippy Shake
The Temptations	Ball Of Confusion (That's What The World Is Today)
	Cloud Nine
	Psychedelic Shack

The Troggs	I Can't Control Myself
	With A Girl Like You
The Turtles	You Showed Me
The Valentinos	It's All Over Now
The Velvet Underground	Rock And Roll
The Ventures	Diamond Head
	God Rest Ye Merry Gentlemen
	I Feel Fine
	Slaughter On Tenth Avenue
	The House Of The Rising Sun
	Underground Fire Radio Spot
	Walk–Don't Run
The Wallflowers	Playboy
The West Coast Pop Art Experimental Band	If You Want This Love
The Who	A Legal Matter
	Anyway, Anyhow, Anywhere
	Baby Don't You Do It
	Circles
	I Can See For Miles
	I Can't Explain
	I'm A Boy
	I'm A Man
	It's Not True
	La–La Lies
	Leaving Here
	Magic Bus
	Mary Anne With The Shaky Hand
	My Generation
	Odorono
	Out In The Street
	Pictures Of Lily
	Relax
	Run Run Run
	See My Way

	So Sad About Us
	Sparks
	Substitute
	Tattoo
	The Kids Are Alright
	Young Man Blues
The Yardbirds	Dazed And Confused
	Heart Full Of Soul
	I Ain't Done Wrong
	I'm Not Talking
	I Wish You Would
	Little Games
	Lost Woman
	Over Under Sideways Down
	The Train Kept A-Rollin'
	You're A Better Man Than I
The Young Rascals	Come On Up
	I Ain't Gonna Eat Out My Heart Anymore
	In The Midnight Hour
	It's Love
	Love Is A Beautiful Thing
	Slow Down
The Zombies	Don't Go Away
	I Love You
	I Remember When I Loved Her
	If It Don't Work Out
	Indication
	Is This The Dream
	It's Alright With Me
	She Does Everything For Me
	Summertime
	This Will Be Our Year
	What More Can I Do
	Whenever You're Ready

	Woman
	You Make Me Feel Good
	You've Really Got A Hold On Me
Them	Baby Please Don't Go
	Here Comes The Night
	I Can Only Give You Everything
	Mystic Eyes
Then There Were Two	Anyone Who Had A Heart
	Don't Fade On Me
	Mother Nature's Son
Thunderclap Newman	Something In The Air
Todd Rundgren	Couldn't I Just Tell You
Tom Petty	I'm Walkin'
Tom Petty & The Heartbreakers	Christmas All Over Again
	Don't Pull Me Over
	First Flash Of Freedom
	Good Enough
	Green Onions
	High In The Morning
	I Just Want To Make Love To You
	I Should Have Known It
	I'm Walkin'
	Lovers Touch
	Running Man's Bible
	The Trip To Pirates Cove
	U.S. 41
Tommy Roe	Everybody
Tommy Tucker	Hi-Heel Sneakers
Tony Jackson & The Vibrations	Bye Bye Baby
Tony Jackson Group	Fortune Teller
Tony Joe	White Polk Salad
Toots & The Maytals	Louie Louie
	Take Me Home, Country Roads
	Time Tough

Traffic	Dear Mr. Fantasy
	Empty Pages
	Forty Thousand Headmen
	Freedom Rider
	Heaven Is In Your Mind
	John Barleycorn Must Die
	Medicated Goo
	Pearly Queen
	Shanghai Noodle Factory
	Something's Got A Hold Of My Toe
	The Low Spark Of High Heeled Boys
	Who Knows What Tomorrow May Bring
	You Can All Join In
Traveling Wilburys	Runaway
Travis Wammac	Fire Fly
	Scratchy
	Tech-Nically Speaking
Van Morrison	Blue Money
	Domino
	Dweller On The Threshold
	In The Days Before Rock 'N' Roll
	Into The Mystic
	Jackie Wilson Said (I'm In Heaven When You Smile)
	Precious Time
	Starting A New Life
	Youth of 1,000 Summers
Van Morrison With Roger Waters	Comfortably Numb
Vanilla Fudge	You Keep Me Hangin' On
Vaughan Bros.	Brothers
Velvelettes	Needle In A Haystack
Wanda Jackson	Fujiyama Mama
	Let's Have A Party

We The People	Declaration Of Independence
	You Burn Me Up And Down
Whiskeytown	16 Days
Wilbert Harrison	Kansas City
Wilco	I Got You (At The End Of The Century)
	Outtasite (Outta Mind)
William Bell	I Forgot To Be Your Lover
Willie Dixon	29 Ways
Willie Mitchell	My Babe Soul Serenade
	That Driving Beat
Wilson Pickett	Engine Number 9
	Hey Jude
	I'm A Midnight Mover
	I Found A True Love
	Mustang Sally
	She's Lookin' Good
	Soul Dance Number Three
Wynonie Harris	Lovin' Machine
	Sittin' On It All The Time
ZZ Top	Brown Sugar
	Just Got Back From Baby's

Suggested Reading

Conversations With Tom Petty by Paul Zollo (Omnibus Press, 2003)
Runnin' Down A Dream, by Tom Petty (Chronicle Books, 2007)

Select Bibliography

Abrahams, Andrew. "Playback." *People* (January 8, 1996): 26.

Author unknown. "Mike Campbell." *The ToneQuest Report* (March 2008, Vol. 9, No. 5).

Author unknown. "Tom Petty and the Heartbreakers" *Melody Maker* (vol 52. No 22. 1977).

Bangs, Lester. "Tom Petty & the Heartbreakers (Capital)." *Circus Magazine* (-------): 15.

Belloni, Matthew. "Tom Petty, Bob Dylan vs. Music Labels: The Industry's New Copyright War." *The Hollywood Reporter* (February 10, 2012).

Blair, Iain. "Moon Shot." *New Music Express* (Vol. 13, Issue 137): 35–38.

Blake, Mike. "He Knew He Was Right." *Q* (July 2012): 56–59.

Bosso, Joe. "Tom Petty Drummer Steve Ferrone Talks Groove" *Music Radar*.

Charone, Barbara. "Tom Petty: Whisky A Go Go, Los Angeles." *Sounds* (September 10, 1977).

Cohen, Mitch. "Tom Petty. Damn the Torpedoes." *Creem* (February 1980): 54–55.

Cohen, Mitchell. "The Pleasure of Petty's Pain." *High Fidelity* (August 1981): 75.

Cohen, Mitchell. "Fugitive Kind of Love: Del Shannon." *Creem* (June 1982).

Collins, Dianne. "Petty Little Thing Called Love." *Rock Express* (number113, 1987): 23–24, 45.

Conway, Ann. "A Good Cause That's Personal." *Los Angeles Times* (February 15, 2004).

Corcoran, Michael. "Raised on Promises." *SPIN* (August 1989): 43–46, 88.

Crowe, Cameron. "Tom Petty Returns for More." *Rolling Stone* (April 20, 1978).

Crowe, Cameron. "Tom Petty's Gonna Get It—His Way." *Rolling Stone* (October 19, 1978): 34–39.

DeCurtis, Anthony. "Tom Petty's New LP: Back to Basics." ------- (-----).

Demorest, Stephen. "Tom Petty: Animus Americus Unpolititucs." *Creem* (August 1978): 28, 77–79.

di Perna, Alan. "Petty on the Inside." *Pulse!* (April 1999): 34–37, 86–87.

Doyle, Patrick. "Q&A: Tom Petty Finishing LP 'Unlike Anything We've Ever Done." *Rolling Stone* (August 5, 2013).

Easterling, Mike. "Feels Like Religion. Jesus and Leon might have left the building, but almost 30 years later, the Church Studio resurrects its legendary music and religious past." *Urban Tulsa Weekly* (November 11, 2009).

Edmonds, Ben. "Tom Petty & The Heartbreakers: Playback (MCA)." *Mojo* (January 1996).

Farber, Jim. "The Heart of the Matter." *New York Daily News* (----, 1999).

Feeney, F.X. and Rosenberg, Howard. "A Chat with Tom Petty." *LA Weekly* (June 26–July 2, 1981).

Flannagan, Bill. "Tom Petty Pulls Together: The Southern Soul of a Hollywood Rocker." *Musician* (-------): 35–42.

Flanagan, Bill. "The Heartbreakers Highway." *Musician* (April 1990): 32–47.

Freff. "Tom Petty & Dave Stewart?!" *Musician* (June 1985): 82.

Forman, Bill. "American Boy: Tom Petty Replants His Roots." *BAM* (May 22, 1987): 42–46/

Gans, David. "Petty: The War Is Over." *Record* (January 1983): 1, 12–13.

Gans, David. "Tom Petty Hot Spell." *Hit Parader* (April 1983): 4–7.

George Warren, Holly. "Tom Petty." *Oxford American* (July/August 2000): 90–95.

Gilmore, Mikal. "Tom Petty's Rock Fervor." *Rolling Stone* (June 30, 1977, number242).

Gilmore, Mikal. "Tom Petty's Real-Life Nightmares." *Rolling Stone* (February 21, 1980): 10–13.

Gilmore, Mikal. "Positively Dylan." *Rolling Stone* (July 17/July 31, 1986): 30–34, 135–136.

Goldberg, Michael. "Back on the Road: Tom Petty Teams Up with New Pal Bob Dylan." *Rolling Stone* (January 16, 1986): 19.

Graff, Gary. "Oh! You Petty Thing." *Revolution* (-----): 47–49.

Graff, Gary. "Tom Petty's New Tales of the Old South." *Creem* (October 1985): 24–25, 62–63.

Graustark, Barbara with Coppola, Vincent. "Rock's New Heartbreak Kid." *Newsweek* (January 7, 1980): 57.

Greene, Andy. "Tom Petty Talks Super Bowl, "Long-Overdue Heartbreakers Record," Corporate Rock: Exclusive." *Rolling Stone* (December 4, 2007).

Greene, Andy. "Q&A: Tom Petty On His Rarities Tour, Writing With Bob Dylan." *Rolling Stone* (June 14, 2013).

Guerra, Tom. "Runnin' Down a Dream: Mike Campbell." *Premier Guitar* (April 2008).

Gundersen, Edna. "But Veteran Think Pop Lacks Snap." *USA Today* (-----): cover story.

Gundersen, Edna. "Petty Runs Down, and Over, American Dream." *USA Today* (October 18, 2002): 6E.

Gundersen, Edna. "No Backing Down." *OIL Magazine* (September 1995): 11.

Hasted, Nick. "Tom Petty: From the *Unchained* Sessions to 'I Won't Back Down.' *Uncut*.

Heller, Greg. "Rick Rubin: Behind the Beard." *Rolling Stone* (December 17, 2001).

Hibbert, Tom. "Tom Petty: Outlaw Blues." Q (July 1989).

Hilburn, Robert. "No Backing Down." *Los Angeles Times* (March 15, 2002): F1, F28–F29.

Hilburn, Robert. "S.F. Smitten by Heartbreakers." *Los Angeles Times* (April 26, 1977).

Hilburn, Robert. "Classic Rock of Tom Petty." *Los Angeles Times* (June 7, 1978).

Hilburn, Robert. "Petty Courts Fans on 'Lawsuit Tour.'" *Los Angeles Times* (July 27, 1979).

Hilburn, Robert. "Tom Petty's New Southern Rock Sound Questions Southern Attitudes." *Los Angeles Times* (-------, 1985).

Hogan, Richard. "Tom Petty Makes Hard Promises' to Rock & Roll." *Circus* (August 31, 1981): 26–30.

Hoskyns, Barney. "Johnny Cash: A Law Unto Himsef." *Mojo* (December 1996).

Hoskyns, Barney. "The Lonely Blue Dream of Roy Orbison." *Mojo* (January 1999).

Jackson, Blair. "Tom Petty: The Promise Fulfilled." *BAM* (June 5, 1981): 23–26.

Jackson, Blair. "Just a Popular Rock 'n' Roll Band." *Trouser Press* (August 1981): 20–24.

Jackson, Blair. "There's a Lot More to The Heartbreakers than Tom Petty." *BAM* (January 28, 1983): 24–28.

Kyle, Russell. "Hearbreak Hit from Tom's Boys." *Glasglow Evening Times* (May 6, 1977).

Lanham, Tom. "Petty on the Inside." *Pulse* (December 1994): 70–76.

Light, Alan. "Tom Petty: Highway Companion." *Rolling Stone* (July 20, 2006).

Loder, Kurt. "Petty to Revive 'Runaway' Rock Legend." *Circus Weekly* (January 9, 1979): 17.

Marsh, Dave. "Tom Petty." *Musician* (July 1981): 42–52.

McCollum, Brian. "Rock Success a Simple Matter for Tom Petty." *Gazette Weekend!* (May 7, 1999): 8W.

Mettler, Mike. "Tom Petty on Recording 'Mojo.' *Sound + Vision* (May 31, 2010).

Miller, Eric T. "If I Had My Way, I'd Tear the Building Down." *Magnet* (January/February 2003): 64–70, 122–123.

Millman, Joyce. "Tom Petty's Rebel Yell." *Rolling Stone* (May 23, 1985).

Mills, Fred. "Album Retrospective: Tom Petty." *Harp* (July 2006).

Moore, Jayne. "Renowned Heartbreakers Drummer Stan Lynch Becomes Top Songwriter & Producer." *SoundwriterUniverse*.

Morse, Steve. "Blonde on Blonde." *Trouser Press* (March 1980): 21–23.

Morse, Steve. "Tom Petty Reaches Back to His Roots." *Boston Globe* (March 31, 1985).

Palmer, Robert. "Tom Petty: Ready to Fight the Good Fight." *The New York Times* (May 7, 1981).

Pareles, Jon. "Tom Petty & the Heartbreakers. Hard Promises." *Creem* (August 1981): 51.

Petty, Tom. "Howie Epstein." *Rolling Stone* (April 3, 2003): 25.

Philips, Chuck. "Recording Stars Challenge Music Labels' Business Practices." *Los Angeles Times* (2001).

Pond, Steve. "Petty Wins Battle Over New LP's Price." *Rolling Stone* (April 30, 1981).

Pond, Steve. "You're Gonna Get It!" *SEE* (July 1999): 24.

Quinn, Michael. "Petty's Peace." *Time* (May 18, 1992): 83.

Regen, Jon. "More Than a Heartbreaker: Benmont Tench on Playing with Tom Petty." *Keyboard* (November 1, 2009).

Ressner, Jeffrey. "Tom Petty Goes It Alone." *Rolling Stone* (April 20, 1989).

Rogers, Sheila. "Supergroup: The Traveling Wilburys." *Rolling Stone* (-----).

Rose, Cynthia. "Tom Petty." *City Limits* (December 3, 1982).

Rose, Cynthia. "Tom Petty & The Heartbreakers: Hard Promises (MCA)." *NME* (March 23, 1981).

Rowland, Mark. "Heartbreaker Straight Ahead! Tom Petty Stops Jamming and Speaks His Mind." *Musician* (September 1987): 76–84.

Rowland, Mark. "Beck Meets Petty." Musician (January 1997): 30–42, 62.

Shapiro, Susin. "The Heartbreak Kid." *Sounds* (April 9, 1977).

Schruers, Fred. "This Is How It Fees." *Rolling Stone* (May 4, 1995): 48–54, 76.

Schruers, Fred. "Tom Petty." *Rolling Stone* (July 8–22, 1999): 88–94.

Scopa, Bud. "Tom Petty: Less is More." *Creem* (August 1987).

Selvin, Joel. "Tom Petty and the Heartbreakers: Fillmore Auditorium." *Mojo* (March 1997).

Sharp, Ken. "Mojo Man: Ron Blair with Tom Petty & The Heartbreakers." *Bass Player* (January 18, 2013).

Sheehan, Tom. "Southern Comfort." *Melody Maker* (May 11, 1985): 24–25, 32.

Simels, Steve. "The Tom Petty Synthesis." *Stereo Review* (----): 114.

Simels, Steve. "Tom Petty and the Heartbreakers: Damn the Torpedoes." *Stereo Review* (---- 1979): 128.

Simels, Steve. "Tom Petty and the Heartbreakers. Hard Promises." *Stereo Review* (August 1981): 78.

Simmons, Sylvie. "Tom Petty: Long After Maturity." *Creem* (April 1983): 28–30, 59–60.

Simmons, Sylvie. "Tom Petty: The Forum, Los Angeles." *Sounds* (February 2, 1980).

Snow, Mat. "Tom Petty." *Mojo* (October 2009).

Snyder, John. "Tommy Petty Leaves Home Again: A Rock Roller Out of Time." *Gainesville Sun* (December 10, 1976).

Sperrazza, Gary. "Tom Petty: The Great White Hope." *Trouser Press* (December 1978).

Spillman, Susan. "Tom Petty's Rowdy Return to the Road." *USA Today* (----).

Sterndan, Darryl. "Guitar Inspires Petty's Mojo." *Toronto Sun* (June 6, 2010).

Strauss, Neil. "Tom Petty's Last Dance." *Rolling Stone* (July 13–27, 2006): 73–78.

Sweeting, Adam. "The Man Most Likely To: Dave Stewart." *Q* (February 1987).

Sweeting, Adam. "Tom Petty: Petty Larceny." *Vox* (September 1991).

Taylor, Jonathan. "Tom Petty: Good Ol' Boy Making Good Music." *Chicago Tribune* (June 22, 1985).

Testa, Fabio. "Tom Petty: Original American." *Rock Scene* (----): 10–11, 56–59.

Thompson, Art. "Heartbreaker Hideout." *Guitar Player* (May 1999): 78–89.

Uhelszki, Jaan. "Won't Back Down." Uncut (June 2012): 42–47.

Uhelszki, Jaan. "Tom Petty: Anatomy of a Rock Star." *Harp* (July/Ausut 2006): 104–110, 144.

Uhelszki, Jaan. "Echo Chamber." *Guitar Magazine* (June 1999): 26–28.

Uhelszki, Jaan. "10 Questions for Tom Petty." *Mojo* (May 1999).

Wallace, Alice. "Memories of Petty: How Singer Found Way in Area." *Gainesville Sun* (September 20, 2006).

Watrous, Peter. "Tom Petty and the Heartbreakers. Pack Up the Plantation: Live!" ------ (----).

Wild, David. "Over the Hump." *Rolling Stone* (August 8, 1991): 39–44, 90.

Young, Charles M. "Tom Petty." *Musician* (March 1983): 42–48.

Young, Jacob and Gold, Todd. "You've Seen 'Em Before, But Now Meet These Wild Wilburys." *People* (October 31, 1988): 48–49.

Zimmer, Dave. "Tom Petty: Once In A Full Moon." *BAM* (May 5, 1989).

http://www.gainesvillerockhistory.com/RickReed.htm accessed 11/20/12

http://sandystringfellow.com/ accessed 11/23/12

http://www.mudcrutch.com/forum/printthread.php?t=1179&pp=12&page=3 accessed 11/23/12

http://www.songfacts.com/blog/interviews/mike_campbell/ accessed 11/25/12

http://www.musicradar.com/news/guitars/mike-campbell-on-30-years-with-tom-petty-and-the-heartbreakers-226467 accessed 11/25/12

http://www.musicradar.com/news/drums/tom-petty-drummer-steve-ferrone-talks-groove-273410

Acknowledgements

First and foremost, thanks to Bob Wise of Music Sales Group for thinking of me when his company was in search of an author for this unofficial biography of Tom Petty. The encouragement of the Omnibus Press UK team, including David Barraclough and Chris Charlesworth, was invaluable during the development of this book.

I'd also like to thank every single music journalist that's ever written about Tom Petty & The Heartbreakers. As a kid I'd clip these stories out of magazines and newspapers and create my own scrapbooks. I had no idea that I would one day also write about the man whose music has inspired our generation. Music criticism is a lost art and I'm indebted to the greats like Lester Bangs, Anthony DeCurtis, Stephen Demorest, Alan di Perna, Stephen Thomas Erlewine, Jim Farber, Bill Flanagan, Mikal Gilmore, Gary Graff, Edna Gundersen, Robert Hilburn, Blair Jackson, Dave Marsh, Steve Morse, Jon Pareles, Steve Pond, Mark Rowland, Fred Schruers, Steve Simels, Neil Strauss, Jaan Uhelszhi, Holly George Warren, David Wild, Charles M. Young and so many others whose work has informed my own.

Many individuals graciously shared their memories of Tom Petty & The Heartbreakers with me and that helped paint a broader picture of the band's shared history. The online community at Ryan Tolone's

Mudcrutch.com was especially helpful. Throughout the years, I've appreciated the kind assistance from everyone at East End Management, especially Mary Klauzer and Tony Dimitriades. Tip of the hat to Kim Stockemer, director of copyright and licensing at Wixen Music Publishing, and Shari Wied, permissions manager at Hal Leonard, who together handled my request to reprint certain Tom Petty lyrics herein.

Very special thanks to my friend and editor-extraordinaire – Barbara Schultz – who combed through the manuscript and offered her perspective before I turned it over to Omnibus Press.

This book was written during a very challenging time in my life. Despite the death of both of my parents during the writing process, I was able to somehow soldier on. It is, no doubt, due to the lessons of perseverance that they so deftly taught me. John and Theresa Rotondo were the best parents a child could hope to have. Thanks also to every member of my family – especially my husband, Leonard Hospidor (the recording engineer in the family) – as well as John, Laura, Jonah and Christopher Rotondo; Lisa, Dan, Alia, Ava and Anna Hampton; Frank Rotondo and Peter Lee; Anthony, Anne, Steven, Kathryn and Marcia Rotondo; Sunny Andracchio; Joanne Miller, Christine Sullivan and Julie Miller-Cacciarelli; as well as John and Maryann Hospidor and John Hospidor, Jr.

My friends inspired me to complete this book and I'm forever grateful to Lori Sgambati, Laurie Flannery, Laura Atkinson, Lisa TE Sonne and Victor Dorff, and Jimmy and Marzena Doherty. Finally, thanks to my precious bearded collies – Logan and Emma – who taught me to live in the moment and enjoy the writing process.